CONTENTS

For Jennifer, who, admittedly, is not quite old enough to enjoy all the delights of Las Vegas, but who is still game for anything.

A Note on *The Brit's Guide*

This *Brit's Guide* is one of an innovative series of travel guides that aim to offer practical, user-friendly guidance for the British traveller abroad. Focusing on clear, honest information, it is one British traveller's advice to another – without the jargon or sales pitch of the brochures. *A Brit's Guide to Las Vegas 2004* gives you the complete rundown on the hotels, restaurants and shows in Las Vegas, plus help in planning a grand tour of the West Coast. The colour plates are organised thematically, so do consult them as you read.

a brit's guide

to

Las Vegas

and

the West

2004-2005

★

Karen Marchbank

foulsham
LONDON • NEW YORK • TORONTO • SYDNEY

foulsham

The Publishing House, Bennetts Close, Cippenham,
Berkshire, SL1 5AP, England

Extra research by Amanda Statham

ISBN 0-572-02926-8

Other books in this series:
A Brit's Guide to New York 2004, Karen Marchbank, 0-572-02917-9
A Brit's Guide to Orlando and Walt Disney World 2004, Simon Veness,
  0-572-02925-X
A Brit's Guide to Disneyland Paris 2004, Simon Veness, 0-572-02949-7
Choosing a Cruise 6th Edition, Simon Veness, 0-572-02946-2

Printed in Great Britain by St. Edmundsbury Press, Bury St. Edmunds, Suffolk.

INTRODUCTION

Like every other American city, Las Vegas, in the state of Nevada, has suffered a loss of international visitors due to both September 11 and the Iraq war. Prior to that, many of the city's top resorts were feeling the pinch from a loss of high rollers and a big drop in Japanese gamblers thanks to the economic downturn in Asia.

This, though, has been good for us punters. Las Vegas, which for years was known for its cheap, all-you-can-eat buffets, 99-cent shrimp cocktails and free drinks, grew much more expensive. Following an upsurge in the number of young and sophisticated inhabitants, attracted by the higher salaries here, and wealthy stylish visitors, the increasingly opulent resort hotels opened a whole raft of upscale dining establishments and celebrity-chef outlets. But today, as a result of the leaner times, there is now also a wider variety of more price-friendly cafés and restaurants.

Another even more important shift has taken place. The notion of Las Vegas as a family-friendly destination has well and truly been laid to rest. Sure, you'll still find hotels that cater for them – Circus, Circus being top of the league – but the executives have worked out that dads don't spend big bucks at the gambling tables, and sex sells big time.

Now, if there is any reference to children in a hotel's literature, it's usually about the babysitting or children's club service, where little ones can be safely dumped – sorry, dropped off – while their parents head out to party.

Let's talk about sex

And they can party big time. Las Vegas – otherwise known as Sin City – has always been synonymous with sex, yet there has still been a distinction between what happens on the main tourist drag, known as the Strip, and the strip club industry, mostly confined to way-out locations on industrial estates! Now the lines are blurring as the major resort hotels – ever watchful for a new way to make a fast buck – are pushing back the boundaries.

It started with the odd topless show on the Strip – such as Jubilee! and Splash – and has branched out to a veritable plethora of adult shows, all of which are reviewed in Chapter 3 Showtime, and which now include risqué productions for the girls, too.

This triggered the arrival of ever more raunchy nightclubs. Now it's not just enough to offer amazing settings, excellent music and wow drinks. A new breed of venues also offers Go-Go girls aplenty and 'seating' arrangements that start with luxurious couches and build up to oversized cushions, ottomans and even beds. The theory is that no one intends actual sex to really take place, but will they, one wonders, be surprised if it does?

And if you think I'm making it up, just bear in mind that Baby's nightclub at the Hard Rock Hotel has been fined $100,000 for 'failing to prevent overt sexual activity'.

Against this backdrop, it's interesting to note that at a recent planning meeting for an upscale new nightclub, it was decided that beds would be included, yet the owner is reported to have said he wanted the place to remain classy. As with so many aspects of Las Vegas, the line between reality and euphemism is a fine one. After all, this is the city where gambling is referred to as 'gaming' and nudity as 'skin'. Perhaps, as one insider said, classy in this case will mean providing condoms!

There may not be any strip clubs on the Strip yet, but surely it is only a matter of time before one of the major resort hotels takes the plunge. In the meantime, the continually classy Caesars Palace provides plenty of titillation in the form of silhouetted topless dancers at its Shadow Bar, while plenty of 'skin' can also be seen at an increasing number of pool parties.

Shop till you drop

However, Sin City is not entirely about sex and gambling! More than half the dosh coming into the city's coffers is through shopping and to prove this the Fashion Show Mall is about to become (early 2004) the only shopping mall in America with eight incredible fashion department stores – including Nieman Marcus, Saks Fifth Avenue, Macy's, Dillard's, Nordstrum and Bloomingdale's – under one roof and more than 250 retail outlets.

It outstrips The Forum Shops at Caesars Palace – an attraction in its own right – as the number one shopping destination in America. Not to be left out, Chelsea Premium Outlets – famous for its New England village-style designer outlet stores – opened its Las Vegas mall in August 2003.

There are loads of other attractions, while the city is also surrounded by some staggeringly beautiful desert scenery and olde worlde towns that can transport you back 100 years to a bygone era of Wild West cowboys. All in all, it's a destination that's hard to beat, so go, enjoy and let your hair down. As the city motto goes, what happens in Las Vegas stays in Las Vegas when you leave the bright lights behind...

ENTERTAINMENT CITY

What the city is all about, useful information, best times to go, what to wear and the weather

Florida and New York are the favourite American destinations for us Brits, but right alongside is Las Vegas – the all-singing, all-dancing, top-of-the-pile city for tourism in the States. Casinos, shows, nightclubs, showgirls – the Sin City has it all, yet it's not until you see the staggering line-up of monster-sized hotels for yourself that the enormity of it sinks in.

In fact, the city never fails to impress. From the revolving restaurants and bars, to the chi-chi lounges, spectacular thrill rides and state-of-the-art nightclubs, it's a jaw-dropping experience from beginning to end.

As you drive up Las Vegas Boulevard South – the Strip, as it is known – from the airport, you'll encounter the triple-pronged Mandalay Bay resort, then the amazing pyramid of the Luxor on your left and the gigantic golden lion of the MGM Grand to your right. Other wondrous sights appear, including the beautiful drawbridge-castle of the Excalibur and a complete replica of New York's skyline at the New York-New York resort. And that is before you even reach what used to be the most famous part of the Strip – the old Four Corners that include the Greco-Roman empire of Caesars Palace and the Flamingo Hilton.

Towering over it all, of course, is the Stratosphere, the world's tallest free-standing observation tower at the top end of the Strip on the way to downtown Las Vegas. Here you'll find the last vestiges of Las Vegas' former neon culture known as Glitter Gulch in the Fremont Street Experience that totally encloses Fremont Street.

There are over 127,000 hotel beds in the city and the number keeps on rising as older hotels are imploded

and replaced with giant resorts. Even so, average occupancy is an amazing 85.6% and more than 35 million visitors came here in 2002.

They never had it so good

Las Vegas is a great place in which to work. Up to 8,000 people move into the area every month from southern California, Utah and beyond. The predictions are that the current population of 1.3 million in Clark County, which encompasses Las Vegas, will have more than doubled to 2.7 million by the year 2018 – after expanding from just 350,000 in 1992. It's not surprising, given that the unemployment rate of 4.2% is the lowest in the country, that the number of jobs will grow by 5.2% every year over the next decade and that the lifestyle is just so good.

But not all the jobs are in the gambling industry. Many other businesses, especially those in the high-tech industry, are attracted by the low property tax and the lack of income or corporate income taxes. For the sixth year in a row POV – the New York business magazine for young entrepreneurs with a smart Point of View – ranks Las Vegas in its top five cities for new businesses. This is based on 19 factors, including quality of life, 'coolness', infrastructure, educated workforce, success rate and taxes.

As a result, a large part of the workforce consists of smart, young professional types, who are lured by the huge wages – salaries in the high-tech sector average out at around $56,000 per annum in comparison with the countrywide norm of $29,000. This has contributed to the explosion of trendy bars, ultra lounges (see page 111), sophisticated nightclubs and an array of celebrity-chef restaurants.

A taste of the action

An increase in younger, trendier visitors has also played a part in the growth of thrill rides, such as the heartline-twister Manhattan Express around New York-New York and Speed at the Sahara Hotel. There are now so many non-casino type attractions that it is even possible to have a family holiday here – and see the fabulous natural sights of the Red Rock Canyon, Valley of Fire, Grand Canyon (by helicopter or plane in a day) and Mount Charleston, not so far away.

You can find a venue for nearly every activity you fancy and there are plenty of opportunities to experience the real West. You can go horse riding at any of the national parks, go on a cowboy trail, meet the Native American tribes north and south of the city, go swimming, water-skiing and fishing at Lake Mead and even go skiing in Lee Canyon in winter. If that's not enough action for you, then try skydiving from Boulder City Airport near the Hoover Dam.

The power of plastic comes into its own in the myriad shopping centres that have sprung up since Caesars Palace's Forum Shops gave a whole new meaning to the word 'mall'. Now locals and tourists spend even more money here than they do on gambling, making Las Vegas the most successful place for the retail industry in all of America.

Walking with the dinosaurs

It's a long way from the days of Bugsy Siegel and, before him, the railroad settlers and Mormons. In fact, the history of southern Nevada reaches back into prehistoric times when it was a marsh full of water and lush vegetation that was home to dinosaurs.

Eventually, as millions of years went by, the marsh receded, rivers disappeared beneath the surface and the wetlands evolved into a parched, arid landscape that can now only support the hardiest of plants and animals. Water trapped underground in the geological formations of the Las Vegas Valley sporadically surfaced to nourish plants and create an oasis in the desert, while life-giving water flowed to the Colorado River.

Hidden for centuries from all but Native Americans, the Las Vegas Valley oasis was protected from discovery by the surrounding harsh and unforgiving Mojave Desert until around 1829 when Mexican trader Antonio Armigo, leading a 60-man party along the Spanish Trail to Los Angeles, veered away from the route and discovered Las Vegas Springs.

On the gold rush trail

The discovery of this oasis shortened the Spanish Trail to Los Angeles and hastened the rush west for the California gold. Between 1830 and 1848, the name Vegas was changed to Las Vegas, which means 'the meadows' in Spanish. In 1844 John C Fremont camped at the springs while leading an overland expedition west and his name is immortalised in the downtown Fremont Hotel and Fremont Street.

In 1855, Mormon settlers from Salt Lake City started to build a fort of sun-dried adobe bricks in Las Vegas to protect pioneers travelling between Utah and Los Angeles. They planted fruit trees and vegetables and made bullets from lead mined at Potosi Mountain, 30 miles (48km) from the fort. They abandoned the settlement in 1858, largely because of Indian raids, but it remains as the oldest non-Indian structure in Las Vegas and has been designated a historic monument.

Working on the railroad

By 1890, railroad developers had chosen the water-rich valley as a prime location for a stop facility and town. When work on the first railroad into Las Vegas began in 1904, a tent-town sprouted, with saloons, stores and boarding houses, and the San Pedro, Los Angeles and Salt Lake Railroad (later absorbed by Union Pacific) made its first run east from California. The advent of the railroad led to the founding of Las Vegas on 15 May 1905. The Union Pacific auctioned off 1,200 lots in a single day in an area that is now known as the Fremont Street Experience.

Gambling got off to a shaky start in the state, which introduced anti-gambling laws in 1910. They were so strict that even the western custom of flipping a coin for a drink was banned. But the locals set up underground gambling dens for their roulette wheels, dice and card games. They stayed illegal but were largely accepted, and flourished until 1931 when the Nevada Legislature approved a legalised gambling bill that was designed to generate tax revenue to support local schools. Now more than 43% of Nevada's income comes from gambling tax revenue and more than 34% of its fund is used to provide state education.

In the same year, construction work began on the Hoover Dam project, which at its peak employed more than 5,000 people, so the young town of Las Vegas was protected from the harsh realities of America's Great Depression. World War Two delayed major resort growth but the seeds for development were sown when Tommy Hull opened the El Rancho Vegas Casino in 1941 on land opposite what is now the Sahara Hotel. During World War Two, the nearby Nellis Air Force Base was a key military installation and later became a training ground for American fighter pilots.

Mob rules

The success of El Rancho Vegas triggered a small building boom in the late 1940s, including several hotel-casinos on the two-lane highway leading into Las Vegas from Los Angeles that has evolved into today's Strip. Early hotels included the Last Frontier, Thunderbird and Club Bingo. By far the most famous was the Flamingo Hotel, built by mobster Benjamin 'Bugsy' Siegel, a member of the Meyer Lanksy crime family. Complete with a giant pink neon sign, replicas of pink flamingos on the lawn and a bullet-proof, high-security apartment for Bugsy, the hotel opened on New Year's Eve in 1946.

Nevertheless, Bugsy was gunned down six months later as he sat in the living room of his girlfriend's home in Beverly Hills. After numerous owners, the Flamingo now belongs to the Hilton Hotel Group. Today, only the name remains as the last of the original motel-like buildings were replaced by a $104-million tower in 1995.

The early building boom continued and Wilbur Clark, a former hotel bellman, opened the Desert Inn in 1950. Two years later, Milton Prell opened the Sahara Hotel on the site of the old Club Bingo. Despite many changes of ownership, the Sahara has survived. So, too, has the Desert Inn, which underwent a $200-million remodelling and construction programme in 1997, and remains a part of Steve Wynn's new Wynn Resort project, due to open in March 2005.

The Sands Hotel, a showroom and once the playground for the 'Rat Pack' of Frank Sinatra and his buddies, high rollers and Hollywood stars, opened in 1952, but was demolished in 1996 to make way for the fabulous new Venetian.

In 1976, Atlantic City, in New Jersey, legalised gambling and so began a new era in Las Vegas's history as hotel-casinos saw they would need to create a true resort destination to compete. Caesars Palace had been the first hotel on the Strip to create a specific theme for its resort hotel when it opened in 1966 and two years later Circus Circus opened its tent-shaped casino with carnival games and rides. But it was not until the late 1980s and early 1990s that the boom in resort hotels began in earnest.

A new day dawns

In 1989, the $630-million upmarket Mirage Hotel opened with a white tiger habitat, dolphin pool, elaborate swimming pool and waterfall and a man-made volcano that belched fire and water. Mirage's owner at the time, Steve Wynn, then built the $430-million Treasure Island resort next door, home to the Sirens of TI show. Wynn also went into a joint venture with Circus Circus Enterprises to develop another luxury resort hotel – the Monte Carlo, which opened in 1996 – and his next venture, the luxurious Bellagio, styled as an Italian lakeside village, opened in 1998 on the site of the former Dunes Hotel. Wynn sold all his holdings in these hotels in June 2000 and snapped up the Desert Inn 10 days later.

The Excalibur medieval castle opened in 1990 with court jesters and King Arthur's jousting knights entertaining visitors to the massive $290-million complex. Circus Circus Enterprises then developed the amazing $375-million Luxor next door, opening in 1993.

In the same year, Grand Slam Canyon Adventuredome opened at the Circus Circus Hotel, as did Treasure Island and the MGM Grand Hotel and Theme Park. Now one of the world's largest resorts, the MGM Grand has three of the largest concert and sports venues in Las Vegas, some of the top restaurants and myriad swimming pools and tennis courts.

In 1997, the £460-million resort hotel New York-New York, which recreates the Big Apple's skyline, added 2,000 rooms. Then came a whole raft of luxury resorts aimed specifically at the sophisticated traveller, including the Mandalay Bay, Paris and Venetian in 1999 – themed as a South Seas island, the French capital and Venice respectively – the Aladdin in 2000 and The Palms in 2001. These hotels are not just the last word in luxury, nor just magnificent creations of a theme, but they have also swelled the cultural and dining coffers of the city.

Bellagio is home to O, a fabulous theatrical feast of human feats by the world-acclaimed Cirque du Soleil® in, on and above water – the title derives from eau, the French word for 'water'. Mandalay Bay has the House of Blues restaurant and live gig joint, plus one of the best nightclubs in town. Between them all, they have enticed more than a dozen top-notch and celebrity chefs from New York, Los Angeles, San Francisco and New Orleans, including Wolfgang Puck, Joachim Splichal, Charlie Palmer, Jean-Louis Palladin and Julian Serrano, to open fine restaurants.

It seems that after going through all its different marketing ploys – the city that never sleeps, a family town, adults only – Las Vegas has finally become the sophisticated Mecca of fun Bugsy Siegel envisaged so many decades ago.

Best times to go

Las Vegas may have a staggering 127,000 rooms, but at certain times of the year it still gets absolutely packed. The busiest times are Christmas, July, August, Easter and the American bank holidays which are: President's Day (George Washington's birthday) – the third Monday in February; Memorial Day – the last Monday in May and the official start of the summer season; Independence Day – 4 July (slap bang in the middle of the high season anyway); Labor Day – the first Monday in September and last holiday of summer; and Thanksgiving – always the fourth Thursday in November.

The best times to visit – providing there are no major conferences or boxing matches going on – are from January to the end of April excluding the bank holidays and Easter, and October and November. May, June and September are busier, but are still good times to go.

Getting around

Las Vegas has been growing at such a phenomenal rate in the last six years that it has only recently solved the problem of a packed Strip, thanks to the opening of the $92-million Desert Inn Super Arterial.

If you arrive by plane, a taxi ride to a Strip hotel (where most of the major theme resorts are located) will cost $14 to $18, and to a downtown hotel between $18 and $22, depending on the route taken. Airport shuttle fares cost from $6 to Strip hotels. They're excellent value for money and can be found immediately on your right as you exit the baggage reclaim area. The ticket office is on your left. In addition, most major hotels run shuttles to and from the airport.

Walking

Let's face it, walking is the way most people want to explore the Strip, yet it can be a highly dodgy activity. The city – like most of those in America – is entirely geared to cars and is not just pedestrian-unfriendly, but downright dangerous. In some parts of the Strip there are no pavements at all, in other parts, where there are pavements and even pedestrian crossings, the crossings have been allowed to erode, and often there is not enough time to get over the road before the lights change. What's worse is that most of the road-users seem to see pedestrians as targets, which is rather odd given the touristy nature of the Strip. However, the hotels and city councillors have been taking action – footbridges have been built at many of the junctions and, although it takes longer, I strongly

advise you to use them!

The monorail

Good news for Las Vegans and visitors alike! A brand spanking new monorail begins service in early 2004. It stretches from the MGM Grand at the southern end of the Strip and goes as far north as the Sahara – effectively taking in most of the Strip resorts – including stops at the Venetian and Las Vegas Convention Center. The cost of travelling on the state-of-the-art monorail is $2.50.

Although the old monorail between the MGM Grand and Bally's has been closed, three other monorails run on the western side of the Strip between Treasure Island and the Mirage, the Bellagio and the Monte Carlo and the Excalibur, Luxor and Mandalay Bay resorts.

In the meantime, an extension has already been approved to connect the Sahara to Fremont Street in the Downtown area, which is due to be completed in 2007.

Buses and taxis

If you're sticking to the main drag, the monorail will be the fastest bet, however the bus service – Citizens Area Transit (CAT) – has a 24-hour service on the Strip and Downtown, plus 40 other routes that operate 5.30am –1.30am daily. For information about routes and schedules, call 702-228 7433.

Over 1,100 taxis service the city but costs will mount if you use them all the time. My caveat would be to avoid using taxis where possible and try to use the monorail. Services

★ ★ ★ BRIT TIP ★ ★ ★

Taking a taxi is not only pricey, but you cannot flag one down on the street, either. You must either pick one up from a hotel (where there's often a queue) or from designated stops.

include: ABC Union: 702-736 8444; Ace Cab Co: 702-736 8383; A North Las Vegas Cab Co: 702-643 1041; A Vegas Western Cab Co: 702-736 6121; Checker Yellow Star: 702-873 2227; Desert Cab: 702-386 9102; Western Cab Co: 702-736 8000; Whittlesea Blue Cab 702-384 6111.

The trolley

The Las Vegas Trolley runs 9.30am–2am every day at roughly 20-minute intervals. Northbound from the Mandalay Bay to the Stratosphere, it stops at the Tropicana, MGM, Bally's, Imperial Palace, Harrah's, Riviera, Hilton and Sahara. Southbound from the Stratosphere, it stops at Circus Circus, Slots of Fun, Stardust, Fashion Show Mall, Caesars, Jockey Club, New York-New York, Excalibur and Mandalay Bay. It costs $1.50 for all journeys and exact change is required. This is a very cheap way of seeing the Strip, but also the slowest – it takes about 50 minutes to travel the entire length in one direction.

Car rental

With the opening of the new monorail, you need only hire a car when you want to take a trip or go touring.

Before hiring a car, read Chapter 14 (see page 196) first so you know exactly what you'll have to pay for. The good news is that Alamo have dropped their one-way drop-off fees for people travelling around Nevada, Arizona and California, but if you're going to use a local Las Vegas car-

★★★ BRIT TIP ★★★

Don't hire a car from the airport or you'll be charged exorbitant airport 'surcharges'. Take a cheap shuttle to your hotel and sort it out from there.

hire firm and intend to leave Nevada, check you won't be charged any extras.

If you do plan to arrange car rental on arrival in Las Vegas, look out for special deals advertised in the local press – you may find excellent prices and extras such as free long-distance phone cards.

★★★ BRIT TIP ★★★

Some trolley stops are harder to find than others – especially at Caesars Palace where there are no signs at all and the bellboys are the rudest on the Strip if you don't brandish a tip. The first stop is on the right-hand side of the road just by the entrance to the Forum Shops. The second stop is at the end of the entrance to Caesars hotel (just by the bus stop).

Car rental companies in Las Vegas include: Airport Rent-A-Car: 702-795 0800; Alamo: 702-263 8411; All State: 702-736 6147; Avis: 702-261 5995; Budget: 702-736 1212; Dollar: 702-739 8408; Enterprise: 702-795 8842; Hertz: 702-736 4900; National: 702-261 5391; Practical: 702-798 5253; Rent A Vette Sports Cars/Exotics/Motorcycle Rentals: 702-736 2592; Thrifty: 702-896 7600.

Some companies have rental sites at many of the major resort hotels. If booking on site in Las Vegas at a quiet time, you may be offered very cheap upgrades, but beware of hard-sell tactics and if you're certain you don't want or need a bigger car, don't be persuaded.

Limos

It won't cost you an arm and a leg to travel in style in Las Vegas – you can rent a limo for the ride into town from the airport for as little as $5 a person if there are several of you. Check out

★ ★ ★   BRIT TIP   ★ ★ ★

Some of the smaller rental companies may be cheaper, but always ensure that your rental agreement will allow you to drive outside the state of Nevada.

★ ★ ★   BRIT TIP   ★ ★ ★

When buying US dollars before your trip always ask for plenty of $1 bills – known as singles – so you can tip porters and taxi drivers on arrival. Also at many American airports it will cost you 1$ to use a baggage trolley.

the deals available on arrival. And if you're having a big night out on the town and want to have a drink, hiring a limo for the night often works out at about the same price as a taxi. Limo companies include: Ambassador Limousines: 702-362 6200; Bell Trans/Limousines and Buses: 702-739 7990 or toll-free 1-800 274 7433; Las Vegas Limousines: 702-736 7990 or toll-free 1-800 274 7433; On Demand Sedan-Black Car Service: 702-876 2222; Presidential Limousines: 702-731 5577 or toll-free 1-800 423 1429.

Practical information

Tips on tipping

Tipping is not just a way of life in America, but a genuine source of income for most employees in the hotel and casino industries and they are even taxed on an expectation of tips received. Sadly, tipping is something that we Brits tend to overlook. There are some fairly loose customs in Las Vegas, but here is a guide to how much we should tip.

Bartenders and cocktail waitresses should generally receive around $1 a round of drinks for parties of two to four people, more for larger groups. It is usual to tip keno runners (see Chapter 7, page 132), slot machine change girls and casino dealers. Some gamblers who play for long periods of time tip casino staff even if they've lost! Hotel maids expect $2 a day at the end of a visit, pool attendants get 50 cents to $1 for towels, pads, loungers, etc. For food servers and room service, the standard 15–20% rule applies.

Many showrooms sell assigned seating tickets, which may include the tip. In resort showrooms that have restaurant-style reservations and seating, you can tip the maître d' (Americans don't have head waiters, they have maître d's like the French!) $5 to $20 to improve your seats. Showroom servers get $5–10 for a party of two to four people at a cocktails-only show, or $10 –20 for a dinner show depending on the service and quality of food.

Taxi drivers expect $1 to $2 per person at the end of the trip. It is normal to tip valet parkers $1 to $2, depending on how quick the service has been.

Medical emergencies

The number for the emergency services is 911.

The **Imperial Palace** has the only 24-hour medical facility on the Strip, phone direct on 702-735 3600.

Many prescription and over-the-counter drugs are produced under different generic names in America. If you take any kind of regular medication, e.g. for a heart condition or epilepsy, it's a good idea to ask your doctor or pharmacy to find out the American name for your particular prescription drug. Keep this written down with your prescription or put both English and American drug names inside a clear plastic case that is easily accessible for medical crews, in case you are involved in an accident. The American term for paracetamol is acetaminophen.

Weather

One thing you can be sure of – you're not going to freeze! Having said that, in November 1995, temperatures only got as high as 7°C (45°F), which is 6°C (12°F) below the daytime norm, and there was the briefest flurry of snow. You'll be pleased to know that those poor Las Vegans did recover from their small taste of our normal springtime! Generally, Las Vegas has about 300 days of sunshine a year, with an average rainfall of 4.2in (10.2cm) throughout the year, making it an arid climate. June to September tends to be the hottest period with daytime temperatures above 38°C (100°F) in July and August, so if you're going out for the day, always make sure you put a good sunblock on before you leave your hotel.

Dress code

Fortunately, given the climate, the dress code is pretty relaxed in Las Vegas with casual clothes permitted around the clock. But wearing swimming costumes inside a casino or restaurant is not acceptable and it is normal to dress up for a big evening out. If you're visiting in early spring or late autumn, take a cardigan or light jacket for the evening and something a bit warmer for winter.

Useful websites

www.vegasfreedom.com – run by the city's Convention and Visitors Authority, this website not only supplies information, but also carries a preview of good deals.

www.ilovevegas.com – this provides current information, supplied by the magazine *What's On, The Las Vegas Guide*, about hotels, casinos, dining, entertainment and recreation.

www.lvrjsun.com – one of the most useful websites with links to entertainment, local news and maps, run by *The Las Vegas Review Journal*.

www.lasvegas.com – an excellent source of information, discounts and pre-booking for restaurants and clubs.

Vocabulary

It has often been said that Brits and Americans are divided by a common language and when you make an unexpected faux pas you'll certainly learn how true this is. For instance, never ask for a packet of fags as this is the American slang word for gays and a sense of humour is not their

MONTH	TEMPERATURE °C/°F MIN	MAX	HUMIDITY % AM/PM	PRECIP. INCHES	SUNSHINE %
January	1/34	13/55	41/30	.50	77
February	3/37	19/66	36/26	.46	80
March	5/41	20/68	30/22	.41	83
April	9/48	25/77	22/15	.22	87
May	15/59	30/86	19/13	.22	88
June	20/68	36/97	15/10	.09	92
July	24/75	40/104	19/15	.45	87
August	22/72	38/100	14/18	.54	88
September	18/64	34/93	23/17	.32	91
October	11/52	27/81	25/19	.25	87
November	5/41	19/66	33/27	.43	80
December	1/34	14/57	41/33	.32	77

Useful numbers

Airport information:	702-261 5743
Airport parking:	702-261 5121
Citizens Area Transit:	702-228 7433
Convention information:	702-892 0711
Directory assistance:	702-555 1212
Emergency Service Dispatch:911	
Highway Patrol:	702-385 0311
Las Vegas Fire Department:	702-383 2888
Las Vegas Transit System:	702-228 7433
Marriage License Bureau:	702-455 4415
Metro Police:	702-795 3111
Poison Information Center:	702-732 4989
Road conditions:	702-486 3116
Show Hot Line:	702-225 5554
Tourist information:	702-892 7575
Weather:	702-736 3854

strong point! There are plenty of other differences, too, so this list should help to avoid confusion. Remember, too, that spellings sometimes vary.

Travelling around:

English	American
Aerial	Antenna
Articulated Truck	Semi
Bonnet	Hood
Boot	Trunk
Caravan	House trailer
Car park	Parking lot
Car silencer	Muffler
Crossroads/junction	Intersection
Demister	Defogger
Dipswitch	Dimmer
Dual carriageway	Four-lane or divided highway
Flyover	Overpass
Give way	Yield
Jump leads	Jumper cables
Lay-by	Turn-out
Lorry	Truck
Manual transmission	Stick shift
Motorway	Superhighway, freeway, expressway
No parking or stopping	No standing
Pavement	Sidewalk
Petrol station	Gas station
Request stop	Flag stop
Ring road	Beltway
Slip road	Ramp
Subway	Pedestrian underpass
Transport	Transportation
Turning	Turnoff
Tyre	Tire
Underground	Subway
Walk	Hike
Wheel clamp	Denver boot
Windscreen	Windshield
Wing	Fender

Eating and stuff:

There are plenty of differences in US and UK food terms. The Americans don't flick fat over the top of the egg when frying it, but turn it over to cook on both sides, so for eggs the way I like them, cooked on both sides but soft, I don't order 'sunny-side up' but 'over easy' and if you like yours well done, then ask for eggs 'over hard'. Many standard American dishes come with a biscuit – which is a corn scone to us! They also have something called grits, which is a porridge-like breakfast dish made out of ground, boiled corn, plus hash browns – grated, fried potatoes.

English	American
Aubergine	Eggplant
Bill	Check or tab
Biscuit (sweet)	Cookie
Biscuit (savoury)	Cracker
Chickpea	Garbanzo bean
Chips	French fries
Choux bun	Cream puff

Cling film	Plastic wrap
Coriander	Cilantro
Corn	Wheat
Cornflour	Cornstarch
Courgette	Zucchini
Crayfish	Crawfish
Crisps	Chips
Crystallised	Candied
Cutlery	Silverware or place-setting
Demerera sugar	Light-brown sugar
Desiccated coconut	Shredded coconut
Digestive biscuit	Graham cracker
Double cream	Heavy cream
Essence (eg vanilla)	Extract
Golden syrup	Corn syrup
Grated, fried potatoes	Hash browns
Grilled	Broiled
Icing sugar	Confectioner's sugar
Jam	Jelly
Ketchup	Catsup
King prawn	Shrimp
Main course	Entree
Measure	Shot
Minced meat	Ground meat
Off-licence	Liquor store
Pastry case	Pie shell
Pips	Seeds (in fruit)
Plain/dark chocolate	Semi-sweet or unsweetened chocolate
Pumpkin	Squash
Scone	Biscuit
Shortcrust pastry	Pie dough
Single cream	Light cream
Soda water	Seltzer
Soya	Soy
Sorbet	Sherbet
Spirits	Liquor
Sponge finger biscuits	Ladyfingers
Spring onion	Scallion
Starter	Appetizer
Stoned (cherries, etc.)	Pitted
Sultana	Golden raisin
Sweet shop	Candy store
Take-away	To go
Tomato purée	Tomato paste
Water biscuit	Cracker

Shopping

English	American
Bumbag	Fanny pack
Chemist	Drug store
Ground floor	First floor
Handbag	Purse
High Street	Main Street
In (Fifth Avenue, etc.)	On
Jumper	Sweater
Muslin	Cheesecloth
Suspenders	Garters
Tights	Pantyhose
Till	Check-out
Trainers	Sneakers
Trousers	Pants
Underpants	Shorts
Vest	Undershirt
Waistcoat	Vest
Zip	Zipper

Money

English	American
Bill	Check
Banknote	Bill
Cheque	Check
1 cent	Penny
5 cents	Nickel
10 cents	Dime
25 cents	Quarter

General

English	American
Air steward(ess)	Flight attendant
Anti-clockwise	Counterclockwise
At weekends	On weekends
Autumn	Fall
Behind	In back of
Camp bed	Cot
Cinema	Movie theater
Coach	Bus
Cot	Crib
Diary (appointments)	Calendar
Diary (records)	Journal
Doctor	Physician
City/town centre	Downtown (not the run-down bit!)
From ... to ...	Through
Lift	Elevator
Long-distance call	Trunk call
Nappy	Diaper
Ordinary	Regular, normal
Paddling pool	Wading pool
Post, postbox	Mail, mailbox
Pram, pushchair	Stroller
Queue	Line, line up
Tap	Faucet
Toilet	Restroom (public) / Bathroom (private)

2 RESORT HOTELS

The biggest and the best hotels and how to choose the right one for you

I t was Howard Hughes, the famously reclusive billionaire, who inadvertently cleaned up Las Vegas by buying up a major chunk of the city's properties from the Mob (see page 9). Holed up on the ninth floor of the Desert Inn, which he also snapped up, Hughes went on a massive spending spree between 1966 and 1973. His presence lent an air of respectability to the city for the first time in its modern-day history, paving the way for the corporations to move in, which led to a major building boom.

Another ground-breaking moment came in 1989 when Steve Wynn, Las Vegas's modern-day casino mogul, opened the swanky new Mirage Hotel – the first major hotel to be built on the Strip in 16 years. With a $630 million price tag, dolphin pool, white tiger habitat, man-made volcano and elaborate swimming pool, it set a new standard and sparked off another massive building boom. Many people believe today's Las Vegas owes much to Wynn, who went on to build the pirate-themed Treasure Island and upmarket Italianate Bellagio before selling out and starting a brand-new project over at the Desert Inn.

The magic line up

To really appreciate the sight of the glittering spectacles that are both resorts and attractions in their own right, it's best to fly into Las Vegas so you can get a bird's eye view as you land at McCarran International Airport – either that, or take a fun helicopter flight. However, it's just as fascinating from the seat of a car.

As you drive north on the Strip from the airport, you'll pass the South Seas paradise of Mandalay Bay on your left, before spotting the

Inside this chapter

unmissable pyramid of the Luxor and the castle-like vistas of Camelot at Excalibur. At the new Four Corners of Las Vegas on the Strip, you will see the Tropicana to your right. Before you've had time to let out a gasp of amazement, you'll be passing the lion of MGM Grand, opposite the towers of New York-New York and its famous Big Apple landmarks. The Monte Carlo is next on the left, a fine re-creation of the ritzy Place du Monaco, then there is the new

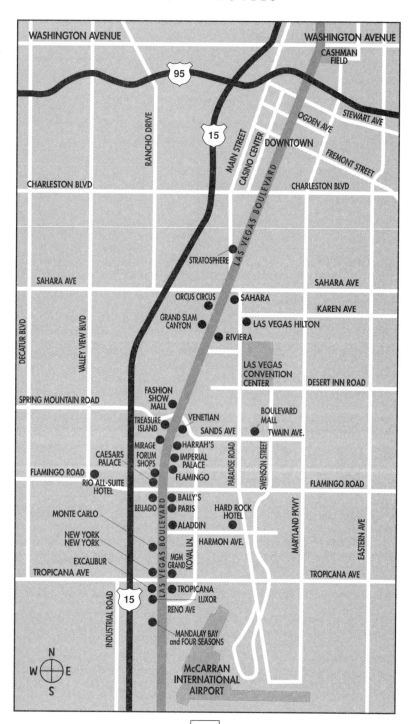

★★★ **BRIT TIP** ★★★

★ For a complete cross reference
★ of all dining options – both fine
★ dining and casual – available in
★ each of the resort hotels, see
★ page 76.

Aladdin on the right, followed by the Eiffel Tower in Paris – but don't forget to glance left for a swift look at the Italian village-setting of the Bellagio.

Now you've reached the old Four Corners, the original section of the Strip that was home to Bugsy Siegel's Flamingo and here you'll see the majestic Caesars Palace with its Greco-Roman empire theme on the left. Opposite the Forum Shops at Caesars is the modern Flamingo Hilton. Then, further north on the right, is the Japanese-inspired Imperial Palace opposite the posh Polynesian resort of the Mirage and its exploding volcano. If arriving any time after 4pm, Treasure Island's pirates of the Caribbean could well be in action at Buccaneer Bay, but don't forget to look right to see the spectacular Venetian with its re–creation of St Mark's Square and the Doge's Palace.

Further north is the circus-dome shape of the Grand Slam Canyon and Circus Circus, a family resort on the theme of a travelling circus, and after that is the spire of the Stratosphere Hotel, the tallest free-standing tower in America.

★★★ **BRIT TIP** ★★★

★ The term 'the Strip' was coined
★ by a former Los Angeles police
★ captain in 1938. Guy McAfee said
★ the stretch of road with its
★ brightly lit hotels and casinos
★ reminded him of Hollywood's
★ Sunset Strip, another Mecca for
★ night owls!

Choices, choices!

It's an amazing line-up – and it's all thanks to money and the making of it. But where do you choose to stay? Undoubtedly, for the best time ever, you stay in one of the main resort hotels – all of which are featured in this chapter. To try to make your life easier – for both choosing a hotel and for seeing them as the attractions they are – I've given a full run-down of their facilities and roughly how much it costs for a room with two people sharing.

I have not given the major resorts a rating for the simple reason that they are aimed at different types of people, so a comparison would not really be appropriate. Also, do remember that in Las Vegas, as in no other city on earth, supply and demand vary greatly and the differences are reflected in hugely fluctuating room prices. My notes on booking your hotel room in Chapter 13 give a more detailed picture of how to find a room not only at the inn of your choice, but also at the right price.

Major resorts on the Strip

The Aladdin

A well-priced mega resort now home to some of the most adult-orientated entertainments on the Strip.
Website: www.aladdincasino.com
Reservations: 702-736 7114
Fax: 702-736 7107
Room rates: from $69 Sunday to Thursday and $99 Saturday and Sunday
Location: the Strip on the corner of Harmon Avenue, south of the Paris resort and almost directly opposite the Bellagio
Theme: 1,001 Arabian Nights
Cost: $1.4 billion
Rooms: 2,567
Shows: Aladdin Theatre concert venue; CenterStage, home to Society of Seven and sexy adult review *X – An Erotic Adventure*; and Sinbad's Lounge for live music

★ ★ ★ **BRIT TIP** ★ ★ ★

Room rates are a rough guide only as they can vary wildly. If there's a large convention booked to stay at the hotel of your choice rack rates can easily rise by $200. Do your homework before booking your flights – see page 194 for details of good websites to check.

Nightclubs: Curve ultra lounge, plus Ibiza USA and Sevilla in the Desert Passage

Restaurants: 8 including seafood and steakhouse Elements, the Italian Tremezzo, PF Chang's China Bistro, Todai Japanese Seafood Buffet and Cheeseburger at the Oasis

Chilling out: 2 sixth-floor outdoor terrace and swimming pool areas overlooking the Strip

Shopping: the Desert Passage at the Aladdin – a massive shopping area with more than 140 shops and 6 fine-dining restaurants including hot city favourites the Commander's Palace from New Orleans, Sevilla, Bice and Anasazi, plus six casual eating outlets

Other amenities: Luxurious 32,000 sq ft (2,980-sq metre) spa and a new wedding chapel

Having opened in 2000, the Aladdin has had one of the bumpiest rides of any major resort hotels in recent time. Of course, it didn't help that the project went massively over budget, nor that the opening was postponed for five months, nor that when it did finally open there weren't enough hotel rooms ready for all the reservations taken. So much for a 'grand' opening!

Financially, the Aladdin has lived on a knife edge for some time, having gone into receivership and needing new investment money, which did finally arrive. The one major factor in the hotel's favour is its prime position – almost directly opposite the

fabulous, upmarket Bellagio with great views of the fountain shows, right next door to the popular Paris resort and within easy striking distance of the chi-chi Venetian.

Luring in the punters: another massive draw is the Desert Passage shopping mall, which wraps around the entire property and which is, along with the Fashion Show Mall, one of the few Strip malls to offer genuinely affordable shopping.

★ ★ ★ **BRIT TIP** ★ ★ ★

The Aladdin is the only major resort hotel on the Strip not to have an entrance on the main drag. You have to enter through a passageway on Harmon Avenue – alternatively use the Desert Passageway's Strip entrance.

The adult twist to many of the eating and entertainment facilities has also given the resort a new edge. Ultra lounges are the hot new trend in Vegas and one of the brightest – Curve – can be found in the hotel's exclusive London Club area. Adult shows are also becoming an increasingly important way of luring in the punters and X, at CenterStage, is one of the raunchiest revues on the Strip. Sevilla and Ibiza USA offer hip nightclub environments, while Commander's Palace, Tremezzo and Elements have all won a loyal following of fans for their excellent fine-dining facilities.

Room-wise, the Aladdin's are not the best on the Strip, but having said that, they are by no means the worst. They are a good size – some are massive – and all come with the latest cable and internet facilities. An added bonus of the hotel, are the two outdoor swimming pool areas, which overlook the madding crowds on the Strip.

The London Club: a taste of English casino action is provided in the heart of the Aladdin with the ultra exclusive

35,000 London Club, which offers baccarat, Pai Gow poker, roulette, blackjack and premium slot machines in its own casino area on the mezzanine level above the Aladdin's casino. Two smaller rooms create the private salons found in many of Europe's most famous casinos. There are also two luxurious bars and the ultra lounge, Curve, while the Club, which is run separately from the hotel, even has its own valet area, its own entrance and private lifts to hotel room floors. A high-class experience that is open to anyone prepared to pay the prices.

Bellagio

Based on an entire village in northern Italy, this truly is a treat for romantics!
Website: www.bellagio.com
Reservations: 702-693 7111
Fax: 702-644 6510
Room rates: from $150 Monday to Thursday; from $500 Friday to Sunday
Location: the Strip at the corner of West Flamingo
Theme: upmarket, romantic Italian lakeside village
Cost: $1.6 billion, plus $375 million for a new Spa Tower
Rooms and suites: 3,005
Show: Cirque du Soleil® theatrical circus spectacular, O
Nightclub: new upmarket nightclub, Light.
Attractions: the Fountains of Bellagio and The Conservatory and Botanical Gardens
Restaurants: 7 fine dining options including the award-winning Picasso,

Aqua and Le Cirque, and 8 casual eateries including the Shintaro sushi bar and The Petrossian Bar for caviar
Chilling out: 6 outdoor pools, 4 spas and 40 private cabanas in a Mediterranean courtyard setting
Shopping: via Bellagio esplanade filled with designer shops including Prada, Chanel, Giorgio Armani, Tiffany & Co, Hermes and Gucci
Other amenities: 2 wedding chapels, a salon for facials, manicures and pedicures and Spa Bellagio with a spa suite, steam rooms, 14 treatment rooms and an exercise room

One of Las Vegas' largest luxury mega-resorts, its 'signature' show is the free **Fountains of Bellagio** – a $30-million aquatic spectacle created by colourful, soaring fountains in a water ballet accompanied by lights and classical music by Copland and Strauss. Another enjoyable freebie is **The Conservatory and Botanical Gardens**. The Conservatory is a 55-ft (17-metre) high, glass-ceilinged edifice with floral displays that reflect the seasons and major American holidays. Each display is planned a year in advance to ensure the necessary flowers, plants and trees are available. The Bellagio is also home to one of the few cultural outlets in the city as it has its own art gallery, though since the departure of former owner Steve Wynn, who took his collection of modern art with him, it now houses travelling exhibitions.

Show stoppers: the real crowd-puller of the hotel is O, the show by the world-famous Cirque du Soleil®. A special $70-million theatre, modelled on the Paris Opera House, was built as a permanent home for the theatrical acrobatics and breathtaking stunts that make Cirque shows so amazing. A new nightclub, Light, combines style with first-class service and a great ambiance, and has attracted the likes of Courteney Cox, Charlie Sheen, Tobey McGuire, Daryl Hannah, Owen Wilson and Matt LeBlanc.

★ ★ ★ **BRIT TIP** ★ ★ ★

★ Be warned – there are no mini ★ bars in your rooms – the hotels ★ want you drinking downstairs ★ where you can gamble too! Nor ★ are there any tea or coffee- ★ making facilities, so remember to ★ buy water or orange juice for ★ yourself in the morning.

Rooms with a view: from each of the many rooms are panoramic views of the 8.5-acre (3.4-ha) lake, classical gardens, elegant pools and landscaped grounds filled with fountains, waterfalls and pools. The restaurants range from casual bistros to the gourmet restaurants Le Cirque and Picasso, which are among the most successful and popular in Las Vegas. When you have a spare moment (and a spare million), try browsing round the esplanade lined with Chanel, Armani, Gucci, Prada and Tiffany boutiques, before taking afternoon tea – one of the more affordable pleasures at the Bellagio!

Wedding belles: Terrace of Dreams is the place where dreams can come true for couples looking for an ultra-romantic outdoor venue to tie the knot. An elegant Romeo-and-Juliet-style balcony with toasted marble flooring and walls tinted a warm, golden patina is the setting before the beautiful Fountains of Bellagio.

My one little quibble about this hotel is that it is pretty crowded, which detracts from creating a truly romantic atmosphere. However, due to its popularity a new $375-million Spa Tower is being added to the spa that will increase the number of rooms by almost 1,000. It is expected to be ready by Christmas 2004.

Caesars Palace

Originally designed for high rollers, it's still posh but is now accessible to all and should at least be on your must-see list.

Website: www.caesars.com
Reservations: 702-731 7110
Fax: 702-731 7172
Room rates: from $109 Monday to Thursday; from $179 Friday to Sunday
Location: on the Strip at the famous Four Corners with Flamingo
Theme: Greco-Roman Empire
Rooms: 3,318
Showrooms: Caesars Palace Colosseum, which is home to Celine Dion's spectacular A New Day; Circus Maximus Showroom, Caesars Magical Empire
Nightlife: Cleopatra's Barge nightclub and Shadow Bar live music lounge
Restaurants: 5 fine-dining establishments including the glittering newcomer, 808, plus four casual outlets featuring the fabulous new self-service-style Cypress Street Marketplace. The Forum Shops at Caesars Palace is home to 5 more upmarket restaurants including the famous Spago, Chinois and The Palm, plus 9 casual dining outlets including the Cheesecake Factory and Planet Hollywood
Chilling out: Garden of the Gods pools and spa
Shopping: Appian Way in the hotel, plus the fabulous Forum Shops
Other amenities: a wedding chapel and a further 3 late-night lounges with live music, plus an outdoor amphitheatre

The first-ever hotel of Las Vegas to be entirely based on a theme, Caesars Palace opened in 1966, specifically aiming at big-money gamblers. Although it allows more ordinary mortals to enter its palatial doors these days, the emphasis is still very much on luxury and opulence. The Palace underwent a $600-million expansion at the turn of this century, which included building the 17-storey Palace Tower, a new Garden of the Gods outdoor area, with pools and landscaped gardens, and a wedding chapel.

Throughout the 80-acre (32-ha) resort are spectacular fountains, majestic cypress trees, gleaming marble statues and beautiful landscaping. The Garden of the Gods area has three outdoor swimming pools inlaid with marble and granite, adjoined by two whirlpool spas and rimmed by lush gardens. There are also three floodlit tennis courts and an intimate outdoor amphitheatre.

A new day dawns: the biggest news at Caesars is the recent opening of the massive Colloseum, which has quickly become a new Strip landmark. Specifically built to house Celine Dion's brand new *A New Day* one-woman show, the 4,000-seat, state-of-the-art venue can also be adapted to accommodate headliners and host major boxing events when *A New Day* is not on.

The hotel has joined the ranks of other major Strip properties in providing more adult-orientated entertainment and its new Shadow Bar – right in the centre of the casino – is one of the places to visit during a stay in Vegas. A relaxed, comfy

lounge by day, by night it is home to topless dancers who perform sexy routines behind backlit screens.

All of the rooms have Jacuzzi tubs and the latest fax/phone gadgetry, while the fabulous Forum Shops are also known as the Shopping Wonder of the World (see page 66). If you want to see how the other half lives, take a wiggle on down to the posh baccarat and VIP high-roller areas. You never know, you may just get a proposal of sorts!

Circus Circus

A great-value, family-fun destination with some surprisingly good restaurants.
Website: www.circuscircus.com
Reservations: 702-734 0410
Fax: 702-734 5897
Room rates: from $39 Sunday to Thursday; from $59 Friday and Saturday
Location: the Strip between West Sahara and the Convention Center
Theme: circus carnival featuring the world's largest permanent circus
Rooms: 4,344
Entertainment: free circus acts; IMAX® theatre and Adventuredome theme park
Casinos: 3, covering 107,500sq ft (1,000sq metres)
Restaurants: 2 fine-dining restaurants and 4 casual eateries including a Mexican and 24-hour café.
Chilling out: 3 swimming pools
Shopping: 20 retail outlets in a 40,000-sq ft (3,720-sq metre) promenade
Other amenities: the Chapel of the Fountain wedding chapel and a beauty salon

The owners of Circus Circus were the second operators to build a theme casino on the Strip. It originally opened in 1968 as the world's largest permanent circus tent plus casino but without any hotel rooms. Now it has three towers housing nearly 5,000 rooms, three major gambling areas, a whole raft of shops and some major family attractions.

Inspired by the turn-of-the-century circuses that used to visit towns throughout America, it aims its services directly at the cost-conscious family market.

★ ★ ★ BRIT TIP ★ ★ ★
★ ★
★ ★
★ Be warned, Circus Circus is so ★
★ popular with families that it can ★
★ seem that you're surrounded by ★
★ wall-to-wall kids! ★
★ ★ ★ ★ ★ ★ ★ ★ ★ ★ ★ ★ ★ ★ ★ ★ ★ ★ ★

The show must go on: the Circus Arena appears in the *Guinness Book of World Records* as the world's largest permanent circus and covers 120,000 sq ft (11,160 sq metres) with a 90-ft (27-metre) high tent-shaped roof. The Carnival Midway is a circus-themed amusement arcade and its centre stage is where free half-hourly shows are presented from 11am to midnight by top circus acts, from high-wire daredevils to flying trapeze artists, acrobats, magicians and jugglers.

The Circus Circus Theme Park – the Adventuredome – is a fully enclosed 5-acre (2-ha) elevated theme park, which is climate-controlled to provide temperatures of 21°C (70°F) all the year round. This first-ever Las Vegas amusement park has been improved over the years and now has thrilling rides in a canyon-like setting (see Chapter 10).

Building blocks: Circus Circus comprises four main building blocks. The Casino Tower has a Renaissance look and is decorated in earth tones. It is actually made up of two 15-storey tower blocks and contains two casinos, the circus arena, Midway, game arcade, several eateries, the betting shop and wedding chapel. The West Tower, a 35-storey, 1,000-room building, is the newest wing and is home to the new central registration lobby and shopping

★ ★ ★ BRIT TIP ★ ★ ★
★ ★
★ ★
★ ★
★ Las Vegas hotels are not known ★
★ for their fantastic rooms. Unless ★
★ you're paying top dollars for ★
★ rooms at the Four Seasons or ★
★ Bellagio, they are fairly plain ★
★ affairs with few facilities. The best ★
★ mid-priced rooms are to be ★
★ found at the Venetian and ★
★ Mandalay Bay. ★
★ ★ ★ ★ ★ ★ ★ ★ ★ ★ ★ ★ ★ ★ ★ ★ ★ ★ ★

promenade, which centrally connects the Adventuredome, Skyrise and Casino Towers. The Skyrise Tower at the west end of the complex, is a 29-storey building, with another full-size casino, restaurants and two pools and, like the West Tower, is decorated in rich tones of purple, green, dark blue or rust.

Bargain hunt: the Manor is a complex of five three-storey buildings, providing budget accommodation with parking outside each building and a moving walkway to the Skyrise Tower.

The resort is committed to providing entertainment in a friendly, low-cost way. If you're a novice and fancy a flutter on the Strip, this is the place to try out your luck on the roulette wheels before moving on to a high-stakes poker game elsewhere (we can dream, can't we?). Despite its emphasis on good prices though, Circus Circus has a host of good eating outlets and two of its fine dining options – The Steakhouse and Stivali's Ristorante – consistently win awards for great food.

★ ★ ★ BRIT TIP ★ ★ ★
★ ★
★ ★
★ Circus Circus provides rooms with ★
★ roll-in showers that have been ★
★ designed for the disabled. It also ★
★ has its own phone line for the ★
★ hearing impaired: 1-800 638 ★
★ 8595. ★
★ ★ ★ ★ ★ ★ ★ ★ ★ ★ ★ ★ ★ ★ ★ ★ ★ ★ ★

★★★ BRIT TIP ★★★

You've got more chance of getting a room – and cheaply – at the resort hotels if you go between Monday and Thursday.

Excalibur

Great for family fun at reasonable prices, it should also be on your must-visit list.

Website: www.excalibur-casino.com
Reservations: 702-597 7777
Fax: 702-597 7040
Room rates: from $45 Monday to Thursday; from $75 Friday to Sunday
Location: the Strip at West Tropicana
Theme: King Arthur and the Knights of the Round Table
Cost: $290 million
Rooms: 4,032
Entertainment: *King Arthur's Tournament* show, free fire-breathing dragon show, strolling entertainers and 2 magic-motion cinemas
Restaurants: 2 fine-dining options – the Steakhouse at Camelot and Sir Galahad's Prime Rib House – and a further 3 casual options
Chilling out: 2 swimming pools
Shopping: Medieval Village
Wedding chapels: 2

The beautiful spires of the Camelot-style entrance building are set between two huge castle-like towers that house the 4,000-odd rooms at this family-orientated resort. Make no mistake though, the free Dragon Battle that takes place every hour on the hour from 10am until 10pm to draw the crowds has the sole purpose of inviting you in to part with your cash in the 100,000-sq ft (9,300-sq metre) casino. But there are plenty of other free entertainments to keep you amused as you wander round the Medieval Village of shops and restaurants, from the strolling entertainers to the free variety acts on the Court Jester's Stage from 10am every day.

You can eat dinner and see *King Arthur's Tournament* at either 6pm or 8.30pm any day of the week, or bop along to live music at the Minstrel's Lounge. The house of fun also has six restaurants and parking is free and relatively accessible by Las Vegas standards!

★★★ BRIT TIP ★★★

Don't miss the medieval-costumed staff at the Excalibur, where entertainers wander around playing medieval trumpets!

Four Seasons

Provides an oasis of elegance – predominantly for business people – as the first non-gambling hotel on the Strip.

Website:
www.fourseasons.com/lasvegas
Reservations: 702-632 5000
Fax: 702-632 5105
Room rates: from $200 Sunday to Thursday; from $300 Friday and Saturday
Location: the Strip, just south of the Mandalay Bay
Theme: understated luxury
Rooms: 424
Restaurants: 3 restaurants and lounges including the Lobby Lounge for afternoon tea and Club Bar, the new Las Vegas power spot
Chilling out: pool and health and fitness club (and the ONLY hotel in Las Vegas to provide those facilities free to guests)

Although the guestrooms of the hotel are located on floors 35 to 39 of the Mandalay Bay, the Four Seasons is very much a hotel in its own right. The only hotel in recent history to open on the Strip without massive theming, it is also the only one without a casino and one of only two with a five-diamond rating in Las Vegas.

Ostensibly geared up to business people – it is the only hotel in Las

Vegas to have a corporate rate – it still attracts tourists, many of whom are dedicated followers of the Four Seasons 'brand'. While guests have access to all the facilities of the Mandalay Bay, they have their own exclusive facilities, too, including the private pool and health and fitness club.

The restaurants – including celebrity chef Charlie Palmer's Steakhouse – have been building up a regular band of loyal locals as well as guests of the hotel. Nor are they overpriced. The Verandah has a set $9 two-course or $21 three-course meal. At the Four Seasons it's all about understated elegance, darlink!

Luxor

Tastefully done theme resort at good value-for-money prices.
Website: www.luxor.com
Reservations: 702-262 4444
Fax: 702-262 4452
Room rates: from $59 Monday to Thursday; from $170 Friday to Sunday
Location: the Strip between Tropicana and Reno
Theme: ancient Egypt
Cost: $375 million, plus a $240-million expansion
Rooms: 4,408
Shows: Blue Man Group and the adult revue *Midnight Fantasy*
Nightlife: Ra nightclub and Nefertiti's Lounge for live music and dancing
Entertainment: adventure rides in IMAX® cinemas at The Pharoah's Pavilion
Restaurants: 5 fine-dining experiences

including the award-winning Isis, the Polynesian Papyrus and the divine Sacred Sea Room, plus 5 casual eateries including a food court, deli and La Salsa Mexican grill
Chilling out: 4 swimming pools and relaxing Jacuzzis in a luxurious oasis setting
Shopping: Giza Galleria promenade plus shops in The Pharoah's Pavilion
Other amenities: spa for over 18s only

For us Brits this is the hotel that is synonymous with Las Vegas extravagance, and staying in the fabulous replica of a pyramid is up there on your must-do list. With its trademark beacon of light that can now be seen from outer space (along with the Great Wall of China), the hotel is one of the most tastefully executed theme resorts in the middle-market sector. You enter the beautiful structure through a life-size replica of the great Temple of Rameses II, which takes you directly into the casino (funny that!) where 120,000 sq ft (11,160 sq metres) of gambling space houses slot and video machines, gaming tables, a sports book, poker and keno.
That's entertainment: Even if you don't want to have a flutter, there's plenty to do as The Pharoah's Pavilion, one floor above the casino, is filled with shopping and attractions that include two IMAX® movies – an IMAX® ride film, a virtual reality roller-coaster,

and *The Tomb & Museum of King Tutankhamun*. On the show front, The Blue Man Group continues to be a great draw, while the Luxor now has its own adult topless revue, *Midnight Fantasy*. The hotel is also home to an all-night club called Ra after the Egyptian God, which has a stage, dance floor, bars, cigar lounge and a 110-seater sushi and oyster bar.

To get to your room, you'll travel at a bizarre 39-degree angle, while there are shops selling Egyptian antiquities, gemstones, charms and limited edition art, and one of the hotel's many fine restaurants, Isis, is consistently voted among the top 10 restaurants in America.

Chill out in one of the attractive swimming pool areas or pay $20 ($25 to non-hotel guests) for a day Spa Pass, which includes use of the hot and cold whirlpools, steam bath, dry sauna, fitness centre and a complimentary fruit juice or mineral water.

Mandalay Bay

A luxury resort filled with must-see shows, must-eat-at restaurants and some of the hippest nightlife venues in town.

Website: www.mandalaybay.com
Reservations: 702-632 7777
Fax: 702-632 7013
Room rates: from $99 Sunday to Thursday; from $139 Friday and Saturday
Location: the Strip, just south of West Tropicana Avenue (entrance off Hacienda Drive)
Theme: South Sea Islands
Cost: $950 million
Rooms: 3,700
Shows: headliners and Broadway productions on a rotating basis
Nightlife: House of Blues, Rumjungle, Beach outdoor island stage and Coral Reef lounge
Restaurants: 6 fine dining restaurants, including the famous Aureole and Trattoria del Lupa, plus the new 3950 seafood and steakhouse and Shaghai Lily, venue of one of the most exclusive nightclubs on a Wednesday evening; 5 casual dining experiences include the Russian-themed Red Square, plus 2 live music outlets – the House of Blues and Rumjungle
Chilling out: sand-and-surf beach and the lazy river ride
Shopping: selection of shops on the South Seas theme, selling everything from cigars to Bali treasures
Other amenities: Spa Mandalay

Aimed at a slightly more sophisticated traveller than its sister property the Luxor, it's still excellent value for money and well worth forking out that bit extra for.

For starters, it's one of the few hotels on the Strip where you don't have to walk through the casino to get to your room and, secondly, many of the rooms have massive soaking/Jacuzzi tubs plus a separate shower. A large number also have fabulous views down the entire Strip and, despite being the nearest hotel to the airport, you don't hear a peep out of those planes thanks to some pretty nifty double glazing.
That's entertainment: Dan Aykroyd's House of Blues, the first of which

opened on Sunset Strip in Los Angeles, has a home here. The live music venue is drawing such crowds that you need to book at least four weeks in advance. And if you just can't get enough of the blues, then ask for a room on the 34th floor of the hotel – it's filled with House of Blues-themed guestrooms.

★ ★ ★   **BRIT TIP**   ★ ★ ★

★ Never use the phone in your hotel room – you'll be charged a small fortune. Instead, get an international phone card before you go. ★

Among the numerous pretty darn posh restaurants are two celebrity-chef restaurants – Charlie Palmer's Aureole, consistently voted number one in New York for American food by the Zagat restaurant survey, and Trattoria del Lupo, owned by Wolfgang Puck, one of the most influential chefs in the US. In addition, there's Red Square, the Russian-inspired homage to vodka and caviar. Celebrities have their own vodka lockers, but the less well-to-do can try the frozen ice bar where there are more than 100 frozen vodkas and infusions, Martinis and Russian-inspired cocktails. You can also dine on an extensive selection of caviars or Russian classics.

Still not enough fun? Then try Rumjungle for some dinner and dancing. Here the food and drinks are turned into works of art from a flaming wall to cascading waterfalls, while volcanic mountains of rum and

★ ★ ★   **BRIT TIP**   ★ ★ ★

★ The Mandalay's wave pool is generally closed for maintenance from around the end of October to March. ★

spirits rise before you at the illuminated bar. Many of the sizzling meals are cooked over a giant open fire pit for that authentic South Seas flavour, while dancing is to Latin, Caribbean and African beats until the small hours.

It's not all fast-paced at the Mandalay though, as there are plenty of ways to unwind in the 11-acre (4.5-ha) tropical water environment. Try out the city's first sand-and-surf beach, take a dip in one of the many swimming pools or just go for a lazy river ride. You can now also get a day pass to the spa or opt for one of the many excellent massages, body treatments or facials.

MGM Grand

Seriously massive resort hotel that is good fun for the whole family, yet provides plenty of adult entertainment.
Website: www.mgmgrand.com
Reservations: 702-891 1111
Fax: 702-891 1030
Room rates: from $69 Monday to Thursday; from $129 Friday to Sunday
Location: the Strip at the new Four Corners with East Tropicana
Cost: originally $1 billion followed by $950-million expansion and theme transformation
Theme: The City of Entertainment
Rooms: 5,005
Shows: EFX in the Grand Theater, sporting events and major concerts in the Grand Garden Arena (seats 16,325), plus smaller gigs in the 650-seat Hollywood Theater and a Comedy Club
Nightlife: Studio 54 nightclub, Tabu ultra lounge, Showbar Lounge for daily live music and Zuri, a 24/7 bar with live entertainment nightly
Entertainment: arcade centre with high-tech virtual reality games, the free Lion Habitat and the Youth Activity Center
Restaurants: a whopping 9 fine-dining outlets including 3 celebrity chef eateries – Emeril's New Orleans Fish House, Mark Miller's Coyote Café and Grill and the Wolfgang

BRIT TIP

★★★ ★★★

If you're staying at the MGM Grand or New York-New York, then head to the south baggage area at McCarran Airport to check in while waiting for your luggage to come off the plane. For an extra fee you can even take the direct shuttle to your hotel.

Puck Café – plus the fab new NOBHILL; and 8 casual outlets including The Rainforest Café.
Chilling out: Grand Pool and Spa
Other amenities: Art-Deco-themed Forever Grand Wedding Chapel, plus Grand Spa and access to golf at Shadow Creek

The MGM Grand is so huge it can be all things to all people. An ugly mass from the outside, once within the confines of its air conditioning, it is easy to get lost in the array of opportunities to eat, drink and generally make merry. In recent years, there has been a shift away from the old-style family-orientated entertainments to a more adult-based scene, yet it still has a high-tech arcade and a Youth Activity Center where parents can drop 3-12-year-olds off and go party.
That's entertainment: the hotel is famous for staging headliner shows and big fights in its Grand Garden Arena and Hollywood Theater, but it still has room for the Grand Theater, the venue for EFX, one of the best productions in town.

In an effort to cater to the adult market, the hotel recently opened Tabu, an ultra lounge, while the Studio 54 nightclub now has a more raunchy twist with Dollhouse night when grown-ups get to dress beautiful 'dolls' in outfits of their choice, and Zuri supplies a 24-hour drinking spot.
The chill zone: the 6.6-acre (2.7-ha) Grand Pool and Spa complex, features five pools, lush landscaping,

a lazy river, bridges, fountains and waterfalls, while you can check out your cardiovascular rating in the state-of-the-art fitness centre at the spa. Afterwards, there are no end of eating choices available with a total of 17 fine and casual dining outlets, and if you wish you can even pop out to the flicks at the neighbouring United Artists Showcase cinema.

BRIT TIP

★★★ ★★★

While most fine dining establishments close around 10pm or 10.30pm, all the major resort hotels have at least one café that's open round the clock (24/7) and many others that stay open late.

Mirage
An elegant taste of paradise, yet within reach of most budgets.
Website: www.themirage.com
Reservations: 702-791 7111
Fax: 702-791 7446
Room rates: from $79 Monday to Thursday; from $350 Friday to Sunday
Location: the Strip, between Flamingo and Spring Mountain
Theme: Polynesian, South Seas oasis
Cost: $730 million
Rooms: 3,044
Shows: Internationally renowned illusionists, *Siegfried and Roy* and Danny Gans, entertainer of the year
Entertainment: the White Tiger Habitat and the Dolphin Habitat
Nightlife: no nightclubs, but a fab lounge scene for live music at the Onda Lounge, Baccarat Bar and outdoor Dolphin Bar
Restaurants: 6 fine dining experiences including the award-winning Onda and Renoir restaurants, plus 4 casual options
Chilling out: 2 pools and cabanas in a lush, tropical setting
Shopping: the Street of Shops promenade
Other amenities: spa and salon

★ ★ ★ BRIT TIP ★ ★ ★

Speed up your check-out times by taking advantage of the new check-out systems now available on many of the hotel's TVs. DO check the bill thoroughly, though, before paying, as mistakes can occur, and always resolve any queries before leaving the hotel.

The entrance garden surrounds you with a mass of foliage and waterfalls that cascade over 50-ft (15-metre) rocks to the lagoon below before you reach the Mirage signature volcano. This erupts every few minutes, spewing smoke and fire 100 ft (30 metres) above the water. The reception area is a tropical rainforest, filled with 60-ft (18-metre) high palm trees, more waterfalls, banana trees and tropical orchids, kept in perfect condition with natural sunlight and a computerised misting system. Behind the check-in desk is a massive coral reef aquarium that is home to sharks, puffer fish and angel fish, swimming among the buildings of a sunken city. The forest provides the delightfully exotic setting for Kokomo's, one of the Mirage's top-notch restaurants, serving steaks and seafood.

Animal magic: opened in 1989, the Mirage's theme of a Polynesian island oasis was a taste of the big things to come in Las Vegas, but has itself stood the test of time. It hosts one of the biggest shows in the city – the *Siegfried and Roy* magical show of illusions featuring tigers, lions, leopards and other animals, and the habitats for both the dolphins and the tigers are attractions in themselves. The Secret Garden, where you can see white lions, and the vast Dolphin Habitat were built to create public awareness of the plight of endangered animals.

Accommodation ranges from luxurious standard rooms to opulent bungalows with their own private garden and pools, and eight two and three-bedroom private residences. Admission to the luxurious day spa and fitness centre costs $20, but is free if you book any one of the pampering treatments.

★ ★ ★ BRIT TIP ★ ★ ★

Don't miss the Secret Garden for a real close-up encounter with the white tigers that perform in the *Siegfried and Roy* show at the Mirage.

Monte Carlo

Posh-but-worth-it hotel with great chilling-out facilities.
Website: www.monte-carlo.com
Reservations: 702-730 7000
Fax: 702-730 7250
Room rates: from $60 Monday to Thursday; from $100 Friday to Sunday
Location: the Strip just north of West Tropicana
Theme: re-creation of the Place du Casino in Monte Carlo
Cost: $344 million
Rooms: 3,261
Shows: *Lance Burton, Master Magician*
Restaurants: 2 fine-dining outlets including the famous André's, and 4 casual eateries including the 210-seat food court
Chilling out: 21,000-sq ft (1,950-sq metre) pool area with waterfalls, spa, children's pool, wave pool and rafting down the Easy River
Shopping: Street of Dreams promenade
Other amenities: a wedding chapel, health spa and exercise room

This elegant, upmarket resort hotel is so popular that it is hard for British travel agents to find you a room here. After its opening at the beginning of 1996, the 32-storey resort was fully

★★★ **BRIT TIP** ★★★

★ Skip the expensive buffet at the ★
★ Monte Carlo and go for one of ★
★ the gourmet restaurants instead. ★

★★★★★★★★★★★★★★★★★

booked for the rest of the year by the end of July. Modelled on the famous Place du Casino in Monaco, the emphasis is definitely on providing an elegant and refined atmosphere in which to part with wads of cash in the casino. Massive chandeliers, marble flooring, ornate fountains and gas-lit promenades all go towards setting the elegant tone. After a hard day seeing the sights, make sure you get back in time to make full use of the water facilities, which include a heated spa, children's pool and wave pool that re-creates both the sound and feel of ocean surf waves. Resident entertainer Lance Burton is one of the top magicians in America and, along with *Siegfried and Roy* at the Mirage, produces some of the most spectacular illusions in the world.

New York-New York

For live-wire, 24-hour action this is the place to be!
Website: www.nynyhotelcasino.com
Reservations: 702-740 6969
Fax: 702-740 6920
Room rates: from $89 Monday to Thursday; from $129 Friday to Sunday
Location: the Strip at West Tropicana
Theme: The Big Apple – doh!
Cost: $460 million
Rooms: 2,033
Shows: *Zumanity* circus extravaganza and Rita Rudner's one-woman show
Nightlife: a cracking range of bars including Coyote Ugly, The Bar at Times Square and the Big Apple Bar
Entertainment: Manhattan Express roller-coaster ride and ESPN Zone
Restaurants: 5 fine-dining restaurants include the new Gonzalez Y Gonzalez and Nine Fine Irishmen, and 7 casual dining outlets include 3 in the ESPN Zone

Chilling out: outdoor pool with three relaxing whirlpools
Shopping: gift shops
Other amenities: wedding chapel, spa and fitness centre

Dubbed the Greatest City in Las Vegas, the resort's façade re-creates the Manhattan skyline with 12 of its most famous skyscrapers from the Empire State Building to the Statue of Liberty, along with a 300-ft (90-metre) long replica of Brooklyn Bridge and a Coney Island-style roller-coaster called Manhattan Express™. From the food to the architecture, to the sights and sounds of America's capital city, this Las Vegas resort recreates the energy and vibrancy of New York – then adds the Central Park casino!

★★★ **BRIT TIP** ★★★

★ It's a good 10-minute walk ★
★ through shops and casinos to get ★
★ to the New York-New York's ★
★ roller-coaster ride, but it's well ★
★ worth the trek! ★

★★★★★★★★★★★★★★★★★

That's entertainment: in recent years owner MGM Mirage – whose empire includes the MGM Grand, Mirage, Bellagio and Treasure Island – has invested heavily in new entertainment at the hotel, building a new Cabaret Theater for Rita Rudner's one-woman show and another for *Zumanity*, a fantastic new production from the people behind *O* and *Mystère*.

They have also created a new ESPN Zone, a sports-themed dining and entertainment complex with more than 165 TV screens so you don't miss a moment's action. The Studio Grill offers classic casual American grub in a sports-themed environment, The Screening Room provides multi-game viewing, direct audio control for all televised games around two 14-ft (4-metre) screens and a dozen 36-in (90-cm) video monitors with tiered seating and The Sports Arena has more than 10,000sq ft (930sq metres) of interactive games.

Best bar none: 3 fantastic new bars provide plenty of live music entertainment and party-style atmosphere. Top of the pile is Coyote Ugly, which is based on a southern-style bar, complete with gyrating female bartenders atop the bar, then there is the Big Apple Bar, a hot new live music joint with speciality drinks and The Bar at Times Square, where you can sing along to tunes played by two pianists.

★★★ **BRIT TIP** ★★★

★ For the complete low-down on
★ getting married in Las Vegas see
★ Chapter 8 Going to the Chapel.

The party-style ambiance is continued into the dining area with the arrival of Gonzalez Y Gonzalez, a New York Mexican-style café already famous for its tequilas, or you can opt for a spot of renewal and pampering at the spa!

Paris Las Vegas

Just like the French capital – overpriced and full of Americans – but without the beautiful buildings to make up for it!

Reservations: 702-946 7000
Fax: 702-967 3836
Room rates: from $125 Sunday to Thursday; from $230 Friday and Saturday
Location: the Strip, south of East Flamingo
Theme: Capital of France!
Cost: $760 million
Rooms: 2,916
Attraction: observation deck on the Eiffel Tower
Nightlife: fabulous ultra lounge Risqué, plus Napoleon's and the Eiffel Tower lounges
Restaurants: 8 fine-dining establishments include the popular Eiffel Tower Restaurant, the wonderful new Ortanique and Mon Ami Gabi,

with outside dining right on the Strip, plus 3 casual eateries including the poolside Le Café du Parc
Chilling out: roof-top swimming pool in a manicured French garden setting and tennis courts
Shopping: French shops in the resort's Rue de la Paix district
Amenities: 2 wedding chapels

Bringing to life the ambience and spirit of the French capital, this theme resort opened in the autumn of 1999 with replicas of the Eiffel Tower, Arc de Triomphe, Paris Opera House and the Louvre. The 34-storey hotel tower is fashioned after the famous Hôtel de Ville. Like the Mandalay Bay and Venetian, the Paris is aimed at the more sophisticated traveller with prices – by Las Vegas standards, at least – to match.

That's entertainment: the hotel is now home to one of the city's chicest new ultra lounges – Risqué – plus Napoleon's, a gorgeous champagne and jazz bar, while the lounge at the Eiffel Tower Restaurant provides some of the best views in the city and an ultra-romantic setting.

All the restaurants – in true French fashion – provide wonderful food, while its newest, Ah Sin, has quickly become a popular spot for both its delish Asian cuisine and outdoor patio dining overlooking the Strip.

There is a caveat, though. While so many aspects of this resort are wonderful, the service is generally poor and prices are on the expensive side. It's as if the American staff – who normally excel at providing great service – have been infected with French-style snootiness.

Another irritating but faintly amusing aspect of the hotel is the silly branding. Look out for signs such as L'Hôtel Elevators and Le Service Captain. On top of this, all the staff have been trained to say *'bonjour'* and *'merci'* but can't actually understand a word of French. Still, it's wickedly amusing to watch French tourists discover this after they've ordered their entire meal in their native tongue!

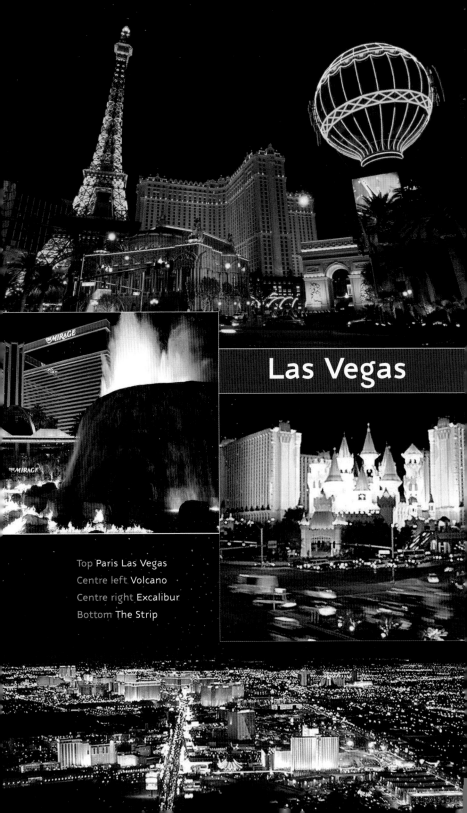

Las Vegas

Top **Paris Las Vegas**
Centre left **Volcano**
Centre right **Excalibur**
Bottom **The Strip**

Las Vegas

Top **Downtown**
Centre right **Lions' Den**
Bottom **Aladdin's casino**

Stratosphere

Extremely good-value hotel and best gambling odds on the Strip
Reservations: 702-380 7777
Fax: 702-383 5334
Room rates: from $39 Monday to Thursday; from $99 Friday to Sunday
Location: at the northern end of the Strip
Theme: tallest building west of the Mississippi
Cost: $550 million
Rooms: 2,500
Shows: *American Superstars* and *Viva Las Vegas*
Nightlife: Crazy Armadillo Oyster Bar, Images Cabaret and Oasis Lounge
Entertainment: highest observation tower in America, world's highest roller-coaster and world's highest thrill ride, the Big Shot
Restaurants: 2 fine-dining experiences including the revolving Top of the World Restaurant on the 106th floor, plus 5 casual dining outlets
Shopping: the Tower Shops
Other amenities: a wedding chapel and state-of-the-art video arcade

Location is such an important part of success in Las Vegas and the Stratosphere has paid the price in the past for being located at the most northern point of the Strip, just that little bit too far from the rest of the action. However, having returned from the brink of bankruptcy, an injection of new capital has allowed the hotel to provide some brilliant party-style bars and eateries.

That's entertainment: at first glance, the Stratosphere may seem like a one-theme wonder – a place where you take the 30-second, high-speed elevator to the observation deck for dramatic views of Las Vegas, have a drink in the bar, allow the world to go round and round (literally) and then return to earth.

But that would be to miss out on the 1,149-ft (350-metre) tower's hidden depths – two of the most amazing thrill rides in the city and Top of the World, one of the best

restaurants in town. The opening of Crazy Armadillo, a fun Oyster Bar with live entertainment daily and singing and dancing Shooter Girls and bar staff, has been a boon. Roxy's Diner is another fun place. Set in the 1950s, it provides classic all-American dishes, while the waiters and waitresses sing and dance along to the rock 'n' roll music.

★★★ **BRIT TIP** ★★★

If you don't want to walk miles to your hotel room, request one near to the lifts. These hotels are massive and rooms can be a considerable distance from the lifts!

The competitively priced rooms are among the cheapest on the Strip – and the amazing odds available in the casino make it the best place to try out your new-found skills on the tables (see Chapter 7)!

Treasure Island

A fun, comfortable resort that's good value for money for young families.
Website: www.treasureisland.com
Reservations: 702-894 7444
Fax: 702-894 7446
Room rates: from $70 Monday to Thursday; from $250 Friday to Sunday
Location: the Strip at Spring Mountain Road
Theme: Robert Louis Stevenson's novel *Treasure Island*
Rooms: 2,891
Shows: Cirque du Soleil's *Mystère*, plus live music in 2 lounges and the Sirens of TI sea show
Entertainment: Mutiny Bay entertainment centre, filled with computer video games, pinball and electronic games
Restaurants: 4 fine-dining including the Buccaneer Bay Club and the new Hawaiian Kahunaville, plus 5 casual eateries

Chilling out: tropical paradise pool with private cabanas
Shopping: the Pirate's Walk shopping promenade
Other amenities: 2 wedding chapels, spa and beauty salon

You arrive at the hotel by crossing the long wooden deck across the waters of Buccaneer Bay and are transported to the bustling, 18th-century pirate town in Buccaneer Bay Village. The village serves as the town plaza and the hub of the resort's attractions, and the theme of a pirate city is extended throughout the resort.

★ ★ ★   BRIT TIP   ★ ★ ★
★   ★
★   If you plan to see the pirate   ★
★   battle at Treasure Island, arrive   ★
★   early to grab a prime spot as   ★
★   crowds build quickly.   ★
★ ★ ★ ★ ★ ★ ★ ★ ★ ★ ★ ★ ★ ★ ★ ★

Built by Steve Wynn, who was also responsible for the Mirage and the Bellagio, the attention to detail in re-creating Robert Louis Stevenson's book is amazing. Now owned by MGM Mirage though, the resort's overtly family orientation is gradually being shifted in a more adult direction.

The signature battle, which takes place outside the resort five times a day, has been given a more grown-up twist. It used to depict a battle between a British frigate and an 18th-century pirate ship, and culminated in huge masts snapping and plunging into the sea, buildings exploding into flames and sailors being catapulted into the air. Now the blood-curdling aspects have been played down and attractive females provide more of the live action, but it still draws the crowds at its showtimes (4pm, 5.30pm, 7pm, 8.30pm and 10pm daily, depending on the weather).

Central to the resort's entertainment are the thrilling, twice-nightly shows by Cirque du Soleil®, who created a spectacle to complement the resort's pirate town theme. Now there is also a stylish, adult offering in the form of the Mist bar and lounge. With state-of-the-art plasma screens, and video poker available at the bar, this is a great new venue for watching sporting events.

The Venetian

All-out sophisticated luxury, which has become a home-from-home for celebs and the beautiful people.
Website: www.venetian.com
Reservations: 702-414 4100
Fax: 702-414 4805
Room rates: from $139 Sunday to Thursday; from $199 Friday and Saturday
Location: the Strip at East Spring Mountain Road
Theme: Renaissance Venice
Cost: $1.2 billion
Rooms: 4,049 suites
Shows: Lord of the Dance, V – The Ultimate Variety Show, plus headliners
Nightlife: V Bar supper club, Venus Lounge, La Scena Lounge, K2 nightclub
Attractions: Madame Tussaud's, Guggenheim Las Vegas and Russia's Hermitage Museum
Restaurants: 5 fine-dining establishments in the hotel itself, including the wonderful Lutece and the award-winning Delmonico Steakhouse, while 6 casual dining outlets include the delightful PS Italian Grill and the WB Stage 16 diner with live music
Chilling out: pool deck with private cabanas
Shopping: Grand Canal Shoppes, which has 5 more fine-dining restaurants, including the award-winning Postrio, plus 3 casual eating outlets
Other amenities: a massive wedding chapel, which can be divided up into three and Canyon Ranch Spa Club – one of the most luxurious on the Strip

Here you will find replicas of everything that Venice stands for, from the Doge's Palace to St Mark's Square, the Grand Canal and Rialto Bridge, all recreated to the finest details by sculptors with the help of two historians to 'ensure the integrity of the design and architecture'. In fact, its beauty and style is only matched by its service, which has established the Venetian as one of the most successful resorts on the Strip.

Towering glory: reflecting that success, the hotel recently opened a new $275 million, 12-storey, all-suite Venezia tower, which added a further 1,013 luxury suites, a lavish pool deck and the hotel's first wedding chapel. The pool deck has been based on a Venetian garden and includes a swimming pool, three spa pools and ornate gazebos.

★ ★ ★   BRIT TIP   ★ ★ ★

★   The Venetian is one of the few

★   Las Vegas hotels to actually

★   provide mini bars in its rooms!   ★

Suite dreams: each of the new suites is a whopping 700sq ft (65sq metres) – making them the largest standard rooms in the world according to the *Guinness Book of World Records*. They contain a spacious private bed chamber with draped canopies, a massive bathroom finished in Italian marble, and a sunken living room furnished with a convertible sofa, two upholstered chairs, a desk and a dining table!

Don't worry if you can't get a room in the new tower, though, as all the rooms in the main hotel are suites and at least double the size of a standard Las Vegas hotel room. The premium standard rooms have the same features as those in the tower, and all rooms come with a safe, mini bar, fax machine and copier, computer printer, three telephones with dual lines and dataport access and two colour televisions.

That's entertainment: as fantastic as the suites are though, you won't be in them long as the Venetian has a host of bars, lounges and restaurants that will entice you out. Newest on the

scene are the swanky V Bar, based on LA's sophisticated Sunset Room, and the glamorous Venus Lounge, home to an exotic range of drinks and Ladies in Red attending to your every whim. Michael Flatley has moved his amazing dance-based show to the Venetian, while the variety show has become a big hit.

The chill zone: if you need refreshing, try the Canyon Ranch Spa Club, next to the 5-acre (2-ha) pool deck, which has private cabanas and is modelled on a Venetian-style garden. The state-of-the-art spa features massage and treatments, a 40-ft (12-metre) rock-climbing wall, Pilates studio, spinning gym, therapeutic Watsu pools and Canyon Ranch Café.

Shopping heaven: the centrepiece of the main shopping mall, known as the Grand Canal Shoppes, is the reproduction of Venice's majestic Grand Canal and St Mark's Square and for a price you can even take a romantic gondola ride. One of the nicest things about the Venetian – depending on your preferences, of course – are the masses of beautiful people wearing fab Italian clobber. They may be the reason the NBC television network has opened a research centre in the Grand Canal Shoppes, where a large portion of new shows and promos will be tested.

Resort hotels off the Strip

Hard Rock Hotel

A big hit with models and celebs, plus trendy young things and their parents.

Website: www.hardrockhotel.com
Reservations: 702-693 5000
Fax: 702-693 5010
Room rates: from $119 Monday to Thursday; from $329 Friday to Sunday
Location: 4455 Paradise Road
Theme: rock 'n' roll
Rooms: 670
Nightlife: The Joint live gig venue, Baby's nightclub and the Center Bar

2

Restaurants: 4 fine-dining experiences including the famous Nobu and Mortoni's, 3 casual establishments including the Mexican Pink Taco, which is great for outdoor seating
Chilling out: pool and spa

A truly trendy hangout and an instant hit when it opened at the end of the 1990s, it has remained a Mecca for celebs and the beautiful people despite new competition in the guise of The Palms. Definitely not for the fainthearted, there is a strong adult vibe, particularly in the hotel's nightlife arenas. Baby's nightclub, for instance, is famous for being filled with glam *über*-babes in skimpy outfits and the celeb clientele has included Gwyneth Paltrow and Ben Affleck.

★ ★ ★   **BRIT TIP**   ★ ★ ★
★   ★
★   Right next to the Hard Rock   ★
★   Hotel is the amazing new Ice   ★
★   nightclub, with state-of-the-art   ★
★   special effects and 4,000sq ft   ★
★   (372sq metres) of dance space.   ★
★ ★ ★ ★ ★ ★ ★ ★ ★ ★ ★ ★ ★ ★ ★ ★ ★ ★

And so to bed: following a recent $100-million expansion, the hotel has added a new 330-room guest tower. Each room features French doors that open with views over the hotel's pool, the Strip or surrounding mountains. Rooms have leather headboards on king- or queen-sized beds, parchment and iron lamps, stainless steel bathroom sinks and various musical touches such as curtains with a musical instrument motif and framed photos of rock legends including Jimi Hendrix and Janis Joplin.

Las Vegas Hilton

Filled with conventioners; best just to visit for the *Star Trek* experience.
Website: www.lvhilton.com
Reservations: 702-732 5111
Fax: 702-732 5584
Room rates: from $89 Monday to Thursday; from $269 Friday to Sunday

Location: Paradise Road and Karen Avenue (behind the Strip)
Rooms: 3,174
Show: *Star Trek: The Experience*
Nightlife: the ever popular The Nightclub
Restaurants: 6 fine-dining restaurants including the delightful Andiamo, Bistro Le Montrachet and Margaritagrille, plus 4 casual outlets including a patio coffee shop and 24-hour diner
Chilling out: pool, spa, tennis courts
Shopping: 2 promenades

★ ★ ★   **BRIT TIP**   ★ ★ ★
★   ★
★   When Elvis first appeared in Las   ★
★   Vegas at the Last Frontier Hotel   ★
★   on the Strip in 1956 he was a   ★
★   flop. He didn't return until 1969   ★
★   when he mostly appeared – to   ★
★   great acclaim, of course – at the   ★
★   Las Vegas Hilton.   ★
★ ★ ★ ★ ★ ★ ★ ★ ★ ★ ★ ★ ★ ★ ★ ★ ★ ★

An understated elegance pervades what is ostensibly an upmarket hotel resort for business people attending one of the millions of conventions held in Las Vegas. For them, its location near the Convention Center is perfect, but it's about a 12-minute walk to the Strip, so it's a little off the beaten track for real tourists. The rooftop recreation deck includes a health club, massive swimming pool, six floodlit tennis courts and a putting green, while The Nightclub has all the latest high-tech nightlife gadgetry and is one of the in-places to be seen. Now, following a collaboration with Paramount Parks, the hotel is home to one of the most exciting theme entertainments in Las Vegas – *Star Trek: The Experience*.

The Palms Casino Resort

A sultry boutique resort, which has rapidly established itself as the city's top place to party, attracting both the hip and the famous.
Website: www.thepalmslasvegas.com

Reservations: 702-942 7777
Fax: 702-942 7001
Room rates: $99–140 Sunday to Thursday; from $140 up to $350 Friday and Saturday
Location: Flamingo Road, west of the Strip, close to the Rio All-Suite Hotel
Theme: sophisticated adult playground
Cost: $265 million
Rooms: 455 deluxe rooms
Entertainment: The Brenden Theater Complex, a state-of-the-art 14-screen cinema complex, a drive-in betting shop and two Bachelor Suites for stag parties and hen nights
Nightlife: Rain In The Desert, a multi-level nightclub and concert venue and Ghostbar, an indoor-outdoor lounge
Restaurants: include Nine from Chicago, Little Buddha Café from Paris, the upmarket Alizé, Garduños Mexican restaurant and the Blue Agave Oyster and Chile Bar
Chilling out: Skin Pool Lounge.
Other amenities: 20,000-sq ft (1,860-sq metre), 3-storey spa featuring candlelit yoga classes and fun and fruity body treatments

The original Aladdin management team could learn a great deal from the Texas-based Malouf family, who opened this party palace in a fanfare of glory in November 2001. David Schwimmer, Cuba Gooding Jr, Tyra Banks, Samuel L Jackson, Caprice and Matt Williams were among the celebrities invited to enjoy the delights of the boutique resort hotel, which has created the ultimate adult playground environment. Since then many more stars have arrived and continue to flock here.

With just 455 rooms – albeit luxury – it's the smallest of all the resort hotels – by thousands of rooms! Yet what it lacks in the bedroom department, it more than makes up for in the entertainment arena, and within 18 months of opening has garnered nearly 20 awards from reader polls conducted by the *Las Vegas Review Journal*. These include Best Hotel Nightclub and Best Nightclub for Rain in the Desert, Best Mexican Restaurant in a Hotel for Garduños, Best Gourmet Restaurant for Alizé, Best Movie Theatre for The Brenden Theatres cinema complex and Best Place to Spot Celebrities.

Here is a run-down of some of the elements that go together to create a smash hit of a hotel:

★ ★ ★   BRIT TIP   ★ ★ ★
★   ★
★   Just to give you an insight into   ★
★   VIP prices: a private room at The   ★
★   Palm's Rain in the Desert in goes   ★
★   from $300 to $1,000 a night!   ★
★ ★ ★ ★ ★ ★ ★ ★ ★ ★ ★ ★ ★ ★ ★ ★ ★ ★

Night owls: Rain in the Desert, located on the casino level, is a multi-story, multi-environment nightclub and concert venue, which opened with a special party featuring Macy Gray. It combines performances by international headliners, with an ultra hip dance club (see page 114) and private event facility, and comes with some amazing special effects including fog, haze, 16-ft (5-metre) fire plumes and 3-ft (1-metre) fireballs, while the bamboo dance floor is surrounded by a computer-programmed river of water with dancing jets and fountains. Ghostbar is a vibrant open-hour lounge on top of the 42-storey hotel tower, which has already won plaudits as a hot nightspot.

Best eats: this resort hotel has a fantastic line-up of restaurants that cover upmarket, steaks, casual and bistro-style dining. Top of the pile is the Alizé, the latest and probably swankiest offering from Las Vegan gourmet masterchef and restaurateur André Rochat. Named after the gentle wind that runs along the Mediterranean, it offers a French Riviera-style dining experience in an amazing glass atrium with aquamarine glass walls that provides spectacular views of the city. VIP tables are in front of the windows and secluded from the rest of the dining room by a curved glass partition. Rochat has won a clutch of awards for his distinctive restaurants, including Most Popular Restaurant in Las Vegas by the 2000 Zagat Survey and numerous awards for Best French Restaurants.

★ ★ ★ BRIT TIP ★ ★ ★

★ If good service is important, then ★ The Palms could be the place for you as the Malouf family is famous for excellent hospitality. ★

That's entertainment: one of the smartest moves the Malouf family made was to include the high-end, state-of-the-art Brenden Theater Complex, which not only provides an excellent spot to watch the latest films, but also gives the resort the chance to host film premiere parties. Masterminded by Johnny Brenden, grandson of Los Angeles' legendary Mann Theater developer, it has already hosted the Las Vegas premiere of *The Italian Job*, with a VIP party hosted by Mark Wahlberg in the swanky Real World Suite and an After-Party at the chic Little Buddha.
In the swim: The Skin Pool Lounge has set a new trend in exotic oasis indulgence with relaxation pools, chaise longues, four bars, billiard tables, outdoor swings, poolside blackjack and trampolines. You can even hire one of the private cabanas that come with TVs, fridges, telephones and VIP amenities, while DJs spin tunes day and night and food can be ordered from the Nine Steakhouse. The whole area is only open to hotel guests during the day, but is turned into a voyeuristic club at night (see page 115).
Suite dreams: The Palms has quickly become one of the most coveted private party spots in Las Vegas and its **Real World Suite** has already been used to host events for Leonardo DiCaprio, Avril Lavigne and Mark

Wahlberg. Ordinary mortals need not miss out on the fun as the hotel also has two **Bachelor Suites**, fitted out with dance poles (think Jamie Lee Curtis in *True Lies!*), a wooden dance floor and sophisticated sound system. The ultimate playrooms, perfect for both stag parties and hen nights, they're decked out in 1960s retro colour patterns, a mirror wall made up of fragmented squares of glass to create the effect of a disco ball, the same type of mirror above the bed, an LED lighting system and plasma TV screens.

Rio All-Suite Hotel

Proving there is life beyond the Strip, the Rio truly is an entertainment city in its own right.
Website: www.harrahs.com
Reservations: 702-252 7777
Fax: 702-253 6090
Room rates: from $65 Sunday to Thursday; from $139 Friday and Saturday
Location: 3700 West Flamingo
Theme: Tropical paradise
Cost: $200-million expansion
Rooms: 2,563 suites
Shows: the amazing Penn & Teller, musical comedy *The Scintas, Tony & Tina's Wedding*, the adult Showgirls revue and *Chippendales – The Show*
Nightlife: great spots include the Tequila Sky Bar, the VooDoo Lounge and Bikinis Beach and Dance Club
Entertainment: Masquerade Show in the Sky
Restaurants: 9 fine-dining restaurants include city favourites Antonio's, Buzios and Fiore Rotisserie and Grille, plus the new Gaylord Indian Restaurant, while 9 casual eateries include the funky VooDoo Café.
Chilling out: sand beach and outdoor recreational area
Shopping: Masquerade Village
Other amenities: 2 wedding chapels
    The Rio is consistently voted the best value hotel in America and has some of the finest restaurants – Buzio's, Fiore Rotisserie, Hamada's Asiana and Rosemary's – in Las

Vegas. It is also home to the city's first Wine Cellar Tasting Room, which has the world's largest collection of fine and rare wines, along with an array of tasting accessories.

★ ★ ★   BRIT TIP   ★ ★ ★

★   ★
★   The Rio may be off the beaten   ★
★   track of the Strip, but if you're   ★
★   near Harrah's, take the free   ★
★   shuttle bus between the two   ★
★   hotels – you don't have to be a   ★
★   guest of either to get a ride.   ★

★ ★ ★ ★ ★ ★ ★ ★ ★ ★ ★ ★ ★ ★ ★ ★

Since a major expansion project, it now has the Masquerade Show in the Sky, in which guests can ride aboard fantasy floats that glide above the crowds in a Mardi Gras-style fiesta of music and dance. This has become a much more adult-orientated show of late with topless girls for the evening performances, while the hotel has generally shifted in a more raunchy direction with the opening of the sexy Bikinis nightclub and two chi-chi lounges for grown-ups – the Tequila Sky Bar and the ever popular VooDoo Lounge.

★ ★ ★   BRIT TIP   ★ ★ ★

★   ★
★   If you arrive at a hotel by car or   ★
★   taxi, one bellhop will take your   ★
★   luggage out of the boot (trunk)   ★
★   – for which you have to tip   ★
★   him – then another takes it   ★
★   up to your room – and, yes,   ★
★   he needs a tip, too.   ★

★ ★ ★ ★ ★ ★ ★ ★ ★ ★ ★ ★ ★ ★ ★ ★

Life's a beach: outside, the Ipanema Beach comes with real sand beaches at the edge of a tropical lagoon, complete with waterfalls, plus four nautical-shaped swimming pools and five jacuzzi-style spas. Here you can bask in the sun or order a variety of services including personal massages, poolside cocktails and food.

When it comes to weddings, the Rio does it in style. An entire floor of the Masquerade Tower has been given over to wedding facilities including two chapels and two themed, 1,200-sq ft (112-sq metre) honeymoon suites and reception areas.

Other resort hotels

The following hotels still have their place in the city's hall of fame, but cannot compete with the big shots!

Imperial Palace

Friendly, reasonably priced hotel in prime location.
Website: www.imperialpalace.com
Reservations: 702-731 3311
Fax: 702-735 8578
Room rates: from $45 Monday to Thursday; from $100 Friday to Sunday
Location: the Strip at West Flamingo
Theme: Japanese
Rooms: 2,700
Show: *Legends in Concert*
Entertainment: Car collection
Restaurants: 9
Chilling out: Olympic-size swimming pool with waterfall and heated spa
Wedding chapels: One
Other facilities: a wedding chapel and the only 24-hour medical facility on the Strip, phone direct on 702 735 3600.

When the reviews of Las Vegas accommodation are given, the Imperial Palace hardly takes centre stage, yet after Circus Circus and Caesars Palace, it was actually one of the first hotels to adopt a theme and is the largest privately owned hotel in the world. Owner Ralph Engelstad favoured the clean lines of oriental design and plumped for a theme based on Japanese temple architecture. Now the resort is home to one of the longest-running shows on the Strip, houses a collection of vintage and special-interest cars and has a good-value full-service spa.

Tropicana

Exotic chilling-out environment for grown-ups.

Website: www.tropicanalv.com
Reservations: 702-739 2222
Fax: 702-739 2469
Room rates: from $59 Monday to Thursday; from $119 Friday to Sunday
Location: the Strip at Tropicana
Theme: tropical paradise island
Rooms: 1,875
Shows: *Folies Bergère* and *Comedy Stop*
Entertainment: live poolside entertainment and Wildlife Walk
Restaurants: 8
Chilling out: water park
Other amenities: the world's only swim-up blackjack table! Plus a wedding chapel

The Tropicana has had millions spent on an upgrade to create a colourful Caribbean Village façade and new main entrance to the Paradise Island, while its 'signature' is a spectacular laser light show on its Outer Island.

Inside, Wildlife Walk, in the covered walkway between the resort's two towers, is a wildlife habitat for tropical creatures from toucans to pygmy marmosets, cockatoos to Amazonian parrots. From here you can also see down to the 5-acre (2-ha) water park – home to peacocks, flamingos, Mandarin ducks, African crown cranes and black swans – and features lagoons, spas, waterfalls, a giant water-slide and the world's largest indoor–outdoor swimming pool. Here, live poolside entertainment will have you tapping your toes and moving your body to the beat of everything from rock to reggae as you gently sip a cocktail or two.

★ ★ ★ **BRIT TIP** ★ ★ ★
★   ★
★   ★
★   Pay a bit extra to get a room in   ★
★   the Tropicana's new tower with   ★
★   stunning views of the Strip – the   ★
★   older garden section is in dire   ★
★   need of an overhaul.   ★
★ ★ ★ ★ ★ ★ ★ ★ ★ ★ ★ ★ ★ ★ ★ ★

The Tropicana has been somewhat eclipsed by the newer, bigger and brighter resort hotels, but an inside source tells me plans have already been drawn up for a brand-new resort to be built on the site. Watch this space!

Hotels in Henderson

Just a 17-mile (27-km) drive from the Strip, Henderson is a small but important location for two gorgeous hotels overlooking the brilliant blue waters of Lake Las Vegas. Ultra-romantic settings with wonderful water-based amenities, they're a great place to base yourself if you want to escape the maddening kerchink, kerchink of slot machines yet be within easy reach of the city's fun-filled attractions.

Hyatt Regency Lake Las Vegas Resort

Great for business people and others looking for a break from the Strip.
Website: www.lakelasvegas.hyatt.com
Reservations: 702-567 1234
Fax: 702-567 6067
Room rates: from $115 Monday to Thursday, from $145 Friday to Sunday
Location: 101 MonteLago Boulevard, Lake Las Vegas Resort, Henderson
Theme: Moroccan
Rooms: 496
Entertainment: 2 live gig areas
Restaurants: 2, plus a gourmet coffee bar
Chilling out: spa and fitness centre, 2 swimming pools, a sandy beach and a golf course.

The hotel's beautiful architecture boasts massive, 2-storey arched windows and deep loggias to create an open-air Moroccan ambience, which is continued with the ornamental ironwork and concrete grills in decorative Moroccan patterns.

Each of the rooms and suites has sweeping views of the lake or mountains and amenities include hand-painted armoires, personal vanities, well-lit desks, two-line telephones and dataports, hair-dryers, coffee-makers, plush bathrobes, safes and fridges.

Overlooking the lake, the Japengo restaurant features fine dining in a dramatic setting. Reminiscent of its acclaimed sister restaurant in La Jolla, California, it serves a diverse menu of Pacific Rim-inspired specialities, while a full sushi bar provides a wide array of fresh sushi.

★ ★ ★   BRIT TIP   ★ ★ ★
★   ★
★   ★
★   One of the major drawbacks to   ★
★   arriving at a mega resort during a   ★
★   busy period is the length of time   ★
★   it will take for your luggage to be   ★
★   brought up to your room by a   ★
★   bellhop. Unless it's very heavy,   ★
★   you'd be advised to take it   ★
★   yourself.   ★
★ ★ ★ ★ ★ ★ ★ ★ ★ ★ ★ ★ ★ ★ ★ ★ ★

A casual restaurant provides a relaxed setting and offers an eclectic menu while the poolside bar and grill serves up a variety of fresh salads, sandwiches and grilled-to-order items. Other bars and lounges include a split-level lobby lounge offering speciality drinks and live entertainment with expansive views of the surrounding lake and mountains, and a casino bar with a permanent stage featuring live entertainment.

The casino is the only one in Las Vegas that is properly separated from the rest of the hotel and also the only casino with windows. The fact that they show off the grand views of the lake and mountains is all the better.

Two pools feature landscaped pool decks, palm-shaded terraces, a spa and fitness centre, tent-like cabanas and a water-slide, as well as a sandy beach along the lake for lounging, relaxing and swimming. Sailing, fishing, windsurfing, kayaking, canoeing and electric boats are all available on Lake Las Vegas.

For golf enthusiasts, the Hyatt has an exclusive hotel/golf club agreement with the Reflection Bay Golf Club, a par-72 Jack Nicklaus-designed resort course set on the tranquil shores of the lake. If it all sounds too good to be true, don't worry, I've been there and seen it all for myself – and it is real!

Ritz-Carlton Lake Las Vegas

An ultra-romantic, deluxe desert retreat-style resort that is still conveniently close to the hustle and bustle of Las Vegas.
Website: www.ritzcarlton.com
Reservations: 702-567 4700
Fax: 702-567 4777
Room rates: from $145 Monday to Thursday; from $170 Friday to Sunday
Location: MonteLago Village, 1610 Lake Las Vegas Parkway, Lake Las Vegas Resort, Henderson
Theme: classic sophisticated elegance
Rooms: 349
Nightlife: Firenze Lobby Lounge with live music
Restaurants: a main restaurant, plus poolside dining and a lobby lounge serving food
Chilling out: pool and gardens, beach and water activities
Other amenities: Spa Vita di Lago, access to 2 golf courses

Four Seasons lead the way, followed by the Hyatt Regency, now the upper crust Ritz-Carlton group has opened a fabulous new hotel right on the sandy shores of the beautiful Lake Las Vegas. Just a short ride from Las Vegas' Strip, this is the perfect place to get the full deluxe desert resort treatment, but still have easy access to the delights of Sin City.

An integral part of the MonteLago Village, guests at the hotel can stroll from their rooms over a quaint stone bridge fashioned after Florence's Pontevecchio, to find themselves in an olde worlde area filled with shops, restaurants and a new casino. The landscaped grounds provide a series of scenic walkways and cycling trails around the lake's shoreline, or guests can take to the waters in canopied water taxis, sailboats or kayaks.

Elegant yet relaxed: the Mediterranean ambience of the resort is reflected in the arched doorways, clay tile roofs, interior courtyards and the palette of sun-washed colours that are reflective of European waterside towns and lakeside villas. The rooms live up to the high Ritz-Carlton standards and come with top-notch Frette bedlinen, oversized marble bathrooms and a casually elegant decor. Many of the rooms also have private balconies that look over the vine-covered trellises, shaded loggias, water features, white sand beach and heated swimming pool. There are also 35 suites and two whopping 2,400-sq ft (223-sq metre) suites.

The fabulous Medici Café and Terrace is set in an incredibly romantic courtyard with pretty Florentine gardens for outdoor dining and views over the lake. Elegant yet relaxed, you can have breakfast and lunch here, while it turns into a fine-dining experience for dinner.

The chill zone: the luxurious, 30,000-sq ft (2,790-sq metre) Spa Vita di Lago is the first spa in America to offer treatments from Italy. La Culla is the signature treatment, inspired by age-old water and desert treatments, and is a multi-sensory experience which includes a steam, skin treatment, facial and massage while bathed in fragrance, light and sound. Describing itself as a wellness and beauty oasis, Spa Vita offers fitness facilities, Pilates, yoga, wellness and beauty consultations plus a range of skin treatments and massages.

Golf: access to the Falls Golf Club, a Tom Weiskopf-designed, 18-hole course with waterfall, canyons and stunning views of the Las Vegas Strip, plus Reflection Bay Golf Club, designed by Jack Nicklaus and ranked the number one golf course in Las Vegas by *Where* magazine.

Coming soon

Wynn Resort

At the former Desert Inn, on the corner of Sands avenue at the Strip.
Planned opening date: spring 2005
Estimated cost: $2.6 billion (really!)
Theme: none. It promises to break the hotel-casino mould in Las Vegas and provide a sophisticated, yet casually elegant environment
Rooms and suites: 2,701
Restaurants: 18 planned including 6 fine-dining restaurants
Entertainment: water-based extravaganza in the 2,080-seat Aqua Theater
Nightclub: One of the most technologically advanced in the city
Shopping: 78,000sq feet (7,254sq metres) of retail space devoted to high-end and designer boutiques
Other amenities: the 50-storey tower will devote an entire floor to a luxury spa, there will also be an outdoor entertainment area with a pool and a maze of lush, tropical-plant filled walkways with hidden cabanas. The hotel will be the only property on the Strip with an 18-hole golf course and a Ferrari and Maserati dealership.

Formerly known as La Rève, there is a dream-like quality about this project. Without a doubt, this is the grandest, biggest, costliest project in Las Vegas to date – and given the size and scope of the mega resorts, that really is saying something.

The story started when Steve Wynn, Las Vegas' most famous casino mogul, sold off his incredibly successful Mirage, Bellagio and Treasure Island resorts to what is now MGM Mirage, and snapped up the Desert Inn for a mere $270 million. He immediately closed the loss-making hotel amid rumours he planned to demolish it to make way for two brand-new ultra luxurious hotels.

Hotel awards

Trendiest hotels
Hard Rock Hotel, The Palms, Mandalay Bay, Venetian
Most sophisticated hotels
Bellagio, Monte Carlo, Mirage, Ritz-Carlton Lake Las Vegas, Venetian
Best hotel pools
Caesars Palace, Hard Rock Hotel, Mandalay Bay, The Palms, Monte Carlo, Tropicana
Friendliest hotels
Excalibur, Four Seasons, Hyatt Regency Lake Las Vegas, Luxor, Mandalay Bay, Ritz-Carlton Lake Las Vegas
Best hotels for nightlife
The Aladdin, The Palms, Hard Rock Hotel, Mandalay Bay, MGM Grand, New York-New York, Rio All-Suite Hotel

Eventually, after an 18-month suspense-filled silence, Wynn announced plans for the La Rève project, which includes a 514-ft (157-metre), 50-storey glass tower with 45 floors devoted to suites and rooms, below-ground valet parking, a massive casino floor, mezzanine floor to watch the action and a spa floor.

Using the same design team that was behind the Mirage and Bellagio, Wynn and his wife Elaine have this time set about ensuring that none of the resort's attractions can be seen from the Strip – unlike the fountains of the Bellagio, the volcano of the Mirage or the pirate ships of Treasure Island. Interestingly, the name La Rève has been dumped, following American backlash against the French for opposing the Iraq war, and replaced with Wynn Resort.

The tight-lipped owners have revealed little about the project except to say it will provide a balance between the type of classic luxury enjoyed by the well-heeled and hip décor to appeal to a younger clientele. Insiders say it is basically just a bigger and better Bellagio. Either way, when it opens it promises to be one of the most exciting attractions in a city already filled with eye-catching mega hotels.

Franco Dragone, who developed Cirque du Soleil's fantastic *O*, *Mystère* and *Zumanity* shows, has been working on a new production that will take place in a specially built Aqua Theater, which has an estimated price tag of around $24 million. A new mega-themed nightclub will have some of the most spectacular special effects of all the amazing Las Vegas clubs – complete with plush sofas and even beds to create a sophisticated-bordering-on-erotic environment.

★ ★ ★ BRIT TIP ★ ★ ★
★ ★
★ ★
★ You cannot register at any hotel ★
★ with a casino if you are under ★
★ the age of 21 – nor, for that ★
★ matter, can you gamble if you are ★
★ under 21. ★
★ ★ ★ ★ ★ ★ ★ ★ ★ ★ ★ ★ ★ ★ ★ ★ ★ ★

The Desert Inn itself is remaining and currently houses Wynn's multi-million-pound collection of modern art by Picasso, Matisse, Van Gogh and Cézanne, and is open to the public. Wynn himself is holed up on the ninth floor of the building – the former home of reclusive billionaire Howard Hughes, with its steel-framed doors and bullet-proof windows. Some say that Wynn, who is almost blind, is taking on some of the qualities of Hughes. Whatever the case may be, no one will know the full story on this mega resort until it finally opens, as all the staff working on it have signed contracts forbidding them to reveal details – or even talk about the project!

3

SHOWTIME

Everything from major production numbers to
magic shows, musical revues, comedy, adult shows
and the major music venues

One of the cornerstones of Las Vegas' early success was its policy of paying big bucks for big-name entertainers who could pull in big crowds. Entertainment is even more important now as a whole raft of top-notch musicals, magical shows and circus-led extravaganzas have elevated the Strip to the second Broadway of America. But, like so many other aspects of the city, it has now become very expensive. It's one thing to fork out $100 to $200 to see a headliner in action, but when you're paying anywhere from $70 to $200 to see a production show, you'll want to ensure it's your kind of thing.

Luckily, there are also many other better-priced productions, revues and music venues, while The City of Entertainment is unique in offering free live music at a whole host of lounges. The drinks prices may get a little steep – up to $12 a hit at some places – but they still offer both excellent value for money and generally a relaxed, casual environment (see Chapter 6).

The city has three other types of entertainment in spades: magic shows – some with music, others with comedy – dedicated and well-priced comedy and, of course, adult shows including everything from topless revues to lap dancers and strip joints.

This chapter covers most of them (see Chapter 6 pages 119–21 for adult clubs) and provides some helpful insights along the way. When it comes to the major production shows though, I have stuck to those booked for indefinite engagements as many others may last only six months

Something for nothing

Don't miss the amazing – and free – **Fremont Street Experience** in downtown Las Vegas. In addition to the multi-million pound electronic light and sound show, which takes place in the enclosed, traffic-free pedestrian mall, the city also provides five blocks of street performers and live music. Street performers include Hip Attitude Girls, Star Mimes, showgirls, violinist Barry Van Wie and blues guitarist Richard Torrance. Live bands usually perform at stages on First Street and Third Street from Tuesday to Saturday and the Fremont Street Experience takes place every hour on the hour from 7pm to midnight.

Call 702-678 5600 for information, visit www.vegasexperience.com or just head Downtown in the evening.

You can get into the carnival spirit at the Rio All-Suite Hotel by either watching or taking part in the **Masquerade Show in the Sky**. This fantastic parade, which takes place high above the casino floor, is an extravaganza of floats and dancers in exotic costumes with an adult twist. Daily shows at 3.30, 4.30, 5.30, 7, 8, 9 and 10pm are free, or you can pay $9.95 to don an exotic costume and ride on one of the main floats. You have to buy them in person at least one hour before the show and they do sell out! Call the Rio for more information on 702-252 7776.

Other free shows include fiery illusion stunts in **Lumineria** at Caesars Magical Empire, daily from 11am to 4.30pm, and free circus acts in the Main Arena of **Circus Circus** from 11am until midnight every day.

or less. Some prices given here include local sales tax, but if not specified, add 7%. There are other acts that are booked on a one or two-night basis and you can check these out before you go at:
www.vegasfreedom.com (the city's official website with details of all current shows), www.lasvegas.com (a comprehensive section on shows, comedians, regular local acts and live music venues); www.lvlocalmusicscene.com (non-hotel resort live music acts).

Also bear in mind you can visit www.ticketmaster.com to book more mainstream events.

Guide to ratings: ***** pure brilliance; **** fantastic; *** a great show; ** poor value for money.

★★★ **BRIT TIP** ★★★
★ ★
★ ★
★ Want to know why you pay so ★
★ much to see some of these Las ★
★ Vegas shows? Michael Flatley got ★
★ $250 million to take his ★
★ production to The Showroom at ★
★ the Venetian until 2007, while it ★
★ is reported that Celine Dion ★
★ signed a $100 million contract ★
★ with Caesars Palace to appear at ★
★ the Colosseum for three years. ★
★★★★★★★★★★★★★★★★★★★★

Major Productions

V – The Ultimate Variety Show

The Showroom at the Venetian, 702-948 3007 or 702-933 4230
Every show includes a breathtaking combination of magic, special effects, death-defying stunts and wild comedy. There is a core of show entertainers, plus a plethora of talented acts who perform elsewhere on the Strip through the week so no two shows are the same. An old yet new concept for a major resort hotel show, this has been taking Las Vegas by storm.
Rating: ***** Top-notch entertainment
Shows: nightly at 6pm

Tickets: $49, $59 and $69 for VIP package, which includes line pass, preferred seating and an autographed poster; $22 for children

A New Day

Colosseum Showroom, Caesars Palace, 702-474 4000 or online at www.ticketmaster.com
Celine Dion has signed an extended, exclusive contract with Caesars to star in her own show at a brand-new $95 million showroom built to look like Rome's Colosseum. The 4,000-seat showroom, with state-of-the-art lighting and oversized screens, creates the illusion of a European town square with picturesque temples and starry sky-scapes. It is the perfect backdrop for Celine's amazing show, which she will perform a minimum of 200 nights a year until at least March 2006. Created by Celine's own company and Franco Dragone, the director and creator behind Cirque du Soleil®, each song transports the audience to a different visual experience with the aid of the largest indoor LED screen in North America and the use of mood lighting. The cast of 58 performers, musicians and singers perform stunning choreography and amazing aerial stunts throughout the show.
Rating: ***** Showstoppingly brilliant, but pricey!
Shows: Wednesday to Sunday at 8.30pm
Tickets: $87.50, $127.50, $150 and $200

★★★ **BRIT TIP** ★★★
★ ★
★ ★
★ If you're determined to see ★
★ Celine Dion book tickets in ★
★ advance through TicketMaster at ★
★ www.ticketmaster.com. ★
★★★★★★★★★★★★★★★★★★★★

Mystère

At Treasure Island on the Strip, 702-894 7111
You're taken on a journey through time that allows the supreme athletes to

show off their strength and extraordinary flexibility with a mesmerising aerial bungee ballet, a precision performance based around Chinese poles and an awe-inspiring trapeze act. This truly is state-of-the-art theatre. The show originally cost $20 million to stage and is rivalled only by its new sister show at the Bellagio. Along with *Siegfried and Roy*, it should definitely be on your must-see list.

Rating: ★★★★★ You'll want to go back again and again

Shows: Wednesday to Sunday at 7.30pm and 10.30pm

Tickets: $88 including tax

★ ★ ★   **BRIT TIP**   ★ ★ ★

★ Try to be in your seats by 7pm to ★
★ enjoy the pre-show show. Arrive ★
★ after 7.15pm and you could ★
★ inadvertently become a part of ★
★ the show! ★

★ ★ ★ ★ ★ ★ ★ ★ ★ ★ ★ ★ ★ ★ ★ ★

O

At the Bellagio on the Strip, 702-693 7722

If you've ever been lucky enough to see the Cirque du Soleil® troupe in action, you'll know what makes these artists so special. The 70-odd cast of dancers, acrobats, actors, clowns, comedians and musicians may represent age-old talents of an old-style circus (without the animals), but that is where any similarities with the past comes to an end. O, like all the shows performed by the troupe, is a surrealist celebration of trapeze, dance, high-flying acrobatics and humour. In this case though, every act is performed in, on and above water in a $70-million theatre that was developed specifically for the Bellagio resort and Cirque du Soleil®.

O takes its title from the phonetic spelling of the French word for water – *eau*. The story takes you on a 90-minute voyage of the history of theatre in the trademark Cirque style with daring displays of aerial

gymnastics, high-flying trapeze numbers, synchronised swimming, fire-eating, mind-boggling contortions, clowns and high-diving stunts.

Rating: ★★★★★ Breathtaking

Shows: Friday to Tuesday at 7.30pm and 10.30pm

Tickets: main floor $121, balcony $99, obstructed view $93.50 all including tax

★ ★ ★   **BRIT TIP**   ★ ★ ★

If you're trying to decide
between *Mystère* and *O*, most
people find *Mystère* more
accessible. *O*, although brilliant,
is more ethereal.

★ ★ ★ ★ ★ ★ ★ ★ ★ ★ ★ ★ ★ ★ ★ ★

EFX Alive!

MGM Grand Theater, the MGM Grand on the Strip, 702-891 7777

This $45-million Broadway spectacular stars Rick Springfield. The 70-strong cast go on a surrealist, high-tech journey through space and time in an adventure that calls for singing, dancing and amazing pyrotechnics and visual effects. Central to it all is Springfield's quest to regain the powers of magic, laughter and imagination to win the heart of his true love. The plot may be a bit thin but the brilliant costumes, singing and dancing make up for it.

Rating: ★★★★★ Spectacular effects and show-stoppers

Shows: Tuesday to Saturday at 7.30pm and 10.30pm

Tickets: adults $55 and $75, children $40 including tax and programme

★ ★ ★   **BRIT TIP**   ★ ★ ★

★ Try not to sit close to the side at ★
★ the front at *EFX* as you may end ★
★ up seeing the machinery rather ★
★ than enjoying the effects! ★

★ ★ ★ ★ ★ ★ ★ ★ ★ ★ ★ ★ ★ ★ ★ ★

Zumanity

New York-New York, 702-740 6815

Billed as the provocative, erotic, adult side of the Cirque du Soleil®, this brand-new show made its debut after going to press with this guide. For this reason I can only tell you what I was told – that the show combines the usual amazing Cirque stunts, acrobatics and high-flying antics that have made *O* and *Mystère* two of the favourite shows in town – only this time with a sensual, passionate twist. The cast of 50 performers and musicians blend erotic rhythm with dance to create a world in which inhibitions are discarded.

★★★ **BRIT TIP** ★★★

Love birds wanting a romantic night out will adore the Love Seats and Duo Sofas that have been specially created in New York-New York's new theatre – custom-built for Cirque's *Zumanity*.

Rating: ★★★★★ Sensual and stunning
Shows: Tuesday to Saturday at 7.30pm and 10.30pm
Tickets: $55 and $75 for cabaret stools and theatre seats; Love Seats are $150 per pair and Duo Sofas $190 per pair

Dance

Lord of the Dance

The Showroom at the Venetian, 702-948 3007 and 702-933 4230.

The great man has moved from the New York-New York hotel into the Venetian for an extended run. A classic extravaganza of dazzling dance sequences from both Michael Flatley and his extraordinarily gifted cast, plus musical performances, this continues to be a major attraction in Las Vegas. My one caveat would be that for the sort of money involved I'd prefer to see a show I could only see

in Vegas, but maybe I'm being picky.
Rating: ★★★★ Amazing
Shows: Tuesday to Sunday at 8pm, plus Tuesday, Wednesday and Saturday at 10.15pm
Tickets: $75

Spirit of the Dance

Theatre Ballroom, Golden Nugget, 702-386 8100

Show-stopping Irish dance plus the passionate Latino rhythms of tango, flamenco and salsa in a breath-taking spectacular.
Rating: ★★★★ Brilliant
Shows: Nightly at 7.30pm
Tickets: $45 adults, $35 for under 12s, both including tax

Other Productions

Blue Man Group: Live at Luxor

Luxor Theater, The Luxor, 702-262 4400

The off-the-wall, off off Broadway production, which has been surprising, terrifying and entertaining theatre-goers in New York, Boston and Chicago, has become a Las Vegas staple. Mainstream this isn't, but it's still highly watchable. My one concern is the cost of the tickets – at more than $70 after tax, they're expensive for a show that requires very little stage decor or special effects.
Rating: ★★★★ Delightfully kooky
Shows: Sunday and Monday at 7pm, Wednesday to Saturday 7pm and 10pm, Saturday matinee at 4pm
Tickets: $69.50 and $79.50 plus tax

Master Magicians

Siegfried and Roy

Theater Mirage, the Mirage on the Strip, 702-792 7777

Siegfried and Roy are not names that strike an immediate chord with us Brits. But don't allow that lack of knowledge to let you miss out on one of the biggest and best shows in Las Vegas. The two illusionists appear in an extraordinary extravaganza that has been choreographed by a top impresario and will appeal to all ages. Central to the production are beautiful white tigers, 2-ton elephants and a host of other rare and exotic animals that are made to disappear in a mystifying series of tricks.

★★★ ★ ★ You can take a closer peek at ★ the animals used in Siegfried and ★ Roy's show by visiting their Secret ★ Garden at the Mirage (see ★ Chapter 10 page 152 for details). ★

Rating: ★★★★★ One of the best shows in town, mesmerising
Shows: Sunday to Tuesday at 7.30pm, Friday and Saturday at 7.30pm and 11pm
Tickets: $100.50 including two drinks, tax, tip and programme

Lance Burton, Master Magician

Lance Burton Theater, the Monte Carlo, 702-730 7160
Dubbed a World Champion Magician by his fellows, Burton demonstrates his powers to mystify and entertain in his own show at a theatre especially created for him. Once described by Johnny Carson as 'the best magician I've ever seen', Burton's show involves classic feats of levitation, Houdini-style escapes and mysterious disappearing acts, all done with the flair and pizzazz expected of modern-day magicians. It all starts with the illusion that won him the Grand Prix at the Federation International Society de Magique. Best of all, after more than four years at the Monte Carlo, his show is as fresh and as fun as the day it started.
Rating: ★★★★ Two hours of awe-inspiring, rib-tickling entertainment
Shows: Tuesday to Saturday at 7pm and 10pm
Tickets: From $54.95 to $59.95 including tax

★★★ ★ ★ To get a better deal on the major ★ shows, pick up as many of the ★ visitor magazines as you can and ★ look through for discount ★ coupons and two-for-one ★ specials. ★

Penn & Teller

Calypso Showroom, Rio All-Suite Hotel, 702-252 7776
The famous duo, recently named two of the funniest people alive in *Entertainment Weekly*'s 50 Greatest Comedians, have brought their famous stage show to Las Vegas for an indefinite engagement. Probably the coolest magicians around, their tricks are mind-boggling. If you failed to catch them during their Emmy award-winning TV show when it was aired in Britain – or in appearances in *Friends* and even *The Simpsons* – then here's the perfect opportunity to see them.
Rating: ★★★★★ Both riveting and funny
Shows: Wednesday to Monday at 8.30pm
Tickets: $55 including tax

Steve Wyrick, Magic to the Extreme!

Sahara Theatre, Sahara Hotel, 702-737 2515
Winner of the 2002 Magician of the Year Ward from the International Magic Society, Wyrick is famous for dangerous, death-defying stunts. After signing an eight-year deal with the Sahara, they built a new theatre for him – complete with a retractable roof for his final illusion. This is a high-energy show with dancing and amazing sleight-of-hand illusions, but one of the real showstoppers includes the moment when he walks through the blades of a spinning turbine engine.
Rating: ★★★★★ Heart-stopping
Shows: Wednesday to Saturday at 7pm and 10pm, Sunday at 7pm

Tickets: $45.95 and $62.45 for adults, $24 for under 13s, including tax and service charge

★★★ **BRIT TIP** ★★★

★ Shows generally last 90 minutes
★ and there are no intervals. You
★ can take drinks into shows in
★ plastic containers.

The Soul of Magic

The Big Easy Showroom, Bourbon Street Hotel & Casino, 702-737 7200

Duo Victor and Diamond have created a lively show that's as famous for its use of Motown, R&B and jazz music as for the stunning illusions. Considered the hippest magic show in town by the local ethnic groups.
Rating: ★★★★ Great
Shows: Tuesday to Sunday at 7.30pm
Tickets: $29.95 including one free drink

The Illusionary Magic of Rick Thomas

Tiffany Theatre, Tropicana Resort, 702-739 2411

A great magician who provides brilliant afternoon entertainment that is fantastic fun for the whole family.
Rating: ★★★★ Excellent value
Shows: Saturday to Thursday at 2pm and 4pm
Tickets: $16.95 for table seating, $21.95 for booth seating. A surcharge is added

★★★ **BRIT TIP** ★★★

★ The Tropicana will soon bite the
★ dust in preparation for the
★ building of an all-new resort
★ hotel, which means shows such
★ as Rick Thomas and the Folies will
★ be out of a home for a while.

Darren Romeo, The Voice of Magic

Siegfried & Roy Theater, the Mirage, 702-792 7777

Siegfried and Roy's protégé combines an amazing singing voice with fascinating illusions.
Rating: ★★★★ Superb
Shows: Tuesday to Saturday at 3pm
Tickets: $30 including tax, tip and one drink

Magical Comedy

The Amazing Jonathan

Theater Ballroom, Golden Nugget, 702-386 8100

Two-time winner of the Best Comic Magician of the Year by the World Magic Awards, Jonathan may not be well-known to British audiences, but is famous in America for his razor-sharp wit and bizarre illusions. Dubbed the Freddy Krueger of Comedy, he has his own TV show and has a long string of TV appearances. His hilarious Las Vegas show includes new assistant Psychic Tania, which has created a comedic duo who are the talk of the town.
Rating: ★★★★★ Crazy, wild, hilarious – don't miss it!
Shows: Tuesday to Sunday at 10pm
Tickets: $40 including tax

The Mac King Comedy Magic Show

Comedy Cabaret, First Floor, Harrah's Las Vegas, 702-369 5111

An anthropology graduate, Mac King spent his summer holidays doing a two-person magic act with fellow college student, the now legendary Lance Burton, before taking his show on the road. Along the way he has made a name for himself as a talented magician with an offbeat, witty twist that gives him a broad appeal, and has appeared on shows such as *The World's Wildest Magic*, *An Evening at the Improv, Penn & Teller's Sin City Spectacular* and *Comic Strip Live*.

Rating: ***** Great fun and excellent value entertainment
Shows: Tuesday to Saturday at 1pm and 3pm
Tickets: $14.95

Stand-up Comedy

Rita Rudner

Cabaret Theatre, New York-New York Hotel, 702-740 6815

It's rare that a woman makes it to the top in comedy without becoming the target for sexist jibes, yet the multi-talented Rita has done just that. Her deadpan, soft-spoken delivery is excellent and is matched by the quality of her observations that never fail to keep an audience in stitches. Unashamedly feminine with her big, blue eyes, beautiful skin and gentle, yet questioning voice, she has added a sophisticated edge to the world of comediennes with wry, quirky comments on everything from relationships to family and cleaning women. A sell-out wherever she appears, this new theatre was specially built for her indefinite Las Vegas engagement. In between shows, she continues to work on Hollywood scripts and after the success of her first novel, *Tickled Pink*, is now working on a second.
Rating: ***** Comedic genius
Shows: Sunday to Thursday at 8pm, Friday at 9pm, Saturday at 7pm and 9pm
Tickets: $46 including tax

Musical Comedy

The Scintas – It's A Family Thing

The Masquerade Showroom, Rio All-Suite Hotel, 702-252 7776

A fantastic blend of singing, dancing, humour and plain old-fashioned fun has made this light-hearted look at the loves and rivalries within an Italian-American family a surprise hit in Las Vegas. Great moments include an impression of Tom Jones, plus renditions of songs by Celine Dion,

Patsy Cline and even the Rolling Stones. What really appeals to the largely American audience though, is the somewhat schmaltzy songs of family devotion, but don't let that put you off!
Rating: **** Musical comedy at its best
Shows: Friday to Wednesday at 7.30pm
Tickets: $49.95

★★★ **BRIT TIP** ★★★

★ You may end up sharing a table ★
★ with strangers at The Scintas, but ★
★ this won't detract from the ★
experience!

Society of Seven

CenterStage Showroom, the Aladdin, 702-785 5000 or through www.ticketmaster.com

The famous American comedy troupe has created a show of music and comedy routines specifically for the new Aladdin showroom. Hilarious character impersonations include Sammy Davis Jr, Little Richard, Liberace, Sonny & Cher, Tina Turner and Michael Jackson.
Rating: **** Very American in flavour, but accessible to Brits too
Shows: Tuesday to Sunday at 8pm
Tickets: $34.95 and $45. Dinner and show packages are available at $55 or $65 with dinner at the award-winning Zanzibar Restaurant

Tribute to Frank, Sammy, Joey & Dean

Greek Isles Hotel & Casino, 702-737 5540

This is a trip back in time to the 1960s Las Vegas Rat Pack days when the boys were busy making the original *Ocean's Eleven* movie by day and partying hard by night.
Rating: ***** A big hit
Shows: Thursday to Sunday at 7pm
Tickets: $39.95. Dinner show $49.95 with seating at 5.30pm

Impressionists

Danny Gans

Danny Gans Theater, The Mirage, 702-791 7111.
Singer, comedian, actor and impressionist Danny Gans portrays everyone from Prince to Sinatra. After wowing locals and tourists alike with his range of 300 voices at the Rio, he has had his own theatre built for him at the Mirage and is still always a sell-out.
Rating: **** Sure-fire winner
Shows: Tuesday to Thursday and Saturday and Sunday at 8pm
Tickets: $80 and $100 for preferred seating (first eight rows)

Wayne Newton

Wayne Newton Theater, Stardust Hotel, 702-732 6325.
Best-known to Brits for his portrayal of 'shock-jock' Howard Wick on *Ally McBeal*, his nickname in America is Mr Las Vegas, thanks to the length of time he has been entertaining people in the city. His head-liner show is a mixture of hit covers and guests doing turns as impersonators.
Rating: **** Great fun entertainment
Shows: Saturday to Thursday at 9pm
Tickets: $54.95. Children over 12 admitted with an adult

★★★ **BRIT TIP** ★★★
★ ★
★ ★
★ Follow the locals and eat ★
★ elsewhere before or after the ★
★ show – the Stardust is not famed ★
★ for its good food or service! ★
★★★★★★★★★★★★★★★★★★★

Lasting Impressions

Flamingo Showroom, Flamingo Hotel, 702-733 3333
Bill Acosta has earned critical acclaim as an international singer and impressionist. A highlight of this show, which also features topless dancers, is Acosta's rendition of President Bill Clinton reminiscing over the Twelve Days of Christmas gifts he received from his celebrity friends – from Andy Williams's partridge in a pear tree to 12 people terminated by a mould.
Rating: *** Hilarious
Shows: Saturday to Thursday at 10pm, plus an extra performance at 7.30pm Tuesday
Tickets: from $49.95 to $69.95 including tax

Legends in Concert

Imperial Theater, Imperial Palace, 702-794 3261
Here's a neat way to see all your favourite music stars from Elton John to Madonna, Michael Jackson to Elvis, the Beatles to Liberace. The look- and sound-alikes truly have *Stars in Their Eyes* and together put on one of the most highly rated and popular shows in town.
Rating: *** Great impersonations let down a little by a lack of exciting choreography
Shows: Monday to Saturday at 7.30pm and 10.30pm
Tickets: $34.50 for adults and $19.50 for under 12s

An Evening at La Cage

Mardi Gras Plaza on the third floor of the Riviera, 702-794 9433
Frank Marino stars in the quicksilver world of lipstick, high heels, nine-button evening gloves and put-down lines to die for in this upmarket drag show that wins the hearts of even the most conservative theatre-goers.
Rating: *** Great fun and good value for money
Shows: every night, except Tuesday, at 7.30pm and 9.30pm
Tickets: $24.95

★★★ **BRIT TIP** ★★★
★ ★
★ ★
★ Arrive early for La Cage to get ★
★ good seats and get your drinks ★
★ before you go in as no drinks are ★
★ served inside the showroom. ★
★★★★★★★★★★★★★★★★★★★

American Superstars

Broadway Showroom, the Stratosphere on the Strip, 702-380 7711 Another testimony to the huge success of the long-running *Legends in Concert* is this celebrity-tribute extravaganza. Here you can see stars such as *Men in Black*'s Will Smith strut his stuff Big Willie Style and a full line-up of the Spice Girls, alongside impressionist favourites Michael Jackson, Madonna and Gloria Estefan.
Rating: *** Fun, but not as good as Legends, this is for real fans of *Stars in Their Eyes*!
Shows: every night at 7pm, except Thursday, plus Wednesday, Friday and Saturday at 10pm
Tickets: adults $29.65 and 5–12s $24.15 including tax

The Second City

Bugsy's Celebrity Theater, the Flamingo Hilton, 702-733 3333 A well-known sketch and improvisation comedy company providing entertainment on a par with the Blue Man Group. The troupe was first formed in Chicago in 1959 and is now famous for both its rehearsed skits and on-the-spot creations – many of which are sparked off by ideas from the audience. Martin Short and Jim Belushi among many other American comedians have made surprise appearances.
Rating: **** Pure entertainment
Shows: Thursday to Tuesday at 8pm, plus Friday and Saturday at 10.30pm
Tickets: $29.95

Comedy Clubs

Carolee's Comedy Club

Carolee's Theatre, Buffalo Bill's, 1-800-FUN STOP
This venue always books a great line-up of acts who regularly appear at top comedy clubs in America.
Shows: Friday and Saturday at 9.30pm
Tickets: $12.95

Catch a Rising Star Comedy Club

Comedy Club, the Excalibur, 702-597 7600
One of America's most famous comedy clubs, which has helped shape the careers of many of the best-known and best-loved comedians of America – from Robin Williams to Billy Crystal, Jerry Seinfeld and more. Las Vegas now has a growing crop of comedy spots, but this remains by far the best, with top big-name comedians headlining
Shows: nightly at 10pm, plus Thursday at 7.30pm
Tickets: $18.95

Improv Comedy Club

The Improv, Harrah's Las Vegas, 702-369 5000
Recently voted Best Comedy Club in the Las Vegas Review Journal by readers and critics for its stand-up routines by up-and-coming stars of comedy.
Shows: Tuesday to Sunday at 8.30pm and 10.30pm
Tickets: $24.95. Dinner packages available at $55

Comedy Theatre

Flamingo O'Shea's Casino, 702-737 1343
Featuring the amazing hypnotist Justin Tranz (get it?) in Hip-Nosis: Playin' With Your Head
Shows: Monday to Friday at 9pm, Saturday at 8pm
Tickets: $35 including tax and tips

Riviera Comedy Club

Mardi Gras Plaza on the first floor of the Riviera on the Strip, 702-794 9433
A nightly line-up of top stand-up comedians and comedy acts, many of whom have appeared on American TV.
Shows: Sunday to Thursday at 8pm and 10pm, Friday at 10pm, Saturday at 9pm
Tickets: $29.50 plus tax and handling fees

The Sandy Hackett Comedy Club

Greek Isles Hotel & Casino, 702-737 5540

A roster of regular performers at this great comedy club include Fats Johnson, Tony d'Andrea, Keith Barany and Shuli Egar. Wednesday night is reserved for female performers only and hosted by Carole Montgomery.
Shows: nightly at 9pm with a steak and shrimp dinner
Tickets: $14.95

Dinner Shows

Ba-Da-Bing

Sazio's Restaurant, The Orleans, 702-365 7111

Hilarious swipe at the world of mobsters in a family-friendly song, dance and variety show with plenty of audience participation. The story follows the plans of all the mob 'families' in Las Vegas to put on a surprise birthday bash for Mr Big, the Godfather of the city. The food that goes with this dinner show is, of course, Italian and includes a choice of rib eye steak and lasagne, homemade Tiramisu, salad, champagne and a piece of Mr Big's birthday cake.
Rating: **** Great fun
Shows: Thursday to Monday at 7.30pm
Prices: $55 and 75 adults, $35 under 10s

Caesars Magical Empire

Sultan Palace and Secret Pagoda at Caesars Palace, 702-731 7333
Caesars Magical Empire is an elaborately themed, multi-chambered restaurant/theatre where dinner is combined with illusions and magic. A centurion guides you to one of 10 dining chambers where you'll be entertained by a wizard during your meal. Afterwards you are guided through misty catacombs for the series of 'shows' and you can take a brief break at the Grotto Bar, nestling in a dragon's mouth cave, or at the Spirit Bar, which is haunted by a mysterious poltergeist who enjoys spooking unwary guests. Each show in the Secret Pagoda lasts 18 minutes with performances every 25 minutes, starting at 6.15pm. The Sultan's Palace has a 35-minute stage show every 50 minutes, starting at 7.10pm.
Rating: ** Great idea but basically an over-priced Disney-style ride

★★★ BRIT TIP ★★★
★ ★
★ ★
★ Prepare for long waits to see the ★
★ different shows that make up the ★
★ dining experience at Caesars ★
★ Magical Empire. ★
★★★★★★★★★★★★★★★★★★

Shows: dinner shows run Tuesday to Saturday from 11am to 10pm. Show-only tickets available from 11am to 4pm. Call in advance for schedule
Prices: $75.50 including tax and tip, $19.50 for 5–12s. Show only tickets are $26.50 for adults, $10 for 5–12s

Tony and Tina's Wedding

Calypso Showroom, Rio All-Suite Hotel, 702-252 7776
This comedy dinner show takes you on a romp through a classic American-Italian wedding as Anthony Nunzio Jr marries Valentina Lynne Vitale. The satire begins with the announcement of the wedding, then members of the audience join in the entire event from wedding ceremony to rowdy reception complete with Italian buffet dinner – allowing for plenty of improvisation along the way!
Rating: **** Great fun
Shows: nightly at 7pm
Tickets: $65 and $75 including tax, hors d'oeuvres, champagne toast and a full Italian buffet

Tournament of Kings

King Arthur's Arena at the Excalibur, 702-597 7600
Central to this re-creation of a knights' battle are the laser lights, fireworks and clouds of billowing water vapour

that give the production an air of mystery and magic. The musical begins when Merlin grants a young boy's wish to be a knight by transporting him back to the Middle Ages and transforming him into the White Knight of Kent. Along the way he meets King Arthur and Queen Guinevere and battles with the treacherous Dark Knight to win a princess's hand in marriage. The trick to seeing this show is to finish off your dinner before you become engulfed in water vapour!

Rating: **** One of the top shows – good for horses, feasts and magic!
Shows: 6pm and 8.30pm
Price: $41.95

Afternoon Shows

Bottoms Up
See review and details opposite

Darren Romeo
See review and details on page 49

The Mac King Comedy Magic Show
See review and details on page 49

Rick Thomas
See review and details on page 49

Viva Las Vegas
At the Broadway Showroom of the Stratosphere on the Strip, 702-380 7711
Combining lively dance numbers, singing, comedy and displays of magic, this is a revue in the old style of variety acts. The highlight is Golden Joe Baker's hilarious rendition of a selection of Elvis classics.

Rating: **** A belter of a show!
Shows: Monday to Saturday at 2pm and 4pm
Tickets: $11

★ ★ ★   BRIT TIP   ★ ★ ★
★   *Viva Las Vegas* is not only a great   ★
★   afternoon show, but you're   ★
★   bound to find free tickets for it.   ★

Adults only on the Strip
Watch out if you go down to the big theme resorts today, for you're more and more likely to find topless shows in what were once considered family-friendly hotels. Of course, adult shows have always been a facet of Las Vegas entertainment, but never quite so blatantly out on the Strip. Is it a reflection of waning interest in traditional shows – unlikely – or just another cleverly disguised attempt to get punters into gambling dens? Your guess is as good as mine, but either way, here are they are.

Bottoms Up
Bugsy's Theater, the Flamingo on the Strip, 702-733 3333
Breck Wall's old-fashioned comedy has won awards and a place in the heart of Las Vegas – hence its appearance twice daily at the Flamingo. This show is filled with both topless dancers and some pretty gorgeous men, too.

Rating: **** Sexy frolics
Shows: Monday to Saturday at 2pm and 4pm
Tickets: $12.95

Crazy Benny's Adult Game Show
Ibiza USA Nightclub, Dessert Passage at the Aladdin, 702-836 0830.
Prepare to find yourself doing and saying the unexpected at one of the funniest adult audience participation shows in town. Benny has more than $1,000 worth of prizes to give away during each show – think sex toys, dolls, watches and leather coats – but you have to earn them!

Rating: ***** Great fun
Shows: Daily at 9pm
Tickets: $29.95 including tax

Dr Naughty – A-rated Comedy Hypnotist
Bourbon Street Comedy Theatre, Bourbon Street Hotel, 120 East Flamingo Road, 702-228 7591

This is one of those acts in which unsuspecting members of the audience are hypnotised and then made to do things they would never ordinarily do. What makes this different is the really naughty edge, which creates perfect entertainment for voyeurs and exhibitionists alike. A perennial favourite is the scenario in which an adult is regressed to the mental age of a child, put in a birthday party setting and then given presents of sex toys.

Rating: ***** Hilarious
Shows: Monday to Saturday at 10.15pm
Tickets: $45 including tax

★★★ You must be over 21 to see any of these adult shows, with the exception of *Jubilee!* for which you must be over 18.

The Folies Bergères

Tiffany Theater in the Tropicana on the Strip, 702-739 2414
A turn-of-the-last-century Parisian music hall is the scene for the opening and final acts of the longest-running show in Las Vegas, a tribute to France's early nightclubs that has been entertaining crowds since 1957. This latest version combines award-winning production numbers from past Folies shows with new production sequences, dazzling costumes and scenery and, of course, the famous Folies showgirls, who perform amazing feats in their high-kicking can-can and chorus-line numbers.

★★★ Choose your seat with care at *Folies* – it can be hard to see from some of the long tables and the plastic seats are uncomfortable after a while.

Rating: *** Well done, but more old-style revue than new spectacle
Shows: every night, except Thursday, at 8pm (covered) and 10.30pm (topless)
Tickets: $44.95 for table seating and $54.95 for booth seating

Jubilee!

Jubilee Theater at Bally's on the Strip, 702-739 4567
A lavish, seven-act tribute to American music, with topless showgirls and scantily clad guys. From the Roaring Twenties to the rock 'n' roll era of Elvis, it also features a seductive Sampson and Delilah sequence, a master magician who makes a 26-ft (8-metre) long helicopter appear, and a spectacular sinking of the *Titanic* in which 2,000 gallons (9,100 litres) of water flood on to the stage. Just to give you some idea of the scale of its lavishness, more than 1,000 costumes are worn by the cast of 100 dancers and singers, while 70 different sets and backdrops and about 100,000 light bulbs are required to create the enchanting spectacles.

Rating: **** Lavish, wonderful over-the-top production numbers
Shows: Saturday to Thursday at 7.30pm and 10.30pm
Tickets: $53 to $70 including tax

★★★ Like a show both men and women can enjoy? *Skintight* is an excellent option as it's the only semi-naked revue to include both male and female dancers.

Skintight

Main Showroom, Harrah's Las Vegas on the Strip, 702-369 5111
This adult revue has everything – dance, music, comedy, hilarious skits – plus *über* fit babes and guys.
Rating: **** Good entertainment
Shows: Monday to Wednesday, plus Saturday at 10.30pm, Friday at

10pm and midnight, and Sunday at 7.30pm and 10.30pm
Tickets: $39.95, dinner packages $65

Splash: Voyage of a Lifetime

Splash Theater, Riviera Hotel, 702-477 5276
Another big-time crowd-puller aimed specifically at adults and, as the name suggests, plenty of water-based show-stoppers feature in this magical extravaganza. You are taken deep beneath the ocean waves in Splash's 'virtual submarine' on a nautical voyage of discovery around the North Pole, the Bermuda Triangle and the lost city of Atlantis. A massve on-stage water tank provides a perfect setting for the synchronised swimmers, divers and mermaids.
Rating: *** Past its heyday, but still great fun
Shows: nightly at 7.30pm and 10.30pm. Adults only for the 10.30pm show
Tickets: $42.40 for reserved seating, $51.50 for VIP reserved seating

Tease

Blue Note Las Vegas, Desert Passage at the Aladdin, 702-862 8307
A sexy new musical comedy that combines a classic Broadway musical with a Las Vegas production show and audience participation dinner theatre. Set in a gentlemen's club, it ostensibly focuses on behind-the-scenes antics during a stag night – the perfect backdrop for a show that involves risqué jokes, amazing songs, clever dance routines and a fair amount of audience participation. The characters include new girl Sue-Ann, bi-sexual Raven, stripper-come-mother-figure Portia, Angel, who dreams of being discovered, Vinny the bus-boy and Billy Bob the groom.
Rating: ***** One of the most entertaining adult shows in town
Shows: Wednesday to Monday at 10pm, with a 7.30pm show on Wednesday and Saturday
Tickets: $39.95 for reserved seating,

$49.95 for VIP seating, high roller booths $59.95 all including tax

★ ★ ★   **BRIT TIP**   ★ ★ ★

If you're looking for a little late-night entertainment after Tease you won't have to go far. The Desert Passage is also home to the Ibiza USA nightclub (see Chapter 6 page 113).

X – An Erotic Adventure

Centrestage, Aladdin Hotel, 702-736 7114
Not just titillation, but a surprisingly entertaining mix of comedy, dancing and singing. This revue doesn't just put the erotic into topless shows on the Strip, but adds a great deal more spice too. The eight sexy dancers are constantly caressing each other, they lie together in a tub, undress each other in bed and act out the part of strict headmistresses admonishing naughty schoolgirls until they finally end up with very little of their sizzling costumes still on. In between, comedian John Padon has the audience in stitches with his wry observations about sex. Each month a different Playboy Playmate is a guest star.
Rating: ***** Excellent fun for adults
Shows: Tuesday to Saturday at 10.30pm
Tickets: $44.95

★ ★ ★   **BRIT TIP**   ★ ★ ★

The early evening performances of *Folies Bergères* and *Showgirls of Magic* are the only two adult shows that are NOT topless.

Showgirls

Crazy Girls Fantasy Revue

The Riviera Hotel, 702-477 5276
Plain old-fashioned topless show.

Rating: *** Enjoyable
Shows: Tuesday to Saturday at
8.30pm and 10.30pm
Tickets: $21.95. VIP seating and
dinner/show combinations are
available

La Femme

La Femme Theater, MGM Grand on
the Strip, 702-891 7777
Billing itself as a show that 'celebrates
beautiful women and the art of the
nude', all the 12 dancers are
members of the original Crazy Horse
dance troupe from one of the hottest
popular nightspots in Paris.
Rating: *** Entertaining but pricey
Shows: Wednesday to Monday at
8.30pm and 10.30pm
Tickets: $59 including tax and
programme

Midnight Fantasy

The Luxor on the Strip, 702-262
4400
Featuring singing, dancing and a lot
more besides in an outrageous and
provocative topless revue.
Rating: **** Filled with sexy ladies
Shows: Tuesday, Thursday and
Saturday at 8.30pm and 10.30pm,
Wednesday and Friday at 10.30pm,
Sunday at 8.30pm
Tickets: $34.95 including tax

Showgirls

Samba Theater, Rio All-Suite Hotel,
702-252 7776
An all-new, sexy, late-night adult show
tracing the history of showgirls
throughout the ages from the famous
Ziegfield Follies right up to Madonna
and MTV video showgirls. The

Headliner Showrooms

Grand Garden Arena: MGM Grand on the Strip, 702-891 7777. The biggest venue in Las Vegas regularly hosts major concerts and sporting events. This is where Holyfield met Tyson for their heavyweight champion title clash and where top-notch performers like Sting, Elton John, Bette Midler, Gloria Estefan, Phil Collins and Billy Joel play when they're in town. The 16,325-seat venue has also hosted the Professional Bull Riders Championships and national league hockey. Tickets are likely to cost anything from $100 up.
Hollywood Theater: MGM Grand, 702-891 7777. The MGM's more intimate venue (a mere 650 seats) is still big enough to attract such names as Smokey Robinson, Gladys Knight, Tom Jones and Wayne Newton.
Circus Maximus Showroom: Caesars Palace, 702-731 7333. Since its gala opening in 1966, Judy Garland, Frank Sinatra, Diana Ross and Liberace have headlined here. More recent stars include David Copperfield, Liza Minnelli, Julio Iglesias and Celine Dion.
Hilton Theater: Las Vegas Hilton, 702-732 5111 for show information. Headliners include Johnny Mathis.
Celebrity Room: Bally's, 702-739 4567 for information, times and reservations. Headliners include Liza Minnelli and Penn & Teller.
Circus Maximus: Caesars Palace, 702-731 7333 for show times, prices and reservations. Recent acts include Huey Lewis and the News, Earth, Wind and Fire and Tony Bennett.
Mandalay Bay Events Center: 702-632 7580. Steely Dan, Ricky Martin and REO Speedwagon have all appeared here recently.
Orleans Showroom: The Orleans, 702-365 7075. Recent headliners include the Everly Brothers, Air Supply and Frankie Avalon.
Congo Room: Sahara on the Strip, 702-737 2515 for information and reservations. The Drifters, the Platters and the Coasters have headlined here.

talented cast don't just strut their stuff, but execute top-notch dance routines
Rating: ★★★★ Great entertainment
Shows: Monday to Saturday at 11pm
Tickets: $39.95

Showgirls of Magic

Parisian Cabaret, Hotel San Remo, 702-597 6028
Now for something a little different: topless showgirls doing magic – and it works. In between the dancers put on some enjoyable routines.
Rating: ★★★★ Enjoyable
Shows: Tuesday to Sunday at 8pm and 10.30pm
Tickets: $25.99 including two drinks

Girls' Night Out

Chippendales – The Show

Club Rio, Rio All-Suite Hotel, 702-252 7776
One of the loudest of the all-male revue shows, which leaves very little – a floss-thin G-string – to the imagination. Think motorcycles, beds and a giant computer monitor and imagine *über*-fit men writhing all over them and you'll build up a good picture of what's in store. Prepare to get your best screaming voice ready!
Rating: ★★★★★ Polished perfection
Shows: Thursday at 8pm, Wednesday and Friday to Monday at 10pm
Tickets: $34.95 and 44.95

Men, The Show!

La Cage Theatre, Riviera Hotel on the Strip, 702-794 9433
There's something here for every taste as the producers scoured the globe for a cast of hot male strippers happy to strut their stuff. Song and dance routines are rampant, audience participation a must and hilariously sexy routines include the now famous marine corps rifle drill team in which

Booking tickets in advance

By and large you should have no problem getting tickets to see most of the shows, and you can usually buy them in advance by phone or in person at the hotel's theatre box office. Just bear in mind that getting show tickets in Las Vegas depends on the time of year, the day of the week and whether there is a huge convention in town. For details of the best times to visit see The Best Times to Go (page 10). In all cases, phone ahead to confirm showtimes, dates and prices as these are subject to change without notice. You can find out exactly who will be performing – including the big top-billing stars during your visit to Las Vegas – by phoning the Las Vegas Convention and Visitors' Authority on 702-892 0711 to request a free copy of *Showguide*. Many of the major tour operators will also be able to book tickets in advance for the major shows or you can try attraction specialists Keith Prowse (01232 232425, www.keithprowse.com).

A cheaper alternative for advance booking is to look at the Las Vegas Host Shows web page on www.lasvegashost.com/lvhshows.htm, email them at: lasvegashosts@mltvacations.com or call 702-798 5246. You can now also buy tickets to shows, tours, attractions and rides through www.showtickets.com which is owned by the Las Vegas-based Allstate Ticketing company.

★ ★ ★ BRIT TIP ★ ★ ★
★   ★
★   ★
★ With so much to see and do in ★
★ Las Vegas, it's unlikely you'll have ★
★ time to go to the movies, but ★
★ there are two advantages: you ★
★ get to see a film before it hits our ★
★ shores and it's the one place you ★
★ can guarantee not to hear the ★
★ sound of slot machines! Tickets ★
★   cost around $8.   ★
★ ★ ★ ★ ★ ★ ★ ★ ★ ★ ★ ★ ★ ★ ★ ★ ★

the boys really do get to play with
their toys!
Rating: ★ ★ ★ ★ ★ Sizzlingly hot!
Shows: Wednesday to Monday at
10pm
Tickets: $47.25

Thunder From Down Under

Merlin Theater, Excalibur on the Strip,
702-597 7600
The trio of top Aussie hotties who
have been entertaining a crowd of
mostly women aged anywhere from
their 20s to their 70s for five years in
the city, last year moved into their
new home at the Excalibur. However,
the troupe remains one of the best all-
male entertainers in town – largely
because they don't take themselves
seriously and because they like to
include members of the audience in
the show. Watch out if you get pulled
on stage, you could find yourself
murmuring 'Oh baby' into a
microphone in your best Meg Ryan-
faking-it voice!
Rating: ★ ★ ★ ★ ★ Prepare to be whipped
into a frenzy!
Shows: nightly at 7.30pm, plus an
11pm show on Friday and Saturday
Tickets: $38.45

Cinemas

Brenden Theaters

The Palms, 4321 West Flamingo
Road, 702-507 4849,
www.brendentheaters.com
A state-of-the-art, 14-theatre cinema
complex at the ultra hip The Palms
hotel resort. The brainchild of Johnny
Brenden, grandson of the legendary
Mann's Chinese Theater developer in
Hollywood, LA, it has wall-to-wall
curved screens, THX digital sound
and stadium seating with comfortable,
high-backed rocking chairs, plus love
seats.
  Brenden Theaters has fast become
the hottest Cineplex in town and now
hosts many film premieres including
Mark Wahlberg's *The Italian Job*, with
post-premiere parties at The Palms'
Little Buddha restaurant.

Crown 14 Theaters

Neonopolis, 450 East Fremont Street,
702-383 9600.
Movies at the Crown 14 usually
begin around noon and go on until
11pm with midnight showings on
Friday and Saturday.

★ ★ ★ BRIT TIP ★ ★ ★
★   ★
★   ★
★ If you head to the Crown 14 ★
★ cinema complex, park at the ★
★ Neonopolis car park for free. ★
★ ★ ★ ★ ★ ★ ★ ★ ★ ★ ★ ★ ★ ★ ★ ★ ★

United Artists Showcase

Showcase Mall, 3785 Las Vegas
Boulevard South, 702-740 4911.
Still the only cinema on the Strip, you
may have a hard time finding it as it's
tucked down the side of the MGM
Grand complex next to the parking
garage. Parking is free if you keep
your cinema ticket for validation.

4 SHOPPING

The other side of Las Vegas – everything from top designer malls to discount shopping outlets

They are a canny lot in Las Vegas – if they don't get you in the casinos, they've come up with another brilliant way to separate you from your cash – and it's called shopping. It is such big business that Nevada shopping malls took a massive $23.4 billion in 2000, with most of that money being spent in the city – more money than the casinos took in gambling in the same year. But then the Las Vegas malls do it in such style and with so much fun that people simply can't resist.

The trend for providing more and more shopping continues and over the last few years so many major American department stores have opened in the city that it now rivals New York and San Francisco for upscale shops. At the top of the pile is now the **Fashion Show Mall**, which has just completed a $1 billion expansion and renovation programme to turn itself into the largest shopping destination on the Strip attracting more than 10 million visitors every year.

The title of biggest and best used to belong to the **Forum Shops at Caesars**, which set new standards for shopping malls when it opened in the 1990s. It's still an excellent shopping destination and remains an attraction in its own right. Other high-end shopping malls can be found at the **Grand Canal Shoppes** at the Venetian and **Via Bellagio** at the Bellagio.

Outside of the Fashion Show Mall, best by far for a rounded shopping experience with more mid-range shopping, is the Arabian-themed **Desert Passage** at the Aladdin, while designer junkies have just got a great shot in the arm with the opening in August 2003 of the **Las Vegas Premium Outlets** right in the heart of Downtown, just minutes away from the Strip. There are many

other discount outlet shopping malls, too, while most of the resort hotels have their own shops. Here's a rundown of what's available.

MAJOR SHOPPING MALLS

Fashion Show Mall

3200 Las Vegas Boulevard South, at Spring Mountain Road, just north of Treasure Island and opposite the site of the Wynn Resort
702-369 0704 (management office) or 702-369 8382 (concierge desk)
www.thefashionshow.com
Open: Monday to Friday 10am–9pm, Saturday and Sunday noon–6pm
Stores: the only mall in America with eight major US department stores under one roof – Neiman Marcus, Saks Fifth Avenue, Macy's, Dillard's, Robinsons-May, Bloomingdale's Home, Nordstrum and Lord & Taylor, plus a further 240 shops
Attractions: The Cloud and The Great Hall with its stage and fashion show runway

Fashion Show Mall Major Stores

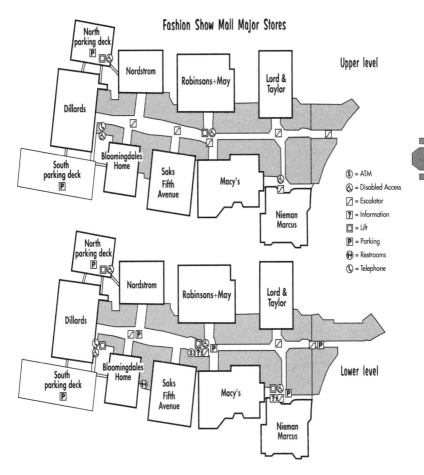

Upper level

Lord & Taylor
Robinsons+May
Nordstrom
North parking deck
Dillards
South parking deck
Bloomingdales Home
Saks Fifth Avenue
Macy's
Nieman Marcus

$ = ATM
= Disabled Access
= Escalator
= Information
= Lift
P = Parking
= Restrooms
= Telephone

Lower level

Restaurants: California Pizza Kitchen, Café Nordstrum, Neiman Marcus Café, Mariposa and a Food Court with 15 food outlets and seating for 1,500 people

For those who are serious about shopping, this is the place to come. Following a massive renovation and expansion programme, the Fashion Show Mall has doubled in size over the last two years and in the process has turned itself into an entertainment experience as well.

Hard to miss is the new **Cloud** structure, which rises 20 storeys above the Strip, and is nearly 500ft (152 metres) long – providing a much-needed shaded area during the day and a giant image projection surface at night. Below it is the 330-ft (100-metre) long **Media Bank** with four extraordinarily-sized LED screens that are used to broadcast videos and events inside the mall and around the city.

The **Great Hall**, a 72,000sq-ft (6,696sq-metre) pedestrian plaza, is home to both the elevated **Food Court** overlooking the plaza and the Strip, and the 28-sq ft (2.6-sq metre) stage and 80-ft (24-metre) retractable runway, which is now used for fashion shows and other events.

Getting around

If you arrive by car, park in the underground car park, which is accessible via Spring Mountain Road and Fashion Show Drive North and take the escalators to the shopping level. Or use the North and South parking decks accessible from Industrial Road West, then follow the signs. There is also complimentary valet parking available at three points around the mall.

Cashpoints (ATMs) and phone booths, where you can use a pre-paid phone card, are dotted around the mall and there's a foreign currency exchange centre.

The **Concierge Desk** can supply directions, concert tickets and show reservations, multilingual brochures, golf tee times and special event information.

Save as you go

Before you start to browse around the shops, join the **Premier Shopper Club** by going to the **Customer Service Center** and filling out the form or using the **Smart Shopper Pavilion** touch screen. Once you have been accepted you can browse through the website and pick up money-saving coupons from the stores. You can also find out about all the latest promotions and activities going on at each of the stores. As a member of the Club, you will automatically be entered into free prize draws simply by swiping your card at the Smart Shopper Pavilion! There are many other bonuses, but most are really aimed at people living in America.

Shopping

There are now eight major anchors to the mall – the most in any American mall and the only one to have all the main department store brands in one location: Macy's, Dillard's, Nieman Marcus, Nordstrum, Lord & Taylor, Bloomingdale's Home, Saks Fifth Avenue and Robinson's May. There are plenty of other shops, too. Here is a rundown of beauty boutiques,

women's stores, men's stores, shoe shops and electronic outlets.

Beauty boutiques

Bath & Body Works: (702-693 5944) natural beauty and skincare products.
Crabtree & Evelyn: (702-732 3609) the renowned British toiletry and home fragrance company.
Fashion Nail: (702-699 9958) a full service nail salon for women and men.
GNC Live Well: (702-651 9090) featuring a create-your-own hair and skin product bar.
H2O Plus: (702-893 1332) with its own line of more than 300 natural products for the whole family.
L'Occitane: (702-369 1286) the high-end French company that specialises in using natural ingredients to create skincare, essential oils, perfumes and home fragrances.
Omni Chemists Pharmacy & Drug Store: (702-731 1162) for exotic products.
Regis Hair Stylists: (702-733 1400) one of the largest and most experienced hair salons in the world.
The Body Shop: (702-737 1198) for all-natural hair and skincare products and make-up.
Victoria's Secret Beauty: (702-796 0110) for modern, sexy fragrances, cosmetics and bodycare.

Women's clothes and accessories

A Pea In The Pod: (702-893 8484) trend-setting and sophisticated maternity fashions.
Abercrombie & Fitch: (702-696 0832) classic and casual clobber for the young at heart.
Ann Taylor: (702-734 8614) America's leading retailer for stylish, professional yet feminine women's clothing.
Ann Taylor Loft: (702-731 0351) the casual branch of Ann Taylor, offering co-ordinating, easy-to-wear pieces.
Arden B: (702-735 0090) everything from dressy to casual wear for sophisticated yet fashion-savvy women.

Bally of Switzerland: (702-737 1968) shoes, clothes and accessories with a strong modern look in bold colours.

★★★ **BRIT TIP** ★★★
★ ★
★ ★
★ One of the things the Americans ★
★ do brilliantly is smart-yet-casual ★
★ outfits at great prices for career ★
★ women. ★
★★★★★★★★★★★★★★★★★★★

BCBG Max Azria: (702-737 0681) shoes, handbags, accessories and clothing with clean, simple lines by the award-winning American designer who has a loyal Hollywood following.
bebe: (702-892 8083) curve-hugging street clobber.
Betsey Johnson: (702-735 3338) funky frocks in flowing fabrics with hippie-inspired detailing and beaded embroidery.
Caché: (702-731 5548) specialising in high-end fashion designers from Europe and America, many of whom are exclusive to the boutique.
Casual Corner: classic and casual kit for career women at good prices.
Chico's: (702-791 3661) high-end designer boutique famous for amazing service.
Cinammon Girl: (702-697 0290) Honolulu-inspired floral-print sundresses for women and teens in exclusive prints, plus gorgeous flip-flops, accessories and bath products.
Claire's Boutique: (702-650 9006) accessories for every occasion and for women and girls of all ages – you'll always be sure to find what you're looking for here, be it earrings or a tiara!
Cleo's: (702-792 2536) good quality anklets, chokers, colourful glass beads, necklaces and bracelets galore.
The Coach Store: (702-759 3451) America's leading accessories store offering good quality, classic yet modern styles. Every mall needs one!
Cole Haan: (702-731 3522) hand-crafted, leather shoes and boots for men and women, plus handbags, wallets and casual outerwear.

Detour: (702-894 5030) sharp, chic looks from soft, silk blouses to little black dresses including clothing by Miss Sixty, Seven jeans, Juicy Couture, Theory and Major Dilemma.
Express: (702-737 8999) ultra-hip fashion clothes almost straight off the catwalk.
GAP: (702-796 0010) a leading retailer offering clothing, accessories and personal care products for both men and women.
Guess: (702-691 2541) a world-wide brand famous for jeans, stylish denim outfits and accessories for women, men and children.
Hot Cats: (702-796 1870) up-to-the-minute styles for men, women, boys and girls sold in an entertaining atmosphere.
J Crew: (702-731 2060) a wide range of clothes, shoes and accessories for women, men and children.
Jessica McClintock: (702-733 4003) contemporary collections from a designer famous for romantic special occasion clothes for women and girls.
Lillie Rubin: (702-731 3042) in town for a wedding? Then here's the perfect location to pick up women's cocktail and evening formal wear.
Lucky Brand: (702-369 4116) classic American denim gear for women and men.
Marshall Rousso: (702-737 5011) unique designs from casual to formal evening wear, plus shoes and accessories.
Petite Sophisticate: fed up with the lack of choice for women under 5ft 4in: (162cm)? Then look no further, this store specialises in perfectly proportioned modern clothing for you!
Rampage: (702-732 0478) everything from casual weekend kit to trendy clubwear, professional women's clothing and accessories, plus aromatherapy oils and bath products.
SoHo Collection: (702-732 4849) up-to-the-minute hair accessories and clothing from trendy New York outlets including French Concept, Jesse USA, Anopia and Kosjuko.

4

Stephanel: (702-892 0883) trendy Italian clothing store offering hip women's knitwear, casuals and sportswear.

Talulah G: (702-737 6000) a hip new boutique chain that has appeared on the Today Show.

Tommy Bahama's: (702-731 6868) fun-yet-chic Bahama-inspired fashion plus shoes, ties, bags, belts and accessories.

Victoria's Secret: (702-737 1313) sexy lingerie and accessories.

Wet Seal: contemporary clothes and accessories for those who lead active lifestyles.

Men's clothing

Abercrombie & Fitch: (702-696 0832) classic and casual clobber for the young at heart.

Bally of Switzerland: (702-737 1968) shoes, clothes and accessories with a strong modern look in bold colours.

Bernini Sport: (702-784 0786) high-end designer clobber from Phat Farm, Versace, Fubu and Sean John among others.

The Coach Store: (702-759 3451) America's leading accessories company offering good quality, classic yet modern styles.

Cole Haan: (702-731 3522) hand-crafted, leather shoes and boots for men and women, plus handbags, wallets and casual outerwear.

GAP: (702-796 0010) a leading retailer offering clothing, accessories and personal care products for both men and women.

Guess: (702-691 2541) a world-wide brand famous for jeans, stylish denim outfits and accessories for women, men and children.

Harris & Frank: (702-737 7545) the finest men's suits, sports coats and sportswear from a shop famous for service and tailoring.

Hot Cats: (702-796 1870) up-to-the-minute styles for men, women, boys and girls sold in an entertaining atmosphere.

J Crew: (702-731 2060) a wide range of clothes, shoes and accessories for women, men and children.

Leather by Michael Lawrence: (702-697 0062) a massive assortment of leather jackets, belts and bags.

Lucky Brand: (702-369 4116) classic American denim gear for women and men.

Lusso: (702-257 0914) a wide selection of luxury Italian menswear with a professional alteration service for both men's and women's clothes.

No Fear: (702-792 3327) young men's casual and lifestyle clothing and accessories.

St Croix Knit: (702-794 4333) fine sweaters, knit shirts and outerwear for men, all hand finished and guaranteed.

Tommy Bahama's: (702-731 6868) fun-yet-chic Bahama-inspired fashion plus shoes, ties, bags, belts and accessories.

Shoes

Adrienne Vittadini: (702-792 1480) casual yet sophisticated Euro-American women's designs for the home, office and leisure time. Plus legwear, handbags, eyewear, jewellery, fragrances, watches, belts and scarves.

Aerosoles: (702-796 4144) stylish and comfortable affordable footwear for women.

Aldo: (702-735 5590) French-based men's and women's fashion shoes.

Ann Taylor: (702-734 8614) America's leading retailer for stylish, professional yet feminine women's clothing and footwear.

Ann Taylor Loft: (702-731 0351) the casual branch of Ann Taylor, offering co-ordinating, easy-to-wear pieces and shoes.

Arteffects: (702-796 7463) innovative designs in leather and fabrics including wedges, clogs, sandals and comfy shoes.

Bakers: (702-737 0108) well-priced sport and formal footwear, plus Baker's own tailored shoes.

Bally of Switzerland: (702-737 1968) shoes, clothes and accessories with a strong modern look in bold colours.

Hotels

Top left Venetian
Top right Bellagio
Centre left Four Seasons
Centre right Luxor
Bottom Excalibur

Hotels

Top left Valley of the Waterfalls at Mandalay Bay

Top right Rainforest Atrium at the Mirage

Centre left New York New York

Bottom left Captain Morgan's Lounge at Treasure Island

Bottom right Fireworks at the Stratosphere

Shows

Top left Splash 2 at the Strip
Top right King Arthur's Tournament at Excalibur
Centre right Rick Thomas
Bottom Mystère at Treasure Island

Shows

Top left Jubilee!

Top right Tribute to Frank,
Sammy, Joey and
Dean

Centre right O at Treasure
Island

Bottom left Jubilee!

Bottom right EFX Alive! at
MGM Grand

BCBG Max Azria: (702-737 0681) shoes, handbags, accessories and clothing with clean, simple lines by the award-winning American designer with a loyal Hollywood following.
Clarks England/Bostonian: (702-732 1801) affordably-priced European-style footwear plus belts, handbags and shoe care products.
Cole Haan: (702-731 3522) hand-crafted, leather shoes and boots for men and women, plus handbags, wallets and casual outerwear.
Easy Spirit: (702-693 4732) comfortable shoes in narrow and wide widths.
Footlocker: (702-369 0401) athletic shoes and clothes for the whole family.
Footworks: (702-369 0048) casual footwear brands for women and children.
Guess: (702-691 2541) a world-wide brand famous for jeans, stylish denim outfits, shoes and accessories for women, men and children.
Johnston & Murphy: (702-737 0114) America's leading outlet for high-end men's shoes and accessories.
Lady Foot Locker: (702-735 7030) athletic shoes and clothes for women.
Marmi: (702-893 2002) fashionable, European-influenced shoes for women in all width sizes.
Marshall Rousso: (702-737 5011) unique designs from casual to formal evening wear, plus shoes and accessories.
Nine West: (702-693 2904) from classics to modern-style footwear.
Steve Madden: (702-733 2904) funky and trendy shoes and accessories for women and teens.
Stiletto: (702-791 0505) eclectic boutique with a wide selection of designer styles, plus novelty handbags and accessories.
Wet Seal: contemporary clothes, footwear and accessories for those who lead active lifestyles.

Cameras and electronics

Apple: (702-650 9550) great store offering customers the chance to learn how to take pictures with a digital camera and put them on their own website, and burn a CD with their favourite music. Also has a giant 10-ft: (3.5-metre) screen on which to view Apple's revolutionary new operating system.

★ ★ ★ **BRIT TIP** ★ ★ ★

★ Just remember that American ★ videos are not compatible with ★ the VHS system used in the UK. ★

Brookstone: (702-650 2048) an assortment of products in an environment in which customers are encouraged to try out products.
EB Games: (702-737 1733) the latest PC entertainment, plus accessories and products.
Futuretronics: (702-387 1818) high-end innovative electronics from Sony, Bose, Nokia, Panasonic and more.
The Sharper Image: (702-731 3113) innovative gifts and gadgets for the whole family.

Cafés

Auntie Anne's: (702-791 0077) a wide variety of soft pretzels including cinnamon sugar, jalapeno and glazin' raisin, plus frozen drinks. Located on the upper level of the West Expansion between Bloomingdale's Home and Saks Fifth Avenue.
Bloomingdale's B-Café: (702-784 5400) an assortment of pastries, cakes, croissants and sandwiches. Located on the lower level of Bloomies.
Cinnabon: aromatic and delish cinnamon rolls direct from the oven.
Espresso King Kafe: (702-474 2435) a wide assortment of drinks, salads, sarnies and breakfast items. Located on the upper level next to The Limited.
Ethel M Chocolates: (702-796 6662) Las Vegas' famous choc factory has an outlet on the lower level of the Fashion Show Mall opposite Victoria's Secrets. It sells gourmet chocs plus a variety of coffees and ice creams.

NM Café: (702-731 3636) contemporary-style lunch and dinner cuisine in a fashionable yet casual setting. Located on the second level of Neiman Marcus. Open daily 10am–8pm.

★ ★ ★   ★ ★ ★
★   ★
★   ★
★ The NM Café has a brilliant Happy ★
★ Hour for Martinis and food,   ★
★ served nightly on the outdoor   ★
★ terrace overlooking the Strip.   ★
★ ★ ★ ★ ★ ★ ★ ★ ★ ★ ★ ★ ★ ★ ★

Nordstrum E-bar: (702-784 1615) open for coffee, smoothies, pastries, muffins, bagels and sarnies. Located on the lower level next to Nordstrum's entrance. Open Monday to Saturday from 8.30am and from 9.30am on Sundays.

Nordstrum Marketplace Café: (702-784 1610) salads, sarnies, pastas, pizzas and an assortment of daily specials, plus a wide variety of drinks. On the third level of Nordstrum, you can even order food and drinks to take out.

Starbuck Coffee Company: (702-794 4010) delish speciality coffees plus pastries and puds. On the lower level of the Fashion Show Mall opposite Bailey Banks.

Tropicana Smoothies and Swenson's Ice Cream: (702-699 9306) a massive selection of fresh fruit smoothies made with crushed ice and/or frozen yogurt or fruit sorbet. On the upper level of the West Expansion between Bloomies and Saks Fifth Avenue.

NB: at the time of going to press details were unavailable for the outlets to be included in the new Food Court.

★ ★ ★   ★ ★ ★
★   ★
★   ★
★ All cafés and food outlets are   ★
★ open at the same time as the   ★
★ mall unless otherwise stated.   ★
★ ★ ★ ★ ★ ★ ★ ★ ★ ★ ★ ★ ★ ★ ★

Restaurants

California Pizza Kitchen: (702-893 1370) part of one of America's leading casual dining chains, it features a wide variety of pizzas, pastas, salads, soups, sarnies, starters and desserts. Located on the lower level of the West Expansion next to Bloomies.

Mariposa at Neiman Marcus: (702-731 3636) a fine-dining establishment on the first floor of the upper crust department store. Serving Mediterranean cuisine with French, Italian and Asian infusions, it even has entrances on the Strip and at Spring Mountain Road. Open for lunch from Monday to Saturday 11am–3pm and for dinner nightly 5.30–10pm: (11pm on Friday and Saturday)

The Forum Shops at Caesars

Right next to Caesars Palace
702 893 4800

Open: 24/7. Most of the restaurants are open from 10am to 11pm and until midnight on Friday and Saturday

Attractions: Festival Fountain show, Atlantis show, the Great Hall show, the aquarium and Race For Atlantis simulator ride.

Cafés and restaurants: fine-dining outlets include Bertolini's Authentic Trattoria, Caviarteria, Chinois, The Palm and Spago. Casual outlets include the Cheesecake Factory, Forum Café, La Salsa Mexican Restaurant, Planet Hollywood, Stage Deli, Café Caesars, Monopoly Coffee Bar, Star Wars Cantina and the Virgin Café.

Parking: either in the Caesars Palace free covered car park or make use of the valet parking in the underground traffic tunnel at Caesars Boulevard.

Services: contact the hotel's concierge desk for wheelchair and buggy rentals and lost and found.

    This is such an amazing place that it should be on your must-visit list for Las Vegas regardless of whether

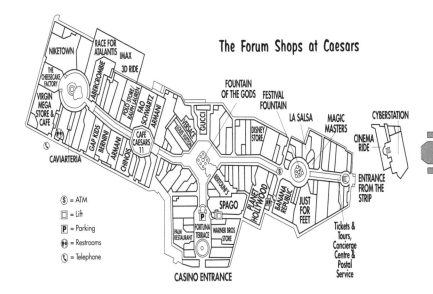

The Forum Shops at Caesars

NIKETOWN
RACE FOR ATALANTIS IMAX
3D RIDE
THE CHEESECAKE FACTORY
ABERCROMBIE
POLO STORE/ RALPH LAUREN
FAO SCHWARZ
ARMANI
VIRGIN MEGA STORE & CAFE
GAP KIDS
BERNINI
ARMANI
CHINOIS
CAFE CAESARS 11
VERSACE
GUESS STUDIO
GUCCI
CAVIARTERIA

FOUNTAIN OF THE GODS
FESTIVAL FOUNTAIN
LA SALSA
MAGIC MASTERS
CYBERSTATION
CINEMA RIDE
DISNEY STORE
BERTOLINI'S
PLANET HOLLYWOOD
BANANA REPUBLIC
JUST FOR FEET
ENTRANCE FROM THE STRIP
SPAGO
PALM RESTAURANT
FORTUNA TERRACE
WARNER BROS STORE
Tickets & Tours, Concierge Centre & Postal Service

CASINO ENTRANCE

$ = ATM
□ = Lift
P = Parking
= Restrooms
= Telephone

4

you want to buy anything. It was deliberately built as an entertainment mall and transports people back in time to the great Roman Empire era with architecture, materials and street lighting to match. Even the piazzas and streets are laid out in the traditional format of a Roman town. The entire mall is enclosed, temperature-controlled and covered with a 'sky' that changes throughout the day from a rosy-mauve dawn to high noon, the fading gold of the afternoon, twilight and finally night-time with twinkling stars.

The original $110-million complex, which opened in 1992, proved so successful that it was expanded and a further 35 stores and entertainment outlets opened in 1997. A second extension opened in the summer of 2000, adding another 240,000sq ft: (22,320sq metres) to the existing 533,000sq ft: (49,569sq metres). On average 50,000 people visit every day, rising to 70,000 at the weekends and even 80,000 a day during the Christmas period.

Once you arrive at the **Festival Fountain** you will see the seven-minute special effects show in which Bacchus, god of merriment and wine, wakes up and decides to throw a party for himself and visitors to the Forum. He enlists the help of Apollo, who provides the music with his lyre, and Plutus, the god of wealth, who brings the fountain to life with cascades of jewel-like effects in the waters, while Venus, the goddess of love, also puts in an appearance. Music, sound effects, animatronics and special scenic projections on the dome combine with a computer-controlled waterscape and theatrical lighting for a dazzling show. After thanking his companions and inviting his guests to enjoy the pleasures of the shops, Bacchus then becomes a marble statue again.

Before leaving the area you can tuck into a sandwich at the nearby deli, grab a bite to eat at **La Salsa** or enter the world of the **Magic Masters**. Designed as a replica of Houdini's private library, Magic Masters features magical demonstrations, and prospective buyers are taken through a secret door to learn how to perform an illusion. Afterwards, drop in at the athletic shoe store **Just for Feet**, where a half-court basketball arena and treadmill machines are provided so you can test out your purchases.

As you head on down towards the **Fountain of the Gods**, you'll pass the **Disney Store** on your right and **Planet Hollywood** on your left. But before you decide to have lunch, just remember that the Forum Shops houses some of the finest restaurants in Las Vegas, including **Bertolini's** Italian restaurant, celebrity chef Wolfgang Puck's two outlets, **Spago** and **Chinois**, and the **Palm Restaurant**.

To the left of the **Fountain of Gods** is the **Fortuna Terrace**, which houses many of the restaurants and the **Warner Bros Studio Store**, which has a video wall showcasing new movie trailers, cartoons and out-takes from classic films.

If you return to the **Fountain of the Gods** you will once again be surrounded by some of the top designer shops that are in the Forum – **Gucci**, **Versace**, **Louis Vuitton** and **Armani**. Head down the promenade to your left and you'll find the **Café Caesars II** restaurant, where you dine al fresco, and continue on to the new **Great Roman Hall**.

Here the **Atlantis** comes to life in a spectacle that has the gods unleashing their wrath on the ancient city. Fire, water, smoke and special effects are used to create a show in which the animatronic characters of Atlas, Gadrius and Alia struggle to rule Atlantis.

Surrounded by a massive saltwater aquarium, the mythical sunken continent rises and falls before your eyes. The **Great Hall** is surrounded by giant projection screens which, together with lasers and other special effects, help create the illusion that you are genuinely part of the action. Shows are held every 90 minutes starting at 10am every day of the year.

★ ★ ★ BRIT TIP ★ ★ ★

★ Arrive early for the Atlantis shows ★
★ as the crowds build up early and ★
★ you'll want a good view of the ★
★ sunken city. ★

Another free 'show' is the dive into the **aquarium** for maintenance and feeding, which takes place several times a day. Inside are sharks and schools of coral-reef fish. Or you can experience the **Race for Atlantis** motion simulator IMAX 3-D experience: (see Chapter 10 page 149).

Afterwards try another fabulous experience – this time the **Caviarteria**, Las Vegas' first caviar, champagne, vodka and martini bar. Caviarteria is America's oldest and biggest distributor of gourmet delicacies and if you're in the mood, you can sample anything from smoked salmon to Icelandic gravadlax salmon, foie gras and a host of champagnes and vodkas.

Afterwards, if you can still walk, wander around the mega **Virgin Megastore**, which has its own café, have a pudding at the **Cheesecake Factory** and see what **Niketown** has on offer for your tootsies.

Desert Passage at the Aladdin

Wrapped around the Aladdin Hotel with entrances on the Strip and Harmon Avenue
702-866 0710 or 1-888 800 8284
www.desertpassage.com
Open: Sunday to Thursday 10am–11pm, Friday and Saturday 10am–midnight
Attractions: rainstorm in Merchants'

Desert Passage

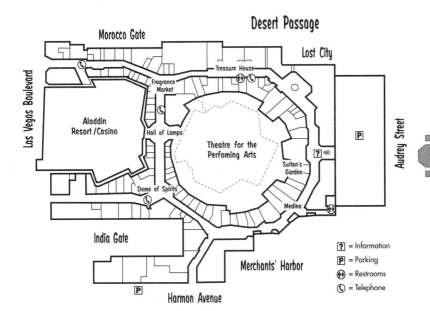

[?] = Information
[P] = Parking
(♿) = Restrooms
(☏) = Telephone

Harbor every hour on the hour Monday to Thursday and every half hour on Friday and Saturday; plus live entertainment from belly dancers, North African acrobats, contortionists and Arabian musicians at 12noon, 2, 4, 6 and 8pm every day except Tuesday.

Cafés and restaurants: fine-dining outlets include Anasazi, Belluga Bar, Bice, Commander's Palace, Joseph's and Sevilla. The casual options are Alacazam, Ben & Jerry's, Cheeseburger at the Oasis, Fat Anthony's and Ferraro, while live music is available at Prana supper club and Ibiza.

Parking: free parking available at the Aladdin.

Services: pedicab rides and henna tattoos.

Designed to provide a shopping 'adventure', you are taken on a journey through the ancient spice routes of North Africa, through distinct lands, bustling street scenes and music and entertainment designed to evoke an emotional connection with each place.

You start at **Morocco Gate**, a

grand portal rising 90ft: (27 metres) high, and immediately enter the land of Morocco. Marrakech and Fez are brought to life through the gorgeous mosaic tiles, intricate iron carvings and pounded mud and straw buildings. Stores in this area include Hugo Boss, Club Monaco, Herve Leger and Max Studio.

The fab **Fragrance Market** can be found here beneath the shade of a majestic olive tree with health and beauty stores such as Aveda, The Body Shop, Clinique, Crabtree & Evelyn, L'Occitane, Sephora and Origins all selling a wealth of lotions and potions.

Next you will see the dramatic desert fortress that guards **Treasure House**. Look up at the sky to see the hand-painted dome ceiling, which depicts the story of Aladdin and the 40 Thieves. Here each storefront is made up of large, sandstone blocks and boutiques include the fun Build-A-Bear-Workshop, GAP and Victoria's Secret.

Next stop is the majestic **Lost City** – a public square nestled amid dome-shaped buildings, towers and a soaring 85-ft: (26-metre) mountainside. Here you will find many restaurants and cafés including Cheeseburger at the Oasis, La Salsa Mexican Cantina and the Sevilla Spanish Steakhouse and Nightclub.

Then comes the **Sultan's Palace** with its 45-ft: (14-metre) high gilded ceiling, iridescent mosaic tile and flamboyant gold monkey chandeliers. Walk through the palace to the **Sultan's Garden**, with its Moorish arches in subdued sandstone that contrast with the vibrant colours and geometric shapes of the hand-painted mosaic tiles. Here you will find stores such as Soho Fine Art Gallery, Wyland Galleries, Z Gallerie and Sharper Image.

★ ★ ★   **BRIT TIP**   ★ ★ ★
★   ★
★   Of all the Strip resort hotel   ★
★   shopping 'malls', the Desert   ★
★   Passage is the only one with   ★
★ direct entrances on the Strip – ie ★
★ you don't have to walk through a ★
★   casino to get to it!   ★
★ ★ ★ ★ ★ ★ ★ ★ ★ ★ ★ ★ ★ ★ ★ ★

Just beyond the palace lies the **Medina**, a fun marketplace with stores such as Ann Taylor Loft and Watch World. Then the **Merchants' Harbor** provides a breathtaking North African harbour-front with Moroccan and Colonial French architecture and pristine Mediterranean whitewashed walls. A 155-ft: (47-metre) European trans-steamer ship is moored permanently in the port, while a sudden breeze announces the beginning of a live rainstorm.

Shops in the area include Aldo, Lucky Brank Dungarees, Steve Madden and Tommy Bahama, and you'll also find the Todai Japanese Seafood Buffet and Merchants' Harbor Coffee House here.

The tour continues with the **Dome of Spirits**, where hand-blown cobalt-blue lamps hang from the 65-ft: (20-metre) high ceiling and stores include

bebe, French Connection and Godiva Chocolatier. The Dome leads on to the **Hall of Lamps**, where more lamps hang from the ceiling, while sophisticated boutiques include Betsey Johnson, Caché, Montblanc and St Croix Knits.

India Gate is the next region, with its carved wood screens and coloured awnings in 18th and 19th-century painting styles. Life-size Indian elephants guard the stores that include Tumi and Brighton Collectibles, while Commander's Palace, one of the best restaurants in town, can also be found here.

Designer fashion stores for men and women at Desert Passage include Alegre, Bisou Bisou, Casablanca Clothiers, Jhane Barnes, Joan Vass, Manrico Cashmere and Napoleon.

Art stores also include Addi Galleries, Bernard K Passman Galleries, Gallery of Legends, Ron Lee's World of Clowns, Russeck Gallery, Tolstoy's Elegant Pens and Watches and Tresor.

Shoe stores include Footworks, Gary's Studio, L'Idea, Palazzo de Scarpi, Rococo and Steve Madden.

Speciality shops include Cashman Photo Magic, Desert Brats, The Discovery Channel Store, Fossil, Houdini's Magic Shop, Magnet Max, Teuscher Chocolates, Toys International and World of Charms.

Grand Canal Shoppes

The Venetian
702-414 4500
Open: Sunday to Thursday 10am–11pm, Friday and Saturday 10am–midnight
Restaurants: fine dining is available at Canaletto, Canyon Ranch Café, Postrio, Tsunami Asian Grill and Zeffirino Ristorante. Casual dining is at Taqueria Canonita and Tintoretto's Bakery, while you can listen to live music at the Venus Lounge.
This is another luxurious shopping environment which has been specifically created to provide entertainment as well as retail outlets.

As you enter from the Strip, you are greeted by extravagant vaulted ceilings adorned with images reminiscent of Italy's great pointed palazzos.

Along the streets of 15th-century Venice are high-fashion luxury boutiques, national branded stores of America, and entertainment retailers. After wandering past some of these shops you arrive at the huge space called St Mark's Square from where you can take a gondola ride – just like those on Venice's fabled canals – and enjoy the illusion created by decorated second-storey balconies.

Posh stores include **Jimmy Choo, Mikimoto**, which is famous for its pearls, **Donna Karan Couture** and **Oliver & Company**, the latter filled with men's fashions by Ralph Lauren, Donna Karan, Giorgio Armani and Borrelli. Other retailers include **Ann Taylor, Banana Republic** and **bébé**. Interesting one-off shops include **Il Prato**, which sells authentic Venetian masks, **Jesurum**, offering fine linen and lace from Venice and **Ripa di Monti** for Venetian glass and collectibles.

The whole process of browsing or parting with your cash is made sweeter by the entertainments with jugglers showcasing their talents along the cobblestone walkways and the glass blowers demonstrating their craft in St Mark's Square.

DISCOUNT SHOPPING

Las Vegas Premium Outlets

875 South Grand Central Parkway, downtown Las Vegas, just off Interstate 15
702-474 7500
www.premiumoutlets.com/lasvegas
Open: Monday to Saturday 10am–10pm, Sunday 10am–9pm
Cafés and restaurants: Auntie Anne's Soft Pretzels, Cajun Grill & BBQ, China Pantry, Dairy Queen/Orange Julius, The Fudgery, Italia Express, JR's Steakery, Makino's, Starbucks Coffee and Subway

Getting there: by car – from the Interstate 15 northbound, take Exit 41B Charleston Boulevard, southbound, exit at Charleston Boulevard. This will take you on to Martin Luther King Boulevard, turn left into Charleston Boulevard and left again into Grand Central Parkway. By taxi – pick up behind Ann Taylor at Suite 1201 and drop off between Adidas and Brooks Brothers, suite 1701

Parking: free and immediately outside the village

Services: go to the management office to collect a map to see the full layout. Here you can also rent a pushchair, wheelchair, get a trolley, arrange for international shipping and buy international phone cards. The village has a food court, other restaurants, three sets of WCs, three cashpoints: (ATMs), foreign currency exchange in the food court and telephones

Additional services: attraction tickets, dinner and show reservations and sightseeing tours available through the Allstate Ticketing/Showtickets.com located in the kiosk in front of Timberland at suite 1901

Discount shopping in Las Vegas took a turn for the better with the arrival of Chelsea Premium Outlets' latest village – Las Vegas Premium Outlets. Run by the same people who run Woodbury Common in New York, this is one of the best discount outfits in America. Each of their village-style settings is picturesque, well laid-out and fully serviced by food and drink outlets and plenty of WCs.

On top of that it provides high-end designer gear at 25–65% of the original price on a year-round basis, while also running fab sales with even cheaper prices – generally held on the major American Holidays and over Christmas.

At the time of going to press, this new centre had not officially opened, but here's a taste of what you will be able to find.

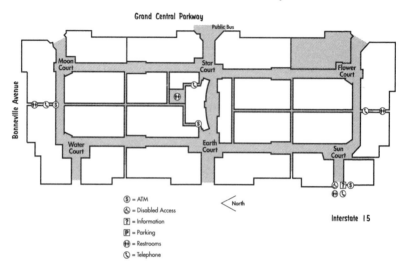

Las Vegas Premium Outlets

Fashion boutiques

The full A-Z: Armani Exchange, Adidas, Bass, Benetton, Bezene, Bernini, Big Dog Sportswear, Billabong, Brooks Brothers, Calvin Klein, Casual Corner, Charlotte Russe, Chico's, Docker's, Dolce & Gabbana, Dress Barn, Ecko Unlimited, Eddie Bauer, Elie Tahari, Front Row Sports, Geoffrey Beene, Guess, Haggar Clothing Co, Izod, Jockey, Jones New York, Kenneth Cole, Lacoste, Leather by Michael Lawrence, Levi's, Liz Claiborne, Maidenform, Maternity Works, Max Studio, Nautica, Nike, Oakley Vault, PacSun, Pancaldi, Perry Ellis, Petite Sophisticate, Polo Ralph Lauren, Puma, Quiksilver, Rave, Reebok, Rip Curl, Rue 21, Samsonite Black Label, Sarar, St John Company Store, Theory, Timberland, Tommy Hilfiger, Van Heusen, Wayne Rogers, Wilsons Leather, Wolford.

Health and beauty

The full A-Z: The Cosmetics Company Store, Crabtree & Evelyn, Designer Fragrances, Perfumania, Perfumes 4U, Vitamin World.

Accessories and jewellery

The full A-Z: Claire's Accessories, Coach, Lids for Less, Seiko The Company Store, Sunglass Hut, Sunglass Outlet, Time Factory Watch Outlet, Totes/Sunglass Station, Ultra Diamond Outlet, Zales The Diamond Store Outlet.

Shoe shops

The full A-Z: Adidas, Aerosoles, Bass, Bostonian Clarks, DC Shoes, Deichmann World of Shoes, Ecco, Etnies exs, Factory Brand Shoes, Hush Puppies, Journeys, Kenneth Cole, Liz Claiborne Shoes, Naturalizer, Nike, Pancaldi, Puma, Reebok, Robert Wayne Footwear, Skechers, Stride Rite Keds Sperry, Timberland, Two Lips Shoes, Vans.

Children's stores

The full A-Z: Carter's, The Children's Place, Dry Ice, Hartstrings, K*B Toy, Little Me, OshKosh, Strasburg Children, Stride Rite Keds Sperry.

Luggage and leather goods

The full A-Z: Coach, Leather by Michael Lawrence, The Luggage

Factory, Samsonite, Wilsons Leather Outlet.

Housewares and home furnishings

The full A-Z: Kitchen Collection, Le Gourmet Chef, Polo Ralph Lauren Factory Store, Welcome Home, Yves Delorme.

Gifts and speciality items

The full A-Z: Book Warehouse, Bose, Fuzziwig's Candy Factory, Harry and David, K*B Toy Outlet.

Factory outlet district

Just a short trip south of the MGM Grand along the Strip is the district of factory shops where many famous brand names are sold at 20–70% discounts. First stop is the **Belz Factory Outlet World** at the corner of Las Vegas Boulevard South and Warm Springs Road. Here, the 625,000-sq ft: (58,125sq metre) mall is home to a permanent laser show plus 140 outlet stores that include **Nike, OshKosh, Off 5th, Saks Fifth Avenue** and **Levis**. A mile: (1.6km) further south is the open-air **Las Vegas Factory Outlet Stores of America** that has a huge range of shops from men's and women's clothing to bookstores and shoe shops. Both are open Monday to Saturday 10am–8pm and on Sunday 10am–6pm.

HOTEL SHOPPING

In addition to the major shopping parades featured at different hotels, earlier in this chapter, here is a full guide to the shops available in each of the major resort hotels. Some offer high-end items – such as the Paris Resort – while many provide shopping that fits in with the theme of the hotel.

Bally's Hotel

Bally's Avenue Shops: (702-736 4111) more than 40 stores from jewellery to fashion, plus men's and women's hair salons, an ice-cream parlour and a place to have your

photo taken in costumes from the 1800s.

Open seven days a week. Most shops open at 9am, closing times vary.

The Bellagio

Via Bellagio: (702-693 7111) the tenants of the Bellagio's shopping 'mall' – a street which winds its way from the hotel down to the Strip – fit in perfectly with the elegant surroundings. **Prada, Georgio Armani** and **Chanel** cater to the Bellagio's well-heeled clientele, as does **Tiffany & Co**, the epitome of subdued shopping style.

Open seven days a week. Most stores open at 10am, closing times vary.

Caesars Palace

Appian Way: (731-7110) despite its proximity to the Forum Shops at Caesars, Appian Way is a fair-sized corridor winding through the hotel and connecting the Roman, Palace and Centurion Towers, which is filled with some of the most exclusive shops and finest salons in the world.

Shops include Ancient Creations, filled with high-quality jewellery and rare coins and artefacts; Cartier, Le Paradis jewellery store; Venus Salon for hair, nail, make-up and skin services; Cottura for hand-painted ceramics; Galerie Michelangelo filled with fine art; Emperors Essentials for Caesars logo merchandise, Piazzas Del Mercato for sportswear, perfumes, golf collections and spa products; Godiva Chocolatier; Colosseum Cigars, Bernini Couture; Cuzzens for men's clothing; Paul and Shark for men's sportswear; Carina for women's designer clothers, shoes and accessories; and Paradiso for swimwear.

Open seven days a week from 10am, closing times vary.

Circus Circus

Circus Circus Shops: (702-734 0410) includes a newsagent plus gift and souvenir shops, a clown shop selling

4

limited-edition collectors' items, clown dolls and figurines, a candy store, novelty photo booth, shoeshine, hair salon and the Grand Slam Trading Post souvenir shop.

Open seven days a week from 10am, closing times vary.

Excalibur Hotel

Excalibur Shoppes: (702-597 7777) fantasy shops on the medieval theme include the Excalibur Shoppe, Castle Souvenirs, Gifts of the Kingdom, Spirit Shoppe, Dragon's Lair and Desert Shoppe, which sell everything from swords and suits of armour to Excalibur merchandise.

Open seven days a week from 10am, closing times vary.

Las Vegas Hilton

Hilton Shops: (702-732 5111) don't forget to pick up your *Star Trek* souvenir merchandise and other goodies at the Hilton shops.

Open seven days a week from 10am, closing times vary.

The Luxor

Giza Galleria: (702-262 4444) the Galleria contains 18 shops selling everything from King Tut's souvenirs to ice cream and sweets. Other shops include the **Scarab Shop** for hieroglyphic T-shirts and sweatshirts, **Innerspace** for limited-edition Egyptian collections, and the **Logo Shop** selling everything from Luxor key chains to stuffed animals and glassware. **Exclusive** is the exciting women's clothing store which has everything from business outfits to cutting-edge designer gear.

Open seven days a week from 10am, closing times vary.

Mandalay Bay

Mandalay Bay Shops: (702-632 7777) a selection of tropically themed shops to match the hotel, selling everything from Bali art to fine cigars, children's and designer clothes, imported rum, toys, rare coins, swimwear and jewellery.

Open seven days a week from 10am, closing times do vary.

MGM Grand

MGM Grand Avenue: (702-891 3300) the City of Entertainment has fun and exclusive shops that provide something for everyone from fine jewellery to men's, women's and children's fashions. You can browse through the luxurious shops along Studio Walk, visit Star Lane Shops on the lower level of the main lobby, or explore the shopping outlets located throughout MGM Grand. **Studio Walk** is a magnificent 115,000-sq ft (10,695-sq metre) shopping promenade located between the casino and the gardens and is designed to look like a Hollywood sound stage, while each of the shops and restaurants has been inspired by some of Hollywood's legendary buildings and landmarks. **Star Lane Shops** has a variety of outlets in a fun and colourful shopping arcade.

Open seven days a week from 10am, closing times vary.

The Mirage

The Street of Shops: (702-791 7111) an exclusive collection of designer boutiques offering everything from unique gifts to beautiful jewellery and designer clothes in a sophisticated Parisian/Italian boulevard setting. Designers include DKNY, Moschino and La Perla, while there are also souvenir shops for Siegfried and Roy and Cirque du Soleil.

Open seven days a week. Sunday to Thursday 10am–11pm, Friday and Saturday till midnight.

Monte Carlo

Monte Carlo Shops, 702-730 7777. Boutiques include a small convenience store, sweet shop, flower shop and the **Lance Burton Magic Shop** with demonstrator shows.

Open seven days a week from 10am, closing times vary.

New York-New York

Soho Village: (702-414-4500) provides a limited number of stores, but still a fun experience. Hailed the Greatest City in Las Vegas, the village is set against a background of New York landmarks and includes both Greenwich Village and Times Square.

Open seven days. Most Stores open at 10am, closing hours vary.

Paris Resort

Le Boulevard: (702-946 7000) high-end shops in their own Rue de la Paix district. Here quaint cobblestone streets and winding alleyways lead you to French boutiques selling wine and cheese, flowers and designer clothes.

Open seven days a week 10am–10pm

Rio All-Suite Hotel

Masquerade Village: (702-252-7777). the $200-million Masquerade Village is actually a combination of shopping, dining, entertainment and gaming woven together by the ongoing carnival atmosphere of the hotel's Masquerade Show in the Sky (see page 152). Here you can stroll down 200-year-old Tuscan-tiled streets filled with boutiques selling designer gear, such as Armani, Versace, Gucci, Rolex and Torras.

Open seven days a week from 10am, closing times vary.

Stratosphere Hotel

Tower Shops: (702-380 7777) visitors pass through themed street scenes reminiscent of Paris, Hong Kong and New York on their way to the Broadway Showroom and elevators to the Observation Deck. More than 50 shops include Bernini Sport, Aerosoles, Swatch, Perfumania, Marshall Rousso and Haagen Dazs.

Open Sunday to Thursday 10am–11pm, Friday and Saturday till midnight.

The Tropicana

Atrium Shopping: (702-739 2222) selection of shops and services such as shoeshines and boutiques.

Shopping hints and tips

Sizes: clothes sizes are one size smaller in America, so a dress size 10 in the US is a size 12 in the UK. It means you can travel out in a size 12 and come back in a size 10! It is the same for men: a jacket size 42 is the English size 44. But it's the opposite with shoes: an American size 10 is our size 9. Measurements: the Americans still work in feet and inches, which is great for anyone over the age of 30!

Taxes: in all cases you will have to add local taxes on to the cost of your goods. This can add anything from 7–9% on to the price, depending on where you are buying. Nevada sales tax is 7.5%.

UK shopping allowances: your duty-free allowance is just £145 and given the wealth of shopping opportunities in Las Vegas, you're likely to exceed this, but don't be tempted to change receipts to show a lesser value as the goods will be confiscated and you'll face a massive fine. In any case, the prices for some goods in America are so cheap that even paying the duty and VAT on top will still work out cheaper than buying it in Britain. Duty can range from 3.5% to 19% depending on the item, eg computers are charged at 3.5%, golf clubs at 4%, cameras at 5.4% and mountain bikes at a massive 15.8%. You pay this on goods above £145 and then VAT of 17.5% on top of that.

Duty free: buy your booze from US liquor stores – they're better value than airports, but remember your allowance is 1 litre of spirits and two bottles of wine.

ood, glorious food abounds in Las Vegas from the classiest gourmet restaurants to the cheap and cheerful diner and from relaxed lounge-style settings to hip and happening bistros. Not so long ago, the city was most famous for its 99-cent shrimp (ie giant prawn) cocktails and the amazing all-you-can-eat buffets – and not a lot else in the dining department. But, like every other aspect of Las Vegas, things have changed as a result of the massive influx of bright young professionals from California and a surge in sophisticated visitors looking for something more than a bit of casino action. Now you cannot walk very far down the Strip without coming across one of the many trendy diners, celebrity-chef eateries or any of the staggering number of smart restaurants that serve delicious food in elegant settings.

★ ★ ★   BRIT TIP   ★ ★ ★

★ Do not assume that because you
★ can smoke anywhere you like in
★ casinos that the same goes for
★ the restaurants. Many of the
★ hotel restaurants are completely
★ non-smoking.

★ ★ ★ ★ ★ ★ ★ ★ ★ ★ ★ ★ ★ ★ ★ ★ ★

Seriously upscale restaurants from all over America – especially New York and California – have been clambering over each other to open new outlets in Las Vegas, while a whole raft of celebrity chefs have been lured to the clutch of sophisticated and hip hotels that have opened including The Palms, Aladdin, Bellagio, Mandalay Bay and Venetian. While there are still plenty of cheap dining options, it is now

possible to part with much larger wads of cash at Charlie Palmer's Aureole (Mandalay Bay), New York's Le Cirque (Bellagio), Mark Miller's Coyote Café (MGM), Julian Serrano's Picasso (Bellagio) and Wolfgang Puck's five outlets – Chinois, Postrio, Spago, Trattoria del Lupa and his Wolfgang Puck's Café.

In addition, there is a whole host of restaurants that provide live entertainment and promise a feast as well as plenty of fun. Whatever you want to eat – caviar and smoked salmon, French, Caribbean, Japanese, dim sum, noodles or Mexican – it is all here in Las Vegas. Hawaiian cuisine has even reached the city, while a whole new raft of party-style restaurants including Crazy Armadillo, have added a new dimension to dining out.

The arrival of all these new and distinguished restaurants has also led to a whole array of awards. The Renoir at the Mirage and the Picasso at the Bellagio have both been named five-star restaurants by the *Mobil Travel Guide*.

Obviously, space dictates that I cannot list all the restaurants on offer, so I have provided information on what are considered to be the finest restaurants in each category. They're

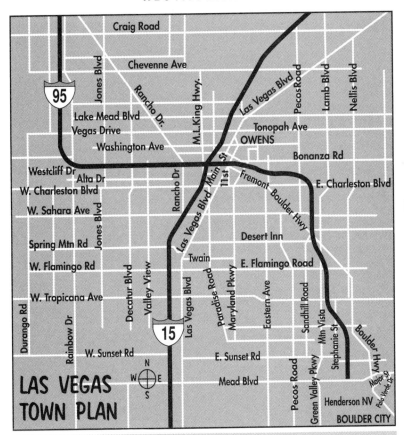

Craig Road
Chevenne Ave
95
Jones Blvd
Rancho Dr.
M.L.King Hwy.
Las Vegas Blvd
Pecos Road
Lamb Blvd
Nellis Blvd
Lake Mead Blvd
Vegas Drive
Washington Ave
Tonopah Ave
OWENS
Bonanza Rd
Westcliff Dr
Alta Dr
W. Charleston Blvd
Rancho Dr
Las Vegas Blvd
Main St
11st
Fremont
Boulder Hwy
E. Charleston Blvd
W. Sahara Ave
Jones Blvd
Desert Inn
Spring Mtn Rd
W. Flamingo Rd
Decatur Blvd
Valley View
Twain
Las Vegas Blvd
Paradise Road
Maryland Pkwy
E. Flamingo Road
Eastern Ave
Sandhill Road
W. Tropicana Ave
Durango Rd
Rainbow Dr
15
Mtn Vista
Stephanie St
Boulder Hwy
W. Sunset Rd
E. Sunset Rd
LAS VEGAS
TOWN PLAN
N
W E
S
Mead Blvd
Pecos Road
Green Valley Pkwy
Major St
Palo Verde Dr.
Henderson NV
BOULDER CITY

Here is a general overview of Las Vegas so you can familiarise yourself with the grid plan. It does not contain all the roads, but does have most of those referred to in this chapter. Remember Las Vegas Boulevard is the Strip and any roads to the right are East, while any to the left are West. The map in the hotels chapter (see page 18) shows you where the major resort hotels are located.

all popular though, so book a table in advance. I have also included a good smattering of extremely well-priced cafés – some of which are open 24/7 (around the clock) – and plenty of non-resort restaurants with enduring appeal.

Price codes

Per head for a three-course meal and one drink:

$	=	under $35
$$	=	up to $70
$$$	=	$81 and over!

Most romantic spots

Eiffel Tower Restaurant	Paris Resort
Gaylord Indian Restaurant	Rio All-Suite Hotel
Le Cirque	Bellagio
Medici Café and Terrace	Ritz-Carlton Lake Las Vegas
Ortanique	Paris Resort
Peppermill Café and Lounge	the Strip
Picasso	Bellagio
Renoir	Mirage

Bistros and Brasseries

NEW! Bleu Blanc Rouge

Mandalay Bay, 702-632 7405. Innovative brasserie-style café combining all the traditional French favourites of pastries, crêpes and ice creams with a raw bar. There is an all-day brunch, light snacks, fresh seafood, plus entrees such as roasted salmon, hangar steak au poivre and braised lamb shank. Open Sunday to Thursday 7am–midnight, and on Friday and Saturday until 1am. **$$**

NEW! PF Chang's China Bistro

The Aladdin, 702-736 7114. Chinese food in an American bistro setting using the freshest ingredients and herbs imported directly from China. The restaurant has two floors and overlooks the hotel's waterfall. Open Sunday to Thursday 11.30am–midnight, Friday and Saturday until 1am. **$–$$**

Pinot Brasserie

The Venetian, 702-414 4100. Famous Los Angeles chef Joachim Splichal brings his Pinot concept to the city. Open daily 11am–11pm. **$$**

Postrio

The Venetian, 702-414 4100. Based on Wolfgang Puck's San Francisco bistro, which serves up American food with Asian and Mediterranean influences, the menu is changed seasonally. House specialities include gourmet pizzas, foie gras terrine with fennel, haricot verts and walnut toast, grilled quail with spinach and soft egg ravioli and Chinese-style duck

★ ★ ★ **BRIT TIP** ★ ★ ★

If you love people-watching, then make the most of Postrio's patio dining area, which gives a great view of the beautiful people who flock to the Venetian.

with mango sauce and crispy fried scallion. By the way, Postrio has been named one of the 10 best restaurants in the world by *Hotels Magazine*. Open daily 11am–11pm. **$$**

RESTAURANTS BY CUISINE

American restaurants

Aureole

Mandalay Bay, 702-632 7777. Charlie Palmer, famous for his New York Aureole, has been enticed to open a second outlet, this time in Las Vegas. The New York restaurant is consistently voted number one for American cuisine by the Zagat survey and Charlie was awarded Best Chef by the James Beard Foundation in 1997. For this restaurant, a four-storey wine tower has been created and wine stewards strap on harnesses to be hoisted up the tower to make their wine selections. Open daily 5.30–10.30pm. **$$$**

Buccaneer Bay Club

Treasure Island, 702-894 7111. One of the best American restaurants in town with a series of nooks and crannies that give a bird's-eye view of the spectacular pirate show outside. You can tuck into lobster bisque,

★ ★ ★ **BRIT TIP** ★ ★ ★

For a bird's eye view of the pirate ship action outside Treasure Island, book yourself a window seat at the Buccaneer Bay Club.

salads, duckling and shrimp. Specials are offered every night and the chef is happy to prepare special orders. The soufflés are the signature desserts of the restaurant. Open daily 5–10.30pm. **$$$**

Cheesecake Factory

The Forum Shops, 702-731 7110. Famous for its extensive menu – there are more than 250 items plus nearly 30 specials – this is more of a place to people-watch than expect gourmet cuisine, yet the food is delicious too. **$**

Grand Lux Café

The Venetian, 702-414 4100. A second outlet in Las Vegas for the wildly successful Cheesecake Factory complete with all the specials. **$**

Nero's

Caesars Palace, 702-731 7731. Nero's specialises in dry-aged prime beef, tender chops and fresh seafood – all artistically presented. House specials include grilled lamb chops on crispy polenta with baby greens and garlic, grilled swordfish with sweet potato purée, herb-roasted onion, pea shoots and lemon aioli, and halibut pan-roasted in lobster oil with braised baby artichokes, steamed clams and saffron couscous. The menu changes according to the season but favourites include crab cakes, carpaccio of beef with shaved Parmesan, salad of frisée, fennel and roasted red peppers and truffle aioli. Open daily 5.30–11pm. **$$$**

Pegasus

Alexis Park Hotel, 375 East Harmon, 702-796 3353. Pegasus offers gourmet dining in a classy environment. Dishes include freshly made pastas, beef, pork and fresh fish that come with delicious vegetables. Open for dinner 6–11pm. **$$**

NEW! Tommy Rocker's Cantina & Grill

4275 Industrial Road, 702-261 6688. It's unlikely you'll be visiting Tommy's unless you're coming here for the music as it's a little off the beaten track. What will surprise you though, will be the half-decent, well-priced, largely American grub that allows you to enjoy the live and DJ music well into the night. **$**

Asian restaurants

Ah-Sin

Paris Las Vegas, 702-739 4111. A new type of dining experience with Japanese sushi, Chinese noodle specialities and a host of favourite cuisines from the Pacific Rim, all prepared by chefs at stations around the dining room. Service begins with a ritual hand-washing ceremony that includes the pouring of pure water scented with jasmine oil. Open from 11am–midnight. **$$**

★ ★ ★ **BRIT TIP** ★ ★ ★

Ah-Sin is right next door to the Risqué ultra lounge (see page 112) where you can relax on the plush couches while tucking into dessert.

Bamboo Garden

4850 West Flamingo Road, 702-871 3262. Popular spot for locals who love the delicious range of unusual dishes at the very reasonable prices. It looks modest enough, but the friendly staff provide excellent service and dishes include cream of seafood soup, Mongolian lamb, firecracker beef, emerald shrimp and Peking duck with Mandarin pancakes. **$$**

Chin Chin

New York-New York Hotel, 702-740 6969. In a restoration of New York Chinatown, you'll find everything from the Pacific Rim to Szechuan and Cantonese food. **$$**

Chinois

The Forum Shops, Caesars Palace, 702-369 6300. Celebrity chef Wolfgang Puck's second outlet in Las Vegas provides dream cuisine from China, Japan and Thailand. The menu features sushi, sashimi, wok-fried and grilled seafood, poultry and meats with fresh, high-quality ingredients and homemade desserts.

5

You have a choice of settings, too – you can dine at the sushi bar, in the 'outdoor' café or the dramatic dining room. Open 11am–midnight. $$

HoWan

3145 Las Vegas Boulevard South, 702-733 4547. Beautifully decorated with tapestries and antiques, and a fish and seafood tank, while the costumed staff provide an excellent service. Many Asians eat here and enjoy tucking into house specialities such as minced squab and crackling shrimp, steamed fish, lobster and seaweed with cabbage and bean curd soup. Open daily 6–11pm. $$$

Papyrus

Luxor Hotel, 702-262 4774. This is the place for romantics to go, with its cosy atmosphere and intimate grass-hut booths. Here you enter the Pacific Basin and dine on Polynesian, Szechwan, Cantonese and other Oriental food that includes such mouthwatering delights as ahi tuna tartare in soy-chilli sauce, Papyrus eight-treasure fried rice, pork loin with Mandarin sauce, Korean-style shortribs with basil mashed potatoes and tempura vegetables. Open daily 6–11pm. $$

NEW! Pearl

MGM Grand, freephone 1-877 793 7111. A stylish, upmarket Chinese-meets-Western restaurant based on Cantonese and Shanghai specialities. The largely seafood dishes include both Maine and Australian lobsters, shark fin and lobster spring rolls and Sian bouillabaisse. An added bonus is the trolley with a range of fine Chinese teas – for a good pick-me-up, try green tea. Open 5.30–10pm. $$–$$$

Shanghai Lilly

Mandalay Bay, 702-632 7409. Classic Cantonese and Szechuan dishes using only the finest ingredients make this one of the best places to enjoy Eastern cuisine. $$$

Thai Spice

4433 West Flamingo Road, 702-362 5308. A friendly restaurant that attracts a lot of the local Asians and tourists alike. Tuck into traditional Thai food from fish cakes to noodles, Thai-spiced beef and pepper-garlic pork. Open Monday to Thursday 11.30am–10pm and on Friday and Saturday until 11pm. $

Cajun/Creole restaurants

Big Mama's Soul Food Kitchen

Utopia Center, opposite Rue de Monte Carlo, 702-597 1616. Good, honest food at rock-bottom prices. Known for its gumbo, fried catfish and BBQ dishes. For a slice of real New Orleans food, try a piece of pecan pie. $

NEW! Big Al's Oyster Bar

New Orleans Hotel, 702-365 7111. Get a flavour of New Orleans-style dining with this Cajun/Creole restaurant with a Bayou oyster bar. Opt for oysters and clams on the half-shell with various oyster shooters from the bar, or choose from a range of southern specials including the classic gumbo, Jambalaya pasta, steamed clams, bouillabaisse and Voodoo mussels. Open Sunday to Thursday 11am–midnight, Friday and Saturday until 1am. $

Commander's Place

Desert Passage at the Aladdin, 702-736 0111. The original restaurant has been wowing well-heeled tourists and resident gourmets in New Orleans for over a century. Now its sister restaurant is doing the same in Las Vegas. $$$

Emeril's New Orleans Fish House

MGM Grand, 702-891 1111. A real must-visit restaurant if you want to experience celebrity chef Emeril Lagasse's New Orleans blend of modern Cajun/Creole cooking. Tuck into seared Atlantic salmon served on a wild mushroom potato hash with herb meat juices and a spicy onion crust or grilled fillet of beef with Creole oyster dressing and homemade hollandaise sauce. Open from 11.30am–2.30pm and 6pm–11pm. Next door is the seafood bar, a walk-up style of eatery featuring fresh shellfish and seafood specials. **$$**

Kiefer's Atop the Carriage House

105 East Harmon Avenue, 702-739 8000. This place has one of the best views of the Strip, which you can look down at while you dine on delicious Creole food from Louisiana at reasonable prices. **$$**

The VooDoo Café

Rio Suite Hotel, 702-252 7777. The VooDoo Café provides superb Cajun and Creole dishes in an elegant New Orleans setting, while the view of the Strip is one of the best in town. Specials include the Blue Water Seafood Platter for starters, the Menage et Trois of filet mignon, lobster and prawns for entrée and Bananas Foster for desert. **$$**

Caribbean restaurants

NEW! Ortanique

Paris Resort, 702-946 4346. A sumptuous palace for Caribbean food from the award-winning team behind Miami's acclaimed Ortanique. Dishes include spicy fried calamari salad, juked double pork chop with guava spiced rum sauce, curried crab cakes and pan-sautéed Bahamian black

★ ★ ★ BRIT TIP ★ ★ ★

★ If you love the Caribbean sounds ★
★ of reggae, steel drums and jazz, ★
★ then you'll enjoy the nightly live ★
★ entertainment at Ortanique. ★

grouper. If you have any room left, try the rum cake or a speciality coffee for afters. Open 5.30pm–1am. **$$**

Rumjungle

Mandalay Bay, 702-632 7777. Here food and drink become the artistic environment with a dancing firewall of food that turns into a soothing wall of water, and volcanic mountains of rum and spirits that rise up behind the illuminated bar. The menu is tropically inspired and many of the dishes are cooked over a giant open fire pit. After your meal you can dance to Latin, Caribbean and African beats until the wee small hours. Open 5pm–4am. **$$**

★ ★ ★ BRIT TIP ★ ★ ★

★ Rumjungle is one of the best ★
★ all-rounders in town. It serves ★
★ superb food, is famous for its ★
★ wide selection of rums, has great ★
★ live music and a fabulous ★
★ atmosphere that attracts the hip ★
★ and the celebs alike. ★

Caviar restaurants

Caviarteria

Forum Shops, 702-792 8560. The setting is perfect for one of the most heavenly experiences in the world as the Caviarteria has done all that is needed to re-create a small but elegant New York-style restaurant. Here you tuck in to top-quality caviar and smoked salmon and wash it all down with some fine champagne. Enjoy! **$$**

The Petrossian Bar

The Bellagio, 702-693 7111. A lavish bar next to the resort's dramatic entrance with its ballustraded walkway overhung by beautiful cypress trees. It specialises in everything from afternoon tea to caviar, champagne and smoked salmon. **$$$**

Red Square

Mandalay Bay, 702-632 7777.
Check out the extensive caviar
selection or try out the menu of
updated Russian classics at the frozen
ice bar, where you can choose from a
selection of more than 100 frozen
vodkas and infusions, Martinis and
Russian-inspired cocktails. **$$$**

Chinese restaurants

Empress Court

Caesars Palace, 702-731 7110.
Empress Court has a watery theme
with a large, salt-water aquarium at
the entrance to reflect the waters of its
cuisine – the more unusual Hong
Kong dishes. Chinese furniture such
as chow tables, tea tables and altar
tables in ebonised wood or aged
silver leaf add an authentic feel to the
room. Open Thursday to Monday
from 6–11pm. **$$$**

Lillie Langtry's

Golden Nugget Hotel, 129 Fremont
Street, 702-385 7111. Provides
downtown gamblers with delicious
and exotic Cantonese dishes in a
brightly decorated setting with great
service. The Great Combination Plate
is a favourite starter, before moving
on to black-pepper steak, stir-fried
shrimp or lemon chicken. Open
5–10.30pm. **$**

The Mandarin Court

1510 East Flamingo Road, 702-737
1234. Designed as a replica of a
Peking palace, this is something of a
landmark locally. However, it is an
excellent place to go to get far from
the madding crowds and enjoy
delicious traditional Chinese food at
good prices. It is also notable for
serving its trademark sweet and sour
dishes until 4am! **$$**

Moongate

Mirage, 702-791 7111. Moongate is
housed in a series of connected
buildings of classical Chinese
architecture surrounding an open

Celebrity chef restaurants

Aqua – Michael Mina and Charles
Candy

Aureole – Charlie Palmer

Border Grill – Mary Sue Milliken
and Susan Feniger aka Too Hot
Tamales

Coyote Café – Mark Miller

Delmonico Steakhouse – Emeril
Lagassé

Drai's – Victor Drai

Emeril's New Orleans Fish House –
Emeril Lagassé

Il Fornaio – Luigi Bomparolo

Le Cirque – Elizabeth Blau

Napa – Jean-Louis Palladin

Olives – Todd English

Picasso – Julian Serrano

Pinot – Joachim Splichal

**Trattoria del Lupa, Chinois, Postrio,
Spago** and **Wolfgang Puck's Café** –
all Wolfgang Puck

courtyard filled with beautiful
flowering cherry trees. The romantic
setting is just right for mouthwatering
classics from Szechwan and Canton.
Open 5.30–11pm. **$$**

English restaurant

Sir Galahad's

The Excalibur, 702-597 7777. This
place serves up traditional English
roast beef and Yorkshire pudding in
its English castle setting with staff in
dress reminiscent of King Arthur's
day. The house speciality is basically
prime rib, but you'll also find chicken
and fish on the menu if you don't
fancy tucking into the main meal,
which is served from a large, copper
cart. Open Sunday to Thursday
5–10pm and Friday, Saturday and
holidays 5pm–midnight. **$**

French restaurants

NEW! Alizé

The Palms, 702-951 7000. Las Vegas' very own celebrity chef and restaurateur, André Rochat, who also owns his own restaurant called André, has created a gourmet dining experience in the hip new Palms hotel. Winner of the Best Gourmet Restaurant in the Las Vegas Review Journal's 2003 Best of Las Vegas awards, delicious entrees include sautéed Muscovy duck breast and market-fresh seafood. This is a top-of-the-pile dining experience, which includes the classic French sorbet between courses for cleansing the palate, a cheese trolley and an extensive wine list. Open Sunday to Thursday 5.30–10pm and Friday and Saturday until 10.30pm. $$–$$$

★★★ **BRIT TIP** ★★★
★　　　　　　　　　　★
★　　　　　　　　　　★
★ As in every other American city, ★
★ top-notch, gourmet restaurants ★
★ have prices to match – ★
★ particularly with bottles of wine ★
★ that can easily cost $200 each, ★
★ so take care when making your ★
★ choice! ★
★★★★★★★★★★★★★★★★★

André's

401 South 6th Street, 702-385 5016. André's has been serving up delicious gourmet food to locals and tourists alike for nearly two decades. Just one block off the Strip, the restaurant is housed in one of the early homes of Las Vegas – dating all the way back to 1930! The menu changes all the time, but mouthwatering offerings include chartreuse of Muscovy duck stewed in Merlot with portabella mushrooms and spring vegetables, sautéed prime fillet of beef with green peppercorn and cognac cream sauce, baked zucchini, gratin dauphinois and baby carrots anglaise and Maine lobster. Open nightly 6–10pm. $$$

Aristocrat

850 South Rancho Drive, 702-870 1977. Another well-established and fine French restaurant which is filled with locals and tourists. Tuck into classics such as mussels in white wine, beef Wellington, filet mignon or any of the fresh fish specialities that are changed daily. Open for lunch weekdays 11.30am–2pm and dinner daily 6–11pm. $$

Le Cirque

The Bellagio, 702-693 7111. Elizabeth Blau, who has been with the Maccioni family's famous flagship restaurant in New York for more than a decade, re-creates its gourmet French dishes with great aplomb, while the views of the Bellagio's famous fountains lend it more than a touch of elegance. $$$

Eiffel Tower Restaurant

Paris, 702-739 4111. The signature dining experience of the new resort hotel is set 17 storeys up on the Eiffel Tower replica and has stunning views of Las Vegas' glittering golden mile. The softly lit ambience includes a romantic piano bar where you can enjoy a glass of champagne or an entire meal while absorbing the views, or try the full gourmet experience in the restaurant. $$$

Frogeez on 4th

Bank of America Center, 300 S 4th St, 702-380 1122. André Rochat and Mary Jane Jarvis of André's fame provide another fine dining experience Downtown. The menu and wine lists are short but sweet, while the atmosphere – particularly with live music at weekends – is always good and the bar is jumping on a Friday night. Open daily 11am–11pm. $

Isis

Luxor Hotel, 702-262 4773. Consistently voted one of the top 10 gourmet restaurants in America by the *Best of the Best Restaurant Guide*. Reproduction Egyptian artefacts are on display inside, many based on those found inside King Tutankhamun's tomb, and the vaulted ceiling is decorated with gold. It certainly is a grand setting in which to dine on house specialities, inspired by gourmet French cuisine and the finest seasonal dishes money can buy. Open daily 6–11pm. **$$$**

Le Montrachet Bistro

Las Vegas Hilton, 702-732 5651. Offers delicious French food in an elegant and luxurious setting and elaborate fresh flower arrangements on each of the tables. The menu changes with the seasons. Open nightly 6–11pm, except Tuesday. **$$$**

Mon Ami Gabi

Paris, 702-946 7000. A Parisian-style café set in the Louvre façade of the Paris hotel. It is on the Strip and you can even opt to sit outside. Open for breakfast, lunch and dinner. **$$**

Napa

Rio All-Suite Hotel, 702-252 7737. Inspired by the Californian wine region, it serves gourmet food by world-renowned chef Jean-Louis Palladin. Open Wednesday to Sunday 6pm–midnight. **$$**

Pamplemousse

400 East Sahara Avenue, 702-733 2066. Like all the top French restaurants, this small but elegant establishment is pricey – but it's worth it. House specialities include roast duckling in red wine and banana rum sauce and veal medallions in cream sauce, plus a huge selection of fresh seafood according to the season from mussels to monkfish and salmon. Open for dinner daily except Monday 6–11pm. **$$$**

Renoir

The Mirage, 702-791 7223. Named a five-star restaurant by the *Mobil Travel Guide*, it serves up meats, seafood and vegetable specialities by head chef Alessandro Shatta. It also

features an à la carte menu and a five-course tasting for $115. The restaurant is decorated in silks and tapestries and is home to original artwork by Renoir. **$$$**

La Rotisserie des Artistes

Paris Resort, 702-739 4111. A wide choice of gourmet dishes include the signature Scottish pheasant brushed with tarragon mustard sauce and served with red-bliss potatoes, and lime oil-brushed swordfish with basil garlic mashed potatoes. Desserts include classics such as crème brûlée and raspberry clafoutis. **$$$**

Fusion restaurants

Fiore Rotisserie and Grille

Rio All-Suite Hotel, 702-252 7702. One of the best restaurants in town, with great food, service and prices that won't break the bank! It has an eclectic range of dishes from chilled, roasted eggplant (aubergine) with balsamic vinaigrette and pesto to spaghettini with pastrami duck breast and cabbage for starters, and Black Forest ham with shiitake mushrooms to Gulf red snapper sautéed with fennel and mushrooms. Cigar lovers will be pleased to note that the restaurant has an excellent selection and a special cigar patio where you can imbibe coffee and cognac. Open for lunch weekdays only 11.30am– 2pm and dinner nightly 6pm– midnight. **$$**

★ ★ ★   **BRIT TIP**   ★ ★ ★

★   Little Buddha offers poolside   ★
★   dining during the summer season ★
★   and is one of the best places in   ★
★   town to spot a celeb or two.   ★
★ ★ ★ ★ ★ ★ ★ ★ ★ ★ ★ ★ ★ ★ ★ ★

NEW! Little Buddha

The Palms, 702-942 7778. Based on the award-winning Buddha Bar and restaurant in Paris, this stylish eatery serves up both Pacific Rim and Chinese dishes with a French twist. There are three dining areas – all decorated in an opulent East-meets-West style, plus a sushi bar. Open Sunday to Thursday 5.30–10.45pm, Friday and Saturday until midnight. $

Mayflower Cuisinier

Sahara Pavilion, 4750 West Sahara at Decatur Boulevard, 702-870 8432. One of the most highly rated restaurants in Las Vegas and consistently appears in the Zagat Top 10. Here you will find Mongolian/Chinese cuisine served Californian-style in a casual, but elegant environment. Book ahead for a table at weekends. Open weekdays only 11am–3pm and Monday to Saturday 5–10pm. $$

NEW! NOBHILL

MGM Grand, freephone 1-877-793 7111. Renowned chef Michael Mina, who created Aqua in San Francisco and at Bellagio, has created a new restaurant to reflect the stylish San Francisco neighbourhood scene. Most of the American-Asian fusion dishes use ingredients from the Bay area around the city and include beef Wellington, rich lobster pot, fish carpaccio and roasted rack of Hop Sing market pork. Open 5.30–10.30pm. $$–$$$

★★★ **BRIT TIP** ★★★
★ Men are advised to wear a jacket ★
★ for dining at the sophisticated ★
★ NOBHILL restaurant – named ★
★ after the famous Nob Hill in San ★
★ Francisco. ★
★★★★★★★★★★★★★★★★

NEW! Rosemary's

Rio All-Suite Hotel, 702-777 7777. A fine dining experience from chefs Michael and Wendy Jordan, the team behind the award-winning Las Vegas restaurant by the same name. An eclectic series of dishes start with Hugo's Texas BBQ Shrimp, pizzas, southern crab cakes and curry Manila clams. Entrees include wood-over-roasted rack of lamb, Maine lobster brochettes, New York strip au poivre and pan-seared scallops. Open 5–11pm, bar opens at 4pm. $$

Spago

The Forum Shops, 702-369 6300. This is one of celebrity chef Wolfgang Puck's famous outlets in Las Vegas and, as with all his other establishments in Los Angeles, is a popular place for celebs and local movers and shakers. You'll find everything from pastas to salads and seafood. Open for dinner Monday to Thursday 6–10pm and until 10.30pm Friday to Sunday. The separate café is open for lunch Sunday to Thursday 11am–11pm and on Friday and Saturday until 1am. $$

WB Stage 16 Restaurant

The Venetian, 702-414 1699. A fusion of Mediterranean, Asian, European and American dishes are served in four settings based on Warner Bros productions. Sets include We're in the Money from *Gold Diggers of 1933*, interiors from *Casablanca*, the Las Vegas 60s Lounge from *Ocean's Eleven* and a Gotham City exterior from *Batman*. $$

Hawaiian restaurants

NEW! 8-0-8

Caesars Palace, 702-731 7731. Chef Jean-Marie Josselin, owner of the award-winning A Pacific Café restaurant in Hawaii, brings a whole new combination of flavours to titillate the palate of Las Vegans and visitors alike. Signature dishes are based on the freshest seafood available and organic Hawaiian produce and then fused with Thai, Japanese, Chinese, Italian, Indian and French flavours to create a unique dining experience. Chef de Cuisine Wesley Coffel prepares the lamb, beef, chicken and veal dishes. Open Wednesday to Sunday 5–11pm. $$$

NEW! Kahunaville

Treasure Island, 702-894 7111. A tropical restaurant setting complete with tiki torches and plants, this features Hawaiian dishes such as teriyaki ginger steak, Hawaiian pork tenderloin and coconut shrimp. It also doubles as a supper club with live entertainment, and there is a great choice of margaritas, coladas, beers and wine. Open daily 8am–11pm, Friday and Saturday to midnight. The bar is open from 11am–3am. $

Irish restaurant

NEW! Nine Fine Irishmen

New York-New York, 702-740 6969. In a town where everything is copied it was only a matter of time before an 'authentic' Irish pub with drink, food, music and entertainment opened its doors. And where better than the New York-New York hotel – evocative of the city that is home to so many Irish-Americans. Dishes have been created by nine of Ireland's top chefs – though the name is based on the lives of nine Irishmen from the 19th century. Open from lunch 11am–3am. The bar is open Sunday to Thursday 11am–3am and on Friday and Saturday 24 hours. $–$$

Indian restaurant

NEW! Gaylord Indian Restaurant

Rio All-Suite Hotel, 702-777 7777. A romantic setting with authentic Indian artefacts in which to enjoy tandoori and Mughlai-style dishes from the creators of the award-winning San Francisco restaurant. One of its main features is the Combination Dinners, in which you can choose different starters and entrees for an all-inclusive price. Lunch buffet 11.30am–2.30pm, dinner 5–11pm. $

Italian restaurants

Al Dente

Bally's Hotel on the Strip, 702-739 4656. Al Dente serves contemporary Italian cuisine in a bright setting with plenty of favourites from bruschetta to gourmet pizzas, antipasti, spinach and chicken dishes. Open Tuesday to Saturday, 6–11pm. $$

Andiamo

Las Vegas Hilton, 702-732 5664. Andiamo specialises in fine northern Italian specialities in a beautiful setting. The exhibition kitchen gives customers the chance to watch chefs preparing the fresh pastas, pastries and sauces. Open 6–11pm. $$

Antonio's

Rio All-Suite Hotel, 3700 West Flamingo Road, 702-252 7777. This, like all the Rio restaurants, makes an excellent choice – this time for those in search of a delicious Italian meal. Dishes include osso bucco, pork loin, lobster and chicken. Open nightly 5–11pm. $$

Battista's Hole in the Wall

4041 Audrie Lane, 702-732 1424. Classic Italian fare served in a fun and friendly atmosphere that makes it a great eating place for locals and tourists alike. Open for dinner only 6–11pm. $$

Bertolini's

Forum Shops at Caesars Palace on the Strip, 702-735 4663. A sidewalk-style café inside the exquisite Forum Shops in the piazza surrounding the Fountain of Gods. Outside you can watch the world go by, but inside there are quieter seats to be found. Pastas and rice dishes, pizzas, soups and salads, chicken and fish. $

Bice

Desert Passage at the Aladdin, 702-736 0111. The American 'chain' of upmarket Italian restaurants has brought its exquisite dishes to Las

Vegas with the arrival of Bice at the Aladdin. **$$$**

California Pizza Kitchen

3400 Las Vegas Boulevard South, 702-791 7353. Part of a growing national chain, which serves mostly delicious pizzas with mouthwatering selections of fresh ingredients. Open Monday to Thursday 11am–midnight and Friday and Saturday until 2am. **$**

Canaletto

The Grand Canal Shoppes at the Venetian, 702-414 4100. Based on a new concept by Il Fornaio's Larry Mindel. Classics include homemade ravioli filled with fresh Maine lobster in a lobster cream sauce topped with shrimp. **$$**

Chicago Joe's

820 South 4th Street, 702-382 5637. Chicago Joe's has been around for more than 20 years and is famous for its Italian sauces. Try the cream garlic dressing with one of the many delicious salads, Mexican Gulf shrimp and Maine lobster. Open for lunch and dinner. **$**

Francesco's

Treasure Island, 702-894 7111. Filled with artwork by celebrities including crooner Tony Bennett, the menu here includes fresh pastas, antipasti, Mediterranean-style seafood and signature freshly baked breads. Open daily 5.30–11pm. **$**

Il Fornaio

New York-New York Hotel on the Strip, 702-740 6969. Superb re-creation of an Italian restaurant from New York's Little Italy neighbourhood. Here you'll find classic Italian cuisine and signature breads, rolls and pastries from the in-house bakery. By the way, most of the waiters migrated to Las Vegas from New York when the hotel opened, so the accents are real! **$$**

Mortoni's

Hard Rock Hotel, 4455 Paradise Road, 702-693 5047. A real hip joint, good for celebrity watching, while pictures of the Rat Pack line the walls. The food's pretty good too, though go for the fish specialities to get a truly tasty meal. Open daily 6–11pm. **$$**

Onda

The Mirage, 702-791 7223. Regional Italian and new American cuisine inspired by Todd English and served up in an elegant setting. **$$$**

Sergio's Italian Gardens

1955 East Tropicana Avenue, 702-739 1544. Consistently rated as one of the best Italian restaurants in town, Sergio's has a delightful garden with Roman columns. Dishes include calamari, Belgium endive salad, sautéed veal and filet mignon Rossini. Open Monday to Friday 11.30am–2.30pm, nightly 5.30–11pm. **$$**

Terrazza

Caesars Palace on the Strip, 702-731 7731. Set in an ornate rotunda overlooking the Garden of the Gods swimming pools and gardens, Terrazza is open for lunch, brunch and dinner. A la carte includes risotto, antipasti, soups, fresh fish and seafood, meats, pastas and freshly baked pizza and focaccia breads. Lunch from Wednesday to Saturday 11.30am–2.30pm, brunch on Sunday 10.30am–3pm and dinner is daily 5.30–11pm (last seating at 10pm). **$$**

Trattoria del Lupa

Mandalay Bay, 702-632 7777. The most recent of celebrity chef Wolfgang Puck's five eating outlets in Las Vegas, this one is pure Italian with traditional recipes cooked in pizza ovens and wood-burning rotisseries. The interior was designed by Adam Tihany, who has re-created a typical small, secluded piazza in Milan with views of pasta, meats and bakery production areas. Open 5.30–11pm. **$$**

5

NEW! Tremezzo

The Aladdin, 702-785 9013. Another excellent offering from the Aladdin, this time under the watchful eye of chef Mario Capone, whose dishes include Manila clams, linguine with grilled Maine lobster, and ahi tuna carpaccio with blood-orange vinaigrette. Already honoured with the Wine Enthusiast Award of Excellence and named one of the 10 best restaurants in Las Vegas by the Zagat survey, the real piece de resistance are the fab views of the Strip. Open Tuesday to Sunday 5–10pm. $$

Venetian

3713 West Sahara Avenue, 702-876 4190. No, not the hotel, but a similarly named restaurant that still stands out a mile due to the exterior and interior murals. When it opened in 1955 it was the first place to serve pizza in Las Vegas! It still does a roaring trade serving everything from pizza to pasta and plenty of other delightful dishes in between – all at great prices. Open for dinner only. $

Japanese restaurants

Benihana Village

Las Vegas Hilton, 702-732 5821. Japanese fantasyland in an enchanting garden setting complete with thunder and lightning storms, lush flowers, flowing ponds and an authentic Torii Arch. There are two restaurants to choose from – the Hibachi where skilled chefs chop, slice and grill your food tableside and the Seafood Grille, where delicious delicacies are the order of the day. You can enjoy drinks and Oriental hors d'oeuvres in the Kabuki Lounge while your table is prepared. Open daily 5–11pm. $$$

NEW! Hamada of Japan

Rio All-Suite Hotel, 702-777 7777 ext 2770. The waitresses are dressed in kimonos which gives this restaurant a touch of authenticity. The main dining room features classics such as beef sukiyaki, shabu-shabu and seafood yosenabe. A second dining room, the Teppan Room, is where food is prepared in front of you by knife-wielding chefs. Delicious dishes are made up from shrimp, lobster, steaks and marinated chicken. It also has a sushi bar. Open 5–11pm. $$

★ ★ ★ BRIT TIP ★ ★ ★

If you want an early evening appetiser, head for the Hamada's cocktail lounge where you can get little plates of deep-fried tempura and sushi with your drinks.

Hyakumi Japanese Restaurant and Sushi Bar

Caesars Palace, 702-734 6116. Home to award-winning executive chef Hiroji Obayashi. For dinner you have a choice of three set-price menus that include a four-course feast of appetisers, miso soup, salad and main course from $64 to $74 or à la carte dishes that include beef, chicken or fish teriyaki, yakitori, shrimp and vegetable tempura. The sushi bar also has a fabulously large selection of delicacies. The main restaurant is open Tuesday to Sunday 6–11pm and on Friday and Saturday the sushi bar stays open until midnight. $$$

Nobu

Hard Rock Hotel, 702-693 5000. Chef Nobu Matsuhisa's ground-breaking temple of Japanese cuisine with Peruvian influences has already set unmatched standards of excellence in Los Angeles, New York and London. The opening of Nobu Las Vegas has been widely hailed as a major coup for the Hard Rock Hotel. Dishes include squid pasta, miso-infused cod and creamy, spicy, cracked crab. $$$

Mediterranean restaurants

Drai's

Barbary Coast, on the Strip at East Flamingo, 702-737 7111. Run by ex-Hollywood producer Victor Drai, this is one of the most popular venues in town among the locals. Tuck into a fusion of French and Mediterranean food to the background sounds of live jazz and blues. Winning dishes include seared jumbo scallops with citrus ginger sauce, crispy duck confit and seven-hour leg of lamb. Open nightly 5.30pm–1am. **$$**

NEW! Medici Café and Terrace

Ritz-Carlton Lake Las Vegas, 702-567 4700. An elegant yet relaxed setting in which to enjoy breakfast, lunch or fine-dining in the evening. Woven fabrics and silks adorn the furniture, European and Italian Renaissance art covers the walls, while the pretty Florentine gardens provide an ultra romantic setting. There is a strong Mediterranean influence to the food and an excellent selection of wines to choose from. Open for breakfast 7–11am, for lunch noon–3pm and for dinner 6–10pm. Sunday brunch is served 11am–3pm. **$–$$**

Olives

Bellagio, 702-693 7111. Todd and Olivia English bring their famous Boston Olives to Las Vegas with Mediterranean-style dishes in a lively café setting. Open 11.30am–11pm. **$$**

Picasso

Bellagio, 702-693 7111. Julian Serano, who dazzled diners at San Francisco's Masa, brings his trademark Spanish-tinged French cuisine to one of the world's most opulent settings for a restaurant – dine here and you'll be surrounded by $52-million-worth of Picasso originals and even some of the artist's ceramics. The menu changes nightly but usually includes Julian's foie gras in Madeira sauce or warm lobster salad with mangoes or potatoes. The views of the Bellagio's dancing fountains finish off a superb dining experience. **$$$**

Mexican restaurants

NEW! Bamboleo

Rio All-Suite Hotel, 702-247 7923. Chef Hector Nunez uses the freshest ingredients to create traditional dishes from Mexico, Brazil and Argentina. Chili relleno, enchiladas and snapper are all on the menu along with excellent margaritas including the two-person house special – a 46oz margarita served in a Rio glass you can keep. Open 11am–11pm. **$$**

NEW! Blue Agave

The Palms, 702-942 7777. A fun, casual dining experience at the über-trendy Palms hotel, named after the plant which gives tequilas their flavour. The house specialities are oysters, seafood cocktails and pan roasts, plus a chili bar with South American favourites. Open Sunday to Thursday 11am–10pm, Friday and Saturday until 1am. **$$$**

★ For a real party atmosphere head to the hip Blue Agave, where along with delish Mexican-based cuisine, there is a range of 150 tequilas and a whopping 350 different margaritas to choose from! ★

Border Grill

Mandalay Bay, 702-632 7777. Mary Sue Milliken and Susan Feniger, the duo known on American TV as Too Hot Tamales, are renowned for their Border Grill in Los Angeles and have now opened an outlet in the new all-jumping hotel, Mandalay Bay. Their bold and

5

tasty Mexican dishes are served in a vibrant beachside setting. **$$**

Cozymel's
Hughes Center, 355 Hughes Center Drive, 702-732 4833. An upscale franchise restaurant serving spectacular seafood specials and delicious fajitas. Open Monday to Thursday 11am–10pm and Friday and Saturday until midnight. **$**

NEW! Crazy Armadillo
Stratosphere, 702-380 7777. 'Flair' bartenders, singing waiters, dancing waitresses and live music make this rowdy cantina-style eaterie a fun place for food. House specialities include meatball soup, baby back ribs, salmon fajitas, tacos and oysters on the half-shell. Enjoy! Open 4–11pm. **$**

NEW! Garduños
The Palms, 702-942 7777. Part of a Mexican cantina chain, this restaurant serves authentic Mexican cuisine and has quickly become a firm favourite in Las Vegas. Margaritas are also available. Open Sunday to Thursday 11am–10.50pm, Friday and Saturday until 11.50pm. **$**

NEW! Gonzalez Y Gonzalez
New York-New York, 702-740 6455. A great spot to soak up the atmosphere of the hotel's outdoor courtyard with lanterns and Spanish piñatas, this serves authentic Mexican cuisine at reasonable prices. Open Sunday to Thursday 11am–11pm, Friday and Saturday until midnight. **$**

★★★ BRIT TIP ★★★

★ The real secret of Gonzalez Y
★ Gonzalez is the long list of
★ margaritas, which can even be
★ served by the yard!

Guadalajara Bar and Grille
Palace Station Hotel, 2411 West Sahara Avenue, 702-367 2411. A 24-hour joint famous for its 99-cent margaritas. It may be a little off the beaten track, but you'll still need to make a reservation! Lunch is served 11am–5pm and dinner 5pm–11am. **$**

Margaritagrille
Las Vegas Hilton, 702-732 5111. One of the best Mexican restaurants in town. Specialities include enchiladas, spicy burritos, chimichangas, crispy tostadas and tacos as well as the chef's own sizzling fajitas. You can also get delicious fresh fruit margaritas from the salsa bar. Open daily 11.30am–3pm and 5–11pm. **$**

Margarita's Mexican Cantina
Frontier Hotel on the Strip, 702-794 8200. Classic Tex-Mex food from burritos to tacos, enchiladas and chimichangas. The tortillas are freshly prepared and come with the usual salsa, guacamole and bean dips. **$**

Pink Taco
Hard Rock Hotel, 702-693 5000. A hip restaurant offering celebrated Californian chef Tacho Kneeland's fresh and modern taste on Mexican classics. Choices include tamales nachos, quesadillas, tacos and a whole range of tequilas – served the traditional way, natch! **$$**

Ricardo's Mexican Restaurant
MGM Grand Hotel on the Strip, 1-800 929 1111. Fun place to go for entertainment and food. Based in the resort's Studio Walk, you'll find a walk-up margarita bar, taco bar and a gift shop (another essential ingredient, it seems, of themed restaurants in Las Vegas!) and classic Mexican dishes. **$**

Viva Mercado's
6182 West Flamingo Road, 702-871 8826. Regularly wins the local daily paper's poll for best Mexican

restaurant in town. That is due to delicious food including chili relleno, carnitas and Mexican-style steak at great prices. **$**

★ ★ ★   **BRIT TIP**   ★ ★ ★

★   Be warned: although Las Vegas is   ★
★   a 24-hour city, most of the top-   ★
★   notch restaurants close as early   ★
★   as 10pm or 10.30pm.   ★

Moroccan restaurants

NEW! Japengo

Hyatt Regency Lake Las Vegas, 702-567 1234. A real Moroccan affair, this superb restaurant focuses largely on products from the sea and even includes a sushi bar that has been rated the best in the Las Vegas valley by the Zagat survey. Best of all, though, are the amazing views of Lake Las Vegas and the mountains. Open daily 6–10.30pm except Sunday. **$$**

Mamounia

4632 South Maryland Parkway, 702-597 0092. Delicious Moroccan dishes are served in a simulated Middle Eastern desert tent setting complete with low benches or pillows, costumed waiters and belly dancers. House specialities include all the Moroccan classics such as hummus, kefta, tabbouleh, briouats, cacik yoghurt dip, shish kebabs and couscous. Great value. Open daily 5.30–11.30pm. **$$**

Marrakech Restaurant

3900 Paradise Road, 702-737 5611. The oldest Moroccan restaurant in town taking the whole eating in the desert thing one stage further than Mamounia by expecting diners to eat with their hands! The house specialities include Moroccan-style chicken in a light lemon sauce and flambéed lamb brochette. Dinner

features a belly-dancing show. Open daily 5.30–11pm. **$$**

Seafood and steakhouses

NEW! 3950

Mandalay Bay, 702-632 7414. Contemporary-yet-classic steak and seafood cuisine served in a bold setting with high-back suede booths and red leather walls. Starters include Beluga caviar, escargot and lobster bisque, while entrees include orange duck, rack of lamb, New York strip steak, grilled swordfish and pan-seared Chilian sea bass. The speciality of the house is the innovative fresh white truffle and lobster macaroni cheese. Open 5–10.30pm. **$$$**

Aqua

Bellagio, 702-693 7111. Michael Mina and Charles Candy's smart San Francisco seafood restaurant is brought to delightful life in Las Vegas by award-winning chef Mark Lo Russo. The five-course, $80 tasting menu includes Dungeness crab cakes on chopped tomatoes, ahi tuna medallion with seared foie gras, spinach, potato cake and portabello mushrooms in a pinot noir sauce. There is also an elaborate caviar service. **$$$**

Beluga Bar

Desert Passage at the Aladdin, 702-736 0111. A traditional steakhouse redesigned to reflect a New England-style hunt club, it offers the finest in steaks, chops and seafood. **$$$**

Burgundy Room

Lady Luck, 206 North 3rd Street, 702-477 3000. If you want to get away from expensive gourmet rooms, then the Burgundy serves up classics like beef Wellington and steak au poivre in an attractive setting at reasonable prices. Open daily 5–10pm. **$$**

5

Búzio's

Rio All-Suite Hotel, 702-252 7697.
Probably one of the best seafood
restaurants in town – not just because
of its extraordinary selection of
seafood dishes, but also because of
its pricing policy – dinner will cost
around $29 per person. This is
another fine restaurant based at the
Rio All-Suite Hotel and well deserves
its appearance in the annual Zagat
survey of top restaurants in Las Vegas.
Open daily 11am–11pm. $$

NEW! Craftsteak

MGM Grand, 702-891 1111. One
of the hotel's newest fine dining
establishments, this was created by
award-winning chef Tom Colicchio,
founder of the critically acclaimed
Craft restaurant in New York. The
philosophy is simple: use the finest
available produce and cook in such a
way to allow the flavours of the
ingredients shine through. A classic
steakhouse, there is a $39, three-
course Market Menu available seven
days a week. Open daily
5.30–10.30pm. Live music Tuesday
to Thursday 8pm–midnight, Friday
and Saturday 9pm–1am. $$–$$$

★ ★ ★   BRIT TIP   ★ ★ ★
★   ★
★   An added bonus of dining at   ★
★   Craftsteak is the live music. Pianist ★
★   Shane Stephens sings a blend of   ★
★   jazz, soul and pop songs every   ★
★   night except Monday.   ★
★ ★ ★ ★ ★ ★ ★ ★ ★ ★ ★ ★ ★ ★ ★ ★

Delmonico Steakhouse

The Venetian, 702-733 5000. Emeril
Lagasse's second outlet in Las Vegas,
it has already won the Ivy Award
from Restaurants and Institutions and
features the food surprises that have
made him famous. Open daily
5.30–10.30pm. $$$

NEW! Elements

The Aladdin, 702-785 9003. A
fabulous newcomer to the Las Vegas
dining scene, Elements has already
been given the Award of Excellence
by *Wine Spectator* magazine and
voted one of the Top 10 restaurants in
the city by Zagat. Located in an
elegant room, it features thick steaks,
fresh seafood, an extensive wine
selection and an authentic Sushi and
Sashimi Bar. Entrees include
peppered ahi with sweet potato purée
and baby fennel in a red wine butter
sauce, and wood-roasted fillet with
green beans, rosti potato and foie
gras in a black truffle sauce. Open
5.30–10.30pm. $$$

Hugo's Cellar

Four Queen's, 202 Fremont Street,
Downtown, 702-385 4011. A
popular choice with locals and visitors
alike, so book ahead to get a table.
Famous for its excellent wine list.
Open daily 5.30–10.30pm. $$

Michael's

Barbary Coast, 3595 The Strip at
East Flamingo, 702-737 7111.
Despite its unprepossessing setting,
this is the choice of Las Vegas high-
flyers so tables are hard to get. The
food is superb, but the prices match.
For real foodies only. Open nightly
6–9.30pm. $$$

Morton's

The Fashion Show Mall on the Strip,
702-893 0703. A branch of the
Chicago-based steakhouse, Morton's
serves huge piles of excellent food at
good prices. Try the broiled sea
scallops wrapped in bacon for
starters before heading on to a huge
selection of massive steaks from
Porterhouse steak to New York sirloin
steak, rib-eye steak and double filet
mignon. For an alternative you can
also tuck into whole Maine lobster,
shrimps or swordfish steak. Open
Monday to Saturday 5–11pm and
Sundays until 10pm. $$

The Palm

Forum Shops at Caesars Palace, 702-732 7256. Following on from the success of the New York restaurant, the Las Vegas version also appears in the Zagat Top 40. Famous for crab cakes, lobster, prime rib and the house speciality, charcoal-burnt steak. Open daily 5–11pm. **$$**

Prime

The Bellagio, 702-693 7223. Award-winning chef Jean-Georges Vongerichten uses only the highest quality meats, seafood and chops to create a fine dining experience. Open daily 5.30–10.30pm. **$$**

Ruth's Chris Steakhouse

3900 Paradise Road, 702-791 7011 and 4561 West Flamingo Road, 702-248 7011. A chain of franchised steakhouses which started in New Orleans, these places have a reputation for serving prime meat on a sizzling-hot platter with butter. Other offerings include lamb, chicken and fish with delicious vegetables from sautéed mushrooms to creamed spinach. Open daily 4.30–10.30pm. **$$**

NEW! Simon

4455 Paradise Road; 702- 693-5000. Kerry Simon's trendy new Palm Springs-style eatery provides good old-fashioned comfort food including excellent steaks, seafood and pasta. **$$**

Smith & Wollensky

3767 The Strip opposite the Monte Carlo next to the MGM Grand, 702-862 4100. Alan Stillman's New York steakhouse group's $10-million, free-standing, three-storey restaurant seats up to 600 diners in a catacomb-like series of rooms, niches and chambers. Open daily 11.30am–11pm. **$$**

Star Canyon

The Venetian, 702-414 4100. Dallas-based chef Stephan Pyles has been awarded Best New Restaurant by *Esquire, Bon Appetit* and *Town & Country.* **$$**

The Steak House

Circus Circus, 702-794 3767. An exception to every other rule at the family-friendly Circus Circus, this is definitely adult-friendly (the kids are running around the lobby outside) and serves some of the best steaks and seafood in town, making it one of the finest in its price range. Open for dinner daily from 5pm. **$$**

The Steakhouse at Camelot

Excalibur 702-597 7777. Gourmet cuisine served in the Excalibur castle overlooking make-believe English countryside creates a truly wonderful eating experience. Epicureans will find everything they are looking for from a fine wine cellar to a cigar room, lounge and private dining chamber, while the casual ambience makes it a friendly place for anyone to enjoy a meal. **$$**

The Tillerman

2245 East Flamingo Road, 702-731 4036. One of the best places in town to get a fabulously fresh seafood dinner – and not at sky-high prices. Pacific salmon, Chilean sea bass and Florida snapper are some of the seafood platters on offer, while you'll also find steaks and pasta. Open daily 5–11pm. **$$**

The Top of the World

Stratosphere, 702-380 7711. The name says it all! More than 800ft (240 metres) up the tallest free-standing building in America, the Top of the World revolving restaurant

★ ★ ★   **BRIT TIP**   ★ ★ ★

The Top of the World restaurant is one of the '10 Great Places to Pop the Question' according to America's wedding website, The Knot (www.theknot.com). Other locations include Paris and New York's Brooklyn Bridge.

5

makes a full 360-degree revolution every 70 minutes. Awarded the Best Gourmet Room award by the Las Vegas Review Journal, the top-notch food includes sizzling steaks and fresh fish and seafood, tasty salads and flaming desserts. Open Sunday to Thursday 5–11pm and Friday and Saturday until midnight. **$$**

Yolie's

3900 Paradise Road, 702-714 0700. A Brazilian steakhouse with large, wood-fired rotisseries that cook the meals in full view of the diners. The selection includes turkey, lamb, brisket, chicken, sausages and steak plus side dishes of fried brown rice, potatoes and vegetables. **$$**

Southern restaurant

House of Blues

Mandalay Bay, 702-632 7777. Dan Aykroyd's famous House of Blues on Los Angeles' Strip has made it to Las Vegas at the majestic Mandalay Bay, and is living up to its 'hot' reputation. You'll find every kind of dish from Southern to Creole and Cajun staples as well as wood-fired pizza and burgers. Gospel fans will enjoy the Gospel Brunch, which features live music and an all-you-can-eat Southern-style buffet. At other times of the week expect blues-inspired and other live music. Open daily 11am–3pm. **$$**

South-western restaurants

The Anasazi

Desert Passage at the Aladdin, 702-736 0111. Based on the award-winning restaurant in Santa Fe, the Anasazi serves up Native American, Northern New Mexico and American Cowboy cuisine. **$$**

Coyote Café and Grill Room

MGM Grand Hotel, 1-800 929 1111. Just about the best South-western coffee-shop-style restaurant in

town serving one of the meanest breakfasts around. Mark Miller's dishes include black beans, blue-corn enchiladas and chicken burritos topped with homemade guacamole and sweetened mild salsas. Margaritas and custom-blended pineapple rum provide delicious afters! Open daily 6–11pm. **$$**

Chili's Grill and Bar

There are three restaurants in this chain: at 2590 South Maryland Parkway, 702-733 6462; 2520 South Decatur Boulevard, 702-871 0500; and 2751 North Green Valley Parkway, 702-433 3333.

★ Don't forget to check out your fun books and local magazines for great two-for-one deals.

Theme restaurants

Allstar Café

3785 The Strip between Harmon and Tropicana, 702-795 8326. Cashing in on the trend of being rich and famous and then opening a restaurant are the tennis stars André Agassi and Monica Seles – and who can blame them? The food might not be brilliant, but it's a fun setting. Open Sunday to Thursday 11am–11pm and till midnight at weekends. **$**

Hard Rock Café

4475 Paradise Road, 702-733 8400. Another chain theme restaurant that won't let you down in the memorabilia and food departments. You can even pick up a Hard Rock T-shirt or other souvenir to prove you've been there! **$**

Harley Davidson® Café

On the Strip at Harmon Avenue, 702-740 4555. The second outlet that pays homage to the 100-year-old motorbike and is hard to miss with its

Best views in the valley

Eiffel Tower Restaurant	Paris Resort
Firenze Lobby Lounge	Ritz-Carlton Lake Las Vegas
Japengo	Hyatt Regency Lake Las Vegas
Kiefer's Atop the Carriage House	East Harmon Avenue
Medici Café and Terrace	Ritz-Carlton Lake Las Vegas
Mon Ami Gabi	Paris Resort
PF Chang's China Bistro	Aladdin
The Top of the World	Stratosphere
VooDoo Café	Rio All-Suite Hotel

28-ft (8.5-metre) high, 15,000-lb (6,800-kg) $500,000 Harley Davidson Heritage Softail Classic bike outside! Inside the 20,000-sq ft (1,860-sq metre), two-storey café is a celebration of the free-spirit lifestyle of Harley Davidsons. And the food and drink lives up to it, too! You can sip on a range of cocktails with names such as Hill Climber, Rockin' Rita and Flat Tracker. Soak up the alcohol with fajitas, hamburgers, barbecue chicken, chillis, pasta or hot dogs. **$**

Mortoni's

Hard Rock Hotel, 702-693 5000. Offers straightforward Italian cuisine in a setting that pays homage to Hollywood of old with vintage photos of legendary stars such as James Dean, Grace Kelly, Marilyn Monroe, Clark Gable, Frank Sinatra, Dean Martin and Peter Lawford among others. Only natural ingredients are used in the dishes that include delicious salads, pizzas, steaks, veal and pasta. Open for dinner every night 6–11pm. **$$**

Planet Hollywood

The Forum Shops at Caesars Palace, 702-791 7827. California comes to Las Vegas with the kind of cuisine you'd expect on the other Strip – Sunset Boulevard! Gourmet pizzas, pastas, fish, burgers and more are served in the usual Planet Hollywood

settings of stunning memorabilia with great sounds. **$**

The Rainforest Café

MGM Grand on the Strip, 1-800 929 1111. A real-life simulation of a rainforest complete with tropical rainstorms featuring thunder and lightning that boom and spark across the entire restaurant. It's an untamed paradise brimming with exotic tropical birds, animated elephants, leopards and gorillas and tropical trees. You enter the dining area by walking under a massive double archway aquarium filled with marine fish from around the world. The food consists of pastas, salads, sandwiches and delectable desserts. Open daily 11am–11pm. **$**

Lounge dining

Lounges are almost unique to Las Vegas. Relaxed yet stylish environments, they all provide live entertainment and in some cases delicious food. Here's a selection.

NEW! Coral Reef Lounge

Mandalay Bay, 702-632 7777. Sushi bar cuisine provides delicious food while you listen to the nightly live music. Open Sunday to Thursday 11am–midnight, and on Friday and Saturday until 1am. **$$**

NEW! Firenze Lobby Lounge

Ritz-Carlton Lake Las Vegas, 702-567 4700. For a light bite in a relaxing and romantic setting, this is the place

★ ★ ★   BRIT TIP   ★ ★ ★

★ For a moment of refinement, try ★
★ Afternoon Florentine Tea at the ★
★ Firenze Lobby Lounge. Fresh ★
★ flower arrangements and a live ★
★ pianist create the perfect setting ★
★ in which to enjoy scones, sarnies ★
★ and savouries while taking in the ★
★ view of Lake Las Vegas and the ★
★ mountains. ★

5

to come. With views of the lake and beautiful art around the walls, you can enjoy hors d'oeuvres, desserts and soufflés before and after your meal. There's live music nightly plus an excellent selection of cocktails, champagne, brandy and liquors. $$

NEW! Nectar

The Bellagio, 702-693 7223. One of the new lounges to crop up on the Strip, this has a futuristic feel with colourful walls, towering columns and slick furniture. The restaurant is run by John Schenk from New York's famous Monkey Bar, and eclectic dishes include fried green tomato and barbecued spare rib salad, buffalo mahi-mahi, oysters, clams, giant Gulf shrimp, crab, lobsters and an iced raw bar. Open Wednesday to Sunday 5–10.30pm. $–$$

NEW! Peppermill Café & Lounge

2985 Las Vegas Boulevard South, 702-735 4177. For a taste of old-style Vegas hospitality, the Peppermill should be on your must-visit list. The

Restaurants with live music

Crazy Armadillo	Stratosphere
Drai's	Barbary Coast
Eiffel Tower Restaurant	Paris Resort
Frogeez on 4th	Downtown
House of Blues	Mandalay Bay
Ibiza	Desert Passage at Aladdin
Jazzed Café	University District
Kahunaville	Treasure Island
Harley Davidson Café	Southern end of Strip
N9ne	The Palms
Ortanique	Paris Resort
Prana	Desert Passage at Aladdin
Rumjumgle	Mandalay Bay
Tommy Rocker's Bar & Grill	4275 Industrial Road
Tres Jazz	Paris Resort
Venus Lounge	Grand Canal Shoppes
VooDoo Café	Rio All-Suite Hotel
WB Stage 16	Venetian

food is excellent and portions are on the large side. Think burgers, sarnies, steak, seafood and huge salads. While you're here, have a drink in the romantic lounge, which is famous for its fireplace, candlelit tables and comfy sofas. $

Cafés and Diners

America

New York-New York, 702-740 6451. A large, open restaurant with a few booths, serves classic casual American food such as roast turkey, meatloaf, pastas, salads and burgers. If all else fails to capture your imagination, try the all-day breakfast. Open 24 hours daily (24/7). $

Binion's Coffee Shop

Binion's Horseshoe Hotel, 128 Fremont Street, 702-382 1600. Binion's gets cram-packed with downtown gamblers so you have to pick your time to avoid long queues. Specialities include Benny Binion's Natural, considered to be one of the best-priced, most delicious breakfasts in town, and Binion's Delight, a hamburger platter with chips. Late-nighters won't go far wrong with the famous $3 steak dinner, which is served 10pm–5.45am. $

Bugsy's Deli

Flamingo Hilton, 702-733 3111. The gangster who created the Flamingo is remembered by the Hilton. The hotel has had a complete overhaul in the last few years and this cafeteria-style coffee shop and diner serves up eggs, hamburgers and roast beef sandwiches to your specifications, plus delicious piping-hot waffles. Good at any time of the day, but a great stop for breakfast. $

NEW! Café Lago

Caesars Palace, 702-731 7110. Just to prove that the Bellagio isn't the only resort in town with water views, Caesars has opened this large café right by the Garden of the Gods Pool

Shopping

Top left **Fashion Show Mall**
Top right **Forum Shops, Fountain of the Gods**
Centre right **Cheesecake Factory**
Bottom left **Venetian Shops**
Bottom right **Via Bellagio**

Restaurants

Top left Margaritas at Kahunaville
Top right Aqua at Bellagio
Centre left House of Lords at the Sahara
Centre right Hard Rock Café
Bottom Rainforest Café

Outdoor and patio dining

Bertolini's	Forum Shops
Gonzalez Y Gonzalez	New York-New York
Mon Ami Gabi	Paris Resort
Moongate	Mirage
Pink Taco	Hard Rock Hotel
Sergio's Italian Gardens	1955 East Tropicana Avenue

Oasis. Serving international dishes and American favourites throughout the day and night, it also offers live music with pianist David Osborne and other soloists in the evening. The one drawback, of course, is that enjoying the beautiful setting doesn't come cheap. **$$**

Café Michelle

1350 East Flamingo Road, inside the local mall, 702-735 8686. The place to go for plenty of cheap grub far from the madding crowds. The red-and-white checked tablecloths and Cinzano umbrellas over tables in the plaza create a European ambience, while you tuck into omelettes, crêpes, salads and seafood. **$**

NEW! Cheeseburger at the Oasis

The Aladdin, 702-735 8600. Polynesia meets casual American in this diner with a difference. Signature dishes include Aloha burger, chicken-salad sandwich with cashews, coconut, mango chutney and ginger sauce, plus calamari scallop combo and a selection of gourmet burgers. Open Sunday to Thursday 8am–11pm and till midnight on Friday and Saturday. Breakfast 8–11am. **$**

Cyber City Café

Target Shopping Center, 3945 Maryland Parkway at East Flamingo, 702-732 2001. Internet addicts will want to make the trip out to the University District on the east side of town to sit in the overstuffed sofas, drink copious amounts of coffee and check out their email for next to nothing. **$**

Enigma Garden Café

918 S Fourth Street, 702-386 0999. One of the best cafés Downtown, it even has live music outside in the garden at weekends. During the summer it's open 24 hours a day (7am–10pm in winter). **$**

Fog City Diner

Hughes Center, 325 Hughes Center Drive, 702-737 0200. Simple diner food given a twist with Japanese-inspired mu shu burritos, first-class seafood and shellfish, plus soups and sandwiches. Open 11.30am–10pm. **$**

Jazzed Café

Napoli Plaza, 2055 East Tropicana in the University District, 702-798 5995. It's worth making the trek out to the east side of town to see how the locals live it up at the hippest café for miles. Check out one of the best wine lists and coffee selections in town, surrounded by dancers, who go for the dark ambience. **$–$$**

Jitters

2457 East Tropicana, 702-898 0056. Jitters specialises in providing one of the biggest and best selections of coffees in town and even roasts its own beans on the premises! Apart from the coffee, you'll also get yourself a decent breakfast, lunch or dinner for under $10. **$**

Best local restaurants

André's	French
Aristocrat	French
Mamounia	Moroccan
Marrakech Restaurant	Moroccan
Mayflower Cuisinier	Asian
Marrakech Restaurant	Moroccan
Moon	Chinese
Pamplemousse	French
Venetian	Italian

5

Lakeside dining

Café Lago	Caesars Palace
Le Cirque	Bellagio
Japengo	Hyatt Regency
	Lake Las Vegas
Medici Café and	Ritz-Carlton
Terrace	Lake Las Vegas
Olives	Bellagio

Mariposa Café

Paradise Plaza, 4643 Paradise Road, 702-650 9009. A real favourite with patrons of the nearby gay and lesbian clubs, this coffee shop opens at 5pm and closes at 5am. $

Mr Lucky's

Hard Rock Hotel, 702-693 5000. The second of only two restaurants at the world's first rock 'n' roll hotel, this is a fun setting for a fun meal. You'll find excellent choices for breakfast, lunch and dinner, while afterwards you can check out the rock 'n' roll memorabilia in the hotel casino, including items once owned by stars such as the Supremes, Elvis and James Brown. $

Ralph's Diner

Stardust Hotel on the Strip, 702-732 6330. This place has jukeboxes on the tables, 1950s' music and other paraphernalia from the original American diner era including black-and-white checkerboard lino and an old-fashioned soda fountain. Blue Plate specials start at $3.95. $

Roxy's Diner

Stratosphere on the Strip, 702-380 7711. A fun place to go to experience a piece of 1950s America – everything from the decor to the uniforms and music pay homage to the rock 'n' roll era. Food includes chicken, fried steak with homemade gravy and Mom's meat loaf with fresh vegetables and real mashed potatoes. Drinks include thick, cold milkshakes in tall, frosty glasses. Open daily 12 noon –10pm. $

Wolfgang Puck's Café

MGM Grand Hotel, 1-800 929 1111. A brightly decorated café with mosaic-tiled booths around the open kitchenette – another of celebrity chef

24/7 Gems

All the following serve excellent grub at under $10 throughout the day and night. These are perfect locations to get a great breakfast after a big night out or stock up on carbs before you hit the town.

Liberty Café: 1700 Las Vegas Boulevard South, 702-383 0196. Just to prove good, old-fashioned grub works, here is an old-fashioned American drugstore with a counter. Famous for its monster breakfasts, it specialises in burgers and chicken-fried steak, while the retro drinks are a speciality. $

Monterey Room: Gold Coast Hotel, 4000 West Flamingo Road, 702-367 7111. Serving classic American grub throughout the day, plus great Chinese cuisine noon–5am, the Monterey is famous for its lunch and dinner specials. Lunch from $6.95 and dinners from $5.95 to $15.95. $

Pelican Rock Café: Castaways Hotel & Casino, 702-385 9123. Traditional American breakfasts include omelettes, waffles and pancakes, lunch soups, salads and sarnies, while dinner offerings include steaks and burgers. This is one of the cheapest joints in town, still famous for its mega-cheap steak and egg deals. $

Ristorante dei Fiore: Hotel San Remo, 115 East Tropicana Avenue, 702-739 9000. Sounds posh, but this is a cheap-as-chips joint serving excellent American and international food. Locals love its prime rib dinner and steak and egg breakfast, both $4.95, which are served 24 hours a day. $

Best gourmet-style dining in a hotel

Alizé	The Palms
Aqua	Bellagio
Aureole	Mandalay Bay
Búzio's	Rio All-Suite Hotel
Elements	Aladdin
Isis	Luxor
La Rotisserie des Artistes	Rio All-Suite Hotel
Onda	Mirage
Nero's	Caesars Palace
Prime	Bellagio
The Renoir	Mirage
Top of the World	Stratosphere

Wolfgang's five outlets in Las Vegas. Tuck into the usual eccentric array of Italian nosh and pizzas. Open daily 11am–11pm. **$**

★ ★ ★   BRIT TIP   ★ ★ ★
★   ★
★ Delis originated in New York and ★
★ are basically the American ★
★ version of our sandwich bars, ★
★ with a heavy Italian feel. ★
★ ★ ★ ★ ★ ★ ★ ★ ★ ★ ★ ★ ★ ★ ★ ★

Hotel restaurants

Many of the best restaurants that have been reviewed and listed are in the top resort hotels. To make life easier I have listed all the eating places at the main resort hotels in town. The hotels also have their own buffets!

Aladdin

702-736 7114. The Aladdin followed the lead of the Bellagio and Mandalay Hotels and opted for tried and tested dining experiences. Despite the hotel's bumpy start, its restaurants have been a great hit.

Fine dining

Elements	Steak and seafood
Tremezzo	Italian

Casual

PF Chang's China Bistro	Chinese
Todai	Japanese seafood buffet
Zanzibar Café	American brasserie
La Salsa Cantina	Mexican
Oyster Bar Seafood & Wine Bar	Seafood
Cheeseburger at the Oasis	American

Desert Passage at the Aladdin

Fine dining

Anasazi	South-western
Belluga Bar	Steakhouse
Bice	Italian
Commander's Palace	New Orleans
Joseph's	Upscale French Brasserie
Sevilla	Spanish Steakhouse

Casual

Alacazam	Coffee shop
Ben & Jerry's	Ice cream
Fat Anthony's	Pizza and pasta
Ferraro	Mediterranean Café

With live music

Prana	Supper club serving Mediterranean cuisine
Ibiza	Mediterranean

Bellagio

702-693 7111. When the Bellagio opened at the end of 1998 it set a new standard both for hotels and restaurants and deliberately went out of its way to attract top celebrity chefs including Elizabeth Blau, Julian Serrano and Todd English. All were a hit from word go and have remained popular ever since.

Fine dining

Le Cirque	French
Picasso	Mediterranean
Aqua	Seafood
Olives	Mediterranean
Circo	Tuscany
Prime	Steakhouse
Jasmine	Chinese

Casual dining

Shintaro	Sushi bar
Noodles	Asian
Nectar	American
Café Bellagio	24-hour dining
The Petrossian Bar	Caviar
Café Gelato	Sarnies and ice-cream
Palio	Pastries and tea
The Buffet at Bellagio	

5

Caesars Palace

702-731 7110. The resort is posh and the restaurants reflect that – serving top-notch and largely pricey meals. If you're feeling flush, you can do no wrong by trying any of the following establishments.

Fine dining

Empress Court	Gourmet Chinese
Hyakumi	Japanese sushi bar
Nero's	Contemporary American
Terrazza	Italian
8-0-8	Hawaiian

Casual

Café Lago	24-hour snacks
La Piazza Food Court	Restaurant/ lounge
Cypress Street Marketplace	Self-service
Java Coast	24-hour coffee shop

The Forum Shops at Caesars Palace

The incredibly upscale Forum Shops have a tremendous number and range of dining options from celebrity chef to other upscale and more casual dining. In some cases you can even dine pavement style and watch the world go by.

Fine dining

Bertolini's Authentic Trattoria	Italian
Caviarteria	Caviar
Chinois	Asian
The Palm	Steakhouse
Spago	American fusion

Casual dining

Cheesecake Factory	American
Forum Café	Café
La Salsa Mexican Restaurant	Mexican
Planet Hollywood	American
Stage Deli	Deli
Café Caesars	Café
Monopoly Coffee Bar	Coffee shop
Star Wars Cantina	Mexican
Vigin Café	American

Circus Circus

702-734 0410. The Steak House is one of the finest of its kind in town and is regularly honoured by local newspaper polls as the Number One steakhouse of Las Vegas.

Fine dining

Steak House	American
Stivali Ristorante	Italian
Blue Iguana	Mexican
The Pink Pony	24-hour café
The Pizzeria	Italian
Barista Café	Coffee shop

Excalibur

702-597 7777. Themes abound at the eating establishments of this resort that pays tribute to King Arthur's day. Sir Galahad's is a Tudor-style rib house, there's Italian cuisine in an Italian setting at Lance-A-Lotta Pasta and live music and country dancing at Wild Bill's Saloon.

Fine dining

The Steakhouse at Camelot	Gourmet dining overlooking the English countryside!
Sir Galahad's Prime Rib House	English

Casual

Regale	Italian Eatery
Village Food Court	Fast food
Sherwood Forest Café	24-hour bistro

Four Seasons

Fine dining

Charlie Palmer's Steakhouse	American

Casual

The Verandah	Eclectic

Hard Rock Hotel

702-693 5000. The rock 'n' roll memorabilia that adorns the first-ever hotel on this theme makes a visit to the casino a must – and while you're there you won't be disappointed by any of the dining establishments.

Fine dining

AJ's Steakhouse	American
Mortoni's	Italian
Mr Lucky's	Coffee shop
Nobu	Japanese

Casual

Pink Taco	Mexican
Simon Kitchen & Bar	American
Starbucks	Coffee shop

Las Vegas Hilton

702-732 5111. The elegant resort hotel has some fine restaurants. The prices are on the high side but then you are getting some of the best ingredients cooked to perfection and served in delightful settings.

Fine dining

Andiamo	Italian
Benihana Village	Japanese
Bistro Le Montrachet	French bistro
Hilton Steakhouse	Steaks
Garden of the Dragon	Chinese
Margaritagrille	Mexican

Casual

Garden Snack Bar	Patio coffee shop
Paradise Café	24-hour diner
Quark's Bar & Restaurant	American
Vegas Subs	Sarnies

Luxor

702-262 4000. Isis, the gourmet French restaurant, is consistently ranked among the top 10 restaurants in all of America, while the Sacred Sea Room and Papyrus are also excellent choices for fine dining.

Fine dining

Isis	Gourmet French
Sacred Sea Room	Casual American
Luxor's Steakhouse	American
Hamada's	Sushi Bar
Papyrus	Polynesian

Casual

Food Court	Self-service
La Salsa	Mexican grill
Nile Deli	Deli
Pharoah's Pheast	Buffet
Pyramid Café	American

Mandalay Bay

702-632 7777. The hotel is in the top-end bracket and aims directly at the more sophisticated traveller in search of fun. It has two cracking live music venues – House of Blues and Rumjungle – within a selection of celebrity chef restaurants.

Fine dining

Aureole	American
Trattoria del Lupa	Italian
Shanghai Lily	Cantonese
China Grill	Chinese

3950	Steak and seafood
Bleu Blanc Rouge	French

Casual

Border Grill	Mexican
Red Square	Caviar
Raffles Café	24-hour dining
The Noodle Shop	Chinese
Bayside Buffet	Buffet

Live music

House of Blues	Southern
Rumjungle	Caribbean

MGM Grand

702-891 7777. Celebrity chefs Wolfgang Puck, Mark Miller and Emeril Lagassé all have restaurants here.

Fine dining

Craftsteak	Steakhouse
Emeril's New Orleans Fish House	Creole/Cajun
Fiamma Trattoria	Italian
Mark Miller's Coyote Café and Grill Room	South-western
NOBHILL	Californian
Pearl	Chinese
Ricardo's Mexican Restaurant	Mexican
Wolfgang Puck Café	Italian

Casual

Cabana Grille	Casual American
Grand Wok and Sushi Bar	Asian
Stage Deli	New York deli
Studio Café	24 hours
The Rainforest Café	Bistro
Farmer's Market	Food Court
Starbucks	Coffee shop
MGM Grand Buffet	Buffet

Mirage

702-791 7111. You won't go wrong dining at any of the eateries here, and many offer fine food at mostly reasonable prices.

Fine dining

Kokomo's	Seafood
Mikado	Japanese
Moongate	Chinese
Onda	Italian
Renoir	French
Samba Brazilian Steakhouse	Steakhouse

5

Casual

California

Pizza Kitchen	Californian
Caribe Café	24-hour coffee shop
The Noodle Kitchen	Casual Chinese
The Mirage Buffet	Buffet

Monte Carlo

702-730 7777. Here you will find one of the best restaurants in town – André's – and three run by top Californian restaurateurs, Salvator Casola, his son Sal and Chipper Pastron. Their Market City Caffé is an Italian eatery featuring fresh homemade bread and pasta dishes. The Dragon Noodle company features the Tea Bar with a range of exotic teas and the Golden Bagel is a replica of a classic New York deli.

Fine dining

André's	Gourmet French
Blackstone Steakhouse	American

Casual

Pub & Brewery	Microbrews
The Café & Sushi Bar	Japanese-American
Dragon Noodle Co	Asian
Market City Caffé	Italian

New York-New York

702-740 6969. Each of the hotel's restaurants provides a themed dining experience based on the New York areas including Little Italy, Chinatown and Manhattan. The quality is good and the prices are reasonable.

Fine dining

Chin Chin	Chinese
Gallagher's Steakhouse	Steakhouse
Gonzalez Y Gonzalez	Mexican
Il Fornaio Panatteria	Italian
Nine Fine Irishmen	Irish

Casual

America	24-hour bistro
Coney Island Pavilion	Food court
Schrafft Ice Cream	Ice-cream parlour
The Village Eateries	Fast food outlets
ESPN Zone	
Haagen-Dazs	Ice-cream parlour
Nathan's Hot Dogs	New York street food
Studio Grill	American

The Palms

702-942 7777. The newest casino hotel on the block is also one of the hippest and has an excellent line-up of restaurants.

Fine dining

Alizé	French
Garduños	Mexican
Little Buddha Café	French
N9ne	American

Casual

Blue Agave Oyster & Chile Bar	Oyster bar
Sunrise Café	American

Paris

702-739 4111. The Paris-inspired resort keeps the French theme in all of its dining outlets ranging from true gourmet to casual. The restaurants have gone from strength-to-strength and new ones have even opened in this successful resort hotel.

Fine dining

Ah Sin	Asian
Eiffel Tower Restaurant	Gourmet French
La Chino	Hong Kong style
La Rôtisserie des Artistes	Gourmet French
Le Provençal	Italian/French
Mon Ami Gabi	Brasserie
Ortanique	French-Caribbean
Très Jazz	Caribbean

Casual

Le Café du Parc	Poolside bistro
Jean Jaques' Boulangerie	Pastries and salads
Le Village Buffet	Buffet

Rio All-Suite Hotel

702-252 7777. Many of the Rio's restaurants are consistently highly rated by the Zagat survey. This is one of the most successful off-Strip resort hotels and has a tremendous range of restaurants and casual dining options to satisfy its ardent fans.

Fine dining

Antonio's	Italian
Bamboleo	Mexican
Búzios	Seafood
Fiore Rotisserie & Grille	Fusion
Fortunes	Oriental/Western

Gaylord India Restaurant	Northern Indian
Hamada's Asiana	Japanese and Chinese
Mask	Oriental
Rosemary's	Italian
Casual	
All-American Bar	American
Beach café	Poolside dining
JW's Tavern	American
Mama Maria's Cucina	Italian
Sao Paulo Café	24-hour diner
Tilted Kilt	Irish-American Tavern
Toscano's Deli	New York deli
Village Seafood Buffet	Buffet
VooDoo Café	Cajun/creole

Stratosphere

702-380 7777. The tallest free-standing tower in America houses the amazing revolving restaurant, the award-winning Top of the World. Then there is the 'fun 50s' Roxy's Diner in which servers are dressed in rock 'n' roll outfits, and the new Crazy Armadillo Oyster Bar and live music venue.

Fine dining

Fellini's Tower of Pasta	Italian
Top of the World	Revolving restaurant
Casual	
Hamada Asian Village	Food court
Lucky's café	Diner
Roxy's Diner	1950s America
The Courtyard Buffet	Buffet
Music	
Crazy Armadillo	Oyster bar

Treasure Island

702-894 7111. The resort tribute to the world of pirates of the Caribbean has some great restaurants.

Fine dining

Buccaneer Bay Club	American
Francesco's	Italian
Kahunaville	Hawaiian
The Steakhouse at Treasure Island	Steakhouse
Casual	
Ben & Jerry's	Ice-cream parlour
Canter's Deli	Deli
The Delicatessan	Deli
Starbucks Coffee	Coffee bar
Terrace Café	American

Tropicana

702-739 2222. There is a distinctly tropical theme to many of the restaurants at this resort hotel – with delicious food to match. After watching the high-roller baccarat players in action you won't go far wrong taking the time out to dine at any of these.

Fine dining

Pietro's	Gourmet
Savanna	Steak and seafood
Mizuno's Teppan Dining	Japanese
Casual	
Calypsos	Caribbean
Legend's Deli	Deli

Venetian

702-414 4100. Aiming at the more sophisticated traveller and diner, this hotel has a host of celebrity-chef restaurants.

Fine dining

Delmonico Steakhouse	Steakhouse
Grand Lux Café	American
Lutèce	Gourmet French
Pinot Brasserie	Gourmet French
Valentino	Italian
Casual	
Noodle Asia	Noodles
PS Italian Grill	Italian American
Royal Star	Californian Chinese
Star Canyon	Texan
With live music	
WB Stage 16	American

Grand Canal Shoppes at the Venetian

Along with everything else about this resort hotel, the shops are beautiful and contain some wonderful restaurants.

Fine dining

Canaletto	Italian
Canyon Ranch Café	American
Postrio	Italian
Tsunami Asian Grill	Asian
Zeffirino Ristorante	Italian
Casual dining	
Taqueria Canonita	Mexican
Tintoretto's Bakery	Deli
With live music	
Venus Lounge	

5

Buffets

These all-you-can-eat-for-little-bucks feasts are what Las Vegas used to be most famous for in the culinary stakes and they are still going strong. The mega-feasts date back to the 1940s when the owner of the El Rancho devised a plan to offer a Midnight Chuck Wagon Buffet – 'all you can eat for a dollar' – and found the crowds rolling in. Other hotels quickly followed suit, introducing breakfast, lunch and dinner spreads and the buffet boom was born.

Now they are known as the gambler's revenge – a way to fill up on food for as little as $3 for breakfast to $15 for dinner – though some of the more upmarket, speciality buffets run to $30 a head. You'll find buffets at just about every hotel on the Strip and Downtown but both the choice and the turnover vary considerably. Circus Circus is famous for its massive buffet and once fed more than 17,600 people in one day, but to be honest the food is not worth the wait.

Buffets on (or near) the Strip

Carnival World Buffet at the **Rio All-Suite Hotel** on West Flamingo is both the biggest and best. The food is laid out in separate kiosks that have different cuisines from around the globe such as American, Chinese, Japanese and Mexican. It's so impressive you'll want to go back again and again, but the long queues may put you off as this is a real favourite with locals. The Rio also does a **Village Seafood Buffet**, in the new Masquerade Village, which is much more expensive than the norm

★ ★ ★ BRIT TIP ★ ★ ★

★ If staying at the Rio All-Suite
★ Hotel or playing in the casino,
★ don't forget to use the VIP queue
★ to get a head start on the
★ crowds!

(around $18) but offers an incredible selection of all the different types of seafood in the world

Stratosphere at the northern end of the Strip has a wide selection of good quality food at very good prices and the **Frontier** in the middle of the Strip is also well worth queueing for. The **San Remo** on Tropicana Avenue, just east of the Strip, has a small but good buffet in an intimate atmosphere. Generally the queues are short here, as this is slightly off the beaten track, and the prices are excellent.

Other places on the Strip that are worth going to but are a little more expensive are at the **Mirage, Caesars Palace** and **Bally's**. The **Excalibur** is one of the biggest and has costumed staff with Robin Hood-style trumpets to add to the atmosphere. The **MGM Grand** is also good but the queues are incredibly long.

★ ★ ★ BRIT TIP ★ ★ ★

★ For a Sunday brunch with a
★ difference, try the Southern
★ cuisine at The House of Blues.
★ Sittings are at 10am and 1pm.

The Brown Derby: a grand champagne brunch at the MGM Grand on Sunday 9am–2pm. Adults $30, children $12.
The Buffet of Champions: champagne brunch at the Las Vegas Hilton on Saturday and Sunday 8am–2.30pm. $12.
Imperial Buffet: champagne brunch in the Imperial Palace on Saturday and Sunday 8am–3pm. $7.
The Luxor Steakhouse: champagne brunch on Sunday 10am–3.30pm. $25.
Mirage: champagne brunch 8am–9.30pm. $14.
Monte Carlo: champagne brunch 7am–3pm. Adults $9 and under 10s $6.
Palatium Buffet: Caesars Palace offers a champagne Sunday brunch

10.30am–3.30pm. Adults $16, under 12s $8.

The Steak House: great champagne Sunday brunch serving 10am–2pm at Circus Circus. Adults $18, under 12s $10.

Sterling Brunch: at Bally's Hotel on the Strip, this is truly expensive ($50) but also truly worth it if you want to splash out on a great dining experience. 9.30am–2pm.

Treasure Island: Champagne brunch 7.30am–3.30pm. $9.

Tropicana: Champagne brunch in the El Gaucho restaurant 10.30am–2pm. Adults $26 and under 10s $16. The hotel's Island Buffet also has a cheaper champagne brunch on Saturday and Sunday 10.30am–2.30pm. $10.

Downtown buffets

Generally these do not have a good reputation, but the **Garden Court Buffet** at Main Street Station on Main Street was reopened in 1996 and since then has been serving a great choice of food in pretty surroundings. You can also try the **Paradise Buffet** at the **Fremont**, which has a magnificent seafood buffet in the evening and an excellent breakfast .

Bourbon Street Hotel: Creole Bloody Mary brunch both Saturday and Sunday 10.30am–2pm for $6.

Fitzgeralds' Hotel: champagne brunch on Saturday and Sunday 8am–4pm. $8.

Main Street Station: champagne brunch 7am–3pm. $8.

The Golden Nugget: champagne brunch 8am–10pm. $12.

Paradise Buffet: champagne brunch at the Fremont 7am–3pm. $8.

Getting the most out of buffets

Generally, avoid breakfast buffets as you won't be able to walk for the rest of the day and the choice is not as good as at other times.

A lot of buffets change from breakfast to lunch at around 11am. Arrive at 10.45am to pay the breakfast rate and get the lunch spread!

Never, ever attempt more than one buffet a day or you will explode! Try to avoid peak lunch and dinner times or you'll find yourself standing in a queue for an hour and a half. At weekends, even going off-peak times, the queues can take 45 minutes.

If the queues are long, take a good book or magazine to read – and opt for comfortable shoes!

Always check out the local magazines for two-for-one coupons.

★ ★ ★   **BRIT TIP**   ★ ★ ★
★   ★
★   ★
★   Weird but true: at some buffets   ★
★   now you have to queue up to   ★
★   get a table after you've queued   ★
★   to get your food!   ★
★ ★ ★ ★ ★ ★ ★ ★ ★ ★ ★ ★ ★ ★ ★ ★ ★ ★

Greater Las Vegas

If you really want to get the best out of a Las Vegas buffet then you will need to travel a little farther afield than the Strip or Downtown. The **Festival Buffet** at the **Fiesta** on Rancho Drive at Lake Mead Boulevard (northwest Las Vegas) was modelled on the **Rio Carnival Buffet** and some locals reckon it now does a better job of things than the Rio! The food is more interesting and the quality and selection on offer is excellent.

In the opposite direction, the **Feast** at Boulder Station on the Boulder Highway provides an excellent stop on your way to or from the Hoover Dam. Here you'll find a good choice of quality foods ranging from tacos to pizzas and rotisserie chicken.

The Broiler: at Boulder Station on the Boulder Highway, a champagne brunch on Sunday 10am–3pm. Under $15.

Garduno's: at the Fiesta on North Rancho Drive at Lake Mead Boulevard, you'll find a margarita Sunday brunch 10am–3pm. $10.

San Remo: champagne brunch runs 7am–2pm Saturday and Sunday. $7.

Bars, lounges, nightclubs, live music venues and strip clubs

Now that the marketing people have well and truly dropped the 'family-friendly' thing, major resort hotels up and down the Strip have been playing up to the adult theme big time. Sure, there have always been strip joints in town – after all, along with weddings and gambling, that's what Las Vegas is famous for – but there's barely been more than a hint of nudity at the major hotels.

The change began with the arrival of more and more topless and raunchy shows (see Chapter 3 Showtime) and has followed with the opening of ever more risqué nightspots. 'Skin' is now the buzz word when assessing the kind of clothes worn by a particular club crowd or the entertainment. Referring to the amount of flesh that can be seen, plenty of skin is now on show at the new breed of down and dirty bars, erotic nightclubs and pool parties.

However, you don't have to reveal all to have a great night out in Sin City, Vegas now has more chi-chi nightclubs, lounges and bars than you can shake a stick at and most of them are conveniently located along the main drag of the famous Strip.

Many hot nightspots start off as restaurants or bars early in the evening and metamorphose into something altogether hotter around 11pm. Other venues are dedicated nightclubs, while live music can be found in the plethora of lounge bars – mostly at hotels and usually free, though the drinks are expensive! – and dedicated live music venues, where drinks are cheaper.

Here's a selection of all types of venues available to keep you well amused during your time in Vegas.

Inside this chapter

Bars

Bar at Times Square

New York-New York, 702-740 6969
The duo of pianists here are famous for trying to outdo each other and have become the best piano show in town. Give them a song and enjoy singing along in the poolside location. Open nightly from 8pm.

Big Apple Bar

New York-New York, 702-740 6969
Happening new venue already known for its huge selection of one-of-a-kind speciality drinks. There are plenty of seats to relax in and to enjoy the live entertainers who perform on a stage that rises above the actual bar. Open nightly from 8pm.

★ ★ ★ **BRIT TIP** ★ ★ ★

You have to be over 21 to buy or drink alcohol in Las Vegas and may often be asked to produce photographic ID, so keep your passport with you.

Bar and club awards

Hottest club in town:	Ghostbar
Swankiest:	Whiskey Bar, Tabu, Ghostbar and Light
Wildest:	The Beach, Bikini's and Rum Jungle
Best for celeb spotting:	Ghostbar and Baby's
Hippest:	Shadow, Ghostbar
Best for beautiful people:	V-Bar, Venus, Tabu and Risqué
Best for cowboys:	Gilley's
Best party time:	Coyote Ugly
Best for salsa:	Ibiza USA and Sevilla

Center Bar

Hard Rock Hotel, 4455 Paradise at Harmon, 702-693 5000.
Flashy circle bar at the heart of the hippest hotel in Vegas, filled with the hottest babes in town flashing their cleavage and G-strings. Drinks are pricey but the people-watching is priceless. Celebs spotted here include Gwyneth Paltrow, Ben Affleck and the Backstreet Boys. The only downside, say insiders, are the desperados trying to hit on 'hot chicks' – you know you've been had when you hear the line, 'Are you a model?'. Open daily 11am–11.30pm.

Coyote Ugly

New York-New York, 702-740 6969
One of the wildest bars in town. Based on the New York namesake, this saloon with a dance floor is designed to look like a southern bar that has seen years of partying. The hot and sassy female bartenders are part of the entertainment – they have not only elevated pouring drinks to an art form, but also get on the bar for an act of sexy dance numbers and amazing stunts from fire-blowing to body shots. Once they've done their thing, female punters are invited to dance on the bar as well and even leave behind some undies on the Bra Wall of Fame. Open nightly 6pm–4am.

Crazy Armadillo's

The Stratosphere, 702-380 7777
A rowdy, south-of-the-border-style bar with 'flair' bartenders who juggle bottles and entertain the crowd as they mix the speciality margaritas. The house special is the Triple Armadillo made with Cuervo Gold tequila, Reposado tequila, Cuervo Tradicional tequila, cointreau, sweet and sour and lime juice. If that's not enough to give you alcohol poisoining, opt for the $20 Tequila Sampler, which offers five different tequila shots.

At the oyster bar you can try oyster shooters such as the Kamikaze Shooter, made from fresh oysters with Smirnoff vodka, triple sec and a splash of lime juice. Just remember, if you feel terrible in the morning you did it to yourself! Along with the singing and dancing Shooter Servers – waitresses who serve tequila shots from their shooter belts – there is also live entertainment nightly. Open nightly 5pm–5am.

Drai's

Barbary Coast at Flamingo, 702-737 7111
A smart/casual joint with some of the most expensive cocktails in town. Don't be put off by its location in the basement of the Barbary Coast Hotel, this is a plush bar with a quiet jazz combo playing and plenty of atmosphere. Open nightly 5.30–11pm.

Gordon Biersch

3987 Paradise Road at Flamingo, 702-312 5247
Filled with beautiful people, this is

6

one of the city's hottest pick-up parlours. Great brews, good food and live swing music make it a fun place to go. Open daily 11.30am–midnight daily and Tuesday to Saturday till 2am.

Lagoon Saloon

The Mirage, 702-7291 7111
Want something a little more on the refined side? Then head to the Mirage and it's picturesque bar under the towering palms beside the waterfall in the hotel's interior lagoon. You'll also enjoy the live music. Open daily 10am–4am.

★ ★ ★   **BRIT TIP**   ★ ★ ★

★ Fancy a pit stop on your way up ★
★ and down the Strip, but don't ★
★ want to sit in a freezing cold, air- ★
★ conditioned bar? Then head for ★
★ the outdoor Lagoon Saloon or ★
★ the poolside Dolphin Bar at the ★
★ Mirage, where it's cool, not cold. ★

Monte Carlo Pub & Brewery

Monte Carlo Resort, 702-730 7423
You can get meals, music and brews with live nightly entertainment from 9pm in the first microbrewery in a resort hotel. Open Sunday to Thursday 11am–3am, Friday and Saturday 11am–4am.

Red Square

Mandalay Bay, 702-632 7407
The place to come for a spot of Russian firewater. Decorated to look like a former tsar's palace-turned-Communist-Party-HQ, drinks range from hardcore fire waters such as Red Army and Yubilev to shooters such as Stolichnaya (try saying that after two!) and a whole range of other vodkas. The other speciality of the house is the vast list of Martinis, for which the bar is famous. Open Sunday to Thursday, 5pm–2am, Friday and Saturday 5pm–4am.

Shadow Bar

Caesar's Palace, 702-731 7110
One of the new breed of hot new hotel bars, this is definitely one place where you'll want to take the weight off your slingbacks and sink into one of the plush booths or comfy couches. Right in the centre of the upmarket hotel's action by Nero's restaurant, the ambience starts off relaxed enough but heats up when the nightly entertainment begins. Silhouetted dancers perform seductive routines behind backlit screens before venturing out to mingle with the crowd. And if that's not your thing then watch the bartenders in action as they create speciality drinks such as Forbidden Fruit, Techno Rush, The Rave and Ultimate Explosion. There's no dance floor, but DJs spin a mix of house and hip hop, while dancers perform 8pm–2am from Sunday to Thursday and 7pm–3am on Friday and Saturday. Open daily noon–4am.

★ ★ ★   **BRIT TIP**   ★ ★ ★

★ Shadow Bar is the perfect place ★
★ for a drink after a show and ★
★ before hitting your chosen ★
★ nightclub. ★

Tilted Kilt

Rio All-Suite Hotel, 702-252 7777
An Irish-American tavern with an extensive list of beers from around the world, plus billiards, darts and an eclectic menu featuring Drunken Clams and Sloppy Janes – a colossal sandwich spin-off of Sloppy Joes. Open daily 4pm–2am with Happy Hour 4–6pm.

Wine cellar

The Wine Cellar Tasting Room, Rio All-Suite Hotel, 3700 West Flamingo, 702-252 7777
The world's largest and most extensive collection of fine wines includes more than 600 different wines once only enjoyed by kings, presidents and the cultural elite. Open

Monday to Thursday 11am–midnight, Friday to Sunday 10am–1.30am.

Zuri

MGM Grand, 702-891 1111
With live nightly entertainment this 100-seat bar just off the hotel's main lobby, specialises in fruit-infused spirits such as frozen Woodford Reserve Bourbon infused with peaches, cinnamon-infused vodka and speciality beer from around the globe. Open 24/7.

★★★ **BRIT TIP** ★★★

★ If you've had a heavy night try ★ Zuri's For The Morning After The Night Before menu, which includes a variety of liquid brunch drinks and Bloody Marys! ★

Hotel Lounges

One of the most wonderful things about Las Vegas is the lounge scene – a phenomenon that's unique to the city. Best of all, there is no entrance fee, although there may be a minimum drink order. The lounges all provide live music and just about every hotel has a good one.

Armadillo Lounge

Texas Station, 2101 Texas Star Lane, 702-631 1000
A real hit with the locals, thanks to the fair prices, this lounge is a happening place most nights of the week. Almost every musical style plays here from rock to blues, jazz, country and reggae. Phone the entertainment hotline for more information on 702-631 1001.

Caramel Lounge

Bellagio, 702-693 7111
Excellent spot to enjoy a pre-show or late-night drink. Opaque marble tables, hand-blown glass sculptures and round ottomans create an elegant and sophisticated setting for a trendy,

yet relaxed lounge. Music ranges from the Rolling Stones to Frank Sinatra and the Beatles. A limited food menu includes the classic Las Vegan Shrimp Cocktail, pâté, smoked salmon and an assorted cheese plate, but the thing to go for here is the signature Martini served in chocolate and caramel-coated chilled glasses. Open Monday to Friday 4pm–4am, Saturday and Sunday 12 noon–4am.

Coral Reef Lounge

Mandalay Bay, 702-632 7777
The hotel's main entertainment lounge with nightly shows and a sushi bar for casual meals.

★★★ **BRIT TIP** ★★★

★ Martini is the drink of Las Vegas – and the best places for it are the Red Square at Mandalay Bay, Caramel Lounge at the Bellagio and Rain in the Desert at The Palms. ★

Fontana Lounge

Bellagio, 702-693 7111
If you want to be in a prime location to enjoy the famous Bellagio fountain show while enjoying a drink, this patio bar is the place to come. An added bonus is the live band playing everything from contemporary to swing and R&B.

Ghostbar

The Palms, 866-725 6768
A sultry indoor-outdoor lounge and sky deck on the 55th floor of The Palms, with 360-degree views of the glittering Las Vegas skyline, that has quickly become the hottest place in town. Decked out in silver, white, greens and greys it has floor-to-ceiling windows, a 30-ft (9-metre) ghost-shaped ceiling that changes colours and custom-made ultra-contemporary lounge furniture. Celebs such as David Schwimmer, Cuba Gooding Jr, Samuel Jackson and Mark Wahlberg

6

have all enjoyed the private VIP lounge and the eclectic music. Miss it and miss out. Open nightly 8pm–4am.

★ Lounges may provide free music, ★ but drinks can start at a pricey $5 ★ and rise to an even more hefty ★ $12 a hit – so sip, don't glug! ★

La Scena Lounge

The Venetian, 702-414 4100
You won't escape the video games here, but you will enjoy the nightly entertainment of high-energy bands performing anything from rock 'n' roll to Motown, disco and Top 40 hits.

Le Cabaret

Paris Las Vegas, 702-739 4111
Designed to create the feeling of sitting outside in a garden area, you can sit under trees laced with twinkling lights while sipping your drinks and enjoying the live entertainment.

Mist

Treasure Island, 702-894 7111
Another stylish yet casual lounge from the same people who created the Light nightclub (see page 112). Mist has state-of-the-art plasma screens, which are used for showing sporting events and music videos, while video poker is also available at the bar. Open daily 4pm–4am.

Tequila Sky Bar

Rio All-Suite Hotel, 702-252 7777
One of the fun new bars that have opened in Vegas, this features specially-trained 'flair' bartenders who entertain guests by juggling bottles from a massive selection of tequila, beer and fine spirits. You can choose from a variety of margaritas and tequila shooters or try the Tequila Sampler, a spiral rack of five hand-blown shot glasses containing five

different varieties of tequila. Have someone on hand though, to walk you home! Open nightly 5pm–5am, Happy Hour 5–7pm. Happy Hour entertainment from Thursday to Monday.

Top of the World Lounge

Stratosphere, 702-380 7777
A casino lounge on the 104th floor. Entrance to the Tower is $6, though you can avoid that by booking a table for dinner at the revolving restaurant (see page 103).

VooDoo Lounge

Rio All-Suite Hotel, 3700 West Flamingo, 702-252 7777
The view of the Strip is fantastic and so are the bottle-juggling bartenders. Sit inside or outside on the terrace while sipping one of the many speciality drinks, such as the Witch Doctor, a mix of four rums and tropical fruit juices. Hot music plays nightly from 9pm. Open 5pm–2.30am.

★ The lifts to the VooDoo Lounge ★ and Café are on the second floor ★ of the Masquerade Tower. ★

Whiskey Bar

Green Valley Ranch, 2300 Paseo Verde Parkway, Henderson, 702-617 7777. For concert tickets call 1-866-264 1818
About a 30-minute drive from the Strip, this haven of old-style Hollywood charm is one of the places to see and be seen. The interior is elegant, but do step outside to enjoy the fantastic views. If you're here for the live music, then you'll see the magical surroundings anyway, as the Whiskey has a unique outdoor concert venue. Open Sunday to Wednesday 5pm–2am, Thursday 5pm–3am, Friday and Saturday 5pm–4am.

★ ★ ★ BRIT TIP ★ ★ ★
★   ★
★   ★
★ It's worth making the trip out to ★
★   Henderson to visit the Whiskey   ★
★   Bar for the views alone. Take   ★
★ your camera to record the valley   ★
★ during the day and the glittering ★
★   lights of Las Vegas at night. ★
★ ★ ★ ★ ★ ★ ★ ★ ★ ★ ★ ★ ★ ★ ★ ★ ★ ★

Non-Hotel Lounges

Fireside Lounge

The Peppermill Coffee Shop, 2985 Las Vegas Boulevard South, 702-735 4177

One of the swankiest and oldest surviving lounges with cosy booths, an intimate atmosphere and the famous firepit – a circular fireplace surrounded by a pool of bubbling water. Recently named one of America's 10 Best Make-Out Bars by *Nerve* magazine, this kitschy spot has attracted the likes of Sharon Stone and Joe Pesci. One of the quirks of the joint is that the waitresses – clothed in long black dresses split to the thigh – sit down at your table to take your order. Try the Scorpion, the giant-sized house special cocktail for two, a 64-oz glass with six shots of various spirits, ice cream and two 2-ft (60-cm) long straws! Open 24/7.

Ice House Lounge

650 South Main Street, Downtown Las Vegas, 702-315-2570

Not just a lounge, this is a new $5-million, two-storey restaurant and gambling venue with two lounges featuring bar tops made of ice to keep drinks cold! The exterior has an Art Deco look with white stucco and

Best lounges for views

Fontana Lounge at the Bellagio
Ghostbar at The Palms
Hush Lounge at the Polo Suites Tower
Top of the World at the Stratosphere
Voodoo Lounge at the Rio
Whiskey Bar at the Green Ranch

LED lights that shine on the building and turn it different colours. Inside you can play video poker or watch sporting events and concerts and the like on any one of the 13 plasma screen TVs or the 100-in (2.5-metre) projection screen. The lounge interior has a retro feel with photos of old downtown Las Vegas and furniture from the 1960s. For a spot of outdoor dining, try the patios available on both levels – even better, the second floor patio has seating around a fireplace. Open 24/7.

Jack's Velvet Lounge

3355 S Las Vegas Blvd opposite the Mirage, 702-414 1699

A great spot for singles with oversized white couches and cocktail waitresses to serve up drinks. The music is a mix of deep and progressive house. Open Sunday to Thursday 6pm–1am.

Ultra Lounges

Is it a bar? Is it a music venue? Is it a nightclub? Is it a decadent den of iniquity? In fact, there is a new breed of nightlife in Las Vegas called the ultra lounge, which combines all of the above. Think luxurious decor, ultra comfy seating, sensuous music and a sense that anything goes and you'll start to build up a picture of the newest kind of scene on the block.

★ ★ ★ BRIT TIP ★ ★ ★
★   ★
★   ★
★ Drink-drive penalties are severe ★
★ and strictly enforced in the city ★
★   so don't even think about it.   ★
★   Besides most of the best bars,   ★
★   lounges and nightclubs are   ★
★   around the Strip so you can   ★
★   either walk or take a taxi   ★
★   (see page 11).   ★
★ ★ ★ ★ ★ ★ ★ ★ ★ ★ ★ ★ ★ ★ ★ ★ ★ ★

Curve

Inside the London Club at the Aladdin, 702-785 5555

The city's hottest new ultra or hyper

6

lounge has already played host to the likes of Nicolas Cage, Dennis Quaid, Ashanti and Snoop Dogg among other celebs. Having opened in the summer of 2003, the $15-million club is now the place where the beautiful people like to gather to dance to great DJ beats. Based on the style of an English manor, it has five elegant rooms with over-stuffed leather chairs and couches, two eclectic DJs each night, sexy VIP booths and two balconies overlooking the Strip. Open Friday and Saturday 10pm–dawn.

Risqué

Paris Las Vegas, 702-946 4589
On the second floor of the chic Paris hotel with dramatic views of the Strip, this ultra lounge combines classic Parisian architecture with contemporary Asian style and discreet lighting elements in which to lounge or dance till dawn. An extension of the fabulous Ah Sin restaurant (see page 79), you can indulge in late-night desserts here prepared by top pastry chef Jean-Claude Canestrier. What makes this place so special, though, are the balconies, plush couches, ottomans, beds, lots of pillows and intimate, lighted dance floor. Open Wednesday to Sunday 10pm–4am.

Tabu

MGM Grand, 702-891 1111
The MGM Grand's cutting edge nightclub for the ultra sophisticated beautiful people combines luxury with state-of-the-art technology and excellent service. The funky furniture, marble tops, wooden floors and gorgeous textiles are highlighted by dynamic images that bounce off every surface with reactive imagery. Music

★★★ **BRIT TIP** ★★★
★ Ensure yourself a reserved table ★
★ at the trendy Tabu by ordering a ★
★ bottle in advance of your visit. ★
★★★★★★★★★★★★★★★★★★

goes from classic lounge tunes earlier in the night to more progressive vocals later in the evening. Open Tuesday to Sunday from 10pm.

Hotel Nightclubs

Baby's

Hard Rock Hotel, 702-693 5555
An underground, state-of-the-art club featuring two rooms of brilliant music. It has the feel of a New York club thanks to the luminescent walls, and the beautiful people love its dance floor, private booths, four bars, dance platforms and exclusive VIP lounge. By the way, if you're after a tame experience, this is definitely NOT the nightclub for you. The Hard Rock Hotel was once fined $100,000 by the Nevada Gaming Commission for failing to prevent overt sexual activity, according to a report in the *Las Vegas Review Journal*! Open Thursday to Sunday 11pm–4am.

★★★ **BRIT TIP** ★★★
★ Baby's nightclub is hard to find – ★
★ look for an unmarked door that ★
★ leads down a staircase beneath ★
★ the Hard Rock Hotel. ★
★★★★★★★★★★★★★★★★★★★★

Cleopatra's Barge

Caesars Palace, 702-731 7110
A theme offering from the Greco-Roman resort. Statues and centurions abound in the beautiful setting where live contemporary dance music is on the menu. Open Tuesday to Sunday 8.30pm–4am.

Club Rio

Rio All-Suite Hotel, 702-252 7777
A video wall surrounds the circular room of this club and a misting system keeps you cool when things get hot! Music includes Top 40 dance hits, 1980s music, Latin, hip hop and house, while ladies get cheap drinks. Be warned it's a popular haunt and is always crowded despite a strict no-

jeans policy and white collared shirts for men. Open Wednesday and Friday 11.30pm–3.30am, Thursday and Saturday 10.30pm–4am.

★ ★ ★ ★ ★ ★
★　　　　　　　　★
★　Las Vegas has no shortage of　★
★　bias. Men pay more to get into　★
★　nightclubs than women and　★
★　many clubs charge out-of-　★
★ towners double. Think anywhere ★
★　from $10 to $20 for men and　★
★　from $0 to $10 for women. In　★
★　fact, if ladies are prepared to　★
★　work their charm, they can often ★
★　schmooze their way in for free! ★
★ ★ ★ ★ ★ ★ ★ ★ ★ ★ ★ ★ ★ ★ ★ ★ ★

C2K

The Venetian, 702-414 1000
Filled with the beautiful people who flock to the Italian-style hotel, this is still one of the hottest clubs in town. Open Friday and Saturday 11pm– 6am.

The Dragon

Mandalay Bay, 702-636 7404
An ultra hip after-hours club in the China Grill restaurant, which really gets going after 1am and always attracts a beautiful crowd. The 1960s design of the restaurant with fab sofas and dramatic lighting is a perfect backdrop for this exotic, multi-tiered club, which has a circular, granite dance floor. Open Wednesday only 10pm–5am.

Ibiza USA

Desert Passage at the Aladdin, 702-836 0830
A trendy, high-energy nightclub that recreates the atmosphere and spirit of the ultra-hip Spanish island clubbing destination. DJs spin a mix of house, retro, techno and hip house music, while go-go dancers, laser lights, flashing strobes and video screens add to the atmosphere. If you don't fancy taking part in the frenzy, you can watch from the chairs that circle

the railing around the dance floor. Open Tuesday to Saturday 10pm–4am.

★ ★ ★　　　　　★ ★ ★
★　　　　　　　　★
★　　　　　　　　★
★　Smart dress is essential to get　★
★　into most nightclubs. Generally　★
★　no trainers, jeans or shorts are　★
★ allowed, while often baggy jeans ★
★　are also banned and tank tops　★
★　for men are a real no-no almost ★
★　　everywhere!　　★
★ ★ ★ ★ ★ ★ ★ ★ ★ ★ ★ ★ ★ ★ ★ ★ ★

Light

The Bellagio, 702-693 8300
Sexy and refined nightclub and lounge with chi-chi decor, excellent service and state-of-the-art electronics, based on the New York nightclub of the same name. On a par with Annabelle's in London, the 7,000-sq ft (650-sq metre) space includes cocktail bars and a lounge with 40 tables that can be pre-booked. DJs spin a mix of hip hop and house, while go-go dancers do their thing. Celebs spotted here include Leonardo DiCaprio, Tobey Maguire, Courteney Cox, Lucy Liu, Matt LeBlanc and Sting. Open Thursday to Saturday 10.30pm–4am.

★ ★ ★　　　　　★ ★ ★
★　　　　　　　　★
★　　　　　　　　★
★ To avoid the long queues to get ★
★　into Light, go before 11pm.　★
★ ★ ★ ★ ★ ★ ★ ★ ★ ★ ★ ★ ★ ★ ★ ★ ★

The Nightclub

Las Vegas Hilton, 702-732 5111
Showcases up-and-coming singers, while top resident DJs provide the kind of music that makes this another of the best nightspots in town. Dressing up to the nines is a must! Open Thursday to Saturday 11pm–4am.

OPM

The Forum Shops at Caesars, 702-369 4998

An ultra-modern club with a state-of-the-art light and sound show and DJs spinning progressive and funk music. The decor is a mix of West meets East with cocktail servers dressed in sensual Asian outfits. Food is available until 3am from one of Wolfgang Puck's cafés. Open Thursday to Sunday 10pm–6am.

★ ★ ★   **BRIT TIP**   ★ ★ ★

Want to experience the VIP treatment? Well money talks in Vegas. You don't need to be a celeb – you just need to hand over the dosh. You may have to part with at least $150–200 for a booth – could be worth it for the special treatment if you're with a crowd. Call in advance to check out the prices.

Ra

Luxor, 702-262 4000
Another all-nighter where you most definitely dress to impress! There are two enormous bars with a central dance floor surrounded by tables and booths for more privacy, while VIPs get their own special area. There are also two cigar lounges, plus a sushi and oyster bar.
Open 10pm to 6am Wednesday to Saturday.

Rain in the Desert

The Palms, 702-942 7777
The massive multi-level Rain doubles as both a nightclub and concert venue and is famous for its special effects, which include water, fire and fog. The back of the stage is flanked by a 16-ft (5-metre), colour-changing water wall and the front by a rain curtain. You enter through a gold-mirrored mosaic tunnel and can either head straight for the elevated bamboo dance floor surrounded by a computer-programmed river of water or find a private booth with water sofas (only eight, so it's best to book

one!). VIPs and the very wealthy can opt for one of the cabanas with mini-bars or a sky box with a private balcony on the third floor.

Food is available and appetisers include shrimp cocktail, smoked salmon canapés, crabcakes, tenderloin skewers with dipping sauce and full oyster and caviar menus. Drink specialities include a sake selection, premium tequilas, champagnes and Martinis. Open Thursday to Saturday 11pm–5am.

Rumjungle

The Mandalay Bay, 702-632 7777.
Still one of the hottest clubs in town. A massive cocktail lounge featuring flaming walls and waterfalls, rum cocktails (natch!), flaming meat skewers and go-go dancers. Celebs spotted here include Brad Pitt, Pete Sampras, Jimmy Smits and 'N Sync. The queues get long, so arrive early. And don't forget a trip to the restrooms, which are very similar to the unisex version in Ally McBeal. Open Tuesday and Wednesday 11pm–2.30am, Thursday, Friday, Saturday and Monday 11pm–4.30am.

Sevilla

The Desert Passageway at the Aladdin, 702-938 7777
This Spanish steakhouse turns into a nightclub at 10.30pm playing a variety of music from rock to hip hop, R&B and even salsa. Open Wednesday to Saturday 10.30pm–4am.

★ ★ ★   **BRIT TIP**   ★ ★ ★

Love your Latin music? The trendy Sevilla is one of the few nightclubs in town to offer salsa music – or visit Venus at the Venetian on a Sunday night.

Studio 54

MGM Grand, 702-891 1111
A high-energy nightclub with state-of-

the-art sound, video and lighting along with a troupe of live dancers. There are four separate dance floors and bars, an exclusive area for invited guests, plus the Rainforest Café, a giant show bar with video screens and music. Tuesday evening is Eden – Erotically Delicious Entertainer's Night – and Thursday is Dollhouse night when guests can dress up beautiful life-size 'dolls' in outfits from the club's reach-in closets. The dolls then serve as hosts in place of cocktail waitresses. Monday to Saturday 10pm–5am.

V Bar

The Venetian, 702-414 3200
One of the coolest nightclubs in town, it is based on both the trend-setting supper club Lotus in New York and Los Angeles's swanky Sunset Room. An upscale lounge, it has opaque glass walls, double-sided leather chaises longues and subdued lighting. The focal point is a custom-designed oversized bed made of pearlised silver leather and hollowed in the centre to allow space for a table holding a selection of exotic cocktails. Open daily 6pm–4am.

Venus

The Venetian, 702-414 4870
The club's Tiki bar is the place for exotic drinks, while the lounge has table seating, service by the Ladies in Red and views of the Strip. Wednesday is ladies' night, Friday's the night for R&B and dance, Saturday is Top 40 night and Sunday is Latin with a live band. If you'd like a table, book in advance. Tiki bar is open daily 5pm–1am, Lounge Wednesday to Saturday 11pm–4am.

The View

Harrah's Las Vegas, 702-369 5222
Located in the hotel's Range Steakhouse, it has spectacular views of the Strip. This is a comfortable, intimate place to dance, drink and dine after hours on a menu of appetisers, while DJs spin dance tracks from the 1970s to the present day. Open Thursday to Saturday midnight–5am.

Whiskey Sky

Green Valley Ranch, 2300 Paseo Verde Parkway, Henderson, 702-617 7777
An innovative nightclub with an 8-acre (3-ha) backyard pool area with private cabanas, day beds and an outdoor bar with gambling tables. The nightclub is right next door to the Whiskey Bar (see page 110). Open daily 4pm–4am.

Hotel Beach Clubs

Bikinis Beach & Dance Club

Rio All-Suite Hotel, 702-252 7777
A year-round indoor beach party with a South Beach-inspired design, the 11,000-sq ft (1,020-sq metre) dance club has a bar and even a shopping area. The real attraction is the sexy bikini and swimming-trunk-clad cocktail servers, bartenders, dancers and lifeguards, who use the beach showers to cool off after entertaining guests from the top of the lifeguard stands. A lava lounge offers old school and disco music from the 1970s and 1980s and there are four bars, but if you get desperate just flag down one of the shot-toting cocktail servers. Sunday night fever with Boogie Knights. Open Thursday to Sunday 9pm–4am.

Skin

Skin Pool Lounge, The Palms, 702-942 7777
By day a luxurious outdoor lounge with two pools, a lavender-shaded swimming pool and the Mermaid Cove – an elevated pool with

6

portholes where mermaids swim after dark – plus private cabanas and fibre-optically lit water salons, four bars, billiard tables, outdoor swings, poolside blackjack, trampolines, massages and other spa services.

Come night-time in the summer, the lounge is transformed into one of the most spectacular outdoor nightclubs and concert venues in Vegas. It has a concert stage, two dance floors, including plexi-glass dance platforms where aqua go-go girls emerge from the depths of the lavender pool. An elevated pool-top dance floor allows you literally to dance on water. Atmosphere is added with amazing lighting and fog effects.

Along with the rest of The Palms' venues, this has become a fast hit with locals and visitors alike – a true haven of voyeurism for adults. And if you're hungry, poolside dining is provided by Nine Steakhouse and include specialities such as sashimi and ceviche.

During the day Skin is only open to hotel residents, in the evening it is open to the public. Cover charges vary depending on the entertainment, while the beach party element is only on during the summer.

Non-hotel Nightclubs

The Beach

365 Convention Center Drive, 702-731 1925
One of the most happening venues in town. Maybe it has something to do with the bikini-wearing waitresses and muscle-bound bartenders. Rock 'n' roll fans will enjoy Wednesday's special night, while Thursday night is Almost Famous night, when live bands, garage bands and up-and-coming artists can show off their talents. Open 24/7.

Club Utopia

3765 South Las Vegas Boulevard, southern end of the Strip, 702-740 4646
Another of the hot nightspots for young trendies, with a different theme every night of the week. Tuesday is ladies' night, Thursday and Saturday techno, and hip hop on Sunday. Saturday is for those into electronica. Open Tuesday to Saturday.

Drink

200 East Harmon Avenue, 702-796 5519
The place to go for a fun, party atmosphere. Full of hip, young locals and tourists, it's a friendly place where you can dance, drink and eat too! If you can make it through the madding crowds, the VIP room above the cigar room is the place to go. Unheard-of drink combinations are served in babies' bottles, test tubes and small plastic buckets. Open Tuesday to Saturday 8pm–5am.

Hush

Polo Towers, 3745 Las Vegas Boulevard South, 702-261 1000
Right on the top floor of the Polo Towers, this is where to enjoy fantastic views on an open-air patio while listening to the sounds of house, down-tempo, lounge and hip hop. Casual dress acceptable, but no baggy, ripped or pool clobber. Open nightly 9pm–3am.

Ice

200 East Harmon Avenue, next to the Hard Rock Hotel, 702-699 5528, www.icelasvegas.com
An amazing new nightclub with five bars, a massive dance space, two DJ booths and a fog system. Not for the fainthearted, the scene is definitely on the lurid side thanks to the heavy tribal rhythms, and favoured skimpy leather outfits and ultra-suggestive dance movements of the punters! Open Friday 10.30pm–5am, Saturday 10.30pm–7am.

Seven

3724 Las Vegas Boulevard South, 702-739 7744
Great restaurant and nightclub with a main dance floor with two bars, plus

two smaller rooms and a sushi bar. The restaurant is swathed in elegant red and filled with swanky booths. The main nightclub has two bars – one featuring a glass top with roses and lights twinkling beneath – a circular dance floor and tiger-skin booths, while DJs spin house, hip hop and dance music.

The club's main feature is its patio overlooking the Strip, which has a bar, couches and tables – a great spot for people-watching. Open Monday to Wednesday 11pm–2am, Thursday to Saturday 11pm–5am.

After Hours

Alesium Afterhours at Seven

3724 South Las Vegas Boulevard, 702-992 7970
In the same venue as Seven, the crowd here is very friendly and relaxed, while the DJs continue the beat with dance, hip hop and house music. Open Thursday to Saturday 2am–9am.

Glo Las Vegas

At Ibiza USA in the Desert Passageway at the Aladdin, 702-310 5060
Glo after hours at Ibiza runs Wednesday, Saturday and Sunday mornings 4am–noon.

HOB: Late night

House of Blues, Mandalay Bay, 702-632 7777
After the live music has finished the DJs do their thing. Friday features 1980s music, Saturday is for the Boogie Knights disco and Sunday is a Service Industry Night. Open Friday to Sunday 11pm–6am.

Live Music Venues

The Boston Bar & Grill

1030 East Flamingo Road at Maryland Parkway next to the Target shopping centre, 702-368 0750, www.thebostonlv.com.
The city's most famous live music venue for local bands has reopened in a new location with more than

10,000sq ft (930sq metres) of space divided between a bar area, sports lounge with 15 large-screen TVs, games room and a few dining room areas. The stage – one of the biggest in town – is in the middle and can be seen from most areas, while the bands tend to play from around 8pm till after midnight, followed by DJ action.

Open 24/7, the restaurant provides breakfast, lunch and dinner menus, which have a big emphasis on seafood, Italian and Irish pub grub.

Admissions $5 weekdays, $7 weekends, free Wednesday.

House of Blues

Mandalay Bay on the Strip, 702-632 7777
The legendary chain of restaurants-come-live-music-venues-and-nightclubs provides an eclectic mix of music to serve all tastes. The venue, which can hold 1,900 people, plays host to every kind of band from rock to R&B, reggae, hip hop, country, jazz and, of course, blues. A Sunday Gospel brunch features the best of gospel music and a Southern-style buffet with seating at 10am and 1pm. Live blues from Thursday to Saturday. The 500-seater restaurant serves everything from the casual to the sublime including the classic Elwood sandwich (named after Dan Aykroyd's character in *The Blues Brothers*), Memphis-style ribs with Jack Daniels sauce, cedar plank salmon with watercress-jicama salad and voodoo shrimp served with rosemary cornbread.

★ ★ ★ **BRIT TIP** ★ ★ ★

Don't hang around the bar area at the House of Blues if you want to catch a good view of the band as the low-lying ceiling will obscure your view.

The Joint

Hard Rock Hotel, Harmon Avenue, 702-226 4650 for live music updates

6

Famous for its cracking live music in a great rock ' n' roll environment.

Tommy Rocker's

4275 South Industrial Road, 702-261 6688

A snazzy grill and cantina for a casual set who like to have fun. A greater selection of beers than most bars, while the rock music makes this a legendary, if extremely loud, live music joint! Open 24/7.

★ ★ ★   **BRIT TIP**   ★ ★ ★
★   ★
★   ★
★   Generally gig tickets go from   ★
★   between $20 and $80, but can   ★
★   rise to a staggering $1,000 a hit if ★
★   you want to see the Rolling   ★
★   Stones, for instance, at The Joint! ★
★ ★ ★ ★ ★ ★ ★ ★ ★ ★ ★ ★ ★ ★ ★ ★ ★

Jazz

Jazzed Café & Vinoteca

8615 West Sahara Avenue on the intersection with Durango Avenue, 702-233 2859

Great restaurant (see page 97) and jazz den offering live music from Tuesday to Thursday 7.30–10.30pm and Friday and Saturday 8–11pm. Open Monday to Friday 5pm–2am, Saturday and Sunday 12noon–2am.

Napoleon's

Paris Las Vegas, 702-739 4111

One of the best champagne bars in the city with more than 100 varieties to choose from, it also has a full-service bar. So enjoy a glass of bubbly and sit back to soak up the

★ ★ ★   **BRIT TIP**   ★ ★ ★
★   ★
★   ★
★   Phone Napoleon's in advance to ★
★   check out current times for   ★
★   Happy Hour, when you get a   ★
★   complimentary carving station   ★
★   roll if you buy a drink.   ★
★ ★ ★ ★ ★ ★ ★ ★ ★ ★ ★ ★ ★ ★ ★ ★ ★

smooth live jazz. The bar also has a fully-stocked cigar humidor and a carving station for fresh rolls piled high with steak, mustard-rubbed roast turkey and wine-braised pork loin. Open Sunday to Thursday 4pm–2am, Friday and Saturday 4pm–3am.

Onda Lounge

The Mirage, 702-791 7111

Just outside the Onda restaurant (see page 87), this is where you can sip wines by the glass or indulge in a cocktail while enjoying the live jazz. Open nightly 5pm–midnight.

Très Jazz

Paris Las Vegas, 702-946 7000.

Located in the passageway between Bally's and Paris, this Parisian-style supper club features new world Caribbean cuisine and live jazz nightly.

Jazz Festival at the Fremont Street Experience

Downtown Las Vegas, 1-800 249 3559

Go to the city during the last weekend in May and you'll enjoy the now annual free Jazz Festival that takes place throughout the five city blocks that make up the Fremont Street Experience.

Country and Western

Gilley's

New Frontier Hotel, 702-794 8434

For the true cowboy experience Las Vegas-style, head for Gilley's, which has become known around town for its amazing barbecue, great music – both live and by DJ – excellent service and the Gilley's Girls. On top of all this, you can try out the famous mechanical bull and take line-dancing lessons. On Friday and Saturday game (and brave!) girls can take part in the bikini bull-riding contest at midnight for $500 in cash and prizes.

Sunday to Wednesday bull rides 4–9pm (first ride free), the DJ starts at 7.30pm. Thursday is ladies' night

with line-dancing lessons
7.30–8.30pm, free bull rides and
drinks for $1 all night from 9pm.
Thursday to Saturday you can opt for
the $10 all-you-can-drink draft beer
after 9pm. The band starts at 10pm,
when it costs $10 to get in.

Other Country & Western venues
include the **Gold Coast Dance Hall**
(4000 West Flamingo, 702-367
7111); **Idle Spurs Tavern** (1113
Rainbow Boulevard, 702-363 7718);
Saddle 'n' Spurs Saloon (2329 North
Jones, 702-646 6292); **Sam's Town
Western Dance Hall** (5111 Boulder
Highway, 702-456 7777), with free
dance lessons; and **Silverado Dance
Hall** (5255 Boulder Highway, 702-
458 8810).

Strip Clubs

The sex industry is big business in Las
Vegas and to prove it a raft of
swanky new clubs have recently
opened. Indeed the latest – Sapphire
– cost $25 million and is so upmarket
you may even feel you've wandered
into the lobby of a five-star hotel. Kid
yourself not though, the club is purely
about titillation with a spot of
elegance thrown in! The following
three are the major topless clubs.

★ ★ ★　　　　　　　★ ★ ★
★　　　　　　　　　　　　　★
★　Hilarious but true: you've no　★
★　excuse for running out of money ★
★　at any of the swanky new clubs – ★
★　Jaguar's, Sapphire and Paradise ★
★　all have their own cashpoints, or ★
★　ATMs as Americans call them!　★
★ ★ ★ ★ ★ ★ ★ ★ ★ ★ ★ ★ ★ ★ ★ ★ ★ ★

Club Paradise

One of the older-style clubs, but
extremely popular thanks to its lack of
seediness (which in Las Vegas equals
classy!). It consists of a large room
with a nightclub atmosphere, one
main stage and two other dance
floors, plus go-go type dance stages
near the ceiling. The club also has a
restaurant and VIP room. Open

Monday to Friday 4pm–6am,
Saturday and Sunday 6pm–6am.
Cover prices: before 9pm $5 for
women, $10 for men; after 9pm $10
for women, $20 for men; lap dance
$20.

Jaguar's

3355 South Procyon Avenue, 702-
732 1116
A luxurious, $15-million club with
Italianate columns, comfy and stylish
chairs, marble walls, chandeliers and
fireplaces. It has three stages for topless
dancers, which can be seen from any
part of the club, three bars including a
bank of televisions in the main bar to
provide coverage of popular sporting
events, a separate lap-dancing area
and an elegant staircase leading up to
the VIP area. The club's sushi
restaurant, Pumi, is open 11am–7pm
every day. Open 24/7.

Cover prices: after 8pm $10 for
locals, $20 for non-residents;
standard lap dance $20. In the VIP
rooms you get four lap dances for
$100 during the day, three for $100
after 8pm, or you can pay $250 for
30 minutes or $500 for an hour.

★ ★ ★　　　　　　　★ ★ ★
★　　　　　　　　　　　　　★
★　Weird but true: women are　★
★　allowed to 'entertain' men, but　★
★　are not allowed entry to　★
★　'gentlemen's' clubs unless they　★
★　arrive with a man!　★
★ ★ ★ ★ ★ ★ ★ ★ ★ ★ ★ ★ ★ ★ ★ ★ ★ ★

Sapphire Gentlemen's Club

3025 South Industrial Road, 702-796
6000
The newest, swankiest, largest club in
town – at 71,000sq ft (6,600sq
metres) – it is massive and at peak
times there can be up to 800 topless
dancers entertaining the crowds. The
huge, multi-layered central stage can
be seen from any part of the club,
while music includes a variety of
dance and Top 40 hits. The three
main bars are the Martini Bar, which

★ ★ ★ BRIT TIP ★ ★ ★
★   ★
★   ★
★ If you really want to get up close ★
★ – but not personal – the going ★
★ rate for a lap dance is generally ★
★ $20.   ★

has an enormous Martini glass as its centrepiece, Pete's Bar and the Off Broadway bar, generally used for private parties. Other facilities include the Stake restaurant, serving steaks, which has its own separate entrance, and VIP Sky Boxes, which allow clients to overlook the main dance floor from a private room. Open 24/7.
Cover prices: free 6am–6pm, then $10 for locals, $20 for non-residents. Lap dances $20; VIP lap dances $100 for three; an hour in the VIP area $400; Skybox $250 an hour including drinks, plus $500 an hour for lap dances.

Other Topless Only Clubs

Cheetas

2112 Western Avenue between West Oakey Boulevard and Sahara Avenue, 702-384 0074
One of the friendliest clubs, it puts a big emphasis on providing coverage of major sporting events. It has five intimate little stages and is a favourite with locals. Open 24/7.
Cover price: $10 between 8pm–5pm.

★ ★ ★ BRIT TIP ★ ★ ★
★   ★
★   ★
★ Make sure you have plenty of ★
★ singles ($1 bills) with you to tip ★
★   the dancers!   ★

Crazy Horse Too Gentleman's Club

2476 Industrial Road at Sahara Avenue, 702-382 8003
Like Cheetah's, this club has been

around forever, but is nowhere near as well laid out. There are only two stage areas and you'll have a long wait to get a ringside seat. Open 24/7.
Cover price: $10 6.30pm–4.30am.

Girls of Glitter Gulch

20 Fremont Street between Casino Center and Main Street, 702-385 4774
Thanks to its location close to the Fremont Street Experience, this attracts a fairly touristy crowd. Open Sunday to Thursday noon–4am, Friday and Saturday noon– 6am. Cover price: minimum of two drinks.

Olympic Garden Cabaret

1531 Las Vegas Boulevard South at Wyoming Avenue, 702-385 8987.
Once one of the largest topless clubs in Vegas – prior to the opening of Jaguar's and Sapphire's – the main room has several stages, while the second has two stages and a catwalk. An exotic male dance revue takes place in the VIP lounge upstairs. Open 24/7.
Cover price: $20 including two drinks.

Total Nudity

For classic dark and steamy, make for any of these old-time strip clubs, which all feature total nudity.

Can Can Room

3155 Industrial Road, one block west of the Stardust Hotel, 702-737 1161
Open 7.30pm–dawn. Cover price: $30.

Déjà Vu Showgirls

3247 South Industrial Avenue, north west of the Fashion Show Mall, 702-894 4167
Open Monday to Saturday 11am–6am, Sunday 6pm–4am. Cover price: $15.

★ ★ ★ BRIT TIP ★ ★ ★
★   ★
★   ★
★ Strip clubs which offer total ★
★ nudity do not serve alcohol. ★

Diamond Cabaret

3177 Highland Drive, north west of the Fashion Show Mall, 702-731 2365

Lacy's

1848 Las Vegas Boulevard North, just opposite Jerry's Nugget, 702-399 3144

Leopard Lounge

3500 West Naples, a mile south of the Rio All-Suite Hotel off Polaris Road, 702-798 6939
Open daily 2pm–dawn. Cover price: $10 after 9pm.

Lil' Darlings

1514 Western Avenue, half a mile south of Charleston Avenue/Interstate 15 intersection, 702-366 1633
Open Monday to Saturday 11am–6am, Sunday 6pm–4am. Cover price: $10 for locals; $20 for non-residents.

Palamino Club

1848 North Las Vegas Boulevard, a quarter of a mile south of the intersection with East Lake Mead Road, 702-385 8987
Open daily 5pm–5am. Cover price: $15 for locals and women, $30 non-residents.

The Playpen

3120 Sirius Avenue, in warehouses behind Scandia Road between Insterstate 15 and Polaris, 702-579 4755
Open daily noon–dawn. Cover price: locals free with one drink minimum ($10), $20 non-residents.

Rick's Tally Ho

2850 South Highland Drive, east of the Sahara Avenue/Interstate 15 intersection, 702-792 9330
Open 24/7. Cover charge: one drink ($12) minimum 7am–6pm, then $12 plus one drink minimum.

Showgirl Video

631 South Las Vegas Boulevard in the downtown area, 702-385 4554
Open daily 8am–5am. Cover price: $1.

Talk of the Town

1238 South Las Vegas Boulevard, one block south of the intersection with East Charleston Road, 702-385 1800
Open daily 4pm–4am. Cover price: free with one-drink minimum ($10).

Wild J's Platinum Babes

2923 South Industrial Road, one block west of Circus Circus Hotel, 702-892 0416
Open 24/7. Cover price: $10 plus one drink minimum ($6), $25 between 5pm–5am plus one drink minimum.

Strip club etiquette

First of all, in Las Vegas anyway, there is a distinction between a strip club and a gentlemen's club – the former offers full nudity and the latter topless only. Both have strict rules governing behaviour.

First off, while many strip clubs don't necessarily have a dress code, you won't get in if you look really scruffy or if you're drunk.

Secondly, if you try to touch one of the girls, you'll find yourself out on your ear pretty pronto.

Thirdly, have plenty of cash. The girls are not paid and work for tips only. It's a big no-no to take in the sights and not tip. And don't even think about sitting stageside without a wad for both drinks and tipping.

Finally, while the dancers are working girls, they're not THAT kind of working girl. Prostitution is illegal in Las Vegas – ironic or what! – so don't even think about it. It's also not on to ask for a date or even suggest dinner.

6

7 GAMBLING

Everything you need to know about having a flutter without blowing all your holiday money

You've seen the erupting volcano, watched the *Sirens of TI* and witnessed amazing circus acts – all in the most opulent, best-that-money-can-buy settings. Now let's get down to the nitty gritty, the *raison d'être* of the city – the casinos.

Most of the Strip resorts have their casinos laid out in such a way that you can't fail to notice them even before you've got to your room. It's no surprise really: you have to accept that there is only one reason for all the glamour and razzmatazz – the making of money, absolutely tons of it. In 2001, casino takings stood at $9.46 BILLION a year in Nevada, with Las Vegas casinos taking the lion's share. All this from the 198,065 slot machines and 6,141 live gambling tables state-wide.

The billions spent in the 1990s on the creation of the mega resorts – the Luxor, the MGM Grand, Treasure Island, New York-New York and the Bellagio plus the newer Mandalay Bay, Paris and Venetian hotels – were triggered by a massive growth in casino income at the beginning of the decade. A location on the Strip is considered so important that an acre (0.4ha) of land there is now worth a cool $10 million.

High-roller baccarat players, the very latest slot machines, state-of-the-art video gambling machines and sports betting are the big money-spinners, and you'll also find everything else from roulette to craps and poker to blackjack.

But it's not all been plain sailing for the casino bosses of Las Vegas. An increase in competition from Atlantic City in New Jersey (it took $4.8 billion in gambling in 2001) and the fact that 22 American states have now legalised gambling has

meant the city has had to reinvent itself as an entertainment destination in its own right, while providing the most sophisticated games and facilities – and all at the most incredible prices.

The massive anti-gambling lobby from politicians, federal bureaucrats and religious organisations hasn't helped, while Congress intends to set up a two-year study on the effects of gambling on states and cities. As a result, the American Gaming Association (gaming being the Las Vegas euphemism for gambling!) has put $200,000 million into a new foundation to study compulsive gambling and develop treatment.

The casinos know that the hard-luck stories of desperate gamblers are bad for business. They want people to win, they want people to have fun and to know when to walk away because they want them to return

★★★ **BRIT TIP** ★★★

Remember the golden rules of gambling: stick to your own limits and always, always quit while you're ahead!

again and again and again. That way, they know, the odds are that they'll always get their money back – and more besides!

To this end, the industry has been working hard to make casinos more user-friendly by providing free lessons in easy-to-find locations. A move to put 'comps' (see page 134) on a more straightforward footing has led to the creation of loyalty cards by many establishments where the amount of money you spend along with the time you spend gambling generates points to put towards free meals, free rooms and free shows.

Whether you intend to spend $20 or $2,000 gambling, or just sit in one of the many bars and watch the action, all these factors mean you can have a fantastic time in Las Vegas without parting with huge amounts of dosh – as long as you follow the rules: **stick to your own limits and always, always quit while you're ahead!**

★ ★ ★   **BRIT TIP**   ★ ★ ★

Money raised from gambling was used to buy uniforms, provisions and bullets for troops fighting us Brits during America's fight for independence from 1775 to 1783.

High rollers

The casinos like to keep all their customers happy, but they go to extraordinary lengths to accommodate high rollers (big betters) – and I mean HIGH! **Baccarat**, the game they tend to play, accounts for a massive 13% of casino takings. The **Las Vegas Hilton** has spent $40 million building three high-roller suites called **Sky Villas**. The massive apartments come with marble floors, chandeliers, five bathrooms, gold-plated bathroom fixtures, private swimming pool, putting green, 24-hour butler, chef, maid and limo service, gym facilities, media room and state-of-the-art entertainment and video equipment. They were built on part of what used to be Elvis Presley's 5,000-sq ft (460sq-metre) penthouse suite and are free of charge – but only to people with a gambling purse starting at $2 million! An exclusive $12-million VIP baccarat facility is available to complement the suites.

Baccarat, with its high-bet limits and liberal odds, is worth a cool $1 billion in gambling income worldwide and other Las Vegas casinos have been working hard to cash in. **Bally's** casino on the Strip has hired a high-roller expert to weed out the big fish – gamblers willing to bet $300,000 to $1 million – from the 'whales', who only bet around $250,000 a hand! Big baccarat players tend to be Asian, Latin and South American, and Asians in particular have been targeted by the **Tropicana**, which recently opened a room specifically for them, called the Jade Palace. The normal limits are $10,000 a hand in games of pai gow, pai gow poker and mini-baccarat.

High-stakes **poker** is big business, too, and **Binion's Horseshoe** casino in downtown Las Vegas has been home to the World Series of Poker title for the last two decades. Thousands of players from all around the world pay a fee to take part in the poker extravaganza that lasts 24 days. Then each May, more than 300 players pay $10,000 each to buy into the four-day World Championship No-limit Texas Hold 'Em competition. The winner is guaranteed $1 million and walks away with the champion poker player of the world crown.

The law

You must be over 21 to gamble in Las Vegas and under 18s are not allowed in arcades from 10pm to 5am during the week and from midnight to 5am at weekends. In a further move to appease the anti-gambling lobby, the city has passed a new law that bans

Fun books and other freebies

Whether or not you intend to do any gambling, always check the casino cages for their free fun books. These will give free goes on slot machines, may entitle you to double a bet at the blackjack table or increase the value of a keno ticket. They will also be full of bargains on food and drink or offer discounts on souvenirs such as T-shirts. These books are also available from car rental agencies, hotels, motels and other locations in the city. Some tour operators – most notably Funway – have put together their own fun books, which include some fantastic deals on excursions and attractions.

The monthly *Las Vegas Advisor* gives subscribers lots of information on deals and freebies available in Las Vegas and sometimes includes valuable coupons or arranges special deals for subscribers. Write to the *Las Vegas Advisor*, Huntington Press, PO Box 28401, Las Vegas, Nevada 89126. Subscriptions are $54 a year, but you'll generally get back that cost in money-saving coupons, let alone all the other tips!

under 18s from walking down or cruising the Strip after 9pm without a parent or guardian.

How to get in on the action

I remember the first time I visited Las Vegas, the bright lights were so overwhelming and the sheer scale of everything so overpowering that it seemed far too daunting to go into the casinos and play a game or two. Removing some of the mystique surrounding these games of chance is not to remove the magic of the setting, but it will give you the right kind of edge.

When it comes to a weekend gambling spree, the average American will allow a budget of between $200 and $500. When a touring Brit arrives in town, their budget of between $20 and $50 is usually simply there to fritter away while downing complimentary drinks. If you do want to have a go, though, here is a guide to the different games, the rules, and the best ways to place your bets so that even if you don't win, you won't blow your entire budget straight away.

The aim of the game is to make your spending money last as long as possible while having fun – and, who knows, you may even come out a

winner! Bear in mind that these tips are aimed at those people who are new to gambling as opposed to those looking for more detailed and advanced information. But I have included details of where you can go for further information and more in-depth advice.

When in a casino always remember Big Brother is watching you! Mirrors or dark glass in the ceilings hide people watching casino action to stop cheating by players or dealers. And there are cameras behind the decorative-looking glass to record action at the tables.

The odds

There are two aspects to every game you play – the chance of you winning inherent in each game (the odds) and the rules designed to favour the house, including payoffs at less than the actual odds or predetermined payoffs, as in slot machines (the edge). It is because of this edge that, no matter how well you are playing or how much luck you seem to be having, the odds will always favour the casinos, who'll win everything back in the long run. That's why when you've come to the end of a winning streak you should always walk away.

Table games with the best odds on winning or on reducing your losses are baccarat and blackjack. Craps is seriously not good, roulette not a lot better and in keno you have about as much chance of winning as you do with our National Lottery, though the cost of the bet is usually lower than $1, so you may not care.

As a general rule, the smaller casinos away from the Strip are what are known as the 'loosest' – they will offer the best returns on slot machines. For some time the downtown casinos have been rated as the 'loosest slots in America' by the *Casino Player* magazine. For instance, slot machines will give anywhere from a 95% to a 99% return on your play. That means if you bet $1, you'll get between 95 and 99 cents back if you win. Downtown, you have more chance of finding machines with a 98% and 99% return.

The exception on the Strip is the Stratosphere, which has made a corporate decision to lure in punters with the promise of the best returns in town. Their deals include 100 times odds on craps, single-zero roulette, hand-dealt double-deck blackjack, double-exposure blackjack (where you see both the dealer's cards), 98% return on 100 $1 slots and more than 100% return on 100 video poker machines. But do bear in mind that there are only a certain number of the high-paying machines, so always check the returns on a particular machine before you play.

Limits

The table limits are an important consideration because the higher the minimum bet, the quicker you'll get through your money. Unless you're a serious gambler, you'll steer clear of baccarat. The minimum at most Strip resorts is $100! Cheapest, though, is New York-New York, which has

games with minimum bets of $10. You can also play mini-baccarat at the Stratosphere with minimum bets of $5 per hand.

Most Strip resorts have a minimum of $5 on blackjack. The cheapest are Circus Circus ($2), Excalibur ($2), Luxor ($2), Monte Carlo ($3), Treasure Island ($3) and Stratosphere ($3). In comparison, you'll find $2 blackjack tables aplenty and $1 roulette at casinos away from the Strip.

★ ★ ★   BRIT TIP   ★ ★ ★
★   ★
★   Limits fluctuate. Minimum bets   ★
★   tend to be higher in the evening, ★
★   at weekends and during special   ★
★   events. The Strip hotels all have   ★
★   higher minimums than   ★
★   downtown casinos.   ★
★ ★ ★ ★ ★ ★ ★ ★ ★ ★ ★ ★ ★ ★ ★ ★

7

Table games

Baccarat

There is normally an aura of glamour surrounding this game as it tends to attract high rollers and is usually played in a separate, often more refined area, cordoned off and staffed by croupiers in posh tuxedos. But don't be put off by the glamour of it all. The mega-bucks, high-roller games will be played in special VIP rooms, so the areas you see really are for mere mortals! What's more, it is an easy game to play and offers the best chance of you beating the casino.

Generally, up to 15 players sit around a table where two cards from an eight-deck shoe are dealt to each of the players and to the bank (see Gambling Lingo, page 127). You can bet either on you winning, the bank winning or there being a tie, but you are only playing against the bank, not the other players. Each time you win, the casino takes a commission, though not if you lose.

The idea is simple: you're aiming to get to a total of either eight or nine and the value of the cards are: ace to nine – face value; tens and face cards – zero. If the cards add up to more than ten, only the second digit is counted. For instance, if your hand contains a nine and a four, it adds up to 13 but is worth three as you drop the first digit from the total. In this case you'd ask the dealer for another card.

The house edge in baccarat is very low, which is why it is such an attractive proposition. The edge when betting on a bank hand is 1.17% (though that is increased by the fact that a commission is always paid to the house on with-bank bets) and the edge on a player is 1.36%.

Blackjack or 21

After baccarat, blackjack, or 21, is one of the easiest games to play and the rows of blackjack tables in casinos reflect the huge number of gamblers who play the game. The object is to get as close to 21 as possible without 'busting'. There can be up to six people around a table, all playing against the dealer.

Bets are placed first, then the dealer gives two cards to each player and himself, the first face down (known as the hole card), the second showing (upcard). Numbered cards count as their face value, face cards count as 10 and aces are worth either one or 11. You can either decide to stand with the two cards you received or take a hit (another card from the dealer) until you're happy with your hand or you go bust.

When all the players have finished, the dealer turns over his hole

Card counters

You will probably have heard of *card counters*. These are people who basically keep a track of the low and high cards that are being played in blackjack to try to determine the likelihood of drawing a high or low card at a crucial moment – eg when you've got a 15, which is unlikely to be enough to win but you can't guarantee you'll get a six or under. There are many different forms of card counting, but the most simple is the one used with single-deck blackjack. Basically, 10, J, Q and K are worth minus two, everything else is worth one. Starting from minus four, you count upwards and down according to the cards dealt. Generally you should bet low when the score is negative (you're more likely to bust) and high when the count is positive or above minus two.

It is not illegal to count cards but the casinos in Las Vegas frown on this misguided attempt by players to cheat them out of money and tend to refuse to let card counters into their casinos. This is why it's best to practise your technique in advance so you won't be noticed!

card and takes hits until his total exceeds 17. If the dealer busts, everyone around the table wins, otherwise only those whose hands are higher than the dealer's win. If the first two cards you are dealt total 21, then you've got what is known as a natural, ie a blackjack, and you automatically win. If both you and the dealer are dealt a blackjack, then it is a stand-off and no one wins.

As a general rule, if you have a hand without an ace against the dealer's seven or higher, you should take hits until you reach at least 17. Against the dealer's four, five or six, you can stand on a 12 or higher; if against the dealer's two or three, hit a 12. With a soft hand (which includes

Gambling lingo

Acorn	Player who is generous with tips
Ante	Money you bet in card games
Bank	Inventory of coins and chips on all table games
Big digger	Ace of spades
Book	Place where bets are made on sporting events
Boxcars	When a gambler rolls two sixes for a point of 12
Boxman	Craps table dealer who sits over the drop box and supervises bets and pay-offs
Bumble puppy	Careless or inexperienced card player
Bust	Exceed the maximum score allowed, for instance 21 in blackjack
Buster	Term used for illegally altered dice
Casino cage	Secure area within the casino for banking services and casino operations
Casino boss	Person who oversees the entire casino
Comp	Free meal, gift, etc (short for complimentary)
Coupons	Redeemable for nearly everything from a free meal to a free pull on a slot machine
Crossroaders	Card cheats who travel across America in search of games
Dealer	Person who conducts table games
Drop box	Locked box on 'live' gaming tables where dealers deposit your cash
Eye in the sky	One-way mirror used for surveillance of the casino area
Flat top	Slot machine with a fixed jackpot, as opposed to a progressive slot machine where the jackpot increases according to the amount of play
Frog skin	Old-time gamblers' name for paper money
Gaming	Las Vegas euphemism for gambling
Green	Gambling chip worth $25, also known as a quarter
High roller	Someone who bets large sums of money
Hit me	What you say when you want another card from the dealer in a blackjack game
In red	If you get a free meal, your name will appear in red on the maître d's reservation list
Ladderman	The person who supervises baccarat games and has the final say over any disputes
Limit	Minimum and maximum bet, as decided by the casino
Loose	Term used to describe slot machines that pay out at the best percentages
Maître d'	Not technically a gambling term, but you'll hear it so often that it's worth mentioning that this is the head waiter
Marker	IOU
Nevada lettuce	$1,000 bill

7

Pit	Area of the casino containing gambling tables
Pit boss	Person who oversees a number of table dealers
Red	Gambling chip worth $5, also known as a nickel
RFB comp	If the casino is impressed with someone's credit rating, they will arrange a free room, food or drink during a hotel stay
Shoe	Contains the packs of playing cards used in blackjack and baccarat
Shooter	Person rolling the dice in craps
Snake eyes	Craps term used when the dice holder rolls a point of two
Soft hand	When you have at least one ace in your blackjack hand. It is counted as either one or 11 so you have two possible totals
Spoon	A device used by slot machine cheats
Stand	To refuse any more cards in blackjack
Stickman	Dealer who moves the dice around on a craps table with a hook-shaped stick
Table games	Everything from blackjack and baccarat to roulette
Toke or gratuity	Tip
Whale	Gambler who is willing to bet $250,000 a hand
Whip shot	In craps, the way of rolling the dice to hit the table in a flat spin so the desired numbers are on top when the dice stop rolling

an ace), hit all totals of 17 or lower. Against the dealer's nine or 10, hit 18.

What gives the house the edge is that you have to play your hand first so even if the dealer busts after you have, you're still a loser. But there are two ways to help you even the odds – you can double down or split pairs. If you feel you may have a good hand and will only need one more card, you double down – ie you double your initial bet and accept one extra card to complete your hand. If you are dealt a pair, you can opt to split them, thereby increasing your chances of winning. You separate the cards to create two hands, thereby doubling your bet, and draw extra cards for each hand. When splitting aces you are only allowed to take one extra card for each ace. If the next card is an ace, though, you can split again. The rule is always to split aces and eights.

A word about '**insurance**'. When the dealer's 'show' card is an ace, you will be offered the chance to insure yourself against the dealer getting a blackjack to win 2–1 if the dealer holds a blackjack, so you break even. But it is not a good bet to make because even if you end up with a blackjack, you'll only get 2–1 on a bet that should pay 9–4.

Another way the casino gets an edge is by using a shoe containing six packs of playing cards. This makes busts less likely, which helps the dealer, who is forced by the rules to take more hits than the player. And blackjacks are also less frequent, another drawback as you get paid 3–2 for those.

If you want to learn more, call into the **Gambler's Book Club** (630 South 11th Street, 1-800 634 6243) where you'll find copies of just about every book ever written about blackjack, and experts on the game – including card counters – who are happy to answer questions.

Nightlife

Top left **Studio 54**

Top right **Coyote Ugly**

Centre left **Les Folies Bergère at Tropicana Tiffany**

Below right **Showgirls of Magic**

Bottom left and right **Baby's**

Gambling

Top left Swimup at the
Tropicana

Top right Sports Book at
the Hilton

Above right Caesars Palace

Centre left Downtown at
night

Bottom Luxor

Craps

We've all seen this game played down New York alleyways in gangster movies, now here's your chance to give it a go! Sadly it is one of the most complicated table games on offer, but it is also the one that seems to produce the most excitement.

You join a game by standing anywhere around the table, start betting any time and wait for your turn to shoot. When rolling the dice you have to do it hard enough for them to bounce off the far wall of the table to ensure a random bounce. Basically, the shooter rolls a pair of dice that determine the outcome of everyone's bets. The first roll is called the 'come-out roll'. If it is a seven or an 11, the shooter and all those who bet with him or her win. If the shooter rolls a two, three or 12, that is craps and the shooter and all those betting with him or her lose. If the shooter rolls a four, five, six, seven, eight, nine or 10, he or she must roll the same number again to win. If the shooter rolls a seven before that number, he or she 'sevens out' and loses.

There is a whole series of bets that can be made – with the most bizarre titles you could imagine – from 'pass lines' to 'don't pass', 'come' and 'don't come', 'field', 'big six' or 'eight', 'any craps', 'hard ways', 'bet the horn', 'any seven' and 'under or over seven'.

The odds on winning and payouts vary wildly:

Best bets: the **Pass Line**, where you are betting with the shooter, and the **Don't Pass Line**, where you are betting against, pay even money. **Come** and **Don't Come** bets are the same as the **Pass** and **Don't Pass** bets, with the same odds, but can only be placed after the first roll of the dice. Best bet of all is the **Free Odds**, which is only available to the above betters, but is not even indicated on the table. Once the point has been established by the first roll of the dice, you can make a bet equal to your original and get true odds (2–1 on the four and 10, 3–2 on the five and nine and 6–5 on the six and eight) rather than even money.

Poor bets: the **Field**, where you bet that any number in the Field, ie not five, six, seven or eight, will be rolled. If the numbers mentioned come up you lose. **Place Bets**, where you bet the four, five, six, seven, eight, nine or 10 will be thrown before a seven, sound like a good idea but the casino edge is so great that you should not consider any bets other than placing the six and eight.

The downright daft!: **Big Six** and **Big Eight** bets on either the six or eight or both can be made at any time and either must appear before a seven is thrown to win. But the bet only pays even money so the casino's advantage is high. Worst bets of all are the **Proposition Bets**, which include the **Hard Ways** and **One-roll** Bets. The casino's advantage is so great that you shouldn't even consider these.

Roulette

This game has been growing in popularity in America since Europeans started visiting the city in greater numbers, but generally it does not carry very good odds. Also, the American roulette table has 36 numbers, plus a green zero and a green double zero – as opposed to the European wheel, which does not have the extra double zero (the only Strip exception is at the Stratosphere).

You place chips on the game board, gambling that either a single number, any of a dozen numbers, a column of numbers, corner of four numbers, red or black, or odd or even numbers comes up on the wheel. After all the chips have been put down, the dealer sends a small metal ball spinning around the roulette wheel, which spins in the opposite direction. When the ball drops into one of the slots, the owner(s) of the chips in that slot collect(s).

The lure is that if your number comes up you're paid at the rate of 35–1, but what makes roulette a poor game for strategists is that it basically involves blind luck. **Best way** to reduce the chance of losing is to stick to betting that the ball will drop on either a red or black number; and odd or even number of numbers 1–18 or 19–36. **Worst bet** is any one number. Other bets include groups of 12 numbers (2–1), groups of six numbers (5–1), groups of four numbers (8–1), groups of three numbers (11–1), groups of two numbers (17–1) and a group of 0, 00, 1, 2 and 3 (6–1).

Card games

Poker

For the real Wild West experience, this is a must! There are many variations, but most follow the same principles: all players play for themselves, paying a certain sum of money per hour of play to the casino, and a regular deck of cards is used. Before joining a game, always check with the dealer to find out the specific game being played.

Seven Card Stud Poker: the easiest poker game in the world. You are dealt two cards face down, then a

third face up. The player with the lowest card makes the first bet, other players can match the bet, raise it or withdraw. Then another card is dealt face up and the player with the highest hand showing starts the betting. This is repeated until four cards have been dealt face up. The seventh and final card is dealt face down to those players still in the game and the final round of betting begins. This is showdown time and players may raise bets up to three times. When the last bet is covered or called, the dealer calls for the showing of hands and the highest one wins.

Poker is a game that requires nerves of steel and the skill to know when to cut your losses and drop out. Professional poker players reckon that you'll have a pretty good idea of your chances by the time the first three cards have been dealt, and there are basic combinations that you need to have if you are going to continue.

The odds on getting three of a kind are about 400–1 and it indicates you've more than likely got a winning hand. But don't overplay your bets or you'll scare off other players, just keep covering the bets until the sixth card is dealt to allow the pot to build and then you can up the ante. A pair of aces or kings is another good start but keep an eye on what cards appear on the table – if something that you really need for your hand turns up elsewhere and your cards haven't improved by card five you should drop out. The same goes for a pair of queens or jacks. Three cards towards a straight flush is a good start but if you haven't improved your hand by card five, drop out.

Texas Hold 'Em: this is the game of the high-stakes World Series of Poker and is similar to Seven Card Stud except that only two of the seven cards are dealt to the player, the other five are dealt face up and used collectively by all the players. Obviously, the first two cards you're dealt are the most important and need to be either a pair of aces, kings, queens or jacks or two high-value cards.

Pai Gow Poker: played with a deck of 52 playing cards plus one joker, which can be used only as an ace to complete a straight, a flush or a straight flush. Players are dealt seven cards which they arrange to make two hands – a low hand of two cards and a high hand of five. The cards are arranged according to high-draw poker rankings, ie the highest two-card hand is two aces and the highest five-card hand is a royal flush. The object is for both hands to beat the banker's hands.

Caribbean Stud Poker™: played with a standard 52-card deck and no joker, it is the first casino table game to offer a progressive jackpot. You start by placing your bet in the box marked 'ante' and then have the option to bet $1 to enter the progressive jackpot, after which all the players and the dealer are dealt five cards. None of your cards is exposed, though one of the dealer's is, but you cannot draw any more cards.

Now you have to decide whether to play or fold; in the latter case your ante is lost. To carry on playing, you have to wager double your ante in the box marked 'bet' to see the dealer's hand. If the dealer's hand is less than ace-king high, then he folds and automatically pays the ante bets at even money. The bet wagers are considered 'no action' and returned to the player regardless of their hand. If the dealer's hand is ace-king high or higher, then he calls all bet wagers. If the dealer's hand is higher than yours, he takes both the ante and the bet. If it's lower than yours, he pays the ante at even money and the bet according to the signposted rates, based on your hand. Regardless of the dealer's hand, if your hand qualifies for the progressive jackpot, you will win the appropriate amount for your hand (shared if there is more than one winner).

Let It Ride Poker™: in this game, you are not playing against the dealer or the other players but simply trying to get a good poker hand. To play, you place three equal bets as indicated on the table layout and then get three cards. After looking at your cards, you can ask for your first bet back or 'let it ride'. The dealer then exposes one of his cards, which becomes all of the players' fourth card. At this point you can either ask for your second bet back or again let it ride, after which the dealer exposes another card to complete the five-card hand. Winning hands are then paid according to the payout schedule.

Pai Gow

In this ancient Chinese game, 32 dominoes are shuffled by the dealer and then placed in eight stacks of four each. Up to eight players are dealt one stack. The object of the game is to set the four dominoes into two pairs for the best ranking combinations – most casinos have charts to show the rankings. The house banks the first hand and throws three dice to determine which player gets the first stack of dominoes. The rest are then dealt in rotation. On every winning hand the house keeps 5% of the winnings.

★★★ BRIT TIP ★★★

The average electricity bill for a large Las Vegas casino is around $3 million a year!

7

131

Keno

This game originated in China more than 2,000 years ago but is basically a form of our lottery. You mark anywhere between one and 15 of the 80 numbers on the keno ticket, then place your bet with the keno writer. You then keep a duplicate ticket to match against the 20 numbers drawn by the casino at a set time. All the casinos have their own rules about winning combinations, so check before playing. The alternative to this game is throwing your money in a bin, but the lure is the massive payouts.

Slots

Las Vegas is home to the most sophisticated, state-of-the-art machinery in the world and gamblers get so mesmerised by the idea of their winning line coming up that they spend hours feeding money into these machines. But slot machines are such big business now that they account for around 60% of total casino earnings – and so fill a staggering amount of floor space in the casinos.

Mechanical penny and nickel slot machines that took one coin at a time have been replaced by **computerised dollar slot machines** that can accept multiple coins simultaneously and now feature poker, keno, blackjack, bingo and craps. Some even accept credit card-style gambling and the linking up of machines has led to massive $10-million-and-more jackpots. You can still play for as little as a nickel a go, but some slots now allow you to use $500-dollar tokens – usually in special VIP slot areas!

★ ★ ★   BRIT TIP   ★ ★ ★

★   Only play on machines that tell   ★
★   you the return and look for a   ★
★   99% return on $1 slots.   ★

Progressive slots are machines that are computer-linked to other machines throughout the States and pay out incredible jackpots. One of the progressive slots is known as **Megabucks**, which is computer-linked to other machines in the state of Nevada. The **CircusBucks** progressives start the jackpot climbing at $500,000, but the most recent **Super Megabucks** starts climbing at $10 million! What's more, gamblers can now phone a toll-free number to find out the current jackpot total on Megabucks and seven other progressive slot networks run by International Game Technology. The number is: 888-448 2946.

Video games

These are basically **interactive slot machines** aimed directly at the new generation who grew up with computers and computer games. Multiple-use videos can offer up to 10 games with anything from poker to keno and blackjack, plus regular slot machines and are activated simply by touching the screen. Some machines even allow you to play for a $1 million poker payout with a 25-cent bet! Another reason for the increase in popularity of video games is that you can play at your own pace, without pressure from dealers, croupiers or other players. The returns that you should be looking for on all the different games are as follows:

All-American Poker: also known as Gator Bonus Poker, go for machines that pay 8–1 on full houses, a flush and a straight.

Bonus Deuces: best machines are those paying 20–1 for a wild royal flush, 10–1 on five of a kind and straight flush and 4–1 on four of a kind and a full house.

Deuces Wild: look for a 5–1 payout on four of a kind, which is considerably better than 4–1 for four of a kind that you'll find on many of these video machines.

Double Bonus Poker: find a 10/7 machine – one that pays 10–1 on a full house and 7–1 on a flush.

Flush Attack: do not play on a machine that needs more than three flushes to go into Attack Mode, then look for one that pays 8–1 for a full house and 5–1 on flushes (known as an 8/5 machine).

Jack or Better: look for 9/6 machines, which pay 9–1 for a full house and 6–1 on flushes.

Joker Wild: kings or better. Look for a machine that pays 20–1 for four of a kind, 7–1 for a full house and 5–1 on a flush.

Sports betting

The **Race and Sports Book**, as it is known, gives you the chance to bet on horse races and major sporting events. For horse races you can bet on a win (first place only), a place (first or second) and a show (first, second or third). Further bets include naming the first two horses in any order, naming the first two horses in correct order or the horses that will win any two specified races.

Details of races, the horses and odds are displayed or you can read local newspapers, racing sheets and other publications before making your mind up. Then watch the action on closed-circuit broadcasts live from race tracks across America. The latest innovation in sports betting are proposals for a progressive prize MegaSports jackpot, where the final payout is determined by the amount of betting over a certain period. The prize pools will start at $1 million.

The surge in televised coverage of sporting events in America has also created a surge in sports gambling. During one Super Bowl weekend (held every February), nearly 200,000 visitors flocked to Las Vegas to bet more than $50 million on their favourite team and spent a further $50 million in the city in the process! At **Caesars Palace Race and Sports Book** – the first to open in Las Vegas – they have a total of 50 different ways to part with your cash, including betting on the number of quarterback sacks or the total field goals.

The internet

World Wide Web Casinos predict they will make $100 million a year with their new internet casino. Around 200 players an hour vie for jackpots worth as much as $10 million, climbing to a potential $200 million. The casino will offer home access to gambling on blackjack, craps, video poker, roulette, bingo and three-dimensional, interactive slot machines.

Gambling lessons

Many hotels are linked to the **Players Network**, which you can access through the TV for tips on how to play different games, table etiquette and sports betting. For 'live' classes, try **Caesars Palace**, where you can learn with low-bet table play in a beautiful setting. Craps is taught at 11am and 5pm, roulette at 12 noon, blackjack at 12.15pm and 3.15pm, pai gow poker at 2pm and mini-baccarat at 4pm. You can also ask for lessons in Let It Ride and Caribbean Stud, which are available Monday to Friday.

The **Tropicana** runs free craps lessons at noon and free Caribbean Stud lessons at 11am, both Monday to Friday. The **Imperial Palace School of Gaming** offers free blackjack and

7

craps lessons twice a day, seven days a week. **Circus Circus** runs free blackjack classes at 10.30am and 3pm, roulette classes at 11am and craps classes at 11.30am Monday to Friday in the main casino.

For tips on how to play all the different video poker machines, then it is worth taking the trip to north-west Las Vegas for **Bob Dancer's** weekly lessons at the **Fiesta Casino Hotel** (2400 North Rancho Drive, 702-631 7000). Circus Circus offers free poker lessons at noon Monday to Friday in the poker room and, along with the Tropicana, offers low-bet games that are perfect for beginners! The Tropicana also offers baccarat games for beginners in a youthful yet sophisticated environment.

Comps

The days of casinos just liberally handing out free drinks have gone, though you'll still get one or two if you find the right coupons in the casino's fun book. But you can still get comps on everything from free rooms to food, show tickets, front-row seats and limos, without being a high roller. It's all a question of having the right kind of nerve to demonstrate to the right person – the pit boss – that you are betting enough and playing for long enough to deserve a freebie. You will be automatically categorised by the amount you bet – 'black-action' players, for instance, usually bet $100 a go and 'quarters' ($25), which will 'earn' you different comps.

To qualify for a comp, you'll need a **player's card**, which you can request from the casino as soon as you arrive. A game of blackjack is your best bet and as soon as you sit down at a table ask to be 'rated', presenting your player's card to the pit boss. This effectively starts the clock on your play and the idea from this point is to make it look as if you're placing good bets for as long a period of time as possible, while reducing your risk of losing money by playing as little as possible. In

blackjack you have a 50–50 chance of winning your first hand, so bet $25 – which will give you a decent rating with the pit boss.

★ ★ ★ BRIT TIP ★ ★ ★
The coin trays of slot machines are not anchored to the machine so that the money falls with a 'play-me' tinkling!

Once the floorperson has walked away, bet as little as you can, depending on the table's minimum. Also, don't play every hand. If the dealer is on a winning streak, tell him or her you're going to sit things out until they've busted a couple of times. A natural break in a game is provided when the dealer starts to shuffle and at this point you can whiz off (not forgetting your chips!) to another table out of your pit boss's jurisdiction, though you must always tell them where you're going. Then lay your chips on the table and chat to the dealer, making it look as if you're playing without actually making one bet. After an hour of 'play', take a break, asking the dealer to mark your seat.

It's a pleasant enough way of spending a few hours, but always remember the golden rule of never going beyond the amount of money you have given yourself to play with. Obviously, you'll need to walk around the casino for a while before you start playing so you know which pit bosses cover which tables. Thereafter, it will be down to your ability to act in a natural way!

Deception and subterfuge are not always necessary when it comes to earning freebies, though. Many of the casinos are so determined to foster good relationships with their customers that they have introduced **loyalty cards**, where the amount of play gives you points that can be put towards meals, rooms, shows or even getting cash back. Ask at your hotel, but the following are a few of the best:

★ ★ ★   ★ ★ ★
★   ★
★   ★
★ If you're a regular gambler or plan ★
★ to gamble a lot when in Las Vegas, ★
★   join a slot club and see what   ★
★   deals you're offered. Apart from   ★
★   free drinks, you may get a comp   ★
★   room or even free show tickets.   ★
★ ★ ★ ★ ★ ★ ★ ★ ★ ★ ★ ★ ★ ★ ★ ★ ★

Island Winners' Club: at the Tropicana, this rewards slot, video poker and table game players. Slot and video poker players can earn both comps and cash by inserting their club card into the slot machine. On average, about two hours of play on a dollar slot with maximum coins played on each 'pull' will earn about $10 cash back. Table game players present their card to a floorperson to earn comp credits at blackjack, craps or roulette tables. Credits are based on the average bets and length of time you play.

Play Rio Card: this card, at the Rio Suite Hotel and Casino in Valley View Boulevard at Flamingo Road, will allow you to earn points during both slot and table play towards reduced-price or comp suites, comp dining or tickets to a show. Sign up at the Play Rio Center.

Emperor's Club: the Caesars Palace card awards points based on the amount of play on slot and video poker machines above 25 cents per play, which are redeemable for cash. In addition, members of the club get discounts at selected shops in Appian Way and The Forum Shops and invitations to hotel getaway weekends, themed parties, cocktail receptions with celebrities and free draws for cash prizes. Sign up at either of the two Emperor's Club booths.

Total Gold: with Harrah's card you build up points at the Las Vegas casino and at all Harrah's resorts including those in Tahoe and Atlantic City in New Jersey.

Club Magic: slot players can join at the Las Vegas Hilton to win cash, comps and merchandise based on the amount of play.

Gold Chamber: with this slot and table club at the Luxor you can get a 98.4% return on slot games, plus other comps.

Ringmaster Players' Club: at Circus Circus, this club allows you to build up points through playing slot machines and table games, which can be redeemed for cash. The Ringmaster VIP club allows you to build up credits for free meals and free rooms. In addition, being a member of the club (ask any of the Ringmaster staff for a form) gives you access to excellent room rates, as well as invitations to special events.

The casinos

As much imagination has gone into the decor of the casinos as in every other part of the resort hotels. At the **Luxor** you'll find a sumptuous setting surrounded by the Nile. The **Las Vegas Hilton** continues its *Star Trek: The Experience* theme into its SpaceQuest Casino, where you can part with your cash in a fabulous sci-fi setting. The largest race and sports book is also to be found at the Hilton and if you're having trouble parking, then you can always place your bets at the new drive-up sports book at the **Imperial Palace**! In fact, more casinos would offer the same service but just don't have the space. The manager at the Imperial drive-up says business is always brisk – especially in summer when gamblers prefer to remain in their air-conditioned cars.

You can beat the heat of the summer at the **Tropicana** by swimming up to the blackjack table, open daily 9.30am–5pm. In the indoor area of the resort's indoor-outdoor swimming pool, up to 14 players sit on marble stools up to their hips in water. They play with plastic cards and use either chips or cash. The paper money is kept in mint condition by specially heated rotating drop boxes that dry the cash in less than 60 seconds!

If you want to see how the other half lives, take a sneak look into the VIP high-limit area at the **MGM Grand**. Here high rollers rub cheeks with celebrities in a setting based on the elegance and style of the grand old casinos of Monte Carlo. Tall, classic columns, rose-coloured curtains and cherry wood and suede tables embroidered with the gold MGM Grand monograms are a real sight!

At **Caesars Palace Forum Casino** you can take a break from gambling and have your photo taken with Caesar and Cleopatra as they stroll around with their royal entourage, while the west corridor is home to animatronic Atlantis statues!

The **Excalibur** casino continues its theme with staff dressed in medieval costume and trumpet players blowing on horns straight out of Robin Hood.

The **Las Vegas Hilton Casino** is one of the most beautifully decorated, with marble, rich woods and tier after tier of crystal chandeliers, while the **Race and Sports SuperBook** is the biggest in the city with an impressive array of more than 40 video monitors to screen nearly every major sporting event and race being televised in America at any time. The new *pièce de résistance* is the **SpaceQuest Casino** where gamblers board a futuristic space station that orbits the earth, with space windows that create the illusion of circling the globe from sunrise to sunset.

Downtown casinos

Now home to the last neon signs of what used to be Glitter Gulch city, the Downtown casinos are generally more friendly and relaxed, have cheaper-play slot machines, better returns and more comps. Regular visitors to Las Vegas may like staying at the ritzy, glamorous Strip hotels, but often enjoy a trip Downtown to play on the nickel slot machines.

Binion's Horseshoe, home to the world poker championships, is famous for its single-deck blackjack and liberal rules, single-zero roulette, great odds-on crap, loose nickel and quarter machines and loads of comps. Binion's is also known for its friendly atmosphere, while the **Golden Gate**, another friendly establishment, still serves up its famous 99-cent shrimp (ie huge prawn) cocktail.

You'll find the world's largest regular slot machine at the **Four Queens Hotel** in Downtown. It is the size of a small motorhome and allows six people to play at the same time! The old **Copper Mine** at the **Gold Spike** has many old-time penny slots that are just perfect for people who hate to waste money and the karaoke bar at the **Gold Coast** is excellent for entertainment (locals dressed as stars such as Roy Orbison, Dean Martin and Elvis) and cheap drinks.

The favoured haunt of locals, though, is **Sam's Town** on Boulder Highway (going out towards the Hoover Dam). The free light and laser show is excellent and you'll find great odds on slots and video machines, and good comps.

★ ★ ★   BRIT TIP   ★ ★ ★

★   So many people are so rude,   ★
★ the waitresses always remember ★
★   the nice punters who tip in   ★
★ advance and make sure they get ★
★   their free drinks.   ★

Smoking

The chances of Nevada following California's lead and banning smoking in all indoor public places where food or drink is served is slim to negligible. When one casino adopted a non-smoking policy, it saw a dramatic downturn in business. After lifting the ban three years later it saw an immediate and 'healthy' increase in business!

8 GOING TO THE CHAPEL

Getting married on any type of budget in the wedding capital of the world

Las Vegas has more chapels per square mile and more options on how you tie the knot than any other city in the world – and it's all so easy. Liberal state laws mean that Nevada is one of the few states that does not require a blood test and to get you quickly on your way to the altar, the Marriage License Bureau is open from 8am to midnight – and 24 hours a day on Friday and Saturday.

If you do decide to go ahead, you'll be in star-studded company – this is where Elvis wed Priscilla, Frank Sinatra wed Mia Farrow, Jane Fonda wed Roger Vadim and Paul Newman wed Joanne Woodward. Others include Bruce Willis and Demi Moore, while Brigitte Bardot, Joan Collins, Bing Crosby, Joan Crawford and Judy Garland all said 'I do' at a chapel in Las Vegas.

The rules

Both parties must go to the Marriage License Bureau. You'll find it on the 1st Floor, Clark County Courthouse, 200 South 3rd Street (702-455 4415, co.clark.nv.us) and it's open Monday to Thursday 8am–midnight and continuously from 8am on Friday until midnight on Sunday. (Once the licence has been issued it is valid for one year.)

Minimum age for adults is 18. Those aged 16-17 must have either a parent present at the time the licence is issued or a notarised affidavit.

You will need your passport.

If you have been divorced, you will need to specify the date and place when it became final.

Inside this chapter

Getting married here is so simple that 280 couples wed every day in the city – an amazing 110,000 a year. The most popular day is Valentine's Day, closely followed by New Year's Eve.

★ ★ ★ **BRIT TIP** ★ ★ ★

★ Avoid Valentine's Day unless you ★
★ want to queue for four hours to ★
★ get your licence! ★

And you can do it all in such style. Dress up as a medieval prince and princess at the Canterbury Chapel in the Excalibur, allow an Elvis impersonator to wed you at Graceland Wedding Chapel or try any of the other themes available from Star Trek to gangsters and rock 'n' roll. Then again, you could decide to make your vows before diving off a bungee-jump platform, soaring high above Las Vegas in a hot-air balloon or flying over the Grand Canyon. You can even stay in your car at the world's first ever drive-up wedding chapel or try the new Tunnel of Love chapel at A Little White Chapel on the Strip.

It costs $55 for a marriage licence, which must be paid in cash, and $35 for the ceremony. A very basic package starts at $100, but the sky's the limit depending on where you wed, what you do and the accessories you choose.

Ceremonies

Like every other aspect of Las Vegas, the business of helping people to tie the knot is booming.

Hotel ceremonies tend to be more ostentatious than those at ordinary chapels, but they have prices to match, too! Like the lucky bride who won the opening wedding at **Caesars Palace**'s Neptune Villa: you could be carried on a velvet sedan chair by four centurions to the fountain entrance of Caesars Palace to be greeted by Caesar and Cleopatra before being escorted to the chapel. The decor is amazing, featuring a two-storey double balustrade staircase encircling a koi pond and rising to a wood-panelled foyer that is framed by exotic fish in a saltwater aquarium. Inside the chapel, the ceremony area is draped with sheer white chiffon and the walls feature a hand-painted mural of ancient Roman ruins under beautiful blue skies. All the pomp and circumstance of the old Roman Empire – and all for just $5,000.

Not quite as expensive, but definitely unusual are the packages at the **MGM Grand** in addition to the ceremonies at their two chapels, the Legacy and the Cherish. The first allows couples to take their vows at the top of the 250-ft (76-metre) Sky Screamer before descending into a 100-ft (30-metre) freefall dive at speeds of up to 70mph (113kph). The second is getting married in the trendy Studio 54 nightclub to the sounds of the 1970s. The third is to get wed on the set of the stage spectacular EFX near a mystical waterfall with Merlin presiding.

Wedding Queen of the West

The most famous chapels in town are the **Little White Chapels** (1301 Las Vegas Blvd, 702-382 5943 www.alittlewhitechapel.com) owned by Charolette Richards, dubbed the 'Wedding Queen of the West'. In her time she has married celebs including Joan Collins, Patty Duke and Bruce Willis.

Her ever-growing empire of chapels includes A Little White Chapel, the Drive-Up Wedding Window, A Little White Chapel in the Sky for balloon weddings, the We've Only Just Begun Wedding Chapel in the Imperial Palace Hotel and the Chapel by the Courthouse. She also owns two of the newest in town – the Tunnel of Love drive-through chapel at A Little White Chapel on the Strip and the Speedway to Love Wedding Chapel for those wishing to get married at the Speedway.

In 1991, Charolette noticed a disabled couple having difficulty getting out of their car to go into her chapel so she hit upon the idea of a drive-up window. It became such a novelty that all kinds of couples began queueing up for the drive-through wedding. They come on motorcycles, rollerskates, in cars, limos, trucks, taxis and even boats!

Now it includes a Tunnel of Love in which couples are surrounded by floating cherubs, twinkling stars, birds on ribbons and signs everywhere saying 'I love you, I want you, I need you and I can't live without you' as you drive through the 14-ft (4-metre) high tunnel. You have been warned!

Charolette also has a Braveheart-themed wedding ceremony in which costumed couples can tie the knot by moonlight in secluded woodland.

At A Little White Chapel you pay anything from $179 for the Economy package that includes a candlelight ceremony, music, four photographs and corsage and buttonhole to $579 for the Joan Collins Special, which includes the candlelight ceremony, music, photographs, bridal bouquets, corsages, buttonholes, garter, champagne glasses, lithograph marriage certificate, video recording, wedding cake and an etched marriage scroll. All the packages include a courtesy limousine service from your hotel to the Marriage License Bureau, on to A Little White Chapel and back to your hotel. The chapel fee is $55, drive-up weddings cost $40, gazebo weddings $55, hot-air balloon weddings start at $1000 and helicopter weddings start at $750. You can also arrange for a video recording at $69, photos at $75 and gown and tuxedo rentals from $100.

Another great place to try is the **Divine Madness Fantasy Wedding Chapel**, recently opened by a Californian designer who has made customised clothes for 22 years. Here you can choose from the simple shotgun wedding for £100, through to getting married in costume as Tarzan and Jane, Caesar and Cleopatra, Romeo and Juliet or Rhett Butler and Scarlet O'Hara among others. Complete costume rental costs between $80 and $250 per person.

At the Excalibur you can get married in the gazebo at the **Canterbury Wedding Chapel**. Here a renewal wedding package costs $250 for the ceremony, music, one red rose, photo and bottle of champagne, while the wedding packages go from $350 to $1,200 – the latter includes room, dinner and breakfast.

Packages at the **Island Wedding Chapel** at the Tropicana start at $399 for the Aloha package and rise to $3499 for the Blue Hawaii, which includes a five-night stay at the hotel.

Ceremonies at the **Flamingo Hilton's Garden Chapel** go from $369 to $1,200, the latter including a mini-suite for one night, pianist at the ceremony, breakfast in bed, dinner and tickets for the cocktail performance of the *Rockettes*.

In addition to the chapels there are several very good wedding specialists.

Co-ordinators

A Viva Las Vegas Wedding

(702-384 0771, www.vivalasvegasweddings.com) arranges an extraordinary number of differently themed weddings from Star Trek to Elvis and rock 'n' roll.

With **Intergalactic**, your special day is presided over by Captain James T Quirk or Captain Schpock in the **Starship Chapel**, surrounded by life-size cut-outs of your favourite characters. The package comes with a Minister Transporter, an illusion entrance, theatrical lighting and lots of fog for $700.

The rock 'n' roll theme takes place in the **Rock 'n' Roll Chapel**, complete with memorabilia and an electric guitar version of the Wedding March, while a rock star impersonator will sing during the ceremony for $650.

The **Camelot** theme includes Merlin or King Arthur as the minister, while you'll be treated like a king and queen. The basic package costs $700 and includes period music, knights, trumpeters and fair ladies. For an extra $100 you can have a soloist perform a medieval tune.

The Las Vegas package includes showgirls, keno runners, cocktail waitresses, card dealers and a Las Vegas-style singer/minister, plus theatrical lights and fog. It costs $650 and for another $250 you can even have Elvis or Marilyn Monroe at your wedding. Other packages include the **Victorian** ($600), the **Disco** ($650) and the **Beach Party** ($650).

Elvis in Blue Hawaii has an Elvis impersonator and dancers from the Tropicana's Folies Bergères at your ceremony, which takes place in the **Elvis Chapel**. In addition to all the Elvis memorabilia, Hawaiian sets, showgirls and hula dancers, there will be theatrical lighting and fog, while 'Elvis' will sing *Love Me Tender, Viva Las Vegas* and *I Can't Help Falling In Love With You* ($700).

8

A–Z of Wedding Chapels

A Chapel by the Courthouse: 203 East Bridger Avenue, 702-384 9099, www.achapelbythecourthouse.com
A Las Vegas Wedding Chapel: 727 South 9th, 702-383 5909
A Little Chapel of Roses: 814 Las Vegas Blvd S, 702-382 9404
A Little Chapel of the Flowers: 301 Las Vegas Blvd S, 702-382 5943, www.alittlechapel.com
A Little White Chapel at the Speedway: North Las Vegas, 702-382 5943, www.alittlewhitechapel.com
A Little White Chapel in the Sky: 1301 Las Vegas Blvd S, 702-382 5943, www.alittlewhitechapel.com
A San Francisco Sally's Victorian Chapel: 1304 Las Vegas Blvd S, 702-385 7777
A Scenic Wedding: PO Box 80601, 702-873 8316, www.vegasvows/ascenicwedding/
A Special Memory Wedding Chapel: 800 South 4th Street and Gass, 702-384 2211, www.aspecialmemory.com
A Wedding on Wheels: 1301 Las Vegas Blvd S, 702-382 5943, www.alittlewhitechapel.com
All Religions Wedding Chapel: 2855 Las Vegas Blvd S, 702-735 4179
Bally's Celebration Wedding Chapel: 3645 Las Vegas Blvd S, 702-894 5222, www.ballyschapel.com
Bellagio (The Wedding Chapels at): 3600 Las Vegas Blvd S, 702-791 7111, www.bellagiolasvegas.com
Candlelight Wedding Chapel: 2855 Las Vegas Blvd S, 702-735 4179, www.candlelightchapel.com
Canterbury Weddings: Excalibur Hotel on the Strip, 702-597 7777, www.excaliburlasvegas.com
Chapel of the Bells: 2233 Las Vegas Blvd S, 702-735 6803, www.chapelofthebellslasvegas.com
Chapel of Dreams: 316 Brideger Av, Suite 103, 702-471 7729, www.lasvegasweddingchapelofdreams.com
Chapel of Love: 1431 Las Vegas Blvd S, 702-387 0155, www.chapel-of-love.com
Chapel of the Fountains: Circus Circus Hotel 2880 Las Vegas Blvd S, 702-794 3777, www.circuscircus-lasvegas.com
Chaplain at Large: 1301 Las Vegas Blvd S, 702-382 5943
China Town Wedding Temple: 4215 Spring Mountain Rd, 702-252 0400
Cupid's Wedding Chapel: 827 Las Vegas Blvd S, 702-598 4444, www.cupidswedding.com
Divine Madness Fantasy Wedding Chapel: 1111 Las Vegas Blvd S, Suite H, 702-384 5660 or toll-free on 1-800 717 4734
Drive Up Wedding Window: 1301 Las Vegas Blvd S, 702-382 5943, www.alittlewhitechapel.com
El Caribe: 2800 West Sahara 83656 Pecos-Mcleod, 702-382 5943, www.elcaribe.com
Emerald Gardens: 891 Las Vegas Blvd S, 702-242 5700, www.emeraldgarden.com
Flamingo Hilton Garden Chapel: 3555 Las Vegas Blvd S, 702-733 3111
Forever Grand Wedding Chapel at the MGM Grand: 3799 Las Vegas Blvd S, 702-891 7984, www.mgmgrand.com
Graceland Wedding Chapel: 6195 Las Vegas Blvd S, 702-474 6655, www.gracelandchapel.com
Harrah's Las Vegas: 3475 Las Vegas Blvd S, 702-369 5000, www.harrahs.com

Hartland Mansion and Café: 525 Park Paseo Drive, 702-387 6700
Heritage Wedding Chapel: 1 South Main Street, 702-313 9333
Hitching Post Wedding Chapel: 1737 Las Vegas Blvd S, 1-800 572 5530,
   www.hitchingpostweddingchapel.com
Island Wedding Chapel: Tropicana Hotel 3801 Las Vegas Blvd S, 702-739
   2451, www.tropicanalv.com
Jet Helicopter Weddings: 3712 Las Vegas Blvd S, 702-736 0013
L'Amour Chapel: 1901 Las Vegas Blvd S, 702-369 5683
Las Vegas Helicopters Inc: 3724 Las Vegas Blvd S, 702-736 0013
Las Vegas Villa: 4982 Shirley Street, 702-795 8119, www.lasvegasvilla.com
Las Vegas Garden of Love Wedding Chapel: 200 West Sahara Avenue, 702-
   385 5683, www.lvgardenoflove.com
Las Vegas Wedding Reservations: 4036 Adelphi Avenue, 702-435 7922
Little Church of the West: 4617 Las Vegas Blvd S, 702-739 7971,
   www.littlechurchlv.com
Long Fung Wedding Temple: 4215 Spring Mountain Rd, 702-252 0400
Monte Carlo: 3770 Las Vegas Blvd S, 702-730 7777, www.monte-carlo.com
Mount Charleston Hotel and Restaurant: 2 Kyle Canyon Road, Mount
   Charleston, 702-872 5500 or toll-free on 1-800 794 3456,
   www.mtcharlestonhotel.com
Neptune's Villa at Caesars Palace: 3570 Las Vegas Blvd S, 702-731 7110,
   www.lasvegastourism.com/ceasars.htm
New York-New York Hotel: 3790 Las Vegas Blvd S, 702-740 6969,
   www.nynyhotelcasino.com
Orleans Hotel and Casino: 4500 West Tropicana, 702-365 7111,
   www.orleanscasino.com
Paris Las Vegas (Wedding Chapels at): 3645 Las Vegas Blvd S, 702-967
   4611, www.paris-lv.com
Rainbow Gardens: 4125 West Charleston, 702-878 4646,
   www.ilv.com/rainbowgardens
Rio Hotel and Casino: 3700 West Flamingo 702-247 7986
Riviera Wedding Chapel: The Riviera Hotel on the Strip, 702-794 9494,
   www.theriviera.com
Sherwood Forest: 7768 West Sahara Avenue, 702-256 3202
Silver Bell Wedding Chapel: 607 Las Vegas Blvd S, 702-382 3726,
   www.silverbell.com
Speedway to Love Wedding Chapel: 4243 North Las Vegas Blvd, 702-644
   3000
Sunset Gardens: 3931 East Sunset Road, 702-456 9986
The Wedding Chapel: Treasure Island Hotel 3300 Las Vegas Blvd S, 702-894
   7111 or toll-free on 1-800 288 7206, www.treasureisland.com
The Wedding Room at the Cellar: 3601 West Sahara, 702-362 6712
Treasure Island at the Mirage: 3300 Las Vegas Blvd S, 702-894 7111,
   www.treasureisland.com
Tropical Gardens: 3808 East Tropicana Avenue, 702-434 4333
Valley Outreach Synagogue: 1692 Long Horizon Lane, 702-436 4901,
   www.valleyoutreach.com
Victoria's Wedding Chapel: 2800 West Sahara, 702-257 7303,
   www.avictorias.com
Wee Kirk o' the Heather: 231 Las Vegas Blvd S, 702-382 9830,
   www.weekirk.com
We've Only Just Begun Wedding Chapel: Imperial Palace 3535 Las Vegas
   Blvd S, 702-733 0011 www.imperialpalace.com

8

At the **Gangster Chapel**, you'll step back in time to a 1940s Mafioso shotgun wedding where the Godfather/minister opens the door to wedded bliss accompanied by two bodyguards and a waiter/soloist singing in Italian ($650). There's also **Bond** wedding ceremony for $1100, which includes a limousine pick up by Bond baddie Odd Job, two dancing Bond girls and a ceremony performed by a 007 impersonator who arrives by sports car.

Wedding Dreams of Las Vegas

(1-888 2 WED N LV, www.weddingdreams.com) provides a comprehensive series of packages.

You can get married in the great outdoors of the **Red Rock Canyon** and even have an Elvis impersonator to provide the music. The price of $499 includes the minister, photos and flowers, while a limo service and 'Elvis' will cost extra. For $699 you can take a **night flight** over the lights of the Las Vegas Strip, have photographs and a video recording of the event as the minister conducts the service in mid-air. Or you can take a one-hour day flight over the **Grand Canyon** with a videographer. It'll cost you $1846 plus tax!

A beautifully romantic high-flying option is the **sunrise balloon flight** with champagne and hors d'oeuvres at $675. If you want a photographer to go up with you that will cost $1,275 and you can have guests at $150 per person.

For daredevils, there is the **Take The Plunge** bungee-jumping option at $499. You take your vows at the top of the 175-ft (53-metre) tower before taking the plunge. Skydivers will be in heaven with **New Beginnings** option ($1,200) which includes private use of a passenger jet liner, jump masters, minister, photos and a video.

Romantics may prefer to get married by the **four lakes** north of the Strip. The basic price of $549 includes minister, photos, bouquets and flowers, and optional extras

include live music, a video and an Elvis impersonator. For an intimate affair, try the **private limo wedding** in which you'll also get champagne ($375) or get married in the privacy of a hotel room or suite for $499. For another $150 you can have a cake and non-alcoholic champagne reception for 15 people in your room.

Las Vegas Host

(2680 Chandler Avenue, Suite 7B, 702-798 5246, www.lasvegashost.com) offers a full service for weddings at three different chapels in Las Vegas. There are five packages to choose from at the pretty **Victorian Little Chapel of the Flowers**, ranging from $195 to $3,150. Here you'll find a cosy atmosphere that includes polished brass chandeliers, etched glass and burnished cherry-wood with Impressionist paintings.

At the romantic **Candlelight Wedding Chapel**, there are four packages ranging from $179 to $499. Opened in 1967 (historic by Las Vegas standards!), this is the only free-standing chapel in the heart of the hotel district on the Strip and is where Whoopi Goldberg, Bette Midler and Michael Caine were wed.

The **Viva Las Vegas Wedding Chapel**, complete with fountain, silk trees and flowers and twinkling fairylights, provides the setting for the ultimate fantasy wedding. Packages start from $125, and include Elvis and other themed ceremonies.

Las Vegas Weddings and Room Coordinators

(2770 South Maryland Parkway, Suite 416, 702-737 6800, www.lasvegasweddings.com) can book your rooms and organise every aspect of your wedding. Open 24/7, they arrange flowers, transport, clothes, reception and entertainments. They have 17 chapels and themes include Elvis and nature weddings.

Or you can choose to take one of the packages arranged by tour operators from Britain (page 182).

GAY LAS VEGAS

A full guide to restaurants, bars and clubs

Surprisingly, for a city that claims to be so adult, there is relatively little available for gays and you have the Mormon history of Las Vegas to thank for that. Nevadan anti-sodomy laws were only repealed in 1995 and many local gays still prefer to stay in the closet. Yet the annual **Gay Pride Parade** in April or May (call 702-733 9800 for details) is testimony to the presence of a gay community.

Gay & Lesbian Center

A good place to start is probably the Gay & Lesbian Center at 912 East Sahara Avenue between 6th Street and Maryland Parkway, 702-733 9800, www.gayvegas.com. Open from Monday to Friday 10am– 7.30pm, call ahead for schedules. It is a relatively new building and a new meeting point for gays. The Center's website is very helpful.

★ ★ ★ **BRIT TIP** ★ ★ ★
★ ★
★ ★
★ Like New York, a lot of ★
★ mainstream clubs, shows and ★
★ restaurants have become popular ★
★ hangouts for members of the gay ★
★ community. ★
★ ★ ★ ★ ★ ★ ★ ★ ★ ★ ★ ★ ★ ★ ★ ★ ★ ★ ★

The Gay Triangle

Get Booked at the Paradise Plaza, 4640 Paradise at Naples Drive, 702-737 7780, is a bookstore at the heart of the **Gay Triangle** at the corner of Naples Drive and Paradise Road, just south of Hard Rock Café. It is open Monday to Thursday 10am–midnight, Friday 10am–2am, Saturday noon to 2am and Sunday noon to midnight. The Gay Triangle

Inside this chapter

area has several bars, Get Booked and the **Mariposa** coffee house. Pick up copies of the two free monthly gay papers – *Las Vegas Bugle* and *Q-Tribe* – at any of those locations.

Accommodation

Blue Moon Resort

2651 Westwood Drive, just off the Strip
Website: www.bluemoonlv.com
Reservations: 702-361 9099
Fax: 702-361 9110
Room rates: from $89 Monday to Thursday and from $139 Friday to Sunday.
The $3.1 million Blue Moon Resort opened in December 2002 providing a full-service gay resort for men only. Amenities include a Jacuzzi Grotto with 10-ft (3-metre) waterfalls to relax and enjoy the sun, a lagoon-style pool and sundeck with a clothing optional area, plus a steam room.
 Parlor suites provide 800sq ft (74sq metres) of space that are ideal for small meetings, entertaining guests or simply watching the TV and have large beds and armoires, large TVs, cable TV and electronic door locks.

Riviera

2901 The Strip at Riviera Boulevard, 702-734 5110
The most openly gay hotel on the Strip, it is the home of La Cage, a top drag show starring Frank Marino as Joan Rivers.

The Ranch

1110 Ralston Drive, near Martin Luther King Boulevard, 702-631 7708
It's expensive and doesn't take credit cards, but is run by lesbians.

Lucky You

702-384 1129
An exclusively gay B&B just two blocks from the Strip within walking distance of gay bars. Well priced but no credit cards accepted.

Cafés

Garlic Café

Decatur Twain Shopping Center, 3650 South Decatur Boulevard, 702-221 0266
The only openly gay-owned café in town, you choose the strength of garlic. It's always busy and serves great food. Open daily 5pm–10pm.

Mariposa

Paradise Plaza, 4643 Paradise Road, at Naples Drive, 702-650 9009
Located in the heart of the Gay Triangle, this is a fun and friendly place with patio seating and great food. Open daily 3pm–3am.

Clubs and Bars

All are open 24 hours a day.

Angles & Lace

4633 Paradise Road at Naples, 702-733 9677
Consists of two bars – Angles for men and Lace for women. Usually the crowd starts here and migrates across the street to the Gipsy.

Apollo Spa

953 East Sahara Avenue, 702-650 9191
Filled with the young, hip and vibrant.

Backdoor Lounge

1415 East Charleston Boulevard, 702-385 2018
Has a Happy Hour every night from 5pm to 7pm. Monday night a free poker party starts at 7pm and there is a free barbecue on Saturday nights at 6pm.

Backstreet Bar & Grill

5012 South Arville Road, about 1 mile (1.6km) west of the Strip on Tropicana, 702-876 1844
Home of the Gay Rodeo Association and probably the friendliest bar in town, the best times to visit are Sunday around 4pm and Tuesday and Thursdays around 7pm when the line-dancing classes get going.

Badlands Saloon

953 East Sahara Avenue, inside the Commercial Center, 702-792 9262
A Country & Western bar, so wear a cowboy hat after 9pm!

Brewed Awakening

2305 East Sahara Avenue, 702-733 9677
With Dick Plummer on Monday and Tuesdays.

The Buffalo

4640 Paradise Road, opposite Angles, 702-733 8355
A Levis and leather club and home of the Satyricons Motorcycle Club.

Cobalt

900 East Karen Avenue, 702-696 0226
A relatively recent arrival on the gay scene.

The Eagle

3430 East Tropicana, about 4 miles (6km) east of the Strip, 702-458 8662
Levis and leather club, famous for its Wednesday Underwear Night.

Flex Lounge

4371 West Charleston Boulevard, 702-385 3539
A great mixed club with drink specials, dancing and live music.

The Freezone

610 East Naples, 702-794 2300
All-round bar with restaurant. Tuesday is the Ladies 4 Ladies revue night, Thursday the all-male revue for Boys Night and What a Drag! is held on Friday and Saturday.

Gipsy II

4605 Paradise Road one block south of the Hard Rock, 702-731 5171
The hottest gay nightclub in town is the revamped version of Gipsy. Open 10pm–dawn.

Good Time Bar & Grill

1775 East Tropicana, 702-736 9494
Happy Hours from 5am to 7am and 5pm to 7pm. Monday is the most popular. No credit cards.

Hamburger Mary's

4503 Paradise Road, 702-735 4400
A popular joint in the Paradise Road enclave.

Ikon of Las Vegas

4633 Paradise Road, 702-791 0100
A great place for guys who want to party.

Inferno

3340 Highland Drive at West Desert Inn Road, 702-734 7336
Mixed club with go-go boys and a Latino night every Thursday. $5 after 10pm.

Keys

100 East Sahara Avenue, 702-731 2200

Las Vegas's first piano bar featuring sing-along entertainment – considered the hottest piano bar in town.

Las Vegas Lounge

900 East Karen Avenue, 702-737 9350
A hip joint for guys.

The Spotlight, Commercial Center

957 East Sahara Avenue, 702-696 0202
Eclectic working-class bar.

Snick's Place

1402 South 4th Street, 702-385 9298
For the mature crowd. Sunday morning from 9am to noon is time for a Bloody Mary special.

Tropical Island

3430 East Tropicana, 702-456 5525. A ladies' bar.

Gay nights

Ibiza USA

Desert Passage at the Aladdin, 702-836 0830
Check out The Room, an alternative lifestyle promotion, held next to Ibiza every Saturday night. The Room is a lounge-style setting tailored for the gay crowd, but comfortable enough for all guests. Doors open at 11pm and admission is $10.

Also at Ibiza USA, Gay and Lesbian night is every Thursday.

10 ATTRACTIONS

Thrill rides, children's attractions, museums and animal habitats

Yes, there really is more to Las Vegas than bright lights and gambling dens. There are a whole host of attractions that appeal to people of all ages, some amazing thrill rides and even a little – overpriced – culture in the form of art museums.

The high-tech wizardry that can be seen in so many nightclubs and production shows is also put to use in heart-thumping simulator rides and 3-D movies. And there is a raft of museums that celebrate aspects of the city's history and people including Liberace, Elvis and the Las Vegas Natural History Museum, while animals can be seen at several resort hotels and the local zoo.

THRILLS AND SPILLS
Conventional Rides

The Adventuredome Theme Park

Circus Circus, 702-794 3939
The desert may be scorching hot outside, but here in this 5-acre (2-ha), fully enclosed elevated theme park – the largest space-frame dome in America – the temperature stays a comfortable 22°C (72°F) year round. Grand Slam Canyon is designed to look like a desert with a large rock canyon that gives way to caverns, pinnacles and steep cliffs, while a stream flows gently through the lush landscape. But this canyon is home to prehistoric creatures – well, life-sized replicas of them at least – who make themselves known between two 140-ft (43-metre) peaks, a fossil wall, archaeological dig and a replica of an Indian cliff dwelling.
Thrill rides: the Canyon Blaster is the only indoor, double-loop, double-

Inside this chapter

corkscrew roller-coaster in America, and sends you careening between canyon walls at 55mph (88kph).

The new two-minute long **Inverter** involves a 360-degree rotation in which you are held upside down with only a harness and a T-bar separating you from the concrete floor 50ft (15 metres) below.

Also new is **Chaos**, which twirls and whirls you anti-clockwise, backwards and upside down on a circular platform amid the tracks of the Canyon Blaster. Lasting two minutes, it creates a 3-D effect as you rise, tilt and spin all at the same time, and due to the variation in speed and motion, no two rides are the same.

The **Rim Runner** is a more relaxing ride, taking you on a scenic journey

★ ★ ★   **BRIT TIP**   ★ ★ ★

Save the Rim Runner thrill ride until the end of your Adventuredome visit as you will get soaked!

through botanical landscaping before plunging over a heart-stopping 60-ft (18-metre) waterfall.

All in all there are 19 rides and attractions in the Adventuredome including **Hot Shots Laser**, where sharpshooters take part in a high-tech war, bumper cars and a swinging ship, plus an IMAX simulator thrill ride (see page 148). Younger children are well catered for from plane and train rides to bumper-mobiles, plus strolling entertainers who juggle, mime and do magic tricks.

Open: daily from 10am. It closes at 6pm from Monday to Thursday, midnight on Friday and Saturday and 8pm on Sundays, though exact hours may vary according to the seasons so phone in advance.

Tickets: the main thrill rides cost $5 each, the large rides cost $4 each, the junior rides $3 each or you can buy an All Day Ride Pass at $13.95 for people 33–48in (84–122cm) tall, and $19.95 for those above 4ft (122cm). Children under 33in (84cm) ride free with an adult.

Adventure Canyon at Buffalo Bill's

Buffalo Bill's Hotel, 31900 South Las Vegas Boulevard, Primm, 702-679 7433 or 1-800 FUN STOP

For amazing thrill rides on a Wild West theme head to Buffalo Bill's in Primm, which is just 35 miles (56km) south of Las Vegas on Interstate 15.

Thrill rides: America's tallest and fastest roller-coaster **Desperado** has a top speed of around 90mph (145kph) and creates a G-force of nearly four. A high-speed dive down a 55-degree hill into a tunnel starts the ride and is then followed by a 155-ft (47-metre) second hill, which leads to a zero-gravity sensation.

Turbo Drop creates a similar sensation to flying straight towards the ground in a jet fighter. Riders are nestled in padded saddles and shoulder harnesses, lifted 200ft (60 metres) up in the air and plunged to earth at 45mph (72kph), creating

positive G-forces close to 4.5.

Other rides: the **Adventure Canyon Log Flume** starts as a classic flume ride with a 35-ft (11-metre) drop, but once you splash down, you continue through an electronic shooting gallery that follows the park's Wild West theme. You take out a pistol as targets are lit up along the way, then if you shoot a bad guy you get points and if you shoot a good guy you lose points! There are plenty of other rides to make your visit worthwhile, plus the **Ghost Town Motion Theaters**.

Open: Monday to Thursday noon–8pm, Friday and Saturday 10am–midnight and Sunday 10am–8pm.

Tickets: the Desperado and Turbo Drop cost $5 each, the log flume $4 and the motion theatres $3 or you can pay $33 for a full-day wristband or $25 for a half-day wristband.

Manhattan Express

New York-New York, 1-800 NYFORME.

Based on the kind of roller coaster that made Coney Island in the real New York so famous, this ride twists, loops and dives around the perimeter and even through the New York-New York hotel. It has the world's first heart-line twist and dive that simulates the sensation felt by a pilot during a barrel roll in an airplane when the centre of rotation actually becomes the same as your centre of gravity! Incidentally, the Manhattan Express has been voted Best Thrill Ride in Nevada by *Nevada Magazine*'s reader survey.

Open: Sunday to Thursday 11am–11pm and Friday and Saturday 11am–11.30pm, weather permitting.

Tickets: $12 per person, second ride $5 or all-day pass $25.

Speed: The Ride and Cyber Speedway

The Sahara Hotel, 702-737 7223
Speed: The Ride is the fastest roller-coaster in Las Vegas and literally

10

slingshots riders at speeds of up to 70mph (112kph). You go through breathtaking loops as you zip your way around the Sahara before repeating the experience in reverse!

Cyber Speedway: you really are in the driving seat on this fun ride. Driving an almost real-sized racing car, you speed around a track modelled on the Las Vegas Motor Speedway at speeds of up to 22mph (35kph) doing seven laps in all against up to seven other drivers.
Open: Monday to Thursday 11am–8pm, Friday and Saturday 10am–11pm, Sunday 10am–8pm.
Tickets: $15 for one ride or $17.95 for a combination package for all-day rides on both attractions.

Stratosphere Tower

Stratosphere Hotel, 702-380 7777 or 1-800 99 TOWER

The **Big Shot** thrusts 16 passengers 160ft (50 metres) into the air along the 228-ft (70-metre) spire at speeds of around 45mph (72kph), producing up to four Gs with negative Gs on the way back down. What is so scary about the ride is not just the speed and force of it all, but the fact that you are so high up in the air in the first place!

Another great ride is the **High Roller** roller-coaster, one of the highest in the world, and the newest ride on the block is **Project X Sky**, an extreme ride that literally takes you over the edge. In an open, floorless vehicle that is attached to a pivoting track, eight passengers are propelled 27ft (8 metres) over the side of the Tower at 30mph (48kph) – repeatedly racing back and forth over the edge.
Open: Sunday to Thursday 10am–1am, Friday and Saturday 10am–2pm.
Tickets: Tower $8, Big Shot $8, High Roller $5; Tower with both rides $17 and an All Day Tower Package $19.95. Project X Sky is expected to cost around $7 per ride.

Simulator Rides and 3-D Movies

Circus Circus IMAX 3-D

Adventuredome Theme Park, 702-794 3939

In **Fun House Express** an amusement park trolley runs off the track and into the depths of a clown's rooms where riders get a horrifying and hilarious insight into the world of clowns.
ReBoot the Ride is a thrilling adventure inside the internet. During the test launch of a new search engine, Megabyte, a nasty virus, threatens to destroy riders and is aided and abetted by Hack and Slash until Bob the gatekeeper comes to the rescue.
Open: 10am–midnight.
Tickets: $5 per ride. You must be over 42in (106cm) tall. All-day passes for the Adventuredome are also available (see page 146).

The Pharaoh's Pavilion

The Luxor, 702-262 4555

The Pavilion is home to a whole series of attractions including two IMAX movie theatres, one IMAX ridefilm, The Tomb & Museum of King Tutankhamun and a virtual reality roller-coaster.
IMAX Ridefilm: Adventures in Motion In Search of the Obelisk tells the story of how a spectacular subterranean civilization was discovered below ground during excavation works to build the Luxor hotel. As you arrive at an archaeological dig it is apparent that evil forces are at work and before long you are taken on a high-speed chase twisting and turning through vast, cavernous areas.

In **Dracula's Haunted Castle: The Ride** the action starts on a dark and stormy night outside a foreboding castle. Two huge wooden doors creak open and an eerie-looking butler appears. You are then carried down dark hallways lit only by lanterns at break-neck speeds with horrifying skeletons jumping out and attacking you with swords and flying bats heading straight for your face!

Fun House Express is the relatively tame story of a ride into the spooky, crazy, underground world of Jimmy the Clown, which will delight children of all ages.
Open: daily 9am–11pm, *In Search of Obelisk* is alternated with *Fun House Express* every few minutes.
Tickets: one pass covers the lot for $24.95.
IMAX Theatre: Current 3-D films include: **The Matrix Reloaded**, which follows the story of Neo (Keanu Reeves) as he begins to master his new powers while protecting the last human enclave on Earth from the dreaded Sentinel machines.

In **Space Station**, a lab on an international space station 250 miles (400km) above Earth is used to study the effects of space travel on the human body and develop drugs to beat diseases such as cancer.

In **Haunted Castle** young musician Johnny is summoned to a mysterious castle. Despite the grim gargoyles on the exterior, he steps inside where a group of knights in armour threaten to attack. Mephisto intervenes and leads him to the evil Mr D who promises eternal youth in exchange for his soul.

Movies change but at the time of going to press *Into The Deep* and *Grand Canyon – The Hidden Secrets* were included.
Open: cinema hours vary but are normally 9am–midnight daily.
Tickets: you can reserve tickets in advance, but you have to reconfirm times on the day. *The Matrix* costs $14, all other films $8.95. Films are not suitable for children under three.

Merlin's Magic Motion Machines

The Excalibur, 702-597 7084
A series of hilarious rides produced by Iwerks Entertainment. In **House of Superstition** you are taken on a spooky roller-coaster ride by Elvira, Mistress of the Dark, in **7th Portal**, you experience a comic adventure

and **Warriors of the Dawn** is a Greek mythology adventure.
Open: daily 11am–11pm.
Tickets: $4 per ride.

★★★ **BRIT TIP** ★★★
★   ★
★   ★
★   The Merlin Magic Motion   ★
★   Machines offer the best-value ★
★   simulator rides on the Strip. ★
★★★★★★★★★★★★★★★★★★★★★★

Race for Atlantis

The Forum Shops at Caesars Palace, 702-733 9000
The world's first giant-screen IMAX 3-D motion simulator ride is a teeth-rattling, hair-raising, computer-animated chariot race through the legendary kingdom. Passengers are 'chosen by gods' to race against a fierce field of competitors – including Neptune, the reigning monarch, and Ghastlius, champion of evil – in a fight to the finish that will determine the ruler of Atlantis for the next millennium. Launched into action by a giant catapult, riders have to dodge evil villains, fantastic obstacles and crashing competitors as 3-D computer-animated visuals take you careening through beautiful vistas and plunging into the depths of the sea.
Open: Sunday to Thursday 10am–11pm, Friday and Saturday 10am–midnight.
Tickets: adults $10, students and seniors $9 and under 12 $7.

Star Trek: The Experience™

Las Vegas Hilton, 3000 Paradise Road, 702-732 5111
Prepare to be beamed up in the $70-million Star Trek ride where you will be transported aboard the *USS Enterprise* and venture on the famous bridge before travelling on a TurboLift and speeding along the Grand Corridor. As you arrive, systems go awry and you are taken on a space adventure in which the Klingons attack the ship. *Star Trek* stars appearing in the film include

10

Jonathan Frakes as Commander William Riker and LeVar Burton and Geordi LaForge.

The promenade in **Star Trek: Deep Space Nine®** been completely re-created here, where you can eat at **Quark's Bar and Restaurant** and even meet Ferengi, Klingons and other interplanetary visitors. A **History of the Future** exhibit claims to have the largest permanent collection of *Star Trek* props and costumes in the world.

Open: daily 11am–11pm.
Tickets: all-day passes cost $24.99 adults, $21.99 for seniors and children under 12. Museum only $14.99. Minimum height 42in (106cm).

Theaters of Sensation

The Venetian, 702-414 4500
A selection of five thrilling 3-D movies presented in two cinemas. The bumpiest is **Time Traveller: The 3-D Ride**, which at eight-and-a-half minutes is the longest motion-adventure in Las Vegas. You are taken back in time to a secret carnival in Venice from where you travel to Egypt to try to defeat the curse of King Tut's Tomb. **Escape From Venice** is shown three times an hour-on the hour, 20 minutes past and 40 minutes past.

Other rides include **Doomed Castle**, which takes you back to King Arthur's lost world, **Red Hot Planet** catapults you to a future on Mars, **Escape from Nemo** has you hurtling on a time machine and **Blue Magic** takes you to a spectacular underwater world in the Bahamas.
Open: Sunday to Thursday 10am–11pm, Friday and Saturday 10am–midnight.
Tickets: each ride $7, Time Traveller $9. Two rides $12 or four $18. Height restrictions vary according to ride.

Splashing Thrills

Wet 'n Wild

2600 Las Vegas Boulevard South, 702-737 7873
Here you will find 15 acres (6ha) of rides, slides, chutes, floats and flumes to beat the summer heat. Wet 'n Wild favourites include the **Lazy River®**, **Der Stuka®** and **Kids' Park**, while you can battle the monster surf of the Wave Pool or tackle the ultimate terror of the **Banzai Banzai®**. Younger children can enjoy the whirlpool wonder of **Willy Willy®** and **Bubble Up**.

Facilities include lockers, changing areas, showers, shops with swimwear, and snack bars, though you are allowed to bring your own picnics.
Open: April to September, times vary according to the season, but from the end of June to early August daily at 10am–11pm.
Tickets: $21.95 for 10 and over, $15.95 for 3–9s. Under 3s free. Parking is free.

★ ★ ★   **BRIT TIP**   ★ ★ ★
★   ★
★   Although you are allowed to   ★
★   bring your own picnics to Wet 'n   ★
★   Wild, do make sure that they are   ★
★   alcohol free!   ★
★ ★ ★ ★ ★ ★ ★ ★ ★ ★ ★ ★ ★ ★ ★ ★

FUN TIMES
Fun Rides

Eiffel Tower Experience

Paris, 702-739 4111
You pay your money, take a lift to about two-thirds of the way up the replica Eiffel Tower and then look out at the desert through an iron mesh. The hotel's tower is, in fact, only two-thirds of the height of the real Eiffel Tower, it is hard to get a decent view of the entire Strip and impossible to take any worthwhile pictures through the grille.

Open: daily 9am–midnight, weather permitting.
Tickets: Monday to Thursday adults $9, seniors and under 13 $7; Friday to Sunday adults $11.95, seniors and under 13 $9.

In my opinion the Eiffel Tower Experience is the biggest rip-off in town. To get similar or even better views, go to any of the rooftop lounges for free or head to the Stratosphere's Observation Deck.

Gondola rides

The Venetian, 702-414 4100
Supplying the full Venetian experience, the hotel puts on gondola rides around the Grand Canal Shoppes. They're pricey, but still cheaper than gondola rides in Venice! Tours start from St Mark's Square.
Open: Sunday to Thursday 10am–10.30pm, Friday and Saturday 10am–11.30pm.
Tickets: adults $12.50, under 13 $5, private gondola $50.

The gondola rides are so popular that tickets sell out every day and the average wait for a ride is one hour.

Observation Deck
Stratosphere Tower

Stratosphere, 702-380 7777
Take a ride up the Stratosphere's lifts to the top of the tallest free-standing observation tower in America, which has an indoor and outdoor Observation Deck where all the landmarks seen from different points

of the circular deck are explained. The best time of day to see the Strip is just before sunset when you can make out all the landmarks before the town goes dark and everything lights up.
Open: Sunday to Thursday 10am–1am, Friday and Saturday 10am–2am.
Tickets: $8 (see page 148 for the details of the tower's thrill rides).

Free Shows

Air Play

Tropicana Hotel, 702-739 2222
Here's a neat way to attract punters to your casino: put on an aerial acrobatic show right above the casino floor. It's well worth watching, though, as acrobats, aerialists and jugglers put on an amazing show on a stage built on top of a bank of slot machines, beneath the Tropicana's famous Tiffany glass ceiling. A team of four dancers and a singer also perform a variety of musical numbers, which change with each performance.
Show times: 3pm, 5pm, 7.30pm and 9.30pm.

Bear in mind that if you are under the age of 21 you won't be able to see Air Play as it takes place in the Tropicana's casino.

Bellagio Fountain Show

In the lake outside the Bellagio
An incredibly stunning visual and audio experience as the now world-famous fountains perform carefully choreographed movements in time to operatic, classical and whimsical music.
Show times: during the week, shows start every half hour 3–7pm and every 15 minutes 7pm–midnight. At weekends shows start at 12 noon.

10

CBS Television City

The MGM Grand, 702-891 1111
A research centre that allows
audiences to view TV shows in
production and comment on them.
Show times: free screenings begin
daily at 9am and are conducted
every 20 minutes.

Masquerade Show In The Sky

Rio All-Suite Hotel, 3700 West
Flamingo, 702-252 7777
A $25-million Disney-esque spectacle
in which dozens of Mardi Gras floats
containing exotically costumed
dancers literally 'float' about 20ft (6
metres) above your head,
accompanied to music.

★ ★ ★   BRIT TIP   ★ ★ ★
★   ★
★   ★
★ If you are travelling with children ★
★ be warned that the Masquerade ★
★ Show In The Sky includes topless ★
★ showgirls during the evening ★
★ performances. ★

Show times: the display happens
every two hours and for a small fee
you can even take part.

NBC Research Center

The Venetian, 702-414 4100
Another research centre, this time for
NBC and at the swanky Venetian
resort. New TV shows and promos
are put under scrutiny as they are
screened to local audiences.

Sirens of TI

Treasure Island, 702-894 7444
Formerly the Buccaneer Bay sea battle
between an English frigate and a pirate

★ ★ ★   BRIT TIP   ★ ★ ★
★   ★
★   ★
★ The Sirens of TI show at the ★
★ Treasure Island resort gets ★
★ packed very quickly so arrive ★
★ early to get a good view. ★

ship in the 18th-century Caribbean, the
all-male cast has been replaced with a
selection of female sirens in a new,
more adult-themed show.
Show times: daily at 4pm, 5.30pm,
7pm, 8.30pm and 10pm, with an
extra show at 11.30pm on Friday
and Saturday.

Animal Magic

Lion Habitat

The MGM Grand, 702-891 1111
A $9-million, multi-level lion habitat
has been opened at the MGM
Grand, in which visitors are encircled
by lions via a see-through tunnel
running through the habitat. Out of
18 lions, who are cared for by a
veteran animal trainer, up to seven
can be viewed in the habitat at any
time. Three of the lions – Goldie,
Metro and Baby Lion – are direct
descendants of MGM Studio's
marquee lion, Metro.
Open: 11am–11pm.
Admission: free, though an 'official'
picture costs around $10.

Nevada Zoological-Botanical Park

1755 North Rancho Drive, 702-648
5955
A small zoo committed to
conservation, education and
recreation, it houses more than 50
species of reptiles and small animals of
the great south-western desert. It is also
home to other animals including an
African lion, Bengal tiger, Barbary
apes, monkeys, wallabies, flamingos,
king vultures and North America's only
tigrina, an endangered tropical cat.
Open: daily 9am–5pm.
Admission: over 12 $5, 2–12 $3
and under 2 free.

Secret Garden and Dolphin Habitat

Mirage Hotel, 702-791 7111
Here is your chance to get a closer
look at the rare breeds of animals
which Siegfried and Roy use in their
magical illusion show. The $15-

million, 2.5-acre (1-ha) natural Secret Garden habitat was specially built to house their Bengal tigers, panthers, snow leopards and Asian elephants. Next door is the massive Dolphin Habitat, which is home to a family of Atlantic bottlenose dolphins. Four connected pools, an artificial coral reef system and a sandy bottom replicate the dolphin's natural environment, which aims to provide a healthy and nurturing home for the marine mammals and educate the public about their role in the ecosystem.
Open: Secret Garden – Thursday to Tuesday 11am–5pm in summer and 11am–3.30pm in winter. Dolphin Habitat – daily 11am–7pm in summer and 11am–5.30pm in winter.
Admission: $12 includes entrance to both habitats. On Wednesday and after the garden closes $6.

Shark Reef

Mandalay Bay, 702-632 7777
An aquarium with some amazing differences – you walk underneath it so you are completely surrounded by water and it contains unusual and dangerous aquatic animals and fish from the world's tropical waters. Nearly 100 species are represented here from a 100-ft (30-metre) nurse shark to a tiny clown fish. Divers in the aquarium talk about the animals and answer questions via a high-tech underwater communications system.

The largest display of golden saltwater crocodiles – it has three – outside of Thailand can be seen here too. This is a seriously endangered species as there are only 12 left in the whole world. Other animals include moray eels, southern stingrays, angelfish, puffer fish, jellyfish and the recent addition of serpents and dragons featuring green tree pythons, known for their vivid green colour and razor-sharp teeth.
Open: daily 10am–11pm; last admission at 10pm.
Admission: adults $14.95, under 13 $9.95, under 5 free.

Tiger Habitat

The Mirage, 702-791 7111
A showcase for the famous white tigers that take part in Siegfried & Roy's magic show, with a pool, waterfalls and all-white background to make the tigers feel at home.
Open: 24/7.
Admission: free

★★★ BRIT TIP ★★★
Make the most of the Mirage's free attractions by taking a look at the enormous tropical fish tank behind the resort's lobby during your visit to see the white tigers.

Wildlife Habitat at the Flamingo

Flamingo Hotel, 702-733 3111
Surrounded by lush pines, palms and magnolia, this is the only place in town where you can see the flamingoes up close. Impeyn and silver pheasants can also be seen here, along with Gambel's quails, a crown crane, two ibis, ducks, turtles, parrots and penguins. The penguins are fed daily at 8.55am and 2.55pm – a sight not to be missed!
Open: 24/7.
Admission: free.

CULTURE AND MUSEUMS

Art Museums and Galleries

Culture, as you can imagine, is thin on the ground in Las Vegas and when it is available it tends to come at quite a premium. For those among you who like to spend money wisely, I'd save money by NOT visiting any of the Vegas art galleries, use the cash for a stopover in New York and see a real art museum. After all $10 to see 13 paintings in the Wynn Collection as opposed to $12 to see 5,000 years worth of art at the Metropolitan Museum of Art... However, there are some fascinating museums such as those on Liberace and Elvis.

Bellagio Gallery of Fine Art

Bellagio, 702-693 7871,
www.bgfa.com
This originally opened to show off the previous owner Steve Wynn's masterpieces, which included Rembrandts, Monets and Picassos, but he took the paintings with him when he sold the hotel to the MGM Grand. Now it showcases travelling art exhibitions and is theoretically non-profit making.
Open: daily 9am–7pm.
Admission: the exhibitions are on a small scale, but cost a steep $15 for adults and $12 for students.

Guggenheim Hermitage Museum

The Venetian, 702-414 4100
Russia's famous Hermitage Museum, which is based in St Petersburg, has joined forces with the Solomon R Guggenheim Foundation in New York to create this fabulous museum at the Venetian. The gallery houses remarkable Russian artefacts and masterpieces that are part of travelling art exhibitions.
Open: daily 9.30am–8.30pm.
Admission: adults $15, students $11, under 13s $7, under 6 free.

Houdini Museum

The Venetian, 702-796 0301
The world's largest collection of Houdini memorabilia built up by Geno Munari since the 1970s includes handcuffs, photos, posters and handwritten letters to family and friends. There is also a wide selection of props – both original and replicas – which were used in Houdini's famous escape tricks. One of the most fascinating aspects of the exhibition is

that it debunks the myth that Houdini died while trying to escape from his water-torture device: he actually died from peritonitis caused by a ruptured appendix at Halloween in 1926.
Open: daily 9am–11pm.
Admission: adults $2, children $1, families $5.

Las Vegas Art Museum

3333 Washington Avenue, 702-647 4300
Fine art exhibits in three galleries that are changed on a monthly basis. The museum also runs art classes for adults and children and art competitions.
Open: Monday to Saturday 10am–3pm and on Sunday noon–3pm.

Moonstruck Gallery

6322 West Sahara Avenue, 702-364 0531
Voted the best gallery in Las Vegas, here you will find limited-edition prints, music, books, pottery, jewellery, handcrafted gifts and musical instruments.
Open: Tuesday to Saturday 10am–6pm.

The Wynn Collection

At the former Desert Inn building, 3145 South Las Vegas Boulevard adjacent to the Fashion Show Mall, 702-733 4100
Here's a very expensive way to see 13 pieces of art. Located off the lobby of the former Desert Inn, casino mogul Steve Wynn's private collection includes Picasso's *Le Reve*, Matisse's *The Persian Robe* and *Pineapples and Anemones* and Manet's *Portrait of Mademoiselle Suzette Lemaire in Profile*. Oh, and there's also a portrait of Steve Wynn himself by Andy Warhol!
Open: daily 10am–5pm.
Admission: adults $10, under 13 $6, under 6 free.

Attractions

Bellagio Conservatory & Botanical Gardens

The Bellagio, 702-693 7111
Billed as a kaleidoscope for the senses, this glorious display of exotic plants and flowers provides row upon row of blooms that create a unique tapestry to reflect each season and holiday. The combination of the fragrances, textures and colours are heavenly, while the inspirational conservatory with its glass-topped atrium and sweeping staircase is simply divine.

★ ★ ★ BRIT TIP ★ ★ ★
★   ★
★   ★
★ Feel a photo opportunity coming ★
★   on? Then the perfect spot to   ★
★ capture yourself in Vegas is at the ★
★   gorgeous Botanical Gardens in   ★
★   the Bellagio.   ★
★ ★ ★ ★ ★ ★ ★ ★ ★ ★ ★ ★ ★ ★ ★ ★

The Cloud

Fashion Show Mall, 702-369 0704
The newest and one of the most eye-catching 'attractions' on the Strip hovers 128ft (39 metres) above a pedestrian plaza right outside the Fashion Show Mall. Nearly 500ft (152 metres) long, the steel canopy is called The Cloud and is a wonderful source of shade during the day. At night giant images are projected on to its surface to highlight promotions and events happening at the mall, while a further four massive LED screens are used to broadcast videos and other live broadcasts from the city. The reality is that whatever it is used for, it is a must-see – and free – sight!

Ethel M Chocolate Factory and Cactus Gardens

Two Cactus Garden Drive, Henderson, 702-433 2500
This large American sweet-making factory, just 5 miles (8km) from the Strip, gives an insight into the entire process. The tour ends with a free sample, but as you'll also find yourself in the factory shop, you won't be alone in deciding to buy a box of chocolates. Take them outside and stroll through the amazing cactus gardens filled with ocotillo, prickly pear and saguaros varieties among many others.
Open: daily 8.30am–7pm.
Admission: free.

Guinness World of Records

2780 Las Vegas Boulevard South, 702-792 3766
Affiliated to the book, record-breakers are brought to three-dimensional life with the help of life-sized replicas, colour videos and computerised databanks. Included are the tallest man, the fattest man and fastest-talking man, plus the musical records of Michael Jackson and videos of world records being set.
Open: daily 9am–6pm.
Admission: adults $6.50, students and seniors over 62 $5.50 and 5–12 $4.50.

Imperial Palace Auto Collection

Imperial Palace Hotel, 702-731 3311
More than 600 cars make up this collection but only 200 are ever on show at one time. Some of the vintage, classic and special-interest cars include the Chaser, the world's fastest petrol-powered police car, a 1986 Ford Mustang, which was specially built for the Nevada Highway Patrol, President Woodrow Wilson's 1917 Pierce Arrow car and a 1961 Lincoln Continental that was once owned by Jacqueline Kennedy Onassis.
Open: daily 9.30am–9.30pm.
Admission: adults $6.95, seniors and under 13 $3.

Madame Tussaud's

The Venetian, 702-414 4100
Five theme areas include **The Big Night**, a special VIP party with Whoopi Goldberg and Brad Pitt

10

among others; the **Sports Arena** with Mohammed Ali, Babe Ruth and Evander Holyfield (who is missing part of his right ear!); **Rock and Pop** with Elton John and Tina Turner; **Las Vegas Legends** with Frank Sinatra and Marilyn Monroe, and the **Finale**, a state-of-the-art tribute to modern Las Vegas legends including Wayne Newton and Siegfried and Roy.
Open: daily 10am–10pm.
Admission: adults $19.95, over 65 and under 13 $14, under 5 free.

Old Las Vegas Mormon Fort

State Historic Park, 908 Las Vegas Boulevard North, 702-486 3511
This is the oldest surviving non-Indian structure in Las Vegas and dates back to 14 June 1855 when the Mormon missionaries arrived in New Mexico Territory. Their aim was to convert the Indians and provide a safe way-station between Mormon communities in Great Salt Lake City to the north and San Bernardino to the east. The 150-sq ft (14-sq metre) adobe-walled fort was still being built when the fort was largely abandoned in 1858 and subsequently was used by lead miners before becoming a ranch.
Open: daily 8.30am–4.30pm.
Admission: adults $2, under 13 $1, under 6 free.

Planetarium and Observatory

Community College of Southern Nevada, 3200 East Cheyenne Avenue, 702-651 5059
Southern Nevada's only public planetarium and observatory has multimedia shows on astronomy plus hemispheric motion pictures. Public observing sessions are held after the last showings.
Open: shows are on Friday 6pm and 7.30pm, Saturday 3.30pm and 7.30pm. Public observing sessions are held at about 8.30pm, weather permitting. The shop is open Friday 5pm–8pm and Saturday 3pm–8pm.
Admission: adults $4, under 12 and over 55 $2.50.

Ron Lee's World of Clowns

330 Carousel Parkway, Henderson, 702-434 1700
Here you can see how clown and animation characters are made in an impressive 35-minute self-guided tour. A Warner Bros production facility, you will see famous cartoon characters including Popeye, Betty Boop, ET and Rocky. Includes a museum of clown memorabilia, Jitters Café and gift shop and a beautiful, jewel-encrusted musical carousel, which you can ride for $1.
Open: Monday to Friday 8.30am–4.30pm, Saturday 10am–4pm.
Admission: free.

The Tomb & Museum of King Tutankhamun

Touted as an exact recreation of King Tut's tomb as it was discovered by Howard Carter in 1922. Hidden for centuries, the tomb and its artefacts had been untouched by grave robbers. The replica includes stone chambers housing statues of the gods, wooden boats intended to carry King Tut on his final voyage to the after life and vessels for food and drink. Most impressive of all replicas is the gold-plated sarcophagus and the *shabtis* – figurines made of semi-precious stones symbolizing workers to help Tut with his duties.
Open: daily 9am–11pm.
Admission: $5 or attraction pass $24.95 (see Pharoah's Pavilion, page 148).

Museums

Clark County Heritage Museum

1830 South Boulder Highway, Henderson, 702-455 7955
Covers a time span of 12,000 years of southern Nevada history and includes Heritage Street, a living history area, and Nevada ghost town. There are old railroad cars, a fully restored 1920s' bungalow built by a pioneer Las Vegas merchant, a replica of a 19th-century frontier print

shop, plus ranching displays and a nature walk.
Open: 9am–4.30pm.
Admission: adults and children $2, under 3s free.

Elvis-A-Rama Museum

3401 Industrial Road (one block west of the Strip), 702-309 7200
You can't miss the great neon gold record and guitar bursting out of the roof! With over $3-million-worth of memorabilia here, you can see hundreds of items belonging to the king of rock 'n' roll. In addition to the displays of his jumpsuits, army uniform and film costumes, there are video displays of Elvis in action throughout the museum. Plus, live performances are featured at the start of every hour by an Elvis impersonator.
Open: daily 10am–7pm daily.
Admission: adults $9.95, seniors and students $7.95, under 12 free with an adult.

★ ★ ★ BRIT TIP ★ ★ ★

The Elvis-A-Rama Museum has a free shuttle service between the museum and any hotel on the Strip between the Stratosphere and Mandalay Bay. Call the museum to arrange a pick up time.

Las Vegas Natural History Museum

900 Las Vegas Boulevard North, 702-384 3466
Wildlife existed in the Las Vegas valley long before man arrived and created casinos! Here you can take a walk on the wild side and discover the scenic and wild natural beauty of southern Nevada. It includes exhibits representing the many different habitats in the Las Vegas area with a diverse variety of plants and wildlife. The historical side is represented by animated dinosaurs, while there is an international wildlife room, small live sharks in the aquarium and a hands-on exploration room for children. There is also an extensive wildlife art gallery with award-winning wood sculptures.
Open: daily 9am–4pm.
Admission: adults $6, students, seniors and over 11 $5, under 12 $3, under 2 free.

Liberace Museum

Liberace Plaza, 1775 East Tropicana Avenue, 702-798 5595
The man known as Mr Showmanship lives on in one of the most popular attractions in Nevada that includes a collection of three buildings near where the artist once lived. One building houses 18 rare and antique pianos including Liberace's favourite Baldwin grand piano, and others owned by Chopin and George Gershwin, plus Liberace's cars. Another building is devoted to his famous stage wardrobe of multi-sequinned, bejewelled and rhinestone-studded costumes and famous rings that used to dazzle audiences around the world. The third contains an extensive collection of Liberace's memorabilia including hundreds of rare Moser crystals from the Czech Republic, a monogrammed set of dinner plates that once belonged to President John F Kennedy, and Liberace's violin, made by the famous violin-maker George Winterling.

★ ★ ★ BRIT TIP ★ ★ ★

The fab Liberace Museum has proved to be so successful it is planning an extension and is now even open for private parties!

All the proceeds of the museum go to the Liberace Foundation for the Performing and Creative Arts, which regularly donates thousands of dollars to schools, universities and other organisations for music, dance, drama, film and visual arts.

10

Open: Monday to Saturday 10am–5pm, Sunday noon–4pm.
Admission: adults $12, seniors, students and over 5 $8, under 6 free. Children must be accompanied by an adult.

Lied Discovery Children's Museum

833 Las Vegas Boulevard North, 702-382 5437
Here children can touch, see, explore and experience more than 100 hands-on exhibits in one of America's largest – and most exciting – children's museums. Children crawl and slide through the **Toddler Towers**, become a star on the **Performing Arts** stage, pilot the **Space Shuttle** or **Gyrochair**, create colour computer prints and toe-tap a tune on the **Musical Pathway**. They can also stand in a giant bubble, play at being a disc jockey at the KKID radio station or use their bodies to generate electricity.
Open: Tuesday to Sunday 10am–5pm.
Admission: adults $6, children aged 1 to 17 $5, seniors and under 1 free. Children under the age of 11 must be accompanied by an adult.

Magic and Movie Hall of Fame O'Sheas

3555 Las Vegas Boulevard South, 702-792 0788
A 20,000-sq ft (1,860-sq metre) hall of magic, ventriloquism and movie memorabilia. **The Magic Museum** has a collection of equipment used by past master magicians including Houdini. **The Movie Museum** has costumes from *Cleopatra* and *Gone with the Wind* and a Frankenstein monster that comes to life.

Open: shows are at 5.30pm, 7.30pm and 9.30pm Monday to Saturday.
Admission: the That's Magic illusion show costs $21.95 for adults and $7.95 for children and includes free entry to the exhibits, a magic gift and one drink.

Neon Museum

East end of the Fremont Street Experience, 702-387 NEON
Rather like New York's Skyscraper Museum, this Downtown experience preserves a famous piece of the city's history. Once the City of Neon, now all that remains of many of Vegas' most famous older hotels are their neon signs. Here you'll find the Hacienda Hotel sign before the building was imploded to make way for the Mandalay Bay, plus the original Aladdin's genie lamp and many other historical neon signs with their spectacular colours, intricate animation and sheer size. A small museum with big appeal!
Open: 24/7.
Admission: free. Guided tour $5 adults, $3 students, under 5 free.

Nevada State Museum and Historical Society

700 Twin Lakes Drive, 702-486 5205
The history of southern Nevada from mammoths to gambling is presented in three galleries – Biology, Earth Science and History/Anthropology. There is also a display explaining how neon has been used in the city.
Open: daily 9am–5pm except major holidays.
Admission: adults $2, under 18 free.

11 OUTDOOR ADVENTURE

Every kind of fun from cowboy cookouts to horseback riding

Las Vegas is a wonderful city, and practically everything you'd like to do in the great outdoors in America is right on its doorstep in a plethora of stunning environments. Nearby are **Red Rock Canyon**, where ponderosa pines and Joshua trees grow out of towering cliffs of Aztec sandstone, the **Valley of Fire**, a Martian landscape of vivid red, pastel and white sandstone, and **Mount Charleston**, which looms 12,000ft (3,658 metres) above sea level.

The biggest jewel in Las Vegas's crown of outdoor splendours though, is the **Grand Canyon**. A whole raft of companies organise plane and helicopter flights to – and even down to the bottom of – the 10-mile (16-km) wide and 1-mile (1.6-km) deep natural wonder. Many of those companies also offer trips a little further north to the stunning **Bryce Canyon** and **Zion National Park**, famous for cascading waterfalls.

On top of that there are a whole host of brilliant ways to experience this great region, from white-water rafting and rock climbing, to horse riding and following the cowboy trail. At certain times of the year, it is possible to go skiing in the morning at **Lee Canyon** on Mount Charleston, then head off to **Lake Mead** for a spot of water-skiing in the afternoon. Where else could you find such a dramatic mix of marvels? Arrive in Las Vegas and you are just moments away from a world of beauty and adventure.

Inside this chapter

Overview of the Great Outdoors
Places to see

PLACES TO SEE

Hoover Dam

South on Highway 93 just past Boulder City, 32 miles (51km) from Las Vegas
Visitors Center: open daily, except Thanksgiving and Christmas Day, 9am–5pm; $10 adults, $5 for 10–16s, free for under 10s
702-293 8321
www.hooverdam.usbr.gov
This amazing construction – it's 726ft (221 metres) high and 1,244ft (379 metres) long and is filled with enough concrete to build a two-lane highway from San Francisco to New York – literally changed the face of America's West. Blocking the Colorado River at the Black Canyon, which spans Nevada and Arizona, the dam put an end to centuries of droughts and floods caused by the mighty Colorado. Work began on the dam in 1931 and the $165-million project was completed by 1935. Its

11

offspring, Lake Mead, now produces drinking and irrigation water for the entire Las Vegas Valley, while the electric power plant creates enough energy to sell to Nevada, Arizona and California.

Since 11 September, it is no longer possible to take an interior tour of the dam for security reasons. Instead the **Discovery Tour** gives you access to the $165-million **Visitor Center,** a three-level, 110-ft (33-metre) in diameter circular building, which stands 700ft (213 metres) above the base of the dam. From the indoor and outdoor observation decks are stunning views of the dam, Lake Mead and the waters of the Colorado River re-entering the Black Canyon after passing through the dam's giant turbines.

★ ★ ★ BRIT TIP ★ ★ ★
★   ★
★   If you're touring in an RV   ★
★   (recreational vehicle, or camper ★
★   van) you will have to park on the ★
★   Arizona side of the dam as they   ★
★   have been banned from the new   ★
★   parking garage at Hoover Dam for ★
★   security reasons.   ★
★ ★ ★ ★ ★ ★ ★ ★ ★ ★ ★ ★ ★ ★ ★ ★ ★ ★

A gallery houses an environmental exhibit, technology exhibit and the story of the settlement of the lower Colorado River area. The rotating theatre is divided up into three segments and you move between the three areas to see three different films about the making and history of the dam.

While you're in the area you can also take a river raft trip (see page 169), try a tandem jump (see page 180) and visit **Boulder City/Hoover Dam Museum** (Boulder Dam Hotel, Boulder City, 702-294 1988; open 10am–4pm for a donation). Here you'll see a free movie about the building of the dam plus historical memorabilia from the workers. While you're there take a peek at the newly renovated home in the museum, which has accommodated movie star

James Cagney and reclusive billionaire Howard Hughes in its time.

An excellent stop-off point during your day trip is **Jitters** (702-293 0099; open 6am–6pm), which serves sarnies and snacks, or try the **Happy Days Diner** (702-293 4637; open 7am–8pm). Boulder's oldest diner, its 1950s-style environment makes for a fun pit stop.

★ ★ ★ BRIT TIP ★ ★ ★
★   ★
★   As you leave Boulder City and   ★
★   head for Hoover Dam watch out   ★
★   for stupendous views of Lake   ★
★   Mead at the junction with   ★
★   Highway 93.   ★
★ ★ ★ ★ ★ ★ ★ ★ ★ ★ ★ ★ ★ ★ ★ ★ ★ ★

Lake Mead

Visitors Center: 4 miles (6km) north-east of Boulder City; open daily 8.30am–4.30pm; admission free 702-293 4041
www.lakemeadguide.com
Other useful numbers: Lake Mead Marina 702-293 3484; Lake Mead National Park Service 702-293 8907; Alan Bible Visitor Center 702-293 8906

The dazzling-blue Lake Mead, created by the construction of the Hoover Dam, is about 25 miles (40km) south of Las Vegas. It is 110 miles (177km) long and has 550 miles (885km) of freshwater shoreline. Here you can try out anything from boating to swimming, scuba-diving, water-skiing, camping and fishing, while six marinas provide docking space for boats, plus restaurants and other services. Every December, a Parade of Lights is held at **Lake Mead Marina**, with a flotilla of powerboats, houseboats and sailboats covered in lights. A newer, annual event is the hydroplane race held in September.

The **Visitors Center** contains a botanical garden and exhibits on natural history. Here you will find details of a self-guided tour, with tape-

Weddings

Clockwise from top left

The Elvis Chapel,

The Canterbury wedding chapel at Excalibur,

Ivy Chapel,

Limo,

Red Rock wedding

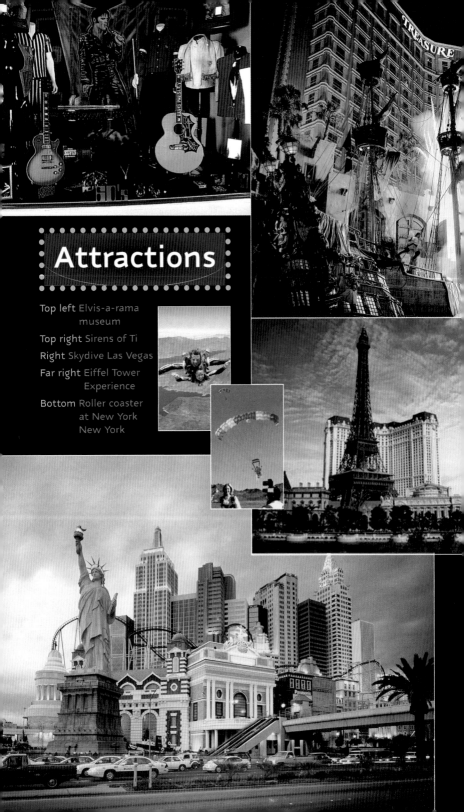

Attractions

Top left Elvis-a-rama museum

Top right Sirens of Ti

Right Skydive Las Vegas

Far right Eiffel Tower Experience

Bottom Roller coaster at New York New York

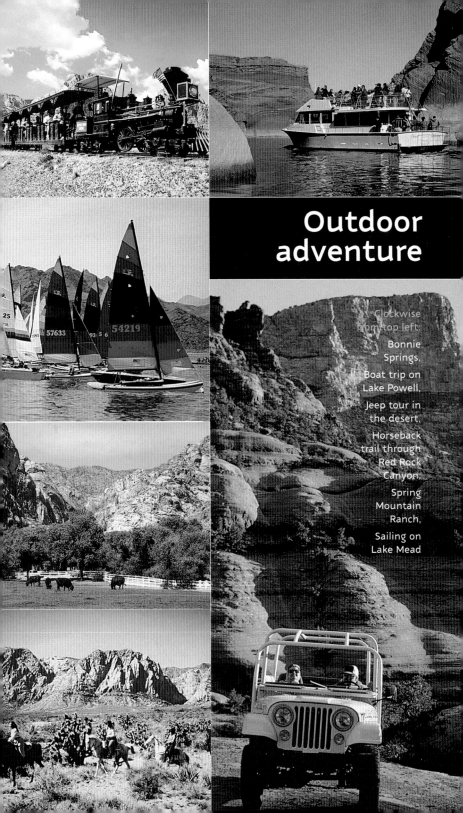

Outdoor adventure

Clockwise from top left:

Bonnie Springs.

Boat trip on Lake Powell.

Jeep tour in the desert.

Horseback trail through Red Rock Canyon.

Spring Mountain Ranch.

Sailing on Lake Mead

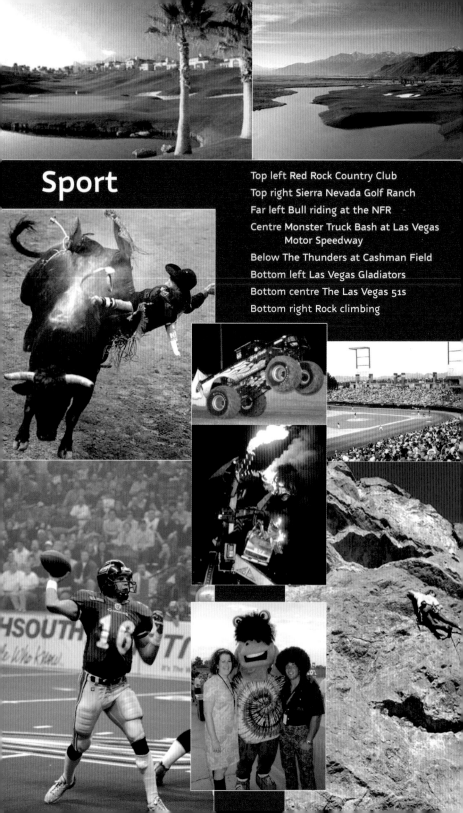

Sport

Top left Red Rock Country Club
Top right Sierra Nevada Golf Ranch
Far left Bull riding at the NFR
Centre Monster Truck Bash at Las Vegas Motor Speedway
Below The Thunders at Cashman Field
Bottom left Las Vegas Gladiators
Bottom centre The Las Vegas 51s
Bottom right Rock climbing

recording, of the lake's Northshore and Lakeshore roads, plus information about facilities and services.

Two not-so-scenic roads – **Lakeside Scenic Drive** (Highway 146) and **Northshore Scenic Drive** (Highway 167) provide access to the marinas around the Nevada shoreline of Lake Mead, which include **Las Vegas Bay Marina** (702-565 9111), **Calville Bay Resort** (702-565 8958), **Echo Bay** (702-394 4000) and **Overton Beach Resort** (702-394 4040). These are all full-service marinas offering houseboat and daily deck cruiser rentals, restaurants and gift shops. At night Callville Bay provides a barbecue on the patio overlooking the lake.

★ ★ ★ **BRIT TIP** ★ ★ ★
★ ★
★ ★
★ For details of jet-skiing, cruising, ★
★ etc., see pages 168–9. ★
★ ★ ★ ★ ★ ★ ★ ★ ★ ★ ★ ★ ★ ★ ★ ★ ★ ★ ★

During the cooler winter and early spring months, you can take a hike in the **Lake Mead National Recreation Area** on Saturday mornings to learn about the history of the people of the area, from the mining era onwards. Each hike is limited to 25 people and you can make reservations by phoning 702-293 8990.

If you'd like to explore a little further afield, head off south to **Lake Mohave** and **Cottonwood Cove Resort and Marina** (1000 Cottonwood Cove Road, Cottonwood, 702-297 1464). It's a full-service marina offering luxury houseboats, small boats and personal watercraft rentals about one and a half hours south of Las Vegas.

Valley of Fire State Park

6 miles (10km) from Lake Mead and 55 miles (88km) north-east of Las Vegas using Interstate 15 and Highway 169, 702-397 2088

Visitor Center: open daily 8.30am–4.30pm. Has exhibits on the geology, ecology and history of the park, plus the nearby region.
Facilities: shaded areas with restrooms at Atlatl Rock, Seven Sisters, the Cabins, near Mouse's Tank trail head and White Domes. The park – the oldest in Nevada – gets its name from the red sandstone formations that were formed from great, shifting desert sand dunes during the age of the dinosaurs 150 million years ago. Complex geological movements and extensive erosion have created the spectacular wind carvings in the colourful rock formations.

This whole area was extensively used by Basket-making peoples and later by the Anasazi Pueblo farmers from the nearby Moapa Valley from 300BC to AD1150. It was probably visited for hunting, food gathering and religious ceremonies, though the lack of water limited their stays. Wonderful reminders of the time these ancient tribes spent here can be seen in the extraordinarily detailed Indian petroglyphs that tell the stories of their lives. The fantastic scenery and fascinating history make it well worth a day's visit.

Nature's way

The whole area is dominated by creosote, burro and brittle bushes, plus several different types of cactus. Spring is a wonderful time to visit as this is the time to see desert marigold, indigo bushes and desert mallow in bloom. The park is visited by many species of birds, but those in residence include raven, house finch, sage sparrow and, of course, the famous road runner – beep beep!

The animals tend to be nocturnal, coming out to forage for food when the desert heat has begun to fade, and include many different types of lizard, snakes, coyote, kit fox, spotted skunk, black-tailed jack rabbit and ground squirrel. The desert tortoise is now so rare it is protected by Nevada state law.

11

One of the best ways to explore the park is by hiking through it and maps of trails are provided at the Visitor Center.

What to see

Atlatl Rock: here you will find outstanding examples of ancient Indian rock art or petroglyphs, including a depiction of the atlatl (at'-lat-l), a notched stick used to throw primitive spears and the forerunner of the bow and arrow.

★ ★ ★   **BRIT TIP**   ★ ★ ★
★   ★
★   Atlatl Rock is a great location for ★
★   campers and the campsite is   ★
★   well-equipped with modern WC ★
★   and shower facilities.   ★
★ ★ ★ ★ ★ ★ ★ ★ ★ ★ ★ ★ ★ ★ ★ ★

Arch Rock: a 2-mile (3-km) scenic loop road provides views of some of the valley's most interesting rock formations, for example Arch Rock and Piano Rock. You'll get a true wilderness experience at the secluded Arch Rock Campground with its primitive facilities!
Beehives: unusual sandstone formations weathered by the eroding forces of wind and water. Nearby are three group camping areas, available by reservation only.
Cabins: now a picnic area, these historic stone cabins were built with native sandstone by the Civilian Conservation Corps in the 1930s as a shelter for passing travellers.
Mouse's Tank: named after a renegade Indian who used the area as a hideout in the 1890s, this is a natural basin in the rock where water collects after rainfall, sometimes remaining for months. A half-mile round trip trail leads to Mouse's Tank from the trail head parking area, passing numerous examples of prehistoric Indian petroglyphs.
Petrified logs: logs and stumps washed into the area from an ancient forest about 225 million years ago

are exposed in two locations.
Rainbow vista: a favourite photo point with a panoramic view of multicoloured sandstone.
Seven Sisters: fascinating red rock formations, which are easily accessible from the road. Picnic areas provide a relaxing stop.
White Domes: sandstone formations with brilliant contrasting colours, picnic area and trail head. White Domes is an 11-mile (17.7 km) round trip drive from the Visitor Center.
Duck Rock is a short hike.
Other sights include the **Clark Memorial, Elephant Rock,** the deep red sandstone of **Fire Canyon** and the amazing **Silica Dome**.

Red Rock Canyon Conservancy Area

An area to the west of Las Vegas which includes the Spring Mountain Range, home of the Spring Mountain Ranch, and Mount Charleston, plus the Red Rock Canyon and Bonnie Springs Old Nevada.

Red Rock Canyon

17 miles (27km) west of the Las Vegas Strip on Charleston Boulevard – Highway 159.
702-515 5350
www.redrockcanyon.blm.com
Once the home of ancient Native American tribes, this magnificent canyon was formed by a thrust fault – a fracture in the earth's crust where one plate is pushed horizontally over another – 65 million years ago. It is home to feral horses and burros (donkeys), as well as native wildlife such as desert bighorn sheep and coyotes, which you can see on the 13-mile (21-km) **Scenic Loop Drive** (see page 163).
The **Calico Vista** points are good stopping points, offering great views of the crossed-bedded Aztec sandstone. For easy access to the sandstone, stop at the **Sandstone Quarry** parking lot where you can see large blocks of stone and other

historic evidence of quarry activity which took place during the turn of the last century. You can have a picnic at **Red Spring** and **Willow Spring**, while there are also great views of wooded canyons and desert washes at **Icebox Canyon, Pine Creek Canyon** and **Red Rock Wash**. The Bureau of Land Management runs the Conservancy Area and there is a new free **Visitors Center** at the entrance to the Scenic Loop Drive for touring information, open 8am–4.30pm from November to March, and 8am–5.30pm from April to October.

★ ★ ★   ★ ★ ★
★   ★
★   ★
★ It is advisable to stop at the ★
★ Visitors Center, before going into ★
★ the park's Scenic Drive Loop, to ★
★ acquaint yourself with the park ★
★ regulations including where you ★
★   can drive and park.   ★
★ ★ ★ ★ ★ ★ ★ ★ ★ ★ ★ ★ ★ ★ ★ ★

Scenic Loop Drive

Open daily 6am–5pm from November to February, 6am–8pm from April to September and 6am–7pm in March and October. Entrance to the loop costs $5 for motorists and $2 for motorcyclists; free for hikers and cyclists.

The 13-mile (21-km) scenic drive is a one-way road. Cyclists are permitted to ride on the scenic drive, but must obey traffic laws. Sightseeing, photography and hiking trails are accessible from the designated pullouts and parking areas. If you would like to go hiking or rock climbing in Red Rock or Mount Charleston, see pages 167–9.

Bonnie Springs Old Nevada

Just 16 miles (26km) west of Las Vegas
702-875 4191
www.bonniesprings.com
Admission to village: $7 per car (up to six people) weekdays; $10 weekends and holidays or $3 per

person on a bus. Price includes access to the zoo

Originally built in 1843 as a stopover for the wagon trains going to California down the Old Spanish Trail, Bonnie Springs has been used as a tourist attraction since 1952. **Old Nevada Village** attractions include gunfights in the street, hangings, an 1880 melodrama, miniature train, US Post Office, blacksmith display and Boot Hill Cemetery. You can go horse riding from here – a one-hour guided horseback ride costs $25 – while there is a petting zoo, duck pond and aviary. Breakfast, lunch, dinner and cocktails are also available. A shuttle service to the village and ranch from Las Vegas is provided through Star Land Tours (702-296 4972).

Spring Mountain Ranch State Park

15 miles (24km) west of Las Vegas, via Charleston Boulevard (Highway 159), in the Red Rock Canyon National Conservation Area
702-875 4141
Open: the park is open daily 8am–dusk. The main ranch house is open daily 10am–4pm. Here you can find information about the ranch and surrounding areas and take a self-guided tour. Guided tours throughout the historic area are available weekdays at noon, 1 and 2pm, weekends at noon, 1, 2 and 3pm.
Admission: $5.
The many springs in these mountains once provided water for Paiute Indians and later brought mountain men and early settlers to the area. This 520-acre (210-ha) oasis was developed into a combination working ranch and luxurious retreat by a string of owners who have given the area a long and colourful history. Chester Lauck of the comedy team Lum & Abner and millionaire Howard Hughes are past owners of the ranch.

In the mid-1830s a campsite was established along the wash that runs through the ranch. The spring-fed creek and grassy meadows formed a

11

welcome oasis for travellers using this as an alternative route to the Spanish Trail through Cottonwood Valley. The use of the site by pack and wagon trains continued until their replacement by the railroad in 1905.

Outlaws and Indians

The remote trail was also perfect for outlaws and was used extensively by those involved in Indian slave trading, horse stealing and raids on passing caravans. One of the most famous was mountain man Bill Williams, after whom the ranch was first named.

In 1876 it was taken over by two men and named Sand Stone Ranch. The name stuck until it was leased in 1944 to Chet Lauck, the Lum part of comedy duo Lum & Abner and renamed Bar Nothing Ranch. A ranch house was built as a family retreat and Lum created a boys' camp. In 1955, German actress Vera Krupp bought the property, expanded the ranching business side and renaming it Spring Mountain Ranch.

At 3,800ft (1,158 metres), it is usually up to 15 degrees cooler than Las Vegas with cold winters and thunderstorms and flash floods in summer. Visitors can see wonderful plants including the Joshua tree, Mohave yucca, indigo bush, desert marigold and globe mallow. Animals are harder to spot as many are nocturnal, but include lizards, snakes, antelope ground squirrels, kit fox, jackrabbits, coyote, rock squirrel, badger, mule deer and bighorn sheep.

What's on

A **Living History** programme recreates the ranch's past in the spring and autumn, including demonstrations of pioneer skills. The Super Summer Theater puts on outdoor performances every June, July and August, while the Theatre Under The Stars features musicals and plays for the whole family. There is also a picnic area.

Mount Charleston

45 miles (72km) north-west of Las Vegas on Highways 95 and 157. 702-873 8800.
Camping: 1-800 280 CAMP. Camping allowed from May to September. Cost $8 per site per day.
Set in the lush Toiyabe National Forest, Mount Charleston looms nearly 12,000ft (3,657 metres) above sea level. One of the most beautiful areas in the Las Vegas Valley, Lee Canyon Road, the Kyle Canyon section of Charleston Park Road and Deer Creek Road have all been designated Scenic Byways because of their extraordinary scenery and panoramic views. The area is about 17°C/30°F cooler than Las Vegas, making it a perfect escape from the city heat for a day.

Camping is popular here, along with horse riding, and in the winter you can ski at Lee Canyon (see Things to do, page 167).

Charleston Peak was the birthplace of the Paiute people, so for the Native Americans it is sacred land. To respect this, the scale and extent of the road system remains fairly limited.

Pahrump Valley Vineyards

3810 Winery Road, Pahrump 702-727 6900
Open: tours 10am–4.40pm, lunch noon–3.30pm and dinner 5pm–9pm (until 8pm on Sunday).
Just north of Red Rock is Nevada's only vineyard and it regularly produces award-winning Chardonnay, Cabernet and Burgundy.

Further afield

Grand Canyon

If you're planning to go on a bit of a tour, then you're bound to want to see the Grand Canyon close up and for real. But it is also possible to take plane and helicopter rides to this, the

most spectacular canyon on earth –
even landing on the canyon floor and
having a spot of lunch on the banks
of the Colorado.

With Heli USA you can combine
a flight to the Grand Canyon with a
river rafting trip. Full details of the
Grand Canyon and activities are
given in Chapter 15 on pages
201–15 and details of air and
bus tours wind up this chapter on
pages 169–73.

Zion National Park

North of Las Vegas and the Grand
Canyon in southern Utah is the
majestic Zion National Park with its
beautiful waterfalls cascading down
red rocks and hanging gardens.
Once a home to the ancient Anasazi,
its history and majesty are presented
in an adventure film on a giant screen
at the **Zion Canyon Cinemax Theater**
(435-772 2400).

Bryce Canyon

Nearby in Utah is the equally beautiful
Bryce Canyon, once home to both
Native Americans and cowboys of the
Old West. Both Zion and Bryce offer
hiking, biking, horse riding, rock
climbing and bird watching.

★★★ **BRIT TIP** ★★★

★ Day trips to the Grand Canyon, ★
★ Bryce Canyon and Zion Canyon ★
★ from Las Vegas are available via ★
★ helicopter, small plane or coach ★
★ (see pages 204–5). ★

Death Valley

West of Las Vegas in eastern
California
760-786 2392
The hottest place on earth with
average summer temperatures of
45°C (131°F), here you will see miles
of sand that has been hardened into
a sea-like landscape by the heat of
the sun, extinct volcanos and wind-
carved rock formations. A full

description of the desert and how to
drive through it is given in Chapter 15,
starting on page 213, but you can see
it on a day trip from Las Vegas.

★★★ **BRIT TIP** ★★★

★ At around $179, Death Valley ★
★ tours are not cheap but Rocky ★
★ Trails (see page 173) do offer a ★
★ great experience if you want to ★
★ see it close up! ★

Many companies offer tours to
Death Valley and to break up the
monotonous terrain on the way, you'll
be taken through the beautiful Titus
Canyon, some ghost towns and be
shown Native American Indian
petroglyphs. Once there you'll be
shown all the Death Valley highlights
including Furnace Creek, Zabriski
Point, Bad Water and Scotty's Castle.

Spooky sights

ET Highway

About 140 miles (237km) north of Las
Vegas. A 98-mile (158-km) stretch of
road on Route 375, a few miles north
of the notorious Area 51 and the
super-secret Groom Lake Air Force
Base
1-800 237 0774 for information kit
This is where the American Air Force
is believed to have tested the Stealth
and U-2 aircraft and where numerous
American TV shows have claimed
aliens from outer space have
undergone examinations at the top-
secret Department of Defense site.
UFO buffs often gather on ridges
above Area 51 and use high-
powered telescopes and binoculars to
spy on the secret location. Their
favourite meeting points are at the
bars in nearby **Rachel**, where they
exchange tales about extra-terrestrials.

Now the road has been officially
dubbed the ET Highway by the
Nevada Commission on Tourism,
which has even created a new

11

Flying to the Grand Canyon

The Maverick Helicopters' pilot looked the spitting image of Tom Cruise and the theme from *Mission: Impossible* was blasting down our earphones as we took off from McCarran Airport. Suddenly the helicopter banked steeply and we five passengers had an altogether too-close-for-comfort view of the ground. Then, just as suddenly as we'd banked to the right, the helicopter straightened up and we found ourselves inching over the 'matchbox' houses at what seemed to be a snail's pace. In reality, we were speeding out of the Las Vegas Valley at 130mph (210kph), heading east to the West Rim of the Grand Canyon.

Within minutes, we were flying over the $1-million homes in the exclusive community of Lake Las Vegas and its two golf courses. Next came the 110-mile (177-km) long Lake Mead, the largest man-made lake in America providing a beautiful blue contrast to the pale brown rocks, and then the Hoover Dam. My thoughts that the scenery had a volcanic look to it were confirmed when our pilot pointed out an extinct volcano.

It took half an hour to reach the Grand Canyon and after a brief flyover, we landed on its rocky floor. Our pilot immediately jumped out and started preparing our champagne drinks with light snacks. It seemed a perfect way to spend 40 minutes – quaffing champagne and looking around at this millions-of-years-old natural wonder.

All too soon, it seemed, we were taking off again, but before we started our return journey we were taken on a small flight through the Canyon. The half-hour ride back to Las Vegas passed all too quickly as we headed for our final treat – a flight down the entire length of the famous Strip for a bird's-eye view of all those amazing buildings. (For information on helicopter flights to the Grand Canyon see page 204.)

programme called the **ET Experience**. You can call the toll-free number above to get an information kit on the highway and nearby attractions. The kit also contains a mileage chart and suggested (earthbound) travel itinerary. If you travel the route and can prove it with receipts from businesses along the highway you can become an official member of the ET Experience Association. Members receive a T-shirt, glow-in-the-dark licence plate frame, bumper sticker and collar pin. Call the Commission on 1-800 NEVADA 8.

Pioneer Saloon

Goodsprings, south of Las Vegas
702-874 9362
Open: daily from 10am
Founded in the old mining town, it

has much historical memorabilia and is worth dropping into to soak up some old-Americana atmosphere. Sitting on top of the US Army Cannon Stove, once used to warm people up on cold winter nights, is a piece of melted aluminium from the airplane in which film star Carole Lombard died. The plane crashed into Double Deal Mountain in January 1942 and her husband Clark Gable sat in the bar for days after, hoping for a miracle.

Bonnie and Clyde's 'Death Car'

Whiskey Pete's Hotel, Pimm (off Interstate 15)
702-679 6624
The original car driven by Bonnie Parker and Clyde Barrow in their final shoot-out with the FBI on 23 May 1934 is on display at Whiskey Pete's

Hotel. The infamous duo who held up gas stations, restaurants and small banks in Texas, New Mexico, Oklahoma and Missouri were shopped by a friend. At a cost of $75,000, Clyde's bullet-ridden and bloodstained shirt is now on display too! Worth visiting if you're going to Buffalo Bill's Turbo Drop and Desperado (see page 147).

Ghost towns

The old gold and silver mining towns are the stuff of many a Western movie and it is possible to visit some of these abandoned sites.

Goldfield Ghost Town (on Interstate 95 north of Scotty's Castle) was once Nevada's largest city after gold was dicovered in 1902. Known for its opulence, it was called the Queen of Camps and had 20,000 residents at its peak, with mines producing $10,000 a day in 1907. A flood in 1913 and a fire in 1923 destroyed much of the town, but still standing are the Courthouse and Santa Fe Saloon among others. For details contact the Goldfield Chamber of Commerce (702-485 6365).

In 1904 gold was discovered in the Amargosa Valley and the town of **Rhyolite** (just outside Beatty on Interstate 95, then 374) was born. At its peak, it housed 10,000 people and had more than 50 saloons, 18 grocery stores and half a dozen barbers. But it became a ghost town in 1911 after losing its financial backing. You can still see the Cook Bank Building, school and jail, plus a house built in 1905 entirely of bottles.

THINGS TO DO

There's plenty to do outside Las Vegas and as the interest in the great outdoors increases, so do the options. These days you can easily do anything from white water rafting to horse riding, jeep tours, hiking and skiing. All the companies offering different types of activities and their contact details are listed in the A–Z on pages 169–73.

Tours

Air tours

You can fly to all the major sights mentioned in this chapter either in a small plane or by helicopter. Flight packages are offered by many of the tour companies listed – **Eagle Scenic** is the largest and some just specialise in helicopter flights. These tours may be pricey – anything up to $450 – but they offer a marvellous opportunity to see amazing scenery in a very short space of time.

Generally, a small flight will include the Las Vegas Strip, Western Grand Canyon, Hoover Dam and Lake Mead and will cost around $99. The next step up will be the above plus a complete aerial tour of the Grand Canyon for around $149. The more expensive prices will include extras such as a champagne lunch on the Grand Canyon rim or, in the case of a helicopter flight, on the Canyon floor next to the Colorado. Combination tours may include lunch with Native Americans, river rafting and hiking. Some companies offer an overnight stay at the Grand Canyon, Bryce Canyon or Monument Valley.

Bus tours

The prices are cheaper, but the days are longer as you get to see all the sights covered by the air tours – only on the ground, of course!

Activities

Hiking

You can hike just about anywhere with **Rocky Trails**, one of the largest dedicated hiking organisations, which specialises in providing geological tours of everywhere from Red Rock to Valley of Fire, Mount Charleston and even Death Valley. Tours cost $139 to $179 including lunch. Or hike down the Grand Canyon – still the best way of seeing one of the most beautiful places on earth. **The Grand Canyon Tour Company** do half-day and full-day hikes with guides who tell you all

11

about the geology and human and natural history of the Grand Canyon. You will be given drinking water, high energy drink mixers and snacks.

Horse riding

Available at Red Rock Canyon, Bonnie Springs Old Nevada, Mount Charleston and Valley of Fire. You can go on horseback rides, custom and group trail rides and pack trips in southern Nevada, Utah and Northern Arizona with **Cowboy Trail Rides Inc**. Trips are tailor-made and can last an hour or seven days.

City slickers can enjoy a taste of the local desert landscape on gentle cowboy-trained trail horses in one- and two-hour trail rides and all-day cattle drives with **Saddle Up** in Primm. **A1 Western** offers Fossil Ridge, Canyon Rim and sunset rides in Red Rock Canyon.

The **Mount Charleston Riding Stables** (702 872 7009) offers a three-hour ride to the Fletcher Canyon filled with beautiful aspen trees and huge evergreens. Overnight wilderness rides are also available. A 90-minute ride through Cedar Ridge will provide panoramic views of the high desert valley below and the surrounding Spring Mountains. Allow four hours to include travel to and from your hotel. Costs $69 per person. An incredible three-hour ride along the legendary trails of Robbers Roost is also available. You will see where the outlaws rode to escape their crimes, follow a trail hidden by dense foliage, see the cave, secret passageway and streams that supplied water – all tucked away in the forest. Allow five hours to include travelling time. Cost $89 per person.

Water activities

Cruising, boating, fishing and jet-skiing are all available on Lake Mead and the largest provider of cruises and jet-skiing is **Lake Mead Cruises**. They run breakfast, midday, dinner and dinner-dance (Friday and Saturday only) cruises on the glassy waters of Lake Mead on board the *Desert Princess*, an authentic 300-passenger paddlewheeler, which is climate-controlled inside. Breakfast cruises cost $21 (under 12s $10), midday cruises $16 (under 12s $6), early dinner cruises $29 (under 12s $15) and dinner-dance cruises $43. Under 2s go free. All prices include tax. You can either board at Hoover Dam or at Lake Mead Marina.

The same company also run a two-hour **Lake Mead Jetski Tours** package ($164), which includes a half-hour orientation class and 90 minutes on the water. Each tour is accompanied by a guide who will narrate the trip via a hands-free, waterproof, two-way radio on each personal jet-ski. A box lunch is served at the end.

Further north at Overton Beach Marina you can hire everything from personal watercraft to patio and fishing boats with **Overton Beach Watercraft** (1-800 553 5452). Overnight packages are even available. Personal watercraft can seat two or three people and have storage compartments with a built-in cooler for your packed lunch. Patio boats for up to 10 people are perfect for fishing or cruising and come with a motor, radio/cassette, cooler, cushioned bench seating and an awning. Fishing boats hold four people and come with a Fish Finder and Pole Holder to increase your odds! Costs in each case are $45 an hour, $125 for half a day and $175 for a full day.

Off-road adventures

ATV Action Tours have the sole licensing permits for many desert regions, mountains and other points of interest in south-west Nevada. They combine the off-road experience in Land-Rovers, Jeep Cherokees and Wranglers with short hiking excursions, climbing large rock formations and searching for petroglyphs. Definitely the most fun way to get back to nature without breaking into a sweat! Tours cost between $65 and $179.

Since ATV set the ball rolling, many other tour companies are now offering Hummer Tours – the term used to describe off-road adventures in 4x4 Hummers. Those companies include **Grand Canyon Tour Company, A1 Western Tours** and **Rebel Adventure Tours**. The Hummer tours can be combined with other activities such as jet-skiing and rafting.

Rafting

Two basic types of rafting are easily available from Las Vegas. You can take a gentle ride in a motorised raft down an 11-mile (18-km) stretch of the Colorado, starting at the base of the mighty Hoover Dam and stopping for lunch (and a cooling swim). Along the way you will see hot water springs bubbling out of cliffs, flora and fauna and the amazing desert bighorn sheep, who think nothing of living on the perilous slopes of the Grand Canyon. These rides usually last around seven hours and cost about $80 with **Black Canyon River Raft Tours**. Plenty of other tour companies offer similar tours. The other kind of rafting is a lot more expensive, but more authentic and involves rapids. One- or two-day trips on rapids with strengths of between four and seven (on a scale of one to 10) are available with Native Americans from the Grand Canyon area. The **Grand Canyon Tour Company** offers trips from Lees Ferry in Arizona (about 2½ hours' drive from the South Rim of the Grand Canyon) that can also be combined with a hike down the Grand Canyon. Otherwise most of their trips start at three days and go up to two weeks between April and October, costing around $225 per day.

With **A1 Western Tours** you can do a two-day trip with a Native American river guide. You'll see the rugged mountains, mesas and deep gorges of the West Rim, travelling into the depths of the Canyon, rafting on rapids rated four to seven. Your overnight accommodation is either at Haulapai Lodge or camping on the canyon floor. These tours cost $612–659.

Rock climbing

Rock climbing is available at Red Rock or Mount Charleston with **Sky's the Limit**. Courses in rock and alpine craft are available daily for small groups and cost anywhere between $110 and $200 per day for rock craft and $160 to $250 for alpine craft depending on the size of the group. All levels are covered and can last up to a week for the serious! For instance, the week-long Basic Alpine Craft course covers balance and technique in face and crack climbing, rope management, climbing signals, belays, anchors, rappelling, multi-pitch climbing, use of ice axe in climbing and self-arrest, route finding, evaluation of hazards and ethics. It costs $900, though, so it's only for the dedicated, but as with all courses, there is a 10 per cent discount for advanced booking and payment.

Skiing and snowboarding

Just 35 minutes away from Las Vegas in Mount Charleston's Lee Canyon you can ski or snowboard from Thanksgiving to Easter. Beginner packages for skiing cost $40 for ski rental equipment, lift ticket and a one-hour group lesson. For snowboarding it costs $59 for the rental equipment, lift ticket and a one-hour group lesson. Lift prices for those with experience are $28 for adults and $21 for under 12s.

In summer (mid-June to October) ski-lift chair rides to the top of the ski runs are only $4 for adults and $2 for under 12s.

A–Z of tour companies

As you can see, the outdoor options are numerous and to make life a little simpler I have tried to list most of the major tour companies in this simple A–Z format. In many cases the companies have their own websites

Cowboys ...

You can't get away from them in Nevada – even the casinos are packed with Stetsons bobbing around among the slot machines. One of the most exciting festivals the city has to offer is the annual National Finals Rodeo held in the second week of December. Great contests include saddle bronc riding, bareback riding, bull riding, calf roping, steer wrestling, team roping, steer roping and barrel racing.

You can get a taste for real-life ranch action at any of the many ranches dotted throughout Nevada, Arizona and California that allow non-cowboys on board for a bit of fun (see page 205 for a full description of the different types and how to get in). One of the nearest – just 45 minutes by helicopter from the Las Vegas Strip – is the new **Grand Canyon West Ranch**, which nestles in the mountainous area between the west end of the Grand Canyon and the 6,000-ft (1,828-metre) Music Mountains of Arizona. **Heli USA** offers overnight packages, including helicopter flight, at this working cattle and guest ranch for $449.

Accommodation consists of rustic two- or four-person cabins with authentic roll-top bathtubs and log fires. A herd of long-horn Corriente cattle roam the ranch along with the wild animals such as deer, mountain lion, bob cats, rattle snakes and lizards. Self-drive packages with cabin stay start at $69 per person mid week.

If time doesn't permit a stay, **Wagons West** runs bus tours to cowboy country with horse-riding trips and highlights include the evening cowboy cook-out dinner in the heart of the Nevada desert. They can even arrange a real cowboy rodeo or Western show. **Pioneer Territory Wagon Tours** and **Cactus Jack's Wild West Tour Company** offer similar deals.

Expect to pay around $40 for a day wagon ride including dinner or $75 for overnight stays at the cow camp in Ash Meadows National Wildlife Meadows Refuge with Pioneer.

Valen Transportation has a Wild West and Bryce Canyon tour which itends to recapture the Wild West Experience through exciting stories of history, geology and Indian culture. The tour takes you on pioneer trails, to Old West towns, into Indian country and to the **Frontier Movie Town**, the old Hollywood Western film centre, in Kanab. There you can have a traditional cowboy Dutch-oven lunch. These tours cost $129. Also see Horse riding (page 168) for other cowboy trails.

About 20 miles (32km) east of Laughlin is **Oatman** in Arizona. Once a thriving mining town during the gold rush, wild burros now wander the streets of this popular TV and Western movie backdrop. At weekends you can take a trip back to the Old West with free cowboy gunfights and showdowns on Main Street. For details phone the Chamber of Commerce on 520-768 3990. Finally, a visit to Bonnie Springs Old Nevada (see page 163) will give you a real taste of the Wild West.

... and Indians

Three tribes have dominated Nevada's Native American history – the Northern Paiute, Southern Paiute and the Shoshone. Between them they have etched their stories in the rock petroglyphs of the Valley of Fire and other sacred places including Mount Charleston. The modern-day Native Americans still remain an important force in Nevada, with major Indian reservations at Moapa plus Fort Mojave Reservation in the southern-most tip of the state. They still live by their ancient codes and, even though they now run their own casinos and restaurants, maintain their heritage through traditional Pow Wows.

Originally, the Pow Wow was designed to bring various tribes together in a friendly way. It was a festive gathering where they exchanged gifts, heard the latest news and sold foods and crafts. Rodeos were an attraction, but the highlight was always the tribal dance competition for which they would dress in tribal regalia.

Pow Wows still take place today and are a wonderful way to experience the Indian culture. Of course, it cannot be guaranteed that a Pow Wow will be organised for your trip, but you can still get a taste of the Indian way of life by visiting the **Moapa River Indian Reservation**, just east of the Valley of Fire off Interstate 15. The store at the entrance is famous for its duty-free tobacco, alcohol and fireworks. But be warned, fireworks are not allowed outside the reservation and police do stop and search cars periodically.

Another great place to go is the **Lost City Museum of Archaeology** (721 South Moapa Valley Boulevard, Overton, 702-397 2193, just north of Red Rock Canyon). Here you will find artefacts from the Anasazis who lived in the Moapa Valley from the first to the 12th Centuries AD. Displays include a reconstruction of the Basket-maker pithouse and pueblo dwellings. The museum is located 66 miles (106km) north-east of Las Vegas on Highway 15 and Highway 169 near Overton. Open daily 8.30am–4.30pm.

Bruno's Indian Museum (1306 Nevada Highway, Boulder City, 702-293 4865) promotes and gives information about the Native American artists of the south-west, of which 2,000 are represented by the museum. Open 9am–5pm.

Most of the major tour companies offer Grand Canyon flights or helicopter tours to the West Rim combined with a barbecue lunch with the **Hualapai Indians** who will tell you about their legends and culture. The trips have been so successful that the Hualapai have even built a tiny village overlooking the Grand Canyon where you can shop for souvenirs or check out the small museum.

Another way to get the 'Indian' experience is to go on a one- or two-day rafting trip with a Native American river guide on the Colorado River. The **Grand Canyon Tour Company** (see page 172) offers rafting from Diamond Creek to Pierce Ferry.

11

through which it is possible to book excursions and trips in advance. This is probably most useful for those planning to do something quite specialist, such as rock climbing, or trying to go off the beaten track as times and dates may be specific.
Adventure Photo Tours 702-889 8687, www.adventurephototours.com. Private or semi-private photo safaris with professional and well-informed guides to Red Rock, Valley of Fire, Lake Mead and ghost towns in seven-seater Ford Expeditions, with pick-up from your hotel.
A1 Western Tours 702-644 7191, www.a1westerntours.com. Bus, air and helicopter tours, plus rafting, Lake Mead cruises, riding and ghost towns.

★★★ **BRIT TIP** ★★★
★ Watch out! Some tour companies ★
★ offer two-for-one or other big ★
★ discounts, making their prices ★
★ appear very competitive, but ★
★ they don't include taxes and ★
★ other extras, which can bump up ★
★ the cost considerably. ★
★★★★★★★★★★★★★★★★★★

ATV Action Tours 702-566 7400, www.atvactiontours.com.
Get to the other side of Las Vegas Valley in a Jeep Cherokee or Wrangler off-roader and then take a short hike. Also offers custom tours – including overnight stays at a dude ranch (see page 205), in a mountain cabin or even camping under the stars.
Black Canyon River Raft Tours 702-293 3776, www.rafts.com.
Cactus Jack's Wild West Tour Company 702-731 9400
Cadillac Reservations and Tours 1-800 556 3566, www.lvhelicopters.com.
Offers a selection of helicopter flights to the Grand Canyon, but they do not land in the canyon.
Cowboy Trail Rides 702-387 2457
Creative Adventures 702-361 5565. Specialists in the Spirits and Ghosts

Tour, which takes you to the wild country along the Colorado to Indian country before touring Searchlight, once a bustling mining town at the turn of the last century.
Desert Action Tours 702-796 9355
Drive Yourself Tours® 702-565 8761, www.grandcanyonwest.com.
Pop a tape in the cassette machine and take yourself off to Red Rock, Valley of Fire, Mount Charleston, Hoover Dam, Lake Mead or the Grand Canyon, listening to information about points of interest. The tapes come with maps.
Eagle Scenic 702-638 3300, www.scenic.com.
Since Eagle Airlines bought out Scenic, this is now the largest air tour company in Las Vegas. It offers every single destination you could think of – and every combination. In addition to the Grand Canyon, Zion Canyon, Bryce Canyon, Monument Valley and Lake Powell, you can also do overnight stops and get the Native American experience. Plus, of course, the night flight over the Strip.
Gourmet Tour 702-221 0376.
Offers two tours – to Hoover Dam/ Lake Mead and the Valley of Fire – combined with a gourmet lunch provided by one of the top restaurants.
Grand Canyon Discount Flights 702-433 7770, www.gcflight.com.
Specialises in Grand Canyon flights and helicopter tours and also combines them with champagne lunches, river rafting and trips to Bonnie Springs Old Nevada.
Grand Canyon Tour Company 702-655 6060, www.grandcanyontourcompany.com.
Another of the very big tour companies, offering all the Grand Canyon flights and helicopter rides to the bottom of the Canyon, bus trips, overnight stays, trips to Bryce and Zion Canyon, plus combinations with rafting, hiking, Hummers, and even a trip on the Grand Canyon Railway.
Gray Line Sightseeing Tours 702-384 1234, www.pcap.com/grayline.htm.
The big bus trip specialist, covering

everywhere from Hoover Dam to Bryce Canyon and Death Valley. If you pay for your tour in advance, you'll get a free round trip transfer from the airport to your hotel or a free Laughlin Day Tour.

Guaranteed Tours 702-369 1000, www.guaranteedtours.com.
Largely bus tours, but also offers some air tours, river rafting and a good selection of destinations.

Heli USA Airways 01462 455323 (UK) or 702-736 8787 (Las Vegas) www.heliUSA.com.
Offers a comprehensive selection of flights to the Grand Canyon with overnight stays, plus exclusive stays at the Grand Canyon West Ranch (see Cowboys panel).

HLA Tourist Services 702-243 2786, www.hlatours.com.

Keith Prowse 028 9023 2425, www.keithprowse.com.
For helicopter, aircraft and land tours.

Kidz Adventure Tours 702-564 6631

Lake Mead Cruises 702-293 6180, www.lakemeadcruises.com.
For both cruises and jet-skiing at Lake Mead.

Las Vegas Airlines 702-735 8007, www.lasvegasair.com/customer.
Specialises in air trips to the Grand Canyon area.

Las Vegas Concierge Sightseeing Tours 1-800 789 4444.
Can arrange for you to see the Hoover Dam, go on a Lake Mead Cruise, have a barbecue in Native American country, go rafting or off-road or take Grand Canyon air tours.

Las Vegas Host 702-798 5246, www.lasvegas.host.
One of the largest agencies for booking tours and attractions at good rates. Covers bus, air and helicopter tours and combinations with Pahrump Valley Vineyard, Harley Davidson Café, Grand Canyon champagne picnics, Native Americans and overnighters. Also offers a $2 discount off entrance to Wet 'n Wild.

Las Vegas Tour Desk 702-310 1320, www.lasvegastourdesk.com.
Specialises in air tours to the Grand Canyon.

Las Vegas Tours 702-895 8996, www.lasvegastours.com.
Champagne picnics at the bottom of the Grand Canyon.

Maverick Helicopter Tours 702-261 0007, www.maverickhelicopter.com.
Custom charters and tours to Grand Canyon, Bryce, Zion, Monument Valley and Death Valley. Also offers personalised videos to take home.

Pioneer Territory Wagon Tours 702-727 8332.
For the real Wild West experience!

★★★ BRIT TIP ★★★

★ Some tour companies offer free ★
★ day-long trips to Laughlin, but ★
★ these are just a classic way to get ★
★ you to spend money at the ★
★ casinos there. ★

Rebel Adventure Tours 702-380 6969, www.rebeladventuretours.com.
Off-road Hummer tours to Lake Mead and Hoover Dam and Grand Canyon, also combined with jet-skiing, lunch with Native Americans and white water rafting.

Rocky Trails 702-869 9991, www.rockytrails.com.
Run by a geologist, this company specialises in hiking tours that give you a real insight into the wonders of Red Rock, Valley of Fire, Mount Charleston and Death Valley.

Sky's The Limit 702-363 4533, www.skysthelimit.com.
Hiking and rock climbing.

Sundance Helicopter Tours 702-736 0606, www.helicopter.com.
Mostly helicopter trips to the Grand Canyon – landing on the canyon floor – but also do combinations with rafting, the Harley Davidson Café and Pahrump Valley Vineyard.

Valen Transportation and Tours 714-956 2252, www.valenbus.com.
Coach trips to the Grand Canyon, Zion and Bryce Canyons, Death Valley and the Wild West Tour.

Wagons West 702-494 8235

Wild West Tour Co 702-731 2425

11

12 GOLF AND OTHER SPORTS

Getting some golf action, plus specatator sports

Las Vegas is most famous for staging big-name fights between boxers, but its climate – especially in the spring, autumn and winter months – makes it perfect for golf and there has been a huge increase in the number of courses built over the last decade.

The irony is that the time when most Brits visit Las Vegas – the summer – is actually low season, so you should get some pretty good deals at golf courses then. The peak season is October to May, as the Americans consider the summer months far too hot to be playing golf! Fortunately, even in the summer golf courses are open early in the morning and later in the afternoon.

★★★ BRIT TIP ★★★

If you want to arrange a round of golf, go for an afternoon slot as the early mornings tend to get very busy. It's also a lot cheaper at many places – ask about 'twilight' rates, which means any time after 1pm.

Many hotels are affiliated to different golf courses, which offer resort guests reduced-price tee fees. All the same, fees for those courses and others in central Las Vegas will be two to three times more expensive than those out of the city, so I have given details of golf courses in Boulder City, North Las Vegas, Laughlin and Pahrump. A few Henderson courses are still well-priced, but most of those in the sought-after Lake Las Vegas area are now very expensive. Generally, the prices given include a cart.

Inside this chapter

A full listing of golf courses open to visitors follows below, but two very useful numbers are:
Stand-By Golf, 702-597 2665 (7am–9pm) for same-day and next-day play at reduced prices at many golf courses in the Las Vegas area.
Golf Reservations of Nevada, 702-732 3119, for advance tee-time reservations for individuals and groups at major courses in the area.

Las Vegas

Angel Park Golf Club

100 South Rampart Boulevard, 702-254 4653,
www.angelparkgolfclub.com
Two 18-hole resort courses. From $65 to $200 depending on the season. Twilight and reduced summer rates available. Reservations up to four months in advance.

Badlands Golf Club

9119 Alta Drive, 702-242 4653,
www.americangolf.com
27-hole resort course. From $90 to $130 depending on season. Twilight rates available. Reservations up to 60 days in advance.

★★★ BRIT TIP ★★★

The Badlands is considered the golfing equivalent of an ultimate thrill ride. Carved through canyons each of the 27 holes is known for dramatic shot values.

Bali Hai Golf Club

5160 Las Vegas Boulevard, 702-450 8000, www.waltersgolf.com
Stunning tropical-themed course just south of the Mandalay Bay with a fab clubhouse. From $150 to $325 depending on the season. Reservations up to six months in advance.

★ ★ ★ BRIT TIP ★ ★ ★

The Bali Hai Golf Club is not only fantastically located just by the Four Seasons and Mandalay Bay hotels, but also has a divine restaurant, Cili, by celebrity chef Wolfgang Puck.

Bear's Best Golf Club

11111 West Flamingo Avenue, 1-866 385 8500, www.bearsbest.com
A collection of Jack Nicklaus's favourite 18 holes in a dramatic setting with a desert-style clubhouse. From $180 to $195 Monday to Thursday and $205 to $235 Friday to Sunday.

Callaway Golf Center/ Divine Nine

6730 Las Vegas Boulevard South at the corner with Sunset Road, 702-896 4100, www.giantgolfacademy.com
From $40 to $60. Driving range hits on to 12 greens with various hazards.

★ ★ ★ BRIT TIP ★ ★ ★

The Callaway Golf Center is also home to the Danny Gans Junior Golf Academy that offers free golf instruction to children aged 11 to 16.

Desert Pines Golf Club

3415 East Bonanza Road, 702-388 4400, www.waltersgolf.com
Named after the hundreds of mature

pines that line the 18-hole public course, it also has covered hitting areas and an automatic ball delivery system. $45 to $165. Reservations up to six months in advance.

Desert Rose Golf Course

5483 Club House Drive, 702-431 4653, www.americangolf.com
Palm trees, water and bunkers highlight the 18-hole County course, which has a wash between the holes. From $75 to $85. Twilight rates available. Tee times seven days in advance.

Las Vegas Golf Club

4300 West Washington, 702-646 3003, www.americangolf.com
18-hole city course. Rates vary according to season. Reservations taken 60 days in advance.

Las Vegas National Golf Club

1911 East Desert Inn Road, 702-382 GOLF, 1-800 468 7918, www.americangolf.com
18-hole public course. From $145 to $175. Twilight rates available. Floodlit driving range. Reservations 60 days in advance.

Las Vegas Paiute Golf Resort

10325 Nu-Wav Kaiv Boulevard, 20 miles (32km) north of city on the Snow Mountain exit near Mount Charleston, 702-658 1400, www.lvpaiutegolf.com
Three 18-hole public courses on the Las Vegas Paiute Tribe Indian Reservation. From $100 to $120. Reservations up to 60 days in advance.

★ ★ ★ BRIT TIP ★ ★ ★

The Snow Mountain course at Las Vegas Paiute Golf Resort is considered the best public access course in Las Vegas by *Golf Digest* magazine.

12

Painted Desert Golf Club

5555 Painted Mirage Drive, 702-645 2568, 1-800 468 7918, www.americangolf.com
18-hole public course. Rates vary according to the season. Reservations up to 60 days in advance.

Rhodes Ranch Golf Club

20 Rhodes Ranch Parkway, 702-740 4114, 1-888 923 4653, www.rhodesranch.com
Rates vary according to the season. Reservations up to 60 days in advance.

Shadow Creek

Phone the Mirage for details on 702-791 7111
18-hole resort course specifically for the MGM Mirage group, which includes the MGM Grand, the New York-New York, Bellagio, Treasure Island and the Mirage. One of the highest ranking courses in America – accessible to MGM Mirage guests from a mere $500!

Tournament Players Club at the Canyons

9851 Canyon Run Drive, 702-256 2000, www.tpc.com

18-hole resort course. Rates vary from $85 to $250 depending on the season. Reservations up to a year in advance.

North Las Vegas

Craig Ranch Golf Course

628 West Craig Road, 702-642 9700
18-hole public course. Rates vary according to season. Reservations seven days in advance.

North Las Vegas Golf Course

324 East Brooks, 702-633 1833
Nine-hole city course (the ninth hole is on a hill and has a great view of Las Vegas). Rates vary according to season. Reservations seven days in advance.

Boulder City

Boulder City Golf Course

1 Clubhouse Drive, Boulder City, 702-293 9236
18-hole city course. Rates from $40 for Clark County residents and $50 for non-residents. Reservations one week in advance.

Henderson/ Green Valley

Black Mountain Golf and Country Club

500 Greenway Road, Henderson, 702-565 7933
18-hole semi-private course. Rates from $70. Tee times up to four days in advance.

DragonRidge Golf and Country Club

552 South Stephanie Street, Henderson, 702-614 4444, www.dragonridgegolfclub.com
With great views of the Las Vegas Valley and bent-grass greens, this will test even the best golfers. From $75 to $195. Reservations can be made up to 30 days in advance.

Legacy Golf Club

130 Par Excellence Drive, Henderson, 702-897 2187, www.thelegacygc.com 18-hole resort course. From $65 to $170 depending on the season. Tee times up to 120 days in advance.

Reflection Bay Golf Club

75 MonteLage Boulevard, Henderson, 702-740 4653
Jack Nicklaus's prestigious course includes five holes played alongside 1.5 miles (2.4km) of Lake Las Vegas shoreline, while other holes are decorated with water features. $165 to $250 daily. Tee times up to 30 days in advance.

★ Jack Nicklaus's nationally ranked ★ Reflection Bay Golf Club is part of ★ the exclusive MonteLago Lake Las Vegas Resort, which includes shops, restaurants, a casino and two waterfront hotels. For more details of the whole area visit www.lakelasvegas.com.

Rio Secco Golf and Country Club

2851 Grand Hills Drive, Henderson, 702-889 2400, www.playrio.com 18-hole resort course owned by the Rio All-Suite Hotel. Mostly for Rio's and Harrah's Hotel guests. Reservations 90 days in advance.

★ The Wildhorse Golf Club's 18th ★ hole is one of the most difficult ★ in the Las Vegas Valley thanks to ★ the surrounding bunkers and four lakes!

Wildhorse Golf Club

2100 Warm Springs Road, 702-434 9000, 1-800 468 7918, www.americangolf.com

18-hole public course. Rates vary seasonally. Reservations up to 60 days in advance.

Laughlin

Emerald River Country Club

1155 West Casino Drive, Laughlin, 702-298 0061
Demanding 18-hole resort course next to the Colorado including five holes along the river, 54 bunkers and plenty of changes in elevation. Rates vary from $45 to $125 depending on the season. Reservations up to 30 days in advance.

★ The Emerald River Country Club ★ has received a three-star rating – ★ the highest – from *Golf Digest*.

Mohave Resort Golf Club

9905 Aha Macav Parkway, Laughlin, 702-535 4653, www.mojaveresort.com
An 18-hole course that hosts the Southern Nevada Golf Association Championships. Rates vary depending on the season. Reservations one week in advance or 30 days with a credit card.

Pahrump

Willow Creek Golf Club

1500 Red Butte, Pahrump, 702-727 4653, www.wcgolf.com
An 18-hole Championship Course

★ The Willow Creek Golf Club – a ★ pleasant 45-minute journey from ★ Las Vegas – has a beautiful course ★ famous for having the best rates ★ in southern Nevada.

Major annual sporting events

March: Big League Weekends (basketball) – Cashman Field Center, 702-386 7200.

April: Spring Pro-Am Golf Tournament – Sunrise Golf Club, 1-800 332 8776; and **Las Vegas Senior Classic** – Senior PGA Golf Tournament, 702-382 6616.

September: Pro-Am Golf Tournament – Sahara Country Club, 1-800 332 8776.

October: Ice Hockey Season. A schedule is available in August for the **Las Vegas Thunder International Hockey League** at the Thomas and Mack Center, 702-798 7825; and for the **Las Vegas Invitational PGA Golf Tournament**, 702-382 6616. This is also the month when the World Championship Wrestling's **Halloween Havoc** event is held every year at the MGM Grand.

December: National Finals Rodeo Christmas Gift Show at Cashman Field Center, 702-386 7100. **National Finals Rodeo** at the Thomas and Mack Center, 702-895 3900. **Las Vegas Rugby Challenge** – 64 American and Canadian teams battle it out at Freedom Park or Sam Boyd Silver Bowl. For a schedule call 702-656 1401. **Las Vegas Bowl Collegiate Football Game** – Big West Conference v Mid-American Conference at Sam Boyd Silver Bowl, 702-731 2115.

surrounded by the Nopah and Spring Mountain ranges. Rates range from $20 to $60 depending on the season. Reservations seven days in advance.

Summerlin

Sun City Summerlin Golf Club

Three courses, 702-254 7010, www.suncity-summerlin.com Palm Valley: 9201-B Del Webb Boulevard. 18-hole semi-private (preference is given to residents). Highland Falls: 10201 Sun City Boulevard. 18-hole course. Eagle Crest: 2203 Thomas Ryan Boulevard. 18-hole course. Rates vary from $45 to $145. Call for reservations.

SPECTATOR SPORTS

Las Vegas has it all still to do in the sporting arena. It doesn't have a professional football or basketball team – both are university (or college, as they are called in America) teams, but sometimes NBA (basketball) friendlies are held during October, which are worth going to see.

The city is most famous for hosting major championship boxing events two or three times a year – and has done so since 1960, largely as a result of the fact that this was the only city in America where you could legally gamble on a winner. Most of the middle and heavyweight fights take place at Caesars Palace, the MGM Grand or the Mandalay Bay. Tickets start at $100 and rise to a steep $1,500 or more for ringside seats. Best place to do your homework is on the TicketMaster website at www.ticketmaster.com.

American Football

Sam Boyd Stadium, Boulder Highway, 702-895 3900
The UNLV team's season runs between September and December. Tickets cost between $15 and $25.

Baseball

Cashman Field, 850 Las Vegas Boulevard North at Washington Avenue, 702-386 7200
Home of the Las Vegas 51s, who play from April to September as part of the Pacific Coast League.

Basketball

Thomas & Mack Center, 4505 Maryland Parkway on the UNLV campus, 702-895 3900, www.thomasandmack.com
The city's team is the UBLV Runnin' Rebels, who play all their games here between November and May. During October NBA teams sometimes play exhibition games here, but tickets are snapped up very quickly.

Las Vegas Speedway Park

6000 Las Vegas Boulevard North, 702-644 7774
Lying 17 miles (27km) north of the Strip, the 1,500-acre (607-ha) Speedway opened in 1996 at a cost of $200 million and seats 107,000. Facilities include a 1.5-mile (2.4km) superspeedway, a 2.5-mile (4-km) road course, a half-mile (0.8km) dirt oval, drag strip, go-kart tracks and racing school. Check out **Midnight Madness** on Fridays and Saturdays for drag racing which starts at 10pm as part of the test and tune sessions that begin at 5pm. Phone ahead for schedules of upcoming events and tickets.

To catch some football action, try the **Canadian Football League** on 702-242 4200 for their schedules. For hockey, try the **Las Vegas Thunder Hockey** on 702-798 PUCK and for general sports events, **UNLV Sports** on 702-895 3900.

★★★ ★★★
★ ★
★ ★
★ Try Nevada Ticket Services on ★
★ 702-597 1588 to book anything ★
★ from basketball to football, ★
★ hockey, baseball, National Finals ★
★ Rodeo, pro bull rides, Superbowl ★
★ and Final Four. ★
★★★★★★★★★★★★★★★★★★

Wrestling

The city doesn't hold its own events, but does play host to several World Wrestling Federation and World Championship Wrestling events.

Either check out the local paper when in town or look at www.wwf.com and www.wcwwrestling.com in advance.

EXTREME SPORTS

There are many different ways to have fun in Las Vegas and if extreme thrills are your thing, then you can do anything from a terrifying bungee jump to taking part in a race at the Speedway.

AJ Hackett Bungee

810 Circus Circus Drive, 702-385 4321
If it's sheer exhilaration you want, jump off the 180-ft (55-metre) tower, then cool off in the pool! Hours are seasonal. Various packages are available with T-shirts and videos.
Open: Monday to Friday 11am–8.30pm, Saturday and Sunday 11am–10pm weather permitting. Last lift goes up half an hour before closing and hours change in autumn and winter.
Cost: for first-time jumpers $54 for one jump. Subsequent jumps $25 each with fourth jump free. Groups of five or more get $5 off per person. T-shirts and jump videos also available.

★★★ ★★★
★ ★
★ You must be a minimum of 13 ★
★ years old to do a bungee jump ★
★ and weigh at least 90lb (40kg). ★
★ Under 18s must also be ★
★ accompanied by a parent or ★
★ legal guardian. ★
★★★★★★★★★★★★★★★★★★★★

Flyaway Indoor Skydiving

200 Convention Center Drive, 702-731 4768
Learn how to fly in America's only indoor skydiving simulator, where the vertical wind tunnel allows you to beat gravity and fly! First-time flyers are given a 25-minute class in safety and body control techniques. Experienced skydivers can also get

12

valuable 'air' time to improve their skills without having to pack a rig and wait for the right weather. Video coaching programmes are also available in which your air tunnel flight is recorded to help you improve your style.
Open: Monday to Saturday 10am–7pm, Sunday 10am–5pm. Classes every half hour from 11am to an hour before closure.
Cost: $50 for first flight, $75 for two flights, $150 for five flights and $250 for learn-to-fly coaching package including five flights, video services and personalised coaching.

★ ★ ★   **BRIT TIP**   ★ ★ ★
★   ★
★   Dress the part for your indoor   ★
★   skydive – make sure you're in   ★
★   comfy clothes with socks and   ★
★   trainers.   ★
★ ★ ★ ★ ★ ★ ★ ★ ★ ★ ★ ★ ★ ★ ★ ★

Laser Quest

7361 West Lake Mead Boulevard, 702-243 8881
You wear a laser-sensing vest and shoot it out with other laser-wielding players in a maze of corners, turns, walkways and mirrored walls. Lasers are, of course, lightbeams, so you can even hit someone from around a corner if you get it to ricochet off the right point. Great for children up to the age of 80!
Open: Tuesday to Thursday 2–10pm, Friday 2–11pm, Saturday noon–11pm, Sunday noon–6pm.
Cost: flat rate of $7 per person for 20 minutes of play.

Las Vegas Skydiving Center

Just behind the Goldstrike Hotel at Jean Airport, 702-877 1010 (south-west of Las Vegas)
Take a tandem skydive after a 20-minute lesson for $159 ($179 including transport from your hotel).
Open: daily from 8am till dusk, jumps are by appointment only.

Las Vegas Mini Grand Prix

1401 North Rainbow Boulevard, 702-259 7000
Take Exit 82a off US 95 for the ride of a lifetime on children's Grand Prix, Nascars, go-karts and kiddie karts. There is also a games arcade and snack bar.
Open: daily 10am–10pm except Christmas Day and depending on the weather.
Cost: $4.95 per ticket or $22.50 for five. Cars available for from four to over 16-year-olds.

Race Car Tours

Las Vegas Motor Speedway, 7000 Las Vegas Boulevard North, 702-644 4444
This is home to the city's NASCAR events and drag races, where you can also get a piece of the action yourself. After minimal instruction you're allowed behind the wheel of a full-sized, 600HP racing car for six laps at speeds of up to 145mph (233kph) at a cost of $375. For a mere $77 you can be a passenger in a two-seater racing car as a professional instructor does six laps around the Speedway. For $129 you can even experience a real race as a passenger in a qualifying run as a professional reaches speeds of up to 180mph (290kph)!

Rocks and Ropes

3065 East Patrick Lane, Suite 4, 702-434 3388
This indoor climbing facility has more than 7,000sq ft (651sq metres) of sculpted and textured walls for climbing, 30-ft (9-metre) ceilings, top rope and lead climbing and a mega-cave with a leadable 40-ft (12-metre) roof so people can learn everything they need to know to go rock climbing for real!
Cost: $45 for a five-visit pass.

Skydive Las Vegas

Boulder City Airport, Boulder City, 702-293 1860 (near Hoover Dam)
You freefall for 45 seconds before

enjoying a seven-minute parachute ride in a tandem jump. By appointment only.

Xtreme Zone

Grand Slam Canyon at Circus Circus, 702-794 3939
A combination of rock climbing and aerial bungee jumping creates an interactive experience with multiple difficulty levels. The Zone's rock-climbing attraction combines traditional harnesses and handholds with cutting-edge belay technology to make it as safe as possible. The aerial trampoline combines a standard trampoline with a hydraulic system and bungee cords so you can climb up to 20ft (6 metres) and then flip and spin yourself back and forth. You must weigh between 40–265lb (18–120kg) to climb the wall and between 30–220lb (13.5–99kg) to experience the bungee.

12

13 GETTING THERE

The low-down on the tour operators, doing it your own way and specialist holiday planners

So that's the big deal... now how do you get there? The options are as extensive as the choices open to you when you decide to visit Las Vegas. Do you use the city as a fantastically cheap base for visiting all the natural wonders on its doorstep; head off on a fly-drive tour; or even start in Los Angeles and San Francisco and take in all the wonderful places that you can reasonably visit in the amount of time available to you?

Then there are the other factors, like how many of you are travelling, will you be visiting friends in, say, LA or San Francisco, in which case you could take advantage of the incredibly cheap offers to Las Vegas that are advertised in the local papers and travel from there. If you have children and teenagers in your party you'll probably be best off with an airline/tour operator that caters well for the family market. You may even want to do a part fly-drive and add on a ranch or golfing holiday or an adventure trek.

The visitor figures show that Brits tend either to go on a long-weekend package to Las Vegas or do a combination of any of the above. It is for this reason that if you have ever picked up a brochure on visiting Las Vegas and California there seems to be so much information and so many options to wade through from multi-centre packages, fly-drives, coach tours, open-jaw flights (see page 184) and so on. It'll take some time to make sense of one brochure, let alone compare a few to see what suits you best. Then there is the other option – to organise your trip totally independently.

To try to make life easier, I've tried to outline the options available, what to look for and what to ask for.

Inside this chapter

Specialist tour operators

I don't mean your local travel agents, though they may have a good working knowledge of Las Vegas, but those who specialise in organising holidays to the region and produce a brochure to display their products. I say this because Las Vegas in particular has quirks all of its own and someone with little 'local' knowledge is unlikely to provide you with the best deals or choice of options.

What's good about the specialist North American tour operators is that the big outfits especially have massive buying power and so can offer the best prices available for both hotels and car-hire services. In many cases you can go for a 'land-only' deal for a nominal charge, which gives you the option to arrange your flights through some of the cheap flight brokers who advertise in the weekend national newspapers (more about that in the independent travel section). Most do not advertise this though, so you will have to ask.

All the main specialist North American operators provide tailor-made packages, which mean that you can take advantage of any special deals and arrangements they may have with, for instance, hotels, theme parks and local airline companies offering scenic flights around the Grand Canyon area and San Francisco.

The bigger guys – such as **American Connections, Virgin, Kuoni, Jetlife, Premier** and **Getaway Vacations** – can pack in a lot of added-value extras such as room upgrades for honeymoon and anniversary holiday-makers, free transfers to the hotel (generally not part of a North American package), free accommodation and/or free meals for children, extra nights free, free flights to London from regional airports and so on. You may also like to know that out of the large tour companies operating in North America, **Virgin Holidays, Kuoni, Travelsphere, Jetsave** and **Page & Moy** did particularly well in the 'would you recommend this tour operator to a friend?' stakes as part of a *Which?* tour operator survey.

Local knowledge

But big is not always best in this market, as good knowledge of the location is very important, along with the operator's determination to provide you with what is best for you (which may involve making alternative suggestions to your own best-laid plans) and offer a generally good

level of service. Smaller outfits such as **Just America** do not claim to be the cheapest, but with a high level of return custom and recommendation-to-friends business, they know their emphasis on getting things right for a slightly higher cost means all the difference between an okay holiday and a fantastic one. Their policy is based on not packing too much into one trip so that you travel to see destinations, not see destinations as you travel. Overall, it makes them very good value for money.

Another smaller UK operator, **Funway**, has a sister company in the US which sends more than one million people a year to Las Vegas, so they have tremendously good buying power and very good access to hotels in Las Vegas. More than 30 hotels are featured in the brochure (the average tends to be about five or six), including all the recently opened resorts such as The Palms.

In addition, Funway's relationship with Las Vegas means they are likely to be able to get you into top resort hotels when other tour operators may not. They also provide a whole raft of extras including a Funway fun book, which is full of two-for-one and free admissions to parks and shows and 25% discounts on helicopter tours to the Grand Canyon. Overall, it makes them one of the best operators to Las Vegas.

★ ★ ★ **BRIT TIP** ★ ★ ★

★ When shopping around for flight ★
★ prices, make sure the figure you ★
★ are given includes all taxes and ★
★ airport fees so you can make a ★
★ proper comparison. ★
★ ★ ★ ★ ★ ★ ★ ★ ★ ★ ★ ★ ★ ★ ★ ★ ★ ★

What to look for

Using a tour operator is great if you want to get everything sewn up before you go, but remember they're in business to make money and, while

13

their brochures may be in one sense accurate, not all of them always give you the full monty, so to speak. Also, it is useful to bear in mind that even if something is not included in the brochure, such as open-jaw tickets (see below) or air passes (see page 186), you should always ask your preferred operator if they can arrange those for you.

Here's how to take the good, watch out for the bad and reject the downright ugly that tour operators have to offer.

Scheduled flights

There is really not much to compare between charter and scheduled flights in the North American market, as only **Unijet** provide charter-only services, but if the European market is anything to go by, this is a good thing as scheduled flights generally provide a far greater degree of satisfaction among customers. For starters, most of the airlines fly every day to a whole range of locations in North America – many at easy-to-catch times of the day – and from a range of regional airports in the UK.

Given the way most Brits tend to move around Nevada, Arizona and California during a holiday to the region, this provides the essential flexibility required when organising a trip. What tends to follow on from scheduled services is the ability to make a stop on the way to your final destination (stopover); fly into one city and out from another (open-jaw) and even fly between cities (using multi-centre packages or air-pass vouchers). And if you tend to do a lot of long-haul travelling, you can even arrange it so that you get frequent-flyer points. Most of the operators offer a minimum of three airline prices, some up to six, except for airline-run operators, eg American Holiday (American Airlines); NorthWest Airlines; United Vacations (United Airlines) and Virgin.

Assessing flight choices

The good news for those who want to get straight to Las Vegas without taking in any other destinations, such as LA or San Francisco, is that Virgin Atlantic has three direct flights a week to the city.

So when comparing prices for flights, the first thing you need to look for is whether you are getting a direct flight with Virgin or whether you are going via a hub city – which you will do with any of the other carriers – and how much longer that will add on to your travel time. When weighing up cost differences do bear in mind that flying into a hub city tends to involve changing planes to a less comfortable domestic plane where you will also be charged for your drinks.

If you do opt to use a non-direct service, also remember that some tickets may provide better stopovers than others, which will make arranging a decent multi-centre deal easier.

The next is to take into consideration any differences between flying at the weekend or midweek – there is normally a surcharge for Friday and Saturday flights.

Finally, always ensure the price you get quoted includes all airport taxes and non-negotiable fees – they can amount to a fair bit and you don't want those kind of surprises!

★ ★ ★   **BRIT TIP**   ★ ★ ★

Always check around for best flight prices before booking, as there may be good deals on offer.

Open-jaw flights

Fly into one city and out from another. It's usually very simple to work out the cost – in most cases, you add the cost of flying to one destination to the cost of flying to the other, divide by two and add a £1. This means you don't have to backtrack and it can save you quite a lot of money on a touring trip. Very few operators advertise open-jaw so you will have to ask whether it can be arranged or shop around.

Multi-centre packages

Fly into one city, look around, fly on to another, look around, fly on to another, look around and then fly home. This kind of package tends to be one of the most popular in the Las Vegas/California holiday market with the trio of Las Vegas, Los Angeles and San Francisco as the leading lights. It's a good idea if you don't want, or don't have, enough time to drive between all the main places you want to see, but it is a more expensive option, generally, than using your full quota of stopovers, or the open-jaw system.

Stopovers

The alternative to the above is to use the stopover system whereby you break your journey at various points. Most of the airlines offer this service, with the first stopover usually free and subsequent stopovers (up to a maximum of three) being charged at around £60 a stop. Some airlines now offer two free stopovers.

If you want to use this system, you have to ensure that the route you are booking is the correct one for you as the first, free, stopover is usually limited to the 'gateway' city, ie the first place where the plane lands in the United States and where you'll go through American immigration. Watch this, as many of the American airlines use 'hub' cities as their gateway cities, such as Detroit or Minneapolis in the case of NorthWest Airlines, and you may not consider Delta's hub cities of Atlanta or Cincinatti to be as exciting a stopover point as New York or Los Angeles, for instance. With other airlines, including NorthWest, it may pay to route your trip via Amsterdam so that you get a more interesting 'gateway' city.

★ ★ ★   BRIT TIP   ★ ★ ★
★   ★
★   To make best use of your free   ★
★   stopover, check your 'gateway'   ★
★   city is a reasonable destination,   ★
★   eg New York or Chicago, rather   ★
★   than Cincinatti or Atlanta!   ★
★ ★ ★ ★ ★ ★ ★ ★ ★ ★ ★ ★ ★ ★ ★ ★ ★ ★

Extra stops

These are similar to stopovers, except you'll pay an extra fee, usually £60. If you want to fly to more than one place not covered by your free stopover allowance, or if the place you want to go to isn't on the route, go for an air pass (see page 186).

Child and youth discounts

Most airlines give child discounts (ages 2–11), usually at 50% off the published price during mid and low seasons and at 40% during peak season. The peak season does vary a little but a rough guide is July–August and the Christmas period between around 15–27 December. Very few airlines offer youth discounts for 12- to 16-year-olds (a paltry 10%, which could be matched by shopping around the flight shops) but your best bets are tour operators who use United Airlines and Virgin.

Infant fares

The old days of tour operators publishing very cheap infant fares, but then adding on up to £60 of taxes are, thankfully, mostly gone, though some still continue this practice. A good fully inclusive price these days is around £70, but do check that the price you have been quoted includes all taxes.

Regional departures

More and more airlines are running routes directly from regional airports in the UK to Las Vegas and California. But neither British Airways nor Virgin does, and in most cases you will have to pay a supplement to

13

Frequent-flyer points

Did you know that every time you fly you could be clocking up frequent-flyer mileage points that will eventually give you free air travel or other perks such as last-minute availability, lounge access and free upgrades or discounts off attractions and excursions in the USA? Very often your holiday booking does give you free air miles, but you may not know about it. Even if you do not claim the benefits, your travel agent still has the right to do so and some like to keep this nice little perk under their hats! So, before you go on holiday, register with the airline for their loyalty scheme and keep your booking passes to prove that the flights were taken. Discounted flights may not qualify, but it's always worth checking.

Many of the North American specialists will automatically offer frequent-flyer points on American Airlines flights, though you may have to pay an additional £49 for the privilege of collecting them. Having said that, AA give you one Advantage mile for every mile you fly, which is over 10,000 if you're flying from London to Los Angeles – enough to earn you one free ticket to certain European destinations.

If you have a family, it is a good idea to register the whole family in the scheme so each person can build up their points. Some schemes such as the Frequent Virgin Club, expects its economy-class passengers to complete three return economy flights before qualifying, though upper class or premium economy passengers qualify immediately. British Airways offer both air miles and travel points, the latter granting lounge facilities and even free travel insurance with enough credits.

When arranging to join a frequent-flyer programme, ask if there is a bonus for joining at that particular time as different airlines offer bonuses. For instance, not so long ago Virgin was offering a bonus of 2,000 points on joining and Continental a special activation bonus of a whopping 5,000 miles when you take your first Continental Airlines holiday. The scheme offers free upgrades and free tickets.

Finally, in the first deal of its kind, the MGM Grand in Las Vegas has teamed up with American Airlines' frequent-flyer programme. So any time you spend money at the hotel you can earn advantage points.

fly to London (though Kuoni offers free flights in connection with transatlantic BA and United Airlines flights). In almost all cases, if you want to fly from Glasgow you will have to pay a supplement of around £45–50. However, United Vacations and US Airtours offer free connections from many regional UK airports.

Air passes

If you plan to visit more than the one city covered by your free stopover or, for whatever reason, are likely to make quite a few flights between certain destinations, an air pass is the way to go. But you must buy before you go as North American residents are not permitted to buy air passes, so they won't be available once you get to the US.

Sadly, as with most open-jaw tickets, most operators don't advertise these air passes, probably because they are a much cheaper (and more flexible) alternative to the extra stopover system – even Trailfinders have dropped them from their brochure. The only tour operators still advertising air passes are Bon Voyage and Jetset, who use the Freedom USA pass from Southwest Airlines.

Four passes are available: **Same**

or **Adjoining State Pass** (£45); the **Western Pass** for travel within the Western time zone – that's from Texas to California inclusive (£69); **Central and Eastern Pass** for travel anywhere except the Western time zone (£69) and the **Anywhere Pass** for travel anywhere within Southwest Airlines' route network (£99). Other US airline companies also offer these passes and if you would like one ask your tour operator to arrange one for you.

★ When booking flights, be sure to
★ claim your free air miles or find
★ out about the airline's loyalty
★ scheme before you go, to be on
★ track for free air travel or other
★ benefits such as priority booking,
★ lounge facilities and upgrades.

The airlines and smoking

Virgin and most of the American airlines have a total non-smoking policy on their transatlantic flights. In fact, smoking is banned by law on all American flights, so even if you do get a transatlantic flight that allows smoking, if you switch to a domestic plane for the final leg of your journey you will not be allowed to smoke on that plane. For the moment you can still puff to your heart's content in the smoking sections of BA flights.

Code share

Many airlines enter into alliances with each other to share routes, which can offer you more choice of routes and fares. It means that your flight is marketed by one airline, with the airline's flight number, but when you board you find the service is operated by a different airline. Some tour operators will inform you in advance, but they may not always know as these alliances are constantly changing. Be careful of this if you have a particular dislike for one airline or know that you definitely

want to fly with a certain company. A 1997 *Which?* survey of airlines found that Virgin was among the most highly rated, yet it currently has a code-share alliance with Continental, who came pretty near the bottom of the same report.

Kids stay free

Many operators offer this as an extra, but it is standard policy at many American hotels to allow children to stay free in the same room as an adult. If you're NOT being offered this as an option, go elsewhere!

Length and type of visit

Weekend breaks

Unijet, charter specialists to Las Vegas, have been known to advertise long weekends to Las Vegas for as little as £400 during the low-season winter months. If that sounds like fun to you, keep your eyes peeled for those newspaper ads! In addition, more and more tour operators are offering weekend breaks.

Fly-drive and tailor-made tours

These have to go hand-in-hand in the North American market as there are so many options it would be daft for any tour company to force people into taking one particular tour (that's what coach trips are for!). Chapter 15 The Grand Canyon and Surroundings gives a good insight into great places to visit within easy striking distance of Las Vegas.

Coach and Tauck tours

If you don't want to worry about car hire, driving and all the other arrangements you will need to make, and you don't mind a coachload of people crowding into an attraction at the same time as you, then this could be the way to go. Coach tours are not necessarily all-inclusive, though, and may not include meals so that you have the option of choosing where to eat.

Tauck tours are the posher version and usually include everything. Run by an American company, you will be greeted and treated as an individual, while the tours themselves tend to be shorter so you have more time to relax and explore sights by yourself. In addition, you are put up in first-class hotels with character.

Extras

Grand Canyon flights

One of the added bonuses of visiting Las Vegas is that you can experience the amazing scenery of Arizona's Canyonlands, plus other natural wonders Bryce Canyon and Zion Park, without the long drive. A whole host of scenic flight operators work out of Las Vegas (details in Chapter 11 Outdoor Adventure), but if you want to make sure of your seat or tie up all loose ends before you go, many of the tour operators are offering these flights. And, again, ask even if they're not advertised as they may be able to arrange a scenic flight for you.

Show tickets

You can buy these in advance to ensure you get a seat, but don't overdo it as you may miss out on cheap deals locally.

Hotel vouchers

The three basic kinds of hotel vouchers are the Liberty and TourAmerica Hotel Passes and the North American Guestcheque. In all cases you buy vouchers at a certain price in advance that are valid for one night at a participating hotel – usually a chain hotel. You can book the hotel in advance and the room will accommodate up to four people. It can be a very good way of planning your holiday budget and pre-paying as far as possible. But one major drawback is that if you buy more than you need, there is usually

a charge for redeeming any unused vouchers. Often it amounts to the value of one voucher and in some cases it can be one voucher plus an administrative charge of £25.

Another drawback is that you do not benefit from any promotions that participating hotels and motels may run locally. And do bear in mind that these chain hotels don't have much character and some may even seem a little soulless. Also:

- Purchasing the vouchers does not automatically give you the right of accommodation, so it is always best to book as far in advance as possible, especially if you intend to travel in the peak seasons (see The seasons, page 189).
- If you intend to arrive after 4pm, you will need a credit card to guarantee your reservation. If it is a hotel/motel in a particularly busy area, such as one of the major sights that is not near a big town or city, I'd recommend you ask them to send or fax the confirmation of your reservation.
- There are often many hotels of the same chain in the same town, so it is best to make a note of the full address so you go to the right one!

The **Liberty Hotelpass** encompasses many of the main hotel and motel chains in America including Days Inn, Howard Johnson, Ramada, Travelodge and Super 8 and you can stay in cities, resorts, near airports and at key touring areas. Most locations have swimming pools, restaurants and facilities for children. Prices per voucher cost between £42 and £45 (including taxes) and you will receive a free directory of participating hotels so you can make advance reservations. In some key touring areas, rooms may require more than one voucher per night, but these are clearly marked in the directory.

The **Tour American Hotelpass** also includes the main chains of Days Inn, Howard Johnson, Travelodge and

Super 8, with over 350 properties along the highways and in major cities, but at £30 a voucher (again for rooms that can accommodate up to four people) it is aimed more at the budget end of the market. As with the Liberty scheme, you will get a directory and some hotels and motels in the key touring areas may require more than one voucher per night.

The **North American Guestcheque** is solely for use with Best Western hotels and motels and there are two voucher prices: £28 (which equates to $44) and £7 (which equates to $11). All the hotel prices in the directory are listed in denominations of $11 so you can purchase the exact number of vouchers required. Fewer tour operators are offering hotel passes, but if you really want them, ask your preferred operator to arrange some for you.

The American Way

Motorbike hire

Okay, so you fancy yourself as a modern-day cowboy enjoying the ultimate touring experience of travelling along those wide-open roads on anything from a Harley Davidson Electra Glide to a Fat Boy or Road King. You can do that from LA and Las Vegas, but it'll be a lot more expensive than a car. The few operators that offer this include **American Holidays** and **Jetlife**.

Amtrak and Greyhound

Greyhound's **International Ameripass** allows you to go where you want when you want, travelling by coach day or night, from £125 for 10 days to £189 for 21 days. Trailfinders is now the ONLY operator offering these.

Amtrak rail passes for Western states start at £122 for 15 days of travel (£158 peak season) and go up to £159 for 30 days of travel (£205 peak season). National and other regions are also available. Amtrak covers all the major destinations and sights in California and there is the new non-stop daily service between Los Angeles and Las Vegas for $99 return. The trip takes 5$^{1}/_{2}$ hours with trains arriving in Las Vegas at 2pm and departing for LA at 4pm every day. Few tour operators advertise Amtrak travel, but others may arrange it for you if you ask.

★ ★ ★   **BRIT TIP**   ★ ★ ★
★   ★
★   ★
★ If you're in Los Angeles check the ★
★   local papers for good deals on   ★
★   the new Amtrak rail service   ★
★   between LA and Las Vegas.   ★
★ ★ ★ ★ ★ ★ ★ ★ ★ ★ ★ ★ ★ ★ ★ ★ ★

Other things you need to know

The seasons

There are four: low or off-peak, low shoulder, high shoulder and peak. Basically, the most expensive times to travel are Christmas, July, August, Easter and during the American bank holidays: President's Day (George Washington's birthday) – the third Monday in February; Memorial Day – the last Monday in May and the official start of the summer season; Independence Day – 4 July (in the middle of the high season); Labor Day – the first Monday in September and last holiday of summer; and Thanksgiving – always the fourth Thursday in November.

Low or off-peak season tends to be November, then January to the end of April excluding the bank

★ ★ ★   **BRIT TIP**   ★ ★ ★
★   ★
★ Don't try to see too much in too ★
★ short a space of time – you don't ★
★   want to spend your whole   ★
★ holiday driving and you may even ★
★   want to leave time for an   ★
★ adventure tour or ranch holiday. ★
★ ★ ★ ★ ★ ★ ★ ★ ★ ★ ★ ★ ★ ★ ★ ★ ★

13

holidays and Easter. May, June and October are low shoulder and all other times are high shoulder.

Best times to travel

Without a doubt, Monday to Thursday. Flights are cheaper, airports less crowded for departure and arrival and hotels in Las Vegas, in particular, are far less busy. The very best days to arrive in Las Vegas are Tuesday to Thursday morning.

THE MAJOR OPERATORS

An A-Z of Specialist Tour Operators

American Connections

London: 01494 473173
Manchester: 0161 835 3655
Glasgow: 0141 332 1311
www.americanconnections.com
Offers a very good 'land-only' section of hotels; also includes ranches and has a special brochure purely for Las Vegas.

The American Holiday

0870 605 0506
Offers 'land-only' deals for a £30 fee, plus free maps and shuttle services at certain destinations. Also offers adventure holidays, horse riding, dude ranching and motorbike hire.

Bon Voyage

01703 330332
www.bon-voyage.com
One of the bigger operators, but surprisingly, offers very few extras.

Funway

020 8466 0222
www.funwayholidays.co.uk
Bonus offers available at certain hotels: free meals and breakfasts for children, free children's clubs, free nights, free shuttle bus service. Plus with every booking fun books, packed with money-saving deals on sightseeing trips, attractions, shows, shopping and dining; free reduced rate phone card; free Rand McNally Travel Planner and VIP shopping discount card in conjunction with the Shop America Alliance. Funway's sister company in America is very big in Las Vegas. It has its own car rental and sightseeing options that can be reserved via its website.

Getaway Vacations

020 8313 0550
With self-drive bookings you receive a free Rand McNally Road Map/Travel Planner.

Jetlife

01322 614200
www.jetlife.co.uk
If you fly with Continental Airlines to the western states, you will get a free car upgrade.

Jetset

0990 555757
Free accommodation for children at certain hotels. Offers Greyhound Ameripass and Air Passes. However, does not give clear details of the 'fully inclusive' insurance and car hire prices, so check that the package DOES include everything you want.

Just America

01730 266588
Has the best value, easiest-to-use arrangements for car hire. Also specialises in a highly personalised, tailor-made service.

Key to America

01784 248777
Bonus scheme at certain hotels: free children's meals, free activities, room upgrades, dining discounts, free breakfasts and fifth night free.

Kuoni

Reservations: 01306 742888
Brochures: 07000 458664
www.kuoni.co.uk
Extra nights free, room upgrades, free sports, meals and drinks and food

discounts. Special deals for honeymooners and those celebrating silver or golden wedding anniversaries (though you'll have to take a copy of your marriage certificate with you!). One of the UK's best longhaul tour operators.

North America Travel Service
020 7938 3737
www.natravel.com
Specialises in fly-drives but very little information about flights and availability of open-jaw and stopovers. Some free night deals at certain hotels. Has separate brochures for coach, Tauck and adventure tours.

NorthWest Airlines
01424 224400
www.nwa.com
Offers flight discounts for teenagers. Tickets come with a complete travel planner and online reservations, plus has its own frequent flyer centre.

Premier Holidays
01223 516688
'Premier Plus' offers include extra nights free at certain hotels; free transport to attractions, breakfasts, upgrades for honeymooners, tea and coffee and use of health clubs.

Trailfinders
020 7937 5400
www.trailfinders.co.uk
The UK's largest independent travel agent, which is renowned for tailor-made itineraries and a good selection of discounted flights. One of the few tour operators still offering Amtrak passes and the only company that still offers the Greyhound Ameripass in its brochure.

Unijet
0990 114114
www.unijet.com
The only company offering chartered flights direct to Las Vegas, it is famous for its amazingly cheap long-weekend and week-long deals.

United Vacations
020 8313 0999
www.unitedvacations.com
No regional departures, unless you fly via Amsterdam, but free connecting flights from regional airports during off-peak times. Books of vouchers for cheaper dining and attraction entrance fees.

USAirtours
0990 280067
www.usairtours.co.uk
Free drinks, breakfasts, shuttle to the Strip in Las Vegas, and free extra nights at certain hotels.

Virgin Holidays
01293 617181
www.virginholidays.co.uk
Free kids' funpack on flights, free breakfasts, free meals for children and extras for honeymoons and anniversaries at certain hotels. Don't forget to join the frequent-flyer programme if you qualify. Plus $50 discount at Virgin Megastores and better deals for single parents.

Escorted tour companies

APT International Tours
020 8879 7444
www.traveleshop.com
Discounts if you have travelled with APT before, plus a travel bag.

Jetsave
01342 313033
www.jetsave.co.uk
'Generous' discounts for groups of 15 or more, plus free places depending on number travelling. No supplements for single travellers if prepared to share a room.

Page & Moy
0116 250 7676
www.page-moy.co.uk
Consistently rated highly by repeat-visit travellers.

13

Travelsphere

01858 410818
www.travelsphere.co.uk
National Express pick-ups to point of departure for £5; savings on hotel airports and regional departures.

AIRPORTS

McCarran International Airport

Just 1 mile (1.6km) from the Strip and 5 miles (8km) from Downtown, McCarran International Airport is one of the slickest, most modern and easy-to-use airports in America. In a passenger survey of 36 major airports – which looked at speed of baggage delivery, ease of reaching gates, ground transport, cleanliness, quality of restaurants, attractiveness, ease of parking and following signs – McCarran came sixth.

The airport is among the 10 busiest airports in the world and deals with 800 flights a day and around 30.5 million passengers a year. A new runway – opened recently at a cost of $80.5 million – will give the airport the capacity to handle 60 million passengers a year in the future. It has direct flights to 62 US airports and nine international destinations and more than 5,000 cars a day use the parking facilities. Like many other aspects of life in Las Vegas, the airport has the very latest technology. There is no need for departing passengers with tickets to go to ticket counters inside the terminals – they can check in their luggage at the ticketing/departure kerb. It is the first airport in America to use Common Use Terminal Equipment (CUTE). This allows airlines to use any gate as needed, which creates more efficient scheduling of gates and faster boarding for passengers. In addition, all facilities are accessible to the disabled and amplified phone sets are dotted throughout the terminal.

Los Angeles International Airport

If you are planning a touring holiday or perhaps an open-jaw flight, you may want to come into or out of Los Angeles airport, a major international airport with all the best facilities.

INDEPENDENT BOOKING

There may be many different reasons why you want to organise all or part of your trip independently. Some people (jammy dodgers I call them!) fly to San Francisco or Los Angeles to visit friends and then decide to go off to Las Vegas and other parts of California or Arizona on little trips. But by nature we Brits are an independent lot and one of the most appealing ideas for us is just to fly to the West Coast of America and hit the open road. Whatever the reason, the following tips will help you to save money in all the right places so you have more to spend on enjoying the sights and buying those essential pairs of trainers etc!

Flights

Competition in the transatlantic flight market is fierce, which is good news for us the customers. It also means that it makes sense to shop around for the best deal you can get. I recommend that you read the Tour Operator section (see pages 190–2) first, so you can acquaint yourself with all the terms and deals available.

Once you have worked out what your priorities are, then you have a pretty good chance of beating the prices quoted in the brochures by phoning round the transatlantic flight bookers who advertise in the weekend newspapers. The *Sunday Times* is particularly good. Remember, too, that the tour operators specialising in the North American market also have access to deals being offered by the airlines, so can often beat their own published prices!

Must-see sights

Left Canon de Chelly in Winter
Above Zion National Park
Below Thor's Hammer at Bryce
Canyon

Left The Grand Canyon
Above Monument Valley

Must-see sights

Clockwise from top left:
Rainbow Bridge at Lake Powell
Yosemite National Park
Mammoth Lakes
Lake Powell
Death Valley

Low and low-shoulder seasons (see The seasons, page 189) are particularly good for brilliant deals, such as flights to Las Vegas or Los Angeles for £200.

You can even go for a totally no-frills, mega-cheap flight with 'consolidated' fares. These are the old-style bucket-shop fares which have now been legalised. The travel agent negotiates deals on your part, so you get very cheap fares and they're happy, too, as they earn better commission rates. The main restriction with these fares is that you can only use one airline and sometimes it may involve flying via that airline's 'home' country, for instance, somewhere in Europe. Also you won't get free or extra stopovers, but you can get around this by buying air passes for internal flights (see page 186). These air passes are not available in the States so you need to buy them before you go.

Hotels

Off-the-cuff: If you're happy touring around Nevada, Arizona and California staying in the rather soulless chains such as Days Inn, Ramada and so on, you could take advantage of many of the special deals that are advertised in local papers and find a room on an ad hoc basis. Generally this is no problem at all in cities and towns, but it may be worth booking a few days in advance for rooms at major sightseeing destinations, such as the Grand Canyon or Furnace Creek in Death Valley. Even if you'd prefer accommodation with a little more character, you can still find cheap deals through agents once you are in America (see page 194).

Las Vegas

This is one of the weirdest cities on earth for hotel prices. In most cities around the world, hotels tend to be busy during the week and offer incentives to fill their rooms at weekends. With Las Vegas the reverse

★ ★ ★ BRIT TIP ★ ★ ★

★ Most hotels will allow children ★
★ under a certain age to sleep for ★
★ free if sharing a room paid for by ★
★ two adults. ★

is true. So many Americans from Salt Lake City to Phoenix and Los Angeles use Las Vegas as a weekend destination that occupancy rates are a staggering 96% on Friday and Saturday nights (even with 127,000 rooms to fill).

On top of that, the city hosts huge conventions and special events such as rodeos and prize fights that tie up hotels, restaurants, transportation, showrooms and traffic for a week at a time. For these reasons, although Las Vegas hotels have their rack (standard) room rates, prices vary wildly above or below that rate according to how busy it is and how much they think they can get away with! Having said that, the price of accommodation is probably cheaper than anywhere else in North America and given the class and quality of facilities on offer, you can live like a king or queen very cheaply at top resorts in Las Vegas. Here's how:

Cheap deals: if you happen to be in southern California in December or January and pick up a local paper, you may see promotional offers direct from Las Vegas hotels in which the rooms are practically being given away. On the basis that an empty room is a liability, they will be happy to do this just to get your foot in the door – and their casino! The deals often include not only incredibly cheap rooms, but also free shows and meals.

In addition, the travel sections of the Sunday papers just about anywhere in the States – and at just about any time of year – are good for picking up fantastic deals to Las Vegas.

13

Wonder websites

Check out the following for up-to-date prices, the best deals and to book:

www.hotelanywhere.co.uk A British-owned website providing discounts on hotels anywhere in the world.

www.quikbook.com A service providing discounts on hotels from coast to coast in America. They promise there are no hidden cancellation or change penalties, and pre-payment is not required.

www.hotres.com A great internet discount reservation service.

www.hotelconxions.com Another good website for checking out availability at well-booked Las Vegas hotels and reserving a room.

By far the best places to buy good Las Vegas deals from are southern California (Los Angeles and San Diego), Phoenix, Denver or Chicago. The package usually includes room, transport and possibly rental car and shows. Even if you've already got your transportation sorted, you can still take advantage of the special deals by asking for the 'land only' part of the deal.

In almost all cases, you will get a better deal on Las Vegas hotels once you are in the States (with the possible exception of Funway, which has access to so many hotels at great prices), especially if you are travelling at low or shoulder seasons.

In the unlikely event that you can't find deals for Las Vegas in the *LA Times* or other local papers, contact airline tour companies such as American Airlines Fly-Away and Delta Dream Vacations and ask if they have special deals at particular hotels.

Good American agents to use include the National Reservation Bureau on toll-free number: 1-800 461 0124 (but don't phone from a hotel room as you'll be charged the hotel phone rates). Prices will vary according to the time of year but when I looked they had rooms at Circus Circus from $46 (approx £28 at $1.60 to the £ or £14 a head for two adults) at the Excalibur from $55 (£17 a head for two) and at the Luxor from $65 (£20 a head for two) among many others. And in all cases the price included free show tickets.

★ ★ ★ **BRIT TIP** ★ ★ ★

Hotel prices in America are for accommodation only and do not include breakfast.

Other Las Vegas agents that will help not just with the price of a room, but actually get you in at the inn, so to speak, include Las Vegas Travel, toll-free on 1-800 286 9195, and Las Vegas Hotels Directory, toll-free on 1-800 732 1191, Accommodations Xpress 609-391 210, Las Vegas Rooms, toll-free on 1-800 233 5594 (they can also organise weddings and car rentals); Las Vegas Backpackers Hostel and Adventure Center, toll-free on 1-800 550 8958, and Gold Reservations, toll-free on 1-800 627 4465.

Remember, most hotels in America work on a per-room price basis, though there may be a maximum number of adults allowed. In addition, the room usually consists of a double or two double beds – the latter can't be guaranteed, but can be requested. In some cases there may be a small extra charge if there are more than two adults, but this won't be much. **No room at the inn:** it is also worth using one of the agents mentioned above if you're having trouble booking yourself into one of the top resort hotels as they are more likely to have rooms. Once agents are given blocks of rooms to sell, as far as the reservations manager is concerned, those rooms are not available.

One word of warning: if booking a hotel yourself, always guarantee your first night with a credit card (even if you do not plan to arrive late). Send a deposit if needed and try to get written confirmation of your reservation. If you're staying in a hotel in San Francisco or LA when booking your hotel in Las Vegas, for instance, they're sure to have a fax you can use to receive a written confirmation. Keep this with you in case you have problems on arrival. Armed with such evidence of your reservation the hotel cannot turn you away. They must find you a room of at least the same rate and standard or better than the one you reserved.

The internet

Take care when making bookings via the internet. As with all independent travel arrangements, you do not have a tour operator to complain to (and, possibly, get money back from) if things go wrong. Stick to bigger hotels and car-hire firms if you are booking some time in advance as you are not covered if the company goes bust before you arrive for your holiday.

Probably the biggest drawback to internet bookings though, is that there have been concerns about the security of sending credit card details over the internet. A good way to do it would be to take details from the internet and make arrangements via the phone, fax or by letter.

The specialists

So you've seen the bright lights of the big cities, taken in the amazing natural wonders of the West and had a flutter in Las Vegas – what more could you want? Well, the truth is that we Brits not only have an independent spirit, we also have romantic notions of the rugged outdoors and cowboy lifestyle. The chances are that if you've gone all the way to the West, you'll want to add on a ranch holiday or 'soft' adventure tour such as rafting, cycling, climbing and motorbiking or perhaps go horse riding, bird watching, play a little golf, do the jazz thing or get a real taste of California wines. The following companies offer those services:

Adventure

Hemmingways: 01737 842735
Outlaw Trails: 01293 529345
Ranch America: 01923 671831
Trailfinders: 020 7938 3939
Trek America: 01295 256777.

Bird watching

Ornitholidays: 01423 821230

Golf

Destination Golf USA: 020 8891 5151
The American Golf Holiday: 01703 465885

Horses

Equitor/Peregrine Holidays Ltd: 01865 511642

Jazz

Ashley Tours: 01886 888335

Ranching

American Round-Up: 01404 881777
North American Representatives: 01344 890525
Ranch America: 020 8868 2970
American Connections: 01494 473173
Getaway Vacations: 020 8313 0550
Jetlife: 01322 614200
Kuoni: 07000 458664
United Vacations: 020 8313 0999
Virgin: 01293 601530

Wine

Arblaster and Clarke: 01730 893344
Winetrails: 01306 712111

13

14 DRIVING AND CAR RENTAL

How to get out and about on the open road

It's the grand dream, isn't it – driving along the American highway, the only car on a stretch of road that goes on for so long you only lose it on the horizon, music blasting, shades on and not a care in the world. Believe me, it truly is an experience not to be missed. You cannot help but get a sense of being so much closer to nature when all around you is space, space, space on an unbelievable scale. And if there is not much of interest to see in some places (as is the case!), the skies are likely to provide some spectacular sights of their own from multi-coloured sunsets to heavenly blue vistas and massive rainfalls that you can see from miles away. I once spent a whole day driving on a straight open road surrounded by Arizona desert landscape, with blue skies each side and a monumentally large downpour straight ahead – and not a drop fell on me until the night (when my tent almost got washed away!), which just gives you a feel of how vast the country is.

I tell you all this to help convey the scale of what you will encounter on a touring trip around the west of America and be warned: unless you particularly want to spend your entire time driving, don't try to see too much on a two-week holiday.

The other point is that while you may have some reservations about your ability to drive on the wrong side of the road in a foreign country, it really is not a problem in America. Recently a friend was planning a trip to Los Angeles but she and her boyfriend were so worried about driving round the city and up to San Francisco that it was putting them off (I might hasten to add that they were jammy dodgers with friends in LA!). I pointed out that driving in America is

not only a lot easier than driving in Britain, but a great deal more fun too, and although I don't understand why, the whole system of getting on and off freeways and turning left and right is so much easier when driving on the right-hand side of the road. So they hired a car and had a wonderful trip, taking in the fantastic vistas along the Pacific Coast Highway to San Francisco – they were so pleased I had encouraged them to go. So if you want to do it, just do it and you'll have the trip of a lifetime.

Car rental

Now you must decide what type of car to hire and who to hire it from. Most of the tour operators have special deals going with Alamo, though one or two use Avis, Budget or Dollar. The prices have become pretty standardised since 2000, but by far the best deal can be found through the tour operator Just America (see page 190), which offers many extras included in the price – and at a lower rate than any other operator.

The costs

Many of the tour operators give the price of hiring the car separately from what it will actually cost you to walk away from the rental desk with your car keys, though others do now show all-inclusive prices. This makes sense as these are charges you must pay in addition to the car hire fees: Extended

Protection, collision damage waiver (CDW), airport user fee, state local surcharges and taxes, cash deposit, additional driver fees, under-age driver fees, child seat (if you need one) and deposit. In any case, when checking the price of hiring a car, make sure you look at the right area and right dates, as prices vary from place to place. Florida and California are cheaper than Western USA prices, which cover Arizona and Nevada.

Extended protection: many Americans do not have any or enough insurance and if they caused the accident, you would have no one to sue for damage to your property or for personal injury (the car is covered by CDW, see below). This type of insurance covers all liabilities and costs $10 per day.

Collision damage waiver (CDW): at $20 per day, this covers you for $10,000–$50,000 worth of damage to your hire car regardless of the cause, plus theft or loss.

Airport user fee: this will cost you up to 10% of the total charge.

State/local surcharges and taxes: from 5 to 15 per cent of the total cost depending on exact location of rental.

Cash deposit: this tends to be around $100 per week. In addition, you will often be asked to provide a credit card in the driver's name to cover any incidentals such as the deposit or under-age driver charges. If you want to leave a cash deposit you'll probably be asked to show three forms of identification, for instance passport, driving licence and airline tickets.

Additional driver fees: $6 per driver per day.

Under-age driver fees: all the UK deals are for drivers with a minimum age of 25 and drivers under 25 will have to pay a further $20 per day.

Child seat and deposit: children up to the age of five must, by law, travel in a child seat in America, and you should book these in advance. The cost will be $5 per day plus $50 deposit.

Environmental tax: a further $2 per day if car rental is arranged in the UK.

★ ★ ★   BRIT TIP   ★ ★ ★
★
★
★   It is worth noting that Virgin's
★   comprehensive insurance cover
★   (car hire with Dollar) includes all
★   the extras covered by Alamo
★   Gold, e.g. additional drivers and
★   child seat.
★ ★ ★ ★ ★ ★ ★ ★ ★ ★ ★ ★ ★ ★ ★ ★ ★ ★

Comprehensive Alamo rentals: the all-inclusive packages and comprehensive insurance cover schemes you take out in advance in the UK tend to cost anywhere between £23 and £30 a day in Las Vegas/Nevada. They include extended protection, CDW, airport user fee and state/local surcharges and taxes, and generally work out cheaper than paying for all the above on arrival (and saves a lot of time when you go to collect your car).

Alamo Gold: many of the tour operators now offer an Alamo Gold scheme which, for a fee of an additional £15 to £25 a week, includes three additional drivers and gives you a free tankful of petrol, worth around $15 to $25 depending on the size of the car hired (though additional driver fees are not payable in California or Nevada).

Rental surcharges: during peak periods, you will be charged a further £23 per week or £5 per day for your car rental. The peak seasons tend to be from 15 July to 31 August and from 20 to 27 December.

One-way drop-off fees: most companies charge if you want to pick up your car in one location and drop it off in another, which can easily add $100 to $300 on to your rental costs. The exceptions tend to be if you pick up and drop off in the same state, though always check. Some tour

14

operators have negotiated free drop-offs between California, Arizona and Nevada on cars over a certain size – check before booking if this will be relevant.

Virgin's Dollar all-inclusive package: includes all your insurance and taxes. For a further £38.50 per week you are also covered for your first tank of petrol, drivers under 25, additional drivers and baby seats – so it is more expensive than Alamo Gold, but a more comprehensive package, too!

Limits: in most cases you will not be allowed to drive your hire car in Mexico or off-road in America.

Documents: you will need a UK driving licence or a driving licence from your country of residence. You do not need an international driving licence, nor is it acceptable.

★ ★ ★ **BRIT TIP** ★ ★ ★

★ Pre-renting can help you avoid ★
★ hard-sell tactics by Alamo staff ★
★ wanting you to take out personal ★
★ insurance. If you have Extended ★
★ Protection and travel insurance ★
★ (see Chapter 12) you'll be well ★
★ covered. ★

Pre-rental: some tour operators are now offering you the chance to fill out all the necessary paperwork before you leave home so when you arrive you can just pick up your car keys and go. Not only does this save you time, but it also means you can bypass efforts by the counter staff at American car-hire firms to give you the upgrade hard sell! In any case, you will generally get a better deal for bigger cars if you arrange this in advance. The possible exception is in Las Vegas where they practically give away upgrades on a quiet week. But be warned, if you arrive in Las Vegas when the city is packed, you may have difficulty finding a car of your choice.

Hiring cars locally: you may only wish to hire a car for a few days while you are on holiday, and this can easily be arranged when you arrive. You'll find phone numbers for all the major car-hire firms in a local phone directory, but remember that the prices they quote you will not include all the extras outlined above, so be sure to include those when you do your calculations. (For names and contact numbers of car-hire companies see page 12.)

Choosing the right car

Sorry, but size _is_ an issue!: where your flight includes car rental, it will normally be for a small, economy-size car, which probably won't be much good for a tour even if there are only two of you. The biggest problem is the boot size – the boots of all American cars are much smaller than their European equivalents and you do have to take into account that you will need to accommodate your luggage.

This is what the different price brands will provide:

- Economy: usually a Chevrolet Metro or similar, equivalent to the UK's Vauxhall Corsa. Considered big enough for two adults sharing.
- Compact: usually a Chevrolet Cavalier or similar, equivalent to a UK Vauxhall Astra. Considered big enough for three adults sharing.
- Intermediate: usually a Pontiac Grand Am, equivalent to the UK's Vauxhall Vectra. Considered big enough for four adults sharing.
- Full Size: usually a Buick Regal or similar, equivalent to the UK's Vauxhall Omega. Again, large enough for four adults.
- Convertible: usually a Chevrolet Cavalier or similar, equivalent to the UK's Vauxhall Astra Convertible. Large enough for three adults.
- Luxury Van: usually a Chevrolet Astravan or similar, equivalent to the UK's VW Sharon. Large enough for seven people.

- 4-Wheel Drive: usually a Chevy Blazer or similar, no UK equivalent. Large enough for five people.

Automatics: all American hire cars will be automatics. Some things may confuse you at first if you are not familiar with automatics, for example you won't be able to drive until you put the car into **D** for drive and you probably won't be able to take the keys out of the ignition until you have put the car into **P** for park. **D1** and **D2** are extra gears, which you only need to use when going up steep hills.

Some larger cars have cruise control, which lets you set the speed at which you want to travel and then take your foot off the gas pedal (the accelerator). There are usually two buttons on the steering wheel for cruise control, one to switch it on and the other to set your speed. You take off cruise control by pressing the on button again or by simply accelerating or braking. In some cases the handbrake may also be a bit different. Some cars have an extra foot pedal to the left of the brake, which you need to press to engage the handbrake. Pull a tab just above it to release or press the main brake pedal.

Air conditioning: all cars come with air conditioning but you must keep the windows closed to make it work and sometimes you will have to switch on the car's fan first to make the A/C or air button work.

Fuel/gas: you've hit the highway and need to fill up, but just bear in mind that for the most part Interstates (the main roads) do not have gas stations – you will have to get off and one though they are not usually too far away. Generally there are two prices: one for self-service and another if the attendant fills up your car. They may also clean your windows (you'll find that essential on long trips) and would expect a tip for this, but there will be equipment for you to do this yourself.

On the road

Rules and regulations

No speeding, please! The speed limits on the main Interstates are well signposted and tend to be between 55 and 70mph (88 and 112kph) – 75mph (120kph) on some lonesome stretches in Nevada – while the MINIMUM allowed is 40mph (64kph).

Be warned, the Americans take their speed limits very seriously. Self-confessed 'gullible traveller' Bob Maddams was on a 65-mph (105-kph) stretch of endless road between Nevada and Utah when boredom set in. He'd not passed a single car for two hours and there was nothing for miles in front or behind him so he decided to put his foot down. He says: 'Less than a minute later the needle was nudging 95 and less than 30 seconds after that a cop car, siren wailing and lights flashing, was waving me down. Where the hell he came from I will never know.'

Facing the prospect of a hefty $200 fine, Bob put on his best Hugh Grant accent, hoping to win over the police officer. But Mr Dark Shades was having none of it and told him: "Are you aware that I am empowered to enforce an immediate jail term for the degree of this offence?" After that Bob was highly delighted to get off with the $200 fine – even if it meant not being able to afford to eat for the next week!

Restrictions: flashing orange lights suspended over the road indicate a school zone ahead, so go slowly. School buses cannot be overtaken in either direction while they are unloading and have their hazard lights flashing. U-turns are forbidden in built-up areas and where a solid line runs down the middle of the road. It is also illegal to park within 10ft (3 metres) of a fire hydrant or a lowered kerb and you should never stop in front of a yellow-painted kerb – they are for emergency vehicles and you will get towed away! Never park on a kerb either.

14

Seat belts: compulsory for all front-seat passengers. It is worth bearing in mind that the legal limit for blood alcohol in America is lower than in Britain and the police are very hot on drink-drivers. It is also illegal to carry open containers of alcohol in the car itself.

★ ★ ★ ★ ★ ★ ★

★ Most accidents that Brits are ★
★ involved in tend to take place ★
★ on left turns, so take extra care ★
★ here. Remember, too, there is ★
★ no amber light from red to ★
★ green, but there is one from ★
★ green to red. ★

★ ★ ★ ★ ★ ★ ★ ★ ★ ★ ★ ★ ★ ★ ★ ★ ★

Accidents and emergencies: if you have even a minor accident, the police must be contacted before the cars can be moved. The car-hire firm will also expect a full police report for the insurance paperwork. In the case of a breakdown there should be an emergency number for the hire company among the paperwork they gave you. Always have your driving licence with you (remember an international driving licence is not valid) and your car-hire agreement forms in case you are stopped by the police at any time. If you are pulled over, keep your hands on the wheel and always be polite. If they find out you're British you could just get away with a ticking off for a minor offence (but not for speeding at 95mph/153kph!).

Signposts and junctions: one of the most confusing aspects of driving around towns in America is the way they hang up road names underneath the traffic lights at every junction. The road name given is not for the road you are actually on, but the one you are crossing. Another thing to be wary of is that there is very little advance notice of junctions, and road names can be hard to read as you approach them, especially at night. So keep your speed down if you think you are close to your turn-off so you can get into the right lane. If you do miss your turning, don't panic, as nearly all roads in American towns are arranged in a simple grid system so it will be relatively easy to work your way back.

Sometimes you will meet a crossroads where there is no obvious right of way. This is a 'four-way stop' and the way it works is that priority goes in order of arrival. When it is your turn, pull out slowly. At red lights, it is possible to turn right providing there is no traffic coming from the left and no pedestrian crossing, unless specified by a sign saying 'No turn on red'. A green arrow gives you the right of way when turning left, but when it is a solid green light, you must give way to traffic coming from the other direction.

THE GRAND CANYON AND SURROUNDINGS

Must-see sights within easy reach of Sin City

ARIZONA AND THE CANYONLANDS

What it's all about

In California it's quite often the people and urban developments that make the state a truly remarkable experience. In Arizona it is the history and natural wonders that make it one of the most beautiful and thrilling of all of America's 52 states. This is the land of cowboys and Indians, of gold-mining and ghost towns, of movie-making and centuries-old history and of one of the seven great natural wonders of the world: the Grand Canyon.

Without a shadow of a doubt it has some of the most spectacular landscapes ever crowded into such a compact area. On top of the Grand Canyon, there is the Petrified Forest, Walnut Canyon, Sunset Crater and Montezuma's Castle.

Arizona is a massive state, encompassing the cities of Phoenix (its capital) and Tuscon. Travelling to these destinations would require a big investment in time. Getting to the Grand Canyon and the Canyonlands, however, is feasible within a matter of hours from Las Vegas.

Going native

Arizona has the largest Native American population and more land devoted to reservations than any other state. In addition, the prehistoric Native American tribes, such as the **Hohokam** of southern Arizona, the **Sinagua** of central and the **Anasazi** (ancient ones) of northern Arizona provide some extremely old historical ruins (rare in America) that are a monument to their high degree of sophistication in dry farming, water management, plus their far-flung trade

routes and jewellery, pottery and textile-making.

And let us not forget, of course, that Arizona was the birthplace of possibly the best known Indian of them all, Geronimo. The Apache Indian warrior engaged nearly three-quarters of America's military ground troops in his pursuit after the Civil War and up to 1886 when he surrendered – having never been captured – at Skeleton Canyon!

Ranching

On the cowboy front, even today mining and ranching are the most important industries of the small communities of **Peeples Valley** and **Yarnell** on Route 89 north of **Wickenburg**. The lush grasslands are home to a thriving cattle industry that has cowboys still riding the plains. The whole area down to Wickenburg is known as the **Dude Ranch Capital of the World** because of all the ranches that allow you to visit and participate in the activities.

Prescott, the old capital of Arizona, surrounded by Prescott National Forest, the pine-covered Bradshaw Mountains and the Yavapai

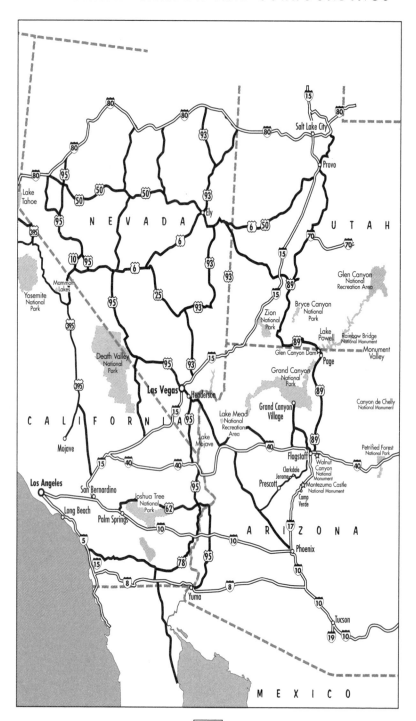

Indian Reservation, is known for its boulder-strewn granite dells and grasslands. Stately Victorian homes are a reminder of its heyday years, while the rowdier side of frontier life is remembered on **Whiskey Row**, where 26 saloons once attracted cowboys from far and wide. The annual **Frontier Days** celebration is held here at the beginning of July, complete with fireworks, dancing, rodeo performances, a parade and cowboy golf tournament.

Further north on Route 89a is **Jerome**, which sprang up during the gold-mining boom on Cleopatra Hill overlooking the Verde Valley. Once the ore diminished, it became known as America's largest **ghost city** and is now home to a colony of artists and visitors who walk the steep, winding streets to see the historic buildings and browse through shops and boutiques.

The best historic sites are the town's **'travelling jail'**, which has moved 225ft (69 metres) since a dynamite explosion dislodged it from its foundations in the 1920s, and **Jerome State Historic Park**, once the mansion of mining developer 'Rawhide' Jimmy Douglas.

To the south-east (along Route 260) is **Campe Verde**, established in 1864 as a cavalry outpost to protect Verde River settlers from Indian raids. The old fort still stands in the middle of the town.

Just north, along Interstate 17, are the well-preserved cliff dwellings at **Montezuma Castle National Monument**, a five-storey, 20-room dwelling built in and under a cliff overlooking Beaver Creek. It was misnamed by early settlers who thought it had been inhabited by Aztecs, but it was actually built by Sinagua Indians in the 12th and 13th centuries.

Further north is **Clarkdale** where you can see the 100-room pueblo that housed 250 people from the 13th century until they mysteriously disappeared some time in the 15th

century. Clarkdale is home to the scenic **Verde Canyon Railroad**, a renovated New York Metro Line train that transports passengers along a 40-mile (64-km) route through cottonwood forests and the base of a desert *mesa* (table). En route you'll see bald eagles, great blue herons, deer and javelina.

Just a little further north is **Flagstaff**, considered to be the gateway to the Grand Canyon.

The Grand Canyon

520-638 7888
www.thecanyon.com
Open: the park is open 24 hours a day. Visitor Center in Canyon View Information Plaza open 8am–5pm
Admission: $20 per vehicle, $10 per person arriving by other means. Admission is for seven days. Under 17s free. Free planning guides are available in advance from the National Park Service. For a Trip Planner, Backcountry Trip Planner or Accessibility Guide, write to **Grand Canyon National Park**, PO Box 129, Grand Canyon, AZ 86023.

Two billion years in the making, the majestic spectacle stands from between 4,500ft (1,370 metres) to 5,700ft (1,740 metres) high for an amazing 277 miles (446km) with an average width of 10 miles (16km). To geologists, it is like an open book, as they can immediately see that the bottom layer is two billion years old while the top is a mere 200 million years old, with the geological ages in between represented in its colourful stony strata.

Viewing it from one of the many vantage points on the South Rim, you will see the myriad rock formations change colour according to the sun's position throughout the day. The best times to see it (and the quietest) are at sunrise or sunset. But in some ways you can only get a feel for its awesome, breathtaking hugeness by descending into its depths by mule. If you don't have the one or two days to spare needed for the trip, you can

15

stop at the new IMAX theatre at **Tusayan** and watch the *Grand Canyon – The Hidden Secrets* film.

★ ★ ★ **BRIT TIP** ★ ★ ★

To avoid the crowds (five million people visit each year) and searing heat, go in March, April, September or October either before 10am or after 2pm.

Seeing the Grand Canyon

More than five million people a year flock to the **South Rim** to view the Grand Canyon. Closer to the Colorado River than the **North Rim**, it also provides better views of the canyon.

You can either drive straight to the **Grand Canyon Village** or head for the **Canyon View Information Plaza** and the Visitors Center and bookstore, where you can pick up a copy of the park's newspaper for up-to-the-minute information on facilities, activities and transportation options, and a map.

From here you can walk to **Mather Point**, which gives wonderful views of the Canyon, before making use of the **free shuttle** service to the Grand Canyon Village for further views.
The film: the IMAX theatre (520-638 2203) at the south entrance in Tusayan has shows at half past the hour 8.30am–8.30pm daily on a 70-ft (21-metre) screen with six-track stereo sound. Adults $8.50, under 12s $6.50.
By train: The Grand Canyon Railway (520-773 1976) runs a 1920s Harriman coach steam train from Williams to the South Rim, travelling through 65 miles (105km) of beautiful countryside.
By bus: guided tours to the South Rim from Flagstaff are run by **Nava-Hopi Bus Lines**. Call 520-774 7715 for times and prices.
By mule: Fred Harvey runs one or two-day inner canyon rides, though you must speak fluent English (to

understand instructions), be at least 4ft 7in (140cm) tall , weigh no more than 200lb (90kg) and not be pregnant. Trips are often booked months in advance, so call 303-297 2757 for information and to make reservations.
Staying on the floor of the Canyon: Phantom Ranch offers 10-bunk dorms with toilet and shower, plus private cabins. For reservations, contact **AMFAC Parks and Resorts**, 14001 East Iliff Avenue, Ste 600, Aurora, CO 80014 or call 303-297 2757.
Horseback rides: with the **Apache Stables** in Tusayan, adjacent to the park. Write to PO Box 369, Grand Canyon, AZ 86023 or call 520-638 2891.
Rafting the Colorado: trips include half-day floating excursions, motor boat trips and 18-day expeditions on rowing boats. You need to book at least six months in advance and companies include: **ARA Wilderness River Adventures** at PO Box 717, Page, AZ 86040 (520-645 3296); **Arizona Raft Adventures** at 4050 East Huntington Drive, Flagstaff, AZ 86004 (520-526 8200); **Arizona River Runners** at PO Box 47788, Phoenix, AZ 85068-7788 (602-867 4866); **Canyon Explorations Inc** at PO Box 310, Flagstaff, AZ 86002 (520-774 4559); **Canyoneers Inc** at PO Box 2997, Flagstaff, AZ 86003 (520-526 0924); **Diamond River Adventures** at PO Box 1300, Page, AZ 86040 (520-645 8866); **Expeditions Inc/Grand Canyon Youth Expeditions** at 625 North Beaver Street, Flagstaff, AZ 86001 (520-779 3769); **Hualapai Tribal River Runners** at PO Box 246, Peach Springs, AZ 86434-0246 (520-769 2210); **Outdoors Unlimited** at 6900 Townsen Winona Road, Flagstaff, AZ 86004 (520-526 4546); and **Wild and Scenic Inc** at PO Box 460, Flagstaff, AZ 86002 (520-774 7343).
Flightseeing: flights by small aircraft or helicopter. Companies include: **Grand Canyon Airlines** at Box 3038, Grand Canyon, AZ 86023 (520-638

2407); **Air Grand Canyon** at PO Box 3399, Grand Canyon, AZ 86023 (520-638 2686); **AirStar Helicopters** at PO Box 3379, Grand Canyon, AZ 86023 (520-638 2622); **Kenai Helicopters** at PO Box 1429, Grand Canyon, AZ 86023 (520-638 2412); and **Papillon Grand Canyon Helicopters** at PO Box 455, Grand Canyon, AZ 86023 (520-638 2419). **Lodging:** for full and up-to-date details of lodges near the rim, write to **AMFAC Parks and Resorts** (see page 204).

North Rim

Through Jacob Lake on Highway 67, this is a lot quieter than the South Rim and home to **Canyon Trail Rides** (801-679 8665), which runs one-hour forest rides, half-day trips into the Canyon and full-day trips to Roaring Springs where you can frolic in the natural pools. Here you can stay at the **Grand Canyon Lodge** from late May to mid October. For reservations, write to AMFAC Parks and Resorts (see page 000). The **Kaibab Lodge**, three miles north of the park, is also open from late May to mid October. For reservations write to Kaibab Lodge, HC64 Box 30, Fredonia, AZ 860022 (520-638 2389).

Howdy pardner!

Arizona is real cowboy country and if there is one way to see the stunning scenery, wide-open expanses and narrow gorges, it is on the back of a horse – as a cowboy. Nowadays, it is very easy to be a real 'city slicker' as a whole host of ranching options are available, depending on your riding abilities and needs for luxury items, such as a bed. The types of ranches are:

Guest ranch: this is where you live as a 'guest' of the ranch owners in an environment that is designed to entertain you while providing plenty of horse riding opportunities and Western activities. It's the soft option that will give you a feel for the way of life but no hands-on experience.

Dude ranch: vacation-based rather than the seriously business-like working ranches, you'll do a lot of riding while Western activities from Wild West shows to rodeo visits, square dances, barbecues and sports provide plenty of fun.

Resort ranch: these offer the Western experience but also have golf, tennis and ballooning, and the whole environment is much more luxurious than dude or working ranches.

Working ranch: still in business to raise livestock and grow crops, these are home to the real cowboys. Depending on the time of year and the work that is necessary on the ranch, you'll be able to learn to drive cattle, brand and rope steers, eat around a camp fire and sleep under the stars. Round-ups take place in spring and autumn when the ranchers prepare their cattle to be moved to summer and winter ranges. It's a high-activity time at the ranches so the hours are long and the work is physically demanding. On the cattle drives you are likely to travel six (9km) to 12 miles (19km) a day but ride at least three times as far, as you bring in strays from the flanks. Evenings spent around the campfire hark back to bygone days in what is a truly wonderful, friendship-forming experience. Horse drives are a much faster version as the horses like to travel at speed. Only for very seasoned riders with lots of cross-country experience, but the long-distance gallops are a real thrill.

Offering the full range of ranches are **American Round-Up** (01404 881777) and **Ranch America** (020 8868 2910), while **Equitour**, part of Peregrine Holidays Ltd (01865 511642), are excellent for working ranches all over America's West and even provide riding clinics to bring you up to speed!

For horse-riding vacations with a difference try **Outlaw Trails** (01293 529345), who runs specially tailored, fully researched trips to the old trails used by outlaws determined to avoid

15

Watch the birdies!

You've seen them in cartoons, now you can see the birds of the Arizona deserts and mountains in real life. The south-eastern corner of the state is the most popular bird-watching area of North America and more than 400 species can be found here from migratory water fowl to native birds, nesting birds, grassland birds and mountain birds.

You can watch greater roadrunners chase lizards across the desert floors, black-chinned hummingbirds buzz around like bees, acorn woodpeckers drill holes in roadside telegraph poles and painted redstarts flit in the dappled light of oak woods with **Ornitholidays** (01243 821230). The company organises a three-week trip at the end of April/beginning of May when the desert is comfortably cool and many birds are nesting while others are starting to migrate to their breeding grounds in the north. All this along with spectacular views of the Grand Canyon.

Another favoured time of the year is in August when the city of Sierra Vista has a birding festival complete with bat stalks and owl prowls.

the long arm of the law. Closest to Arizona is the **Robbers Roost trail** in Utah in which you'll see the way stations and trail used by the Wild Bunch of Butch Cassidy and the Sundance Kid, the Hole in the Wall Gang and Robbers Roost Gang. Robbers Roost land is sprawled across 320sq miles (830sq km) of high desert and you'll ride through pinion, sage and cedar flats, a maze of rock gorges and canyons, plus long mesas, arches, pinnacles and high-shouldered buttes. If you attempt any of the 'climbs' used by the outlaws, you'll get a pretty good idea of what brilliant horsemen they were! The seasons and numbers are limited

because of the weather and nature of the trips, but the trails are perfect for lovers of the historical West who want a great big chunk of adventure.

Other Arizona marvels

Once you've been there, done that at the Grand Canyon, don't miss out on many other natural and historical wonders Arizona has to offer. Leave the South Rim on Highway 64 and take the 89 south to **Sunset Crater Volcano National Monument** (520-556 7042). An active volcano more than 900 years ago, it now rises to 1,000ft (305 metres) and rangers here offer geology, seismology and other tours while the Visitors Center can provide you with maps for self-guided trails.

Further south join the Interstate 40 going east and take in **Walnut Canyon National Monument** for an awe-inspiring view of how Sinagua Indians lived in homes built out of the limestone cliffs. The **Visitors Center Museum** (520-526 3367) displays artefacts that make it possible to imagine how they existed.

Nearby is **Meteor Crater**, which dates back 22,000 years when an enormous meteor travelling at 33,000mph (53,100kph) plunged into Earth. Because of its resemblance to the lunar landscape, the 570-ft (174-metre) deep crater was used as a training site for Apollo astronauts and the museum (520-289 2362) displays a 1,406-lb (638-kg) meteorite, the largest found in the area.

Further east is the **Petrified Forest National Park** and **Painted Desert Visitors' Center and Museum** (520-524 6228). There are more fossilised trees to be found here than anywhere else in the world with million-year-old agate logs lying in profusion on the ground.

Further north on Route 191, you can view the Indian cliff-dwelling ruins at **Canyon de Chelly National Monument**. At the base of sheer red cliffs and in canyon walls, the ruins date back to the 12th century and you can get to them on scenic rim drives, four-wheel-drive vehicles, horseback or on foot. Phone 520-674 8443 for details. Rich with history, the Anasazi Indians lived here until 1300 and the Navajo arrived in 1700, using it as a base to raid nearby Indian and Spanish settlements.

Take Highways 59 and 163 to see **Monument Valley**, probably one of the best-used locations for filming Westerns such as John Wayne's Stagecoach. To the left of this area is the **Navajo Nation**, the largest of all the Indian reservations – extending across 25,000sq miles (64,750sq km), it is bigger than the state of West Virginia – which is home to just 175,000 Native Americans, who welcome visitors for sightseeing and shopping (buy silver and turquoise jewellery, exquisitely woven rugs, intricate kachinas and other crafts).

The land encompasses mile upon mile of desert and forest land, interrupted only by spectacular mesas, buttes and rock formations. The Navajos provide hiking, horseback or four-wheel-drive tours through some of the most popular sites such as Canyon de Chelly and Monument Valley.

From this area, take Route 98 up to the shores of **Lake Powell**, a 25-million acre (10-million ha) lake with more shoreline – 1,960 miles (3,154km) – than California, which was formed by the completion of the Glen Canyon Dam in 1963. Today it's a home for houseboats and pleasure craft that explore the 96 canyons discovered and mapped by intrepid, one-armed explorer John Wesley Powell in the 19th century.

Rainbow Bridge Natural Monument, a natural stone arch carved by the relentless forces of wind and water, only became easily accessible after the lake came into being. It is an amazing 290ft (88 metres) high and 275ft (83 metres) wide. Now boat rentals, tours and

accommodation are all available at the **Wahweap Lodge and Marina** on the lake's southern-most shore.

Glen Canyon Dam offers self-guided tours and day-long and half-day float trips along the Colorado River from the base of the dam, from March to October. For details phone 520-645 2471. The town of **Page**, founded as a construction camp for crews building the dam, has plenty of restaurants and accommodation.

★ ★ ★   **BRIT TIP**   ★ ★ ★

★ Did you know that more people ★
★   have died of drowning in the   ★
★   desert than of thirst? It's all due   ★
★   to flash floods, and the reason   ★
★   why they've got such a high   ★
★   mortality rate is that they are so ★
★   violent and so quick you literally ★
★   have no time at all to react.   ★

★ ★ ★ ★ ★ ★ ★ ★ ★ ★ ★ ★ ★ ★ ★ ★ ★

UTAH AND THE WILD WEST

Often overlooked thanks to the fame of the neighbouring Grand Canyon and Arizona, the south-western corner of Utah is home to an area known as the **Grand Circle**. Stunning national parks include Zion National Park, Kolob Canyons and Bryce Canyon. The Grand Circle also takes in Lake Powell and the Glen Canyon National Recreation Area, which straddles Utah and Arizona, and Nevada's Lake Mead National Recreational Area (see page 160).

The beauty of Utah's natural wonders is matched by its sense of wilderness. Despite an increase in visitors, it is still an untamed environment with often only primitive facilities available, while the rich cowboy and outlaw history touches many sights and locations throughout the region.

15

Zion National Park

Within remarkably easy striking distance of Las Vegas, it takes just two hours to drive to the south-western end of the Grand Circle along Interstate 15 in the direction of St George. The entrance is on the south side just beyond the town of Springdale, where you will find the Visitor Center and two camping sites. **Visitor Center:** 435-772 3256. Open year-round 9am–4.30pm except Christmas Day and provides everything from books, to information, maps, an introductory video and backcountry permits and even has a small museum.

www.zion.national-park.com

Admission: seven-day pass $20 per car or $10 per person. Back country permit $5.

★ ★ ★ **BRIT TIP** ★ ★ ★

★ Within Zion National Park is the ★
★ Kolob Canyons area, which has ★
★ its own Visitor Center. ★

The natural rock sculptures and vividly coloured cliffs that tower above the floor of Zion Canyon pull in nearly 2.5 million visitors a year, making it one of the most popular sights in the region. To the Mormon pioneers who discovered it after the **Paiute Indians** had left, the beautiful rock structures so resembled natural temples they called it Little Zion. An early Methodist minister was so awe-struck that he gave many of the towers and cliffs that rise up 3,000ft (914 metres) into the sky biblical names such as **Three Patriarchs, Angels Landing** and the **Great White Throne**.

Seeing the sights

One of the easiest ways to appreciate its beauty is to take the **Zion Canyon Scenic Drive**, a short, 7-mile (11-km) trek along the canyon floor – a

narrow, deep gorge that is the centrepiece of the park, surrounded by wondrous monoliths that stand between 2,000ft (610 metres) and 3,000ft (914 metres) high. Along the bottom of the canyon flows the **Virgin River**. It may look small, yet it has the power of the once-mighty Colorado and is almost single-handedly responsible for carving the gorge – admittedly over a 13 million-year period!

The **Zion-Mount Carmel Highway** is a 13-mile (21-km) drive up steep switchbacks and through tunnels to Checkerboard Mesa. The road was considered an engineering marvel when it was completed in 1930 and cuts a swathe through rough up-and-down terrain to connect lower Zion Canyon with the high plateaus to the east.

Two narrow tunnels, including one over a mile (1.6km) long, were blasted through the cliffs to complete the job. As you travel from one side of the tunnel to the other, the landscape changes dramatically. On one side are the massive cliff walls of Zion Canyon, on the other is an area known as **Slickrock Country**. Here rocks coloured in white and pastels of orange and red have been eroded into hundreds of fantastic shapes and etched through time with odd patterns of cracks and grooves. It is followed by the mountains of sandstone known as **Checkerboard Mesa** – one of the best examples of naturally sculptured rock art.

Seasons in the sun

Each season provides a spectacular array of colours in Zion. Spring sees the waterfalls cascading into the Virgin River. Summer – easily the busiest time of year – is the time to enjoy the striking sight of the deep red cliffs peeking out above the lush green foliage. Come autumn those leaves turn brilliant red and gold, while in winter a layer of snow adds a pristine cleanliness to the rugged landscape.

★ ★ ★ BRIT TIP ★ ★ ★

The best times to visit Zion National Park are May and September, when the weather is at its finest and the crowds are at their smallest.

Things to do

You can cycle, take a tram ride or go on a horse ride through the park, yet most people agree that the best way to experience the full majesty is to **hike**. Guided walks are offered along fairly easy trails - some of which are accessible by wheelchair. True adventurers, though, will want to do the 16-mile (26-km) hike through **The Narrows**, which involves wading through the Virgin River. Be aware, though, that advance preparation and a permit are necessary to do this.

Guided **horse rides** are available from the end of March to early November. Call 435-772 3967 or 435-679 8665 for information.

★ ★ ★ BRIT TIP ★ ★ ★

It is not advised to drink untreated water from streams or springs. Water can be bought at the Visitor Center, campgrounds, Zion Lodge, Grotto Picnic Area and the Temple of Sinawa.

Bicycles are only permitted on established roads and the Pa'rus Trail, which leads from the campgrounds to the Scenic Drive junction.

Camping is allowed only in the campgrounds or in designated back country sites with a permit.

Climbing is possible and information is available at the Visitor Center. But many of Zion's cliffs are sandstone with much loose or 'rotten' rock and climbing tools and techniques used for granite are often

less effective here.

Kolob Canyons

In the north-western reaches of Zion National Park, just off Interstate 15 at Exit 40 about 45 miles (72km) from the entrance to Zion
Visitor Center: 435-586 9548

Kolob Canyons Road is one of two scenic routes, which provides stunning views of the spectacular finger canyons, carved out by springs along the edge of **Kolob Terrace**. It will take you 5 miles (8km) into the red rock, running perpendicular to the walled Finger Canyons and providing a high viewpoint at the end.

The Kolob Terrace Road overlooks the white and salmon-coloured cliffs at the left and right forks of North Creek. Both routes climb into forests of pinyon and juniper, ponderosa pine and fir, while aspen trees are found at **Lava Point**. In early spring the Kolob is still buried under thick snow, and in summer there is still a feel of mountain coolness to the air.

Lodging in Zion National Park

Zion Lodge, 303-29-PARKS
Open year-round and provides a choice of motel rooms, cabins and suites. It is the only lodge in the park and the only restaurant. There is also a gift shop and post office.

Springdale:
The Zion Park City

Bumbleberry Inn, 97 Bumbleberry Lane, 435-772 3224
Large, spacious rooms with private balconies or patios overlooking wonderful scenery in a quiet, off-road location. Facilities include a heated pool, indoor Jacuzzi, indoor racquetball, games room, restaurant and gift shop.
El Rio Lodge, 995 Zion Park Boulevard, 435-772 3205
Clean, quiet and friendly 10-roomed lodge with a green shady lawn, sundeck and fantastic views of Zion Park.

15

Canyon Ranch Motel, 668 Zion Park Boulevard, 435-772 3357
New and remodelled cottages, some with kitchens, around a quiet, shady lawn with panoramic views of Zion. Amenities include new pool and Jacuzzi.

Cliffrose Lodge & Gardens, 281 Zion Park Boulevard, 435-772 3234
At the entrance to Zion National Park along the Virgin River. All rooms have excellent views, while there is also a large pool and 5 acres (2ha) of lawns, trees and flower gardens.

Virgin and Rockwell

On Highway 9, just outside Zion National Park.

Hummingbird Inn B&B, 37 West Main, Rockville, 405-772 3632
All four guest rooms have private baths and a large country breakfast is included. The inn has a Jacuzzi plus an upstairs deck and a library/games room loft. Outside activities include croquet, horseshoes and badminton.

Kolob Mountain Ranch, Virgin, 405-628 0743.
Luxurious rooms, gourmet meals, swimming, tennis, Jacuzzi and horse rides. There is also a ping-pong room, arcade and game room, racquetball, volleyball, western dancing, fishing, hiking and snow-mobiles.

Hurricane

Halfway between Zion National Park and St George.

Pah Tempe Hot Springs, 825 North 800 East, 35-4 Hurricane, 435-635 2879
A tiny retreat where no smoking or alcohol is allowed, but where massage and therapy programmes are available, plus a relaxing hot mineral pool along the Virgin River.

Park Villa Motel 6, 650 West State Street, 435-635 4010
Luxury units with fridge and microwave, just 1 mile (1.6km) from mineral hot springs. Facilities include heated pool and spa, laundry, kitchen and cable TV.

Bryce Canyon

72 miles (116km) from Zion National Park. Follow Highway 89 towards Hatch, then turn into Highway 12 to Bryce village and the Visitor Center is just inside the entrance on Highway 63.
Visitor Center: 435-834 5322. Open daily 8am–4.30pm except Thanksgiving, Christmas and New Year's Day. Extended hours in spring, summer and early autumn. Provides information, books and back country permits. **The park** is open daily 8am–8pm daily except as above. A short introductory video on the park is shown on the half hour and on the hour and short geology talks are given in the Visitor Center Museum.
www.bryce.canyon.national-park.com
Admission: seven-day pass $5 per person. You can buy a National Parks Pass by phone on 1-888-467 2757 or by visiting their website at www.nationalparks.org/index.html.

The shape of things to come

Bryce Canyon National Park consists of 37,277 acres (15,097ha) of scenic, colourful rock formations and wonderful desert and has been home to Indian tribes for about 12,000 years – including the Anasazi and Fremont. The most recent tribe to inhabit the region was the **Paiute**, who were still here when explorers John Wesley Powell and Captain Clarence E Dutton 'discovered' the area in the 1870s.

In 1875, Ebenezer Bryce settled in the **Paria Valley** to harvest timber from the plateau and neighbours called the nearby canyon Bryce's Canyon – a name that stuck!

The canyon is a geological wonder – home to a series of horseshoe-shaped amphitheatres carved from the eastern edge of the **Paunsugunt Plateau**. Erosion has shaped colourful Calron limestones, sandstones and mudstones into thousands of spires, pinnacles and fins that together provide unique formations known as **hoodoos**.

The Paiutes called the hoodoos

Legend People who had been turned to stone by coyote because of their evil ways. In fact, they are fantastically shaped and incredibly tall pillars of rock that have been created by a series of massive land movements and river erosions.

The result is a geological paradise filled as it is with wonderful examples of the effects of sedimentation from both fresh and sea waters, erosion through wind, water and ice and earthquake and volcanic action over a period of millions and millions of years. The plateaus, staggering vertical columns, gullies and canyons are a joy to behold, while the high elevations – between 6,000ft (1,830 metres) and 9,000ft (2,740 metres) – provide panoramic views of three states and a perfect spot for stargazers.

Sights to look out for include the monoliths of **Thor's Hammer, Deformation, Uplift** and the **Grand Staircase**.

★ ★ ★ **BRIT TIP** ★ ★ ★

The best times to see large mammals in Bryce Canyon are on summer mornings and evenings in roadside meadows.

Nature's way

The differing and diverse soil and moisture conditions throughout Bryce Canyon have allowed more than 400 species of wild flowers to grow including rare gentian, bellflower, yarrow, gilia, sego lily and manzanita.

The meadows and forests are also home to many animals from foxes to deers, coyote, mountain lions and black bears. Elk and pronghorn antelope, reintroduced nearby, can also sometimes be spotted in the park.

On top of that there are more than 160 bird species who visit the park every year. Most migrate to warmer climates in the winter, but those that stay include jays, nuthatches, ravens, eagles and owls.

Scenic Drives

A scenic drive along the 18 miles (30km) of the main park road affords outstanding views of the park and southern Utah scenery. From many overlooks you can see further than 100 miles (160km) on clear days. On crisp winter days, views from **Rainbow** or **Yovimpa** points are restricted only by the curvature of the Earth. Driving south from the Visitor Center to Rainbow Point, you gradually climb 1,100ft (335 metres). En route you will notice how the pines change to spruce, fir and aspen.

Agua Canyon displays some of the best contrasts of light and colour in the park. Look for small trees atop a hoodoo known as the **Hunter**, while in the distance you will also be able to see the rims of southern plateaus and canyons.

Fairyland Canyon/Point offers fab views of the **Fairyland Amphitheater** and its fanciful shapes, the **Sinking Ship, Aquarius Plateau** and **Navajo Mountain** in the distance. Because Fairyland Canyon lies between the entrance station and the park boundary, and 1 mile (1.6km) off the main road, many visitors miss this viewpoint, yet it has some of the most spectacular views in the park.

Farview Point provides a panoramic view of the neighbouring plateaus and mountains and far to the south-east even the **Kaibab Plateau** of the Grand Canyon's North Rim.

The Natural Bridge is actually an arch that was formed by the combined forces of rain and frost erosion rather than the work of a stream.

Paria View looks out across hoodoos in an amphitheatre carved by **Yellow Creek**. The Paria River valley and **Table Cliffs Plateau** form the backdrop. To the south, the White Cliffs, weathered out of Navajo sandstone, can also be seen.

15

★ ★ ★ BRIT TIP ★ ★ ★

Picnic tables, water and WCs are available at Sunset Point, Yovimpa Point and the south end of the north campsites. There are also picnic tables along the road to Rainbow Point, but no amenities.

The area of **Ponderosa Canyon** reveals a series of multi-coloured hoodoos that are framed by pine-covered foothills and the Table Cliffs Plateau to the north.

The **Sunrise, Sunset, Inspiration** and **Bryce Points** ring **Bryce Amphitheatre**, the largest natural amphitheatre in the park. The **Queen's Garden Trail** begins at Sunrise Point. From Sunset Point, you can hike to **Thor's Hammer** and **Wall Street**. Inspiration Point offers the best view of the **Silent City**. The **Under-the-Rim Trail** begins at Bryce Point. From each point you can see as far as the **Black Mountains** in the north-east and **Navajo Mountain** in the south.

Yovimpa and **Rainbow Points** provide magnificent views of a large chunk of southern Utah. On most days you can see **Navajo Mountain** and the **Kaibab Plateau**, which is 90 miles (145km) away in Arizona. On the clearest day you can even see as far as New Mexico. In the foreground are the colours of the long-eroded slopes and remnant hoodoos. While you are here, search out **The Poodle** to the north west of Rainbow Point, and the **Pink Cliffs** behind it.

The park road ends at Rainbow Point with a road loop that turns you back towards the park entrance.

Things to do

You can avoid driving round the park by using the shuttle bus system, which has three different shuttle lines and leaves every 10 to 15 minutes.

Cycling is only allowed on paved roads and there are no mountain biking trails.

You can join a **National Park Service ranger** to explore the Canyon's natural and cultural history and learn about the forces that shaped the landscape. Schedules for ranger activities are available at the Visitor Center.

Guided **horse rides** are available in the morning and afternoon from April to October. For details contact Bryce Canyon Lodge (435-834 5500).

The Visitor Center also provides details of birding, camping, hiking, photography, star gazing, wildlife watching and trail rides.

Lodging in Bryce Canyon

Bryce Canyon Lodge, 435-834 5500. Write to Amfac, 14001 East Lliff Avenue, No 600, Aurora, CO 80014
Provides 114 rooms including suites, motel rooms and cabins. The lodge also has a restaurant, gift shop and post office, and provides the only hotel accommodation inside the canyon.

There are also two **campsites** in the canyon itself, while back country camping is possible for a fee of $5.

Bryce

Town at the entrance to the canyon
Best Western Ruby's Inn, Highway 63, 435-834 5341, www.rubysinn.com
Provides 369 rooms including suites, handicapped rooms and non-smoking room. Facilities include in-room spa, cable TV, indoor swimming pool, spa, hot tub, restaurants, general store, gallery and gift shops. Also offers trail rides, air tours, chuckwagon cookouts, rodeo, ATV rides and cross-country skiing.

Bryce Canyon Pines Motel, Highway 12, 435-834 5441
Has 51 rooms including two with kitchenettes and a room for the disabled. Facilities include a restaurant, swimming pool, gift shop, campsite and horse riding.

Pink Cliffs Bryce Village Inn, at the junction of highways 12 and 63, 435-834 5351
The 53 rooms include 14 bunkhouses that are open seasonally. Amenities include a restaurant, café, swimming pool, trading post and barbecue dinners.

CALIFORNIAN ADVENTURES

Death Valley National Park

From Las Vegas you can reach the park's southern end via Highway 95, which takes you to Amargosa Valley and Death Valley Junction. You can also get there by heading to Pahrump and then following the State Line Road to Death Valley Junction.
Furnace Creek Information Center, 760-786 2331.
www.nps.gov.deva
Open: daily 8am–8pm.
This is the largest of all America's national parks outside of Alaska and covers more than 5,156sq miles (13,354sq km). At the bottom of the 300-mile (483-km) long Sierra Nevada mountain range that stretches to Lake Tahoe in the north, it is the hottest place on earth. In summer the average temperature is 45°C (131°F) and the rocks almost reach water-boiling point. The lowest point – 282ft (86 metres) below sea level – in all of America is in the heart of the Valley.

Wimps can visit in March and April when it is just 18°C (61°F) and admire the desert spring blooms that shoot out of the sculpted rocks. But let's face it, the whole point of going to Death Valley is to drive through it at the hottest time of year! I would, however, advise giving yourself – and your car – an even chance of making it across in one piece by setting off early in the morning and making sure both your car radiator – and you – have plenty of water.

The National Parks of California warn you not to stop your car in the heat of the day (it'll probably not restart until night-time) and don't drive too quickly, again to prevent overheating. Always ensure you have enough petrol as stations are thin on the ground, but can be found at Furnace Creek, Stovepipe Wells, Scotty's Castle and Panamint Springs.

Just bear in mind that if you do break down you'll be on your own for some time as there is no public transport in the Valley and not many Americans are daft enough (mad dogs and Englishmen and all that) to go through in the summer. However, if you're sensible you will survive and will be amazed by the breathtaking beauty of the miles and miles of sand and rocks that have been hardened into a sea-like landscape by the melting sun.

★ ★ ★   BRIT TIP   ★ ★ ★

★ Death Valley may be the extreme ★
★ when it comes to heat, but ★
★ summertime in all the regions ★
★ surrounding Las Vegas is very hot, ★
★ so always ensure you have plenty ★
★ of water with you – dehydration ★
★ is no fun. ★

The main sights include **Furnace Creek**, the ruins of **Harmony Borax Works, Zabriskie Point** with its gorgeously golden hills that are best seen at sunrise or sunset, **Badwater** and the amazing heights of **Dante's View** where you get precisely that – a spectacular vista of the white salt lakes that stretch to the **Panamint Mountains**.

Other sights include **Scotty's Castle**, an incongruous mansion retreat built for American millionaire Albert Johnson in the 1920s, **Ubehebe Crater**, a 500-ft (152-metre) deep hole, which is all that remains of a volcano, the 700-ft (213-metre) high **Eureka** sand dunes and **Racetrack Valley**, so named because it is a dry mud flat covered in wind-blown boulders.

15

If you're mad enough to go hiking, try the 14-mile (22.5-km) round trip to the top of **Telescope Peak**, which does at least get cooler as you get higher!

Some people opt to stay at Furnace Creek, though I can't see the point of being boiled alive for quite so long! However, if you do wish to stay, head for the rustic **Furnace Creek Ranch** (760-786 2361, www.furnacecreekresort.com) which has a pool, stables, restaurant, bar, shop, tennis courts and even an 18-hole golf course – the lowest anywhere on Earth!

Mammoth Lakes

A short one-and-a-half-hours' drive north of Big Pine in Death Valley National Park on Highways 190 and 136 is the majestic world of Mammoth Lakes.
Mammoth Lakes Visitors Bureau: toll free in the US (800) GO MAMMOTH, from elsewhere 760-934 2712

At the gateway to Yosemite, it is one of the best places in the Sierra Nevada for outdoor activities and is second only to Tahoe as a ski resort in winter. The magical setting and 50-mile (80-km) trail make it popular with mountain bikers, while expert guides offer climbing, kayaking and hang-gliding.

The whole area is also good for golf, canoeing, swimming and searching out wildlife, gold mines and ghost towns. Recent investment in Mammoth Mountain mean there is now a new 18-hole championship golf course and a pedestrian resort, **Gondola Village**, with shops, restaurants, a skating pond and gondola, which connects the centre of town to the heart of the mountain for unmissable views.

Lodgings include: **Holiday Inn** (3905 Main Street, 760-924 1234); Mammoth Mountain Inn (1 Minaret Road, 619-934 2581); **Minaret Lodge** (6156 Minaret Road, 760-934 2416) and **Sierra Nevada Inn** (164

Old Mammoth Road, 760-934 2515). Or you can write to the **Mammoth Lakes Visitor Bureau** at PO Box 48, Mammoth Lakes 93546 (760-934 2712) for a free vacation planner.

Good for breakfast and lunch are **Blondies** (3599 Main Street, 760-834 4048) and **Café Vermeer** (3305 Main Street, 760-934 4203). Good for dinner are the **Matterhorn** (6080 Minaret Road, 760-934 3369) and **Alpenrose** (343 Old Mammoth Road, 760-934 3077).

Good for getting around in town is the **Mammoth Shuttle** on 760-934 6588.

Other useful contacts include **Devil's Postpile National Monument** (760-934 2289); **Consolidated Gold Mine** (760-924 5500); **Mammoth Museum** (5489 Sherwin Creek Road, 760-934 6918); **Mammoth Mountain Bike Park and Adventure Challenge Course** (1 Minaret Road, 760-934 0706); **Mammoth Mountain Ski Resort** (760-934 2571) and **Tamarack Cross-Country Ski Area** at Mammoth Lakes (760-934 2442).

Yosemite National Park

Visitors Bureau: 209-683 4636
This has to be one of the most stunning natural sights in America. Mile-high cliffs gouged out by glaciers thousands of years ago are topped with pinnacles and domes from which waterfalls cascade. Coyote and black bears roam the valley floor, which is never more than a mile wide. In winter, roads in the park get blocked by snow and in summer by the thousands of visitors who flock to the area.

Guided tours, including trips around the valley and into the mountains, are bookable through

★ ★ ★   **BRIT TIP**   ★ ★ ★

★   Fill up with petrol on your way ★
★   into Yosemite as there are no ★
★   petrol stations at all in the park. ★
★ ★ ★ ★ ★ ★ ★ ★ ★ ★ ★ ★ ★ ★ ★

The specialists

The Grand Canyon and Surroundings, featured in this chapter, offer a fabulous array of opportunities for those in search of real adventure. Going white-water rafting, mountain biking, walking, hiking, riding amid red rocks, waterskiing on Lake Powell and taking jeep tours around Indian country before camping cowboy-style all provide wonderful thrills. Good UK tour operators include **Hemmingways** (01737 842735), **North American Representatives** (01344 890525) and **Trek America** (01295 256777).

most of the hotels in the area. Full details of mountain biking, fishing, boating at Bass Lake, steam train, the historic park and Native American museums are available from **Yosemite Sierra Visitors Bureau**. Write to them at 41729 Highway 41, Oakhurst 93644 for a visitors' guide.

Another useful office is the **Yosemite Area Traveller Information Centre** (369 West 18th Street, Merced 95340, 209-723 3153), which can give you all the latest information on park and surrounding road conditions (essential at all times except summer), transport, recreation, lodging, camping and dining options.

Yosemite View Lodge, adjacent to the wild and scenic Merced River, opened **Camp Grizzly** early in 1999. Based on a theme of a 1950s summer camp, it provides educational nature trails, barbecue-style dining, country line dancing and other special events. To book and get more information on motels in the area, write to **Yosemite Motels**, PO Box 1989, Mariposa, CA, 95338, or call 209-742 7106.

★ ★ ★ BRIT TIP ★ ★ ★

Some roads close from late autumn to early summer – check in advance and have tyre chains at the ready for sudden falls of snow if driving in winter.

★ ★ ★ ★ ★ ★ ★ ★ ★ ★ ★ ★ ★ ★ ★ ★

Other useful numbers include **Yosemite Mountain Sugar Pine Railroad** (209-683 7273) which runs steam trains through the Sierra National Forest near Yosemite Park; **Yosemite Sightseeing Tours** (209-877 8687); **All-Outdoors Whitewater Trips** (1-800 24 RAFTS) for half, one, two and three-day rafting trips from April to November; and **Whitewater Voyages** (1-800 488 RAFT) for wonderful runs down the Merced with guides, food and equipment.

15

No one wants to think about anything going wrong with their dream holiday, but it is worth thinking about a few common-sense aspects of safety and security so that you can avoid any preventable problems.

General hints and tips

Don't allow your dream trip to Las Vegas and beyond to be spoilt by not taking the right kind of precautions – be they for personal safety or of a medical nature.

In the sun

Let's face it, most Brits tend to travel to America at the hottest time of the year – the summer – and most are unprepared for the sheer intensity of the sun. Before you even think about going out for the day, apply a high-factor sunblock as it is very easy to get sunburnt when you are walking around, sightseeing or shopping. Also, re-apply regularly throughout the day. It is also a good idea to wear a hat or scarf to protect your head from the sun, especially at the hottest time of the day from 11am to 3pm, so you do not get sunstroke. If it is windy, you may be lulled into thinking that it is not as hot, but this is a dangerous illusion – especially in the desert valley of Las Vegas! If you are spending the day by the pool, it is advisable to use a sunshade at the hottest time of the day, and apply waterproof sunblock regularly, even when you are in the pool, as the UV rays travel through water. Always make sure you have plenty of fluids with you when travelling. Water is best and try to avoid alcohol during the day as this will have an additional dehydrating effect.

At your hotel

In America, your hotel room number is your main source of security. It is often your passport to eating and collecting messages, so keep the number safe and secure. When checking in, make sure none of the hotel staff mentions your room number out loud. If they do, give them back the key and ask them to give you a new room and to write down the new room number instead of announcing it (most hotels follow this practice in any case). When you need to give someone your room number – for instance when charging a dinner or any other bill to your room – write it down or show them your room card rather than calling it out.

When in your hotel room, always use the deadlocks and security chains and use the door peephole before opening the door to strangers. If someone knocks on the door and cannot give any identification, phone down to the hotel reception desk.

When you go out, make sure you lock the windows and door properly and even if you leave your room just for a few seconds, lock the door.

★ ★ ★ **BRIT TIP** ★ ★ ★

Use a business address rather than your home address on all your luggage.

Cash and documents

Most hotels in tourist areas have safety deposit boxes, so use these to store important documents such as airline tickets and passports. When you go out, do not take all your cash and credit cards with you – always

have at least one credit card in the safe as an emergency back-up and only take enough cash with you for the day. Using a money belt is also a good idea. Keep a separate record of your travellers' cheque numbers. If your room does not have its own safe, leave your valuables in the main hotel safe.

Emergencies

For the police, fire department or ambulance, dial 911 (9-911 from your hotel room).

If you need medical help in Las Vegas you can go to the **Resort Medical Centers** at 3535 Las Vegas Boulevard South, 8th Floor, Suite 1, or 3743 Las Vegas Boulevard South, Suite 106 (702-735 3600 or 702-736 6311). Both are on the Strip, are open 24 hours a day and offer medical care for tourists. There is a free shuttle service, no appointment is necessary, medications, laboratory and X-ray facilities are available on site and the doctors will even do hotel calls.

Cars

Most of the advice is obvious, but when we go on holiday we sometimes relax to the point of not following our basic common sense. Never leave your car unlocked and never leave any valuable items on the car seats or anywhere else where they can be seen.

Travel insurance

The one thing you should not forget is travel insurance when travelling anywhere around America – medical cover is very expensive and if you are involved in any kind of an accident

you could be sued, which is very costly indeed in America.

If you do want to make savings in this area, don't avoid getting insurance cover, but do avoid buying it from tour operators as they are notoriously expensive.

The alternative, particularly if you plan to make more than one trip in any given year, is to go for an annual worldwide policy directly from insurers. The worldwide annual policies can make even more sense if you're travelling as a family.

In all cases, you need to ensure that the policy gives you the following cover: Actual **coverage of the United States** – not all plans include America. **Medical cover** of at least £2 million in America. **Personal liability cover** of at least £2 million in America. **Cancellation and curtailment cover** of around £3,000 in case you are forced to call off your holiday. **Cover for lost baggage** and belongings at around £1,500. Most premiums only offer cover for individual items up to around £250, so you will need additional cover for expensive cameras or camcorders. **Cover for cash** (usually around £200) and documents including your air tickets, passport and currency. **24-hour helpline** to make it easy for you to get advice and instructions on what to do. **Membership of the Financial Ombudsman Service** in case you are unhappy with the outcome of a claim.

Check and check again

Shop around: You do not *have* to buy your policy from your tour operator so don't let them include it as a matter of course. You will almost certainly be able to get a better deal elsewhere. **Read the policy:** Always ask for a copy of the policy document before you go and if you are not happy with the cover offered, cancel and demand your premium back – in some cases you will only have seven days in which to do this.

16

Don't double up on cover: If you have an 'all risks' policy on your home contents, this will cover your property outside the home and may even cover lost money and credit cards. Check if this covers you abroad – and covers your property when in transit – before buying personal possessions cover.

Look at **gold card cover:** Some bank gold cards provide you with insurance cover if you buy your air ticket with the gold card, so it is worth checking, although there will be terms and conditions so check the details carefully.

Check **dangerous sports cover:** In almost all cases mountaineering, racing and hazardous pursuits such as bungee jumping, skydiving, horse riding, windsurfing, trekking and even cycling are not included in normal policies. There are so many opportunities to do all of these activities that you really should ensure you are covered before you go. Backpackers and dangerous sports enthusiasts can try **The Travel Insurance Club** on 01702 423398 or visit their website at www.ticltd.co.uk. They specialise in insurance for backpackers aged 18–35 and the cover includes walking holidays, sports and activities, skiing and scuba diving, bungee jumping and abseiling.

Make sure you qualify: For instance, if you have been treated in hospital in the six months prior to travelling or are waiting for hospital treatment, you may need medical evidence that you are fit to travel. Ask your doctor for a report giving you the all-clear (you will have to pay for this) and if the insurance company still says your condition is not covered, shop around.

Insurance policies

This is a competitive market, so it pays to shop around to find the best policy for you. Some companies offer discounts if you already have another policy with them. These companies are worth checking out for annual-cover or single-trip travel insurance.

Atlas Direct (0800 0131213, www.atlasdirect.net)
Citybond Travel (0870 444 6431, www.citybond.co.uk)
CostOut (www.costout.co.uk)
Direct Travel (0190 3812345, www.direct-travel.co.uk)
Eagle Star (0800 555200, www.eaglestar.co.uk)
Egg (08451 222888, www.egg.com)
Family Care (08705 561224)
Flexicover Direct (0870 990 9292, www.flexicover.com)
Halifax (0800 7310180, www.halifax.co.uk)
James Hampden (0870 243 0756, www.jameshampden.co.uk)
Leading Edge (01892 836622, www.leadedge.co.uk)
Marks & Spencer Financial Services (0800 068 3918, www.marksandspencer.com)
More Than (0800 300866, www.morethan.com)
MRL Insurance Direct (0870 876 7677, www.mrlinsurance.co.uk)
National Australia Group: Clydesdale Bank (0870 400 4878, www.cbonline.co.uk)
Nationwide BS (0500 302012, www.nationwide.co.uk)
TravelPlan Direct (08707 747377, www.travelplan-direct.com)
Worldwide Travel (01892 833338, www.worldwideinsure.com)

Other useful contacts

The Association of British Insurers (ABI) (020 7600 3333, www.abi.org.uk)
Financial Ombudsman Service (0845 080 1800, www.financial-ombudsman.org.uk)
General Insurance Standards Council (GISC) (020 7648 7810, www.gisc.co.uk)

BRIT TIP

Be warned – American banknotes are all exactly the same green colour and size regardless of denomination.

ACKNOWLEDGEMENTS

The author wishes to acknowledge the help of the following in the production of this book:
Las Vegas News Bureau, Las Vegas Convention and Visitors' Authority, Cellet Travel Services, Nevada Commission on Tourism, Visit USA Association, Funway Holidays, Just America, Virgin Holidays and Virgin Atlantic, Airtours, Air Vacations, American Connections, The American Holiday, APT Tourism, Bon Voyage, Getaway Vacations, Jetlife, Jetsave, Jetset, Key To America, Kuoni, NorthWest Airlines, Page & Moy, Premier, Trailfinders, Travelsphere, Unijet, United Vacations, The Aladdin, Bally's, Bellagio, Caesars Palace, Circus Circus, Cirque du Soleil, Excalibur, Fashion Show Mall, Four Seasons, Harrah's, Imperial Palace, Lance Burton, Las Vegas Airlines, Las Vegas Hilton, Luxor, Mandalay Bay, MGM Grand, Mirage Resorts, Monte Carlo, New York-New York, Rio Suite, Stratosphere, Venetian, Sundance Helicopters, Maverick Helicopters, Wet 'n Wild, Joann 'JJ' José and Rob Powers (Las Vegas Convention and Visitors' Authority), Myram Borders (News Bureau), Stephen Hughes and Kristian Perry (Funway), Mike Easton (Just America), Colin Brain (Table Rock Lake Chamber of Commerce), Diane Court (Cellet), Arizona Tourist Board, San Francisco Convention and Visitors' Bureau, Los Angeles Convention and Visitors' Bureau, California Tourist Board, Hotel Nikko, Long Beach Area Convention and Visitors Bureau, Disneyland Resort® in California, Universal Studios, Warner Bros, San Diego Convention and Visitors' Bureau, Sea World of California, Palm Springs Desert Resorts® Convention and Visitors' Bureau, Palm Springs Tourism Board, Margaret Melia (Disneyland), Stacey Litz and Carol Martinez (LACVB), Makoto Earnie Yasuhara (Hotel Nikko). Plus special thanks to the divine Kirsty Hislop, gullible traveller Bob Maddam, Simon Veness and Lucy Quick of Perform stage school.

Picture Acknowledgements
The author and publisher gratefully acknowledge the provision of the following photographs:
Front cover: Corbis, Powerstock, Las Vegas News Bureau. Back Cover: Las Vegas News Bureau. Colour page 1: Philip Greenspun (Paris, Las Vegas), Vegas-online.de (Volcano Hotel, Mirage, The Ship), Las Vegas News Bureau (Excalibur). Colour page 2: Philip Greenspun (Downtown), Lee-Spencer.com (Lions' Den), The Aladdin. Colour page 3: Las Vegas News Bureau (Venetia n, Bellagio, Four Seasons, Luxor, Excalibur). Colour page 4: Las Vegas News Bureau (Stratosphere, New York-New York, Mandalay Bay, Mirage, Treasure Island). Colour page 5: Masquerade Events (Splash 2), Excalibur, Best Read Guide (Rick Thomas), John Gurzinski (Mystère). Colour page 6: MGM Grand, Jubilee! Treasure Island, Best Read Guide (tribute to Frank, Sammy, Joey and Dean). Colour page 7: Best Read Guide (Fashion Show Mall), vegas-online.de (Venetian Shop), Fountain of the Gods, Cheesecake Factory, Via Bellagio. Colour page 8: Best Read Guide (Kahunaville, Bellagio, House of Lords, Hard Rock Café, Rainforest Café). Colour page 9: Studio 54, coolvegas.com (Coyote Ugly, Baby's), Best Read Guide (Les Folies Bergère, Showgirls of Magic), babyslasvegas.com (Baby's). Colour page 10: Philip Greenspun (Downtown), Best Read Guide (swimup at Tropicana), Las Vegas News Bureau (Sports Book at the Hilton, Caesars Palace), Luxor. Colour page 11: Elvis Chapel, Excalibur, Las Vegas Wedding Bureau (Ivy Chapel, Red Rock), Jennifer Parry (Limo). Colour page 12: Elvis-a-rama, Las Vegas News Bureau (Sirens of TI), Skydive Las Vegas, Best Read Guide (Eiffel Tower Experience). Colour page 13: Alan Benoit (jeep tour in the desert, Lake Powell). Colour page 14: Red Rock Country Club, Sierra Nevada Golf Ranch, Amy Beth Bennet (bull riding), Las Vegas Motor speedway (monster truck bash), Las Vegas Gladiators, Las Vegas 5[15], Dr Byron Bennet & Thor K (limestone climbing). Colour page 15: Alan Benoit (canon de chelly, Monument Valley), Zion National Park, Garfield County Travel Council (Thor's Hammer), Kathleen Jo Ryan (Grand Canyon). Colour page 16: Alan Benoit (Rainbow Bridge at Lake Powell), Robert Holmes (Yesemite National Park), Alan Levine (Death Valley), J Shannon Scott (Mammoth Lake).

16

INDEX

16

16